Progressing to Distributed Multiprocessing

ISBN 0-13-095683-X

90000

9 780130 956835

Progressing to Distributed Multiprocessing

Harry Singh, Ph. D.

Prentice Hall PTR
Upper Saddle River, NJ 07458
http://www.phptr.com

Library of Congress Cataloging-in-Publication Data

Singh, Harry.
    Progressing to distributed multiprocessing / by Harry Singh.
       p. cm.
    Includes bibliographical references and index.
    ISBN 0-13-095683-X (case)
    1. Electronic data processing—Distributed processing.
  2. Multiprocessors.I. Title.
  QA76.9.D5S54435 1999
  004'.36—dc21   98-47479
                                                        CIP

Editorial / production supervision: BooksCraft, Inc., Indianapolis, IN
Cover design director: Jerry Votta
Cover design: Kiwi Design
Acquisition editor: Mike Meehan
Manufacturing manager: Pat Brown
Marketing manager: Kaylie Smith

The publisher offers discounts on this book when ordered in bulk quantities. For more information contact:

Corporate Sales Department
Phone: 800-382-3419 Fax: 201-236-7141
E-mail: corpsales@prenhall.com
Or write:
Prentice Hall PTR
Corp. Sales Dept.
One Lake Street
Upper Saddle River, NJ 07458

Printed in the United States of America

10 9 8 7 6 5 4 3 2 1

ISBN 0-13-095683-X

Prentice-Hall International (UK) Limited, *London*
Prentice-Hall of Australia Pty. Limited, *Sydney*
Prentice-Hall Canada Inc., *Toronto*
Prentice-Hall Hispanoamericana, S.A., *Mexico*
Prentice-Hall of India Private Limited, *New Delhi*
Prentice-Hall of Japan, Inc., *Tokyo*
Simon & Schuster Asia Pte. Ltd., *Singapore*
Editora Prentice-Hall do Brasil, Ltda., *Rio de Janeiro*

To mankind and my family in constantly striving for innovations.

To my children, Sarita, Sushila, Sanjay, and Samita, and to my
grandchildren, Brandon, Nolan, and Preston, for their unconditional love.

To my brothers, Narinder, Ishar, and Shamsher, and my sisters,
Jiswant and Rajinder, for their prolonged faith; and to my parents,
for their high ethics and convictions during my growing years.

Contents

Part I: Need for Distributed Technologies

Part II: Distributed Technologies

Part III: Implementations

Part IV: Managing Distributed Implementations

Preface

"None of us are as smart as all of us."—Japanese Proverb

This book is a treatment of technologies as we progress from standalone centralized systems to distributed multiprocessors. It covers the principles of distributed systems and their application to real-world solutions. I place particular emphasis on the areas of multiprocessing and distribution, both as integral parts of these systems and as examples of complex distributed applications. The book reflects the openness of distributed systems, which are largely constructed from open services built around a standard communication framework.

PURPOSE

Systems are distributed for one or both of these reasons:

☞ An organization and its information systems can be inherently distributed.

☞ An organization can take inherently centralized information processing systems and distribute them to achieve higher reliability, availability, safety, or performance, or all of the above.

A distributed system consists of a number of components, which are themselves computer systems. The components are connected by some communications medium, usually a sophisticated network. Applications execute by using a number of processes in different component systems. These processes communicate and interact to achieve productive work within the application. A distributed system has a number of advantages over a single computer system:

☞ A distributed multiprocessor can be more fault tolerant. It can be designed so that if one component of the system fails the others will continue to work. Such a system will provide useful work in the face of quite a large number of failures in individual component systems.

☞ A distributed system can be made up from a number of different components. Some of these components may be specialized for a specific task, others may be of general purpose.

☞ More processing, storage, or other power can be obtained by increasing the number of components.

☞ When a single large computer system becomes obsolete all of it has to be replaced in a costly and disruptive operation. A distributed system may be upgraded in increments by replacing individual components without a major disruption.

On the other end of the spectrum, distributed systems also introduce several problems not encountered in centralized systems:

☞ They are significantly more complex.

☞ They introduce the problem of maintaining consistency of data.

☞ They introduce synchronization problems between processes.

☞ In general, no central management entity controls the whole system.

As technologies and industries converge, a new global information industry is emerging. Distributed multiprocessor systems will be of increasing importance. In distributed multiprocessor systems, shared data may be the only thing that binds together different subsystems. Thus the key paradigms and concepts of distributed systems should be associated with data considerations. Designing a distributed multiprocessor system so that the data required by its individual components, applications, and processes is available in the proper form when needed, with appropriate security, is a substantial engineering task.

Distributed information systems are a combination of distributed applications and supporting distributed computer systems. Architecture in this context considers the overall requirements of an information system and merges hardware and software considerations into a coordinated and integrated view. As shared data provides the basis for coordination and integration, we need to view distributed computer architecture from a data engineering perspective.

If the sharing of data plays a key role in distributed systems, then both communication and database issues are of great importance. Those issues extend far beyond the classical perspective of communications and centralized databases. It is hard to establish a clear line of demarcation between computing (e.g., node database operations and computation) and communications functions (e.g., data transport and associated data manipulation). Thus there is a single problem—that of distributed multiprocessor systems.

I believe that there is a gap between the books available on distributed computer architecture and the needs of the information systems. The research and literature on multiprocessor computers are increasing. Still, there is little that addresses in a comprehensive and fundamental sense the heterogeneous, widely spaced computer and database systems that make up distributed multiprocessor systems.

It is to be expected that such systems will continue to play an ever-increasing role in enterprise computations. That trend is driven by ever-expanding technological innovations, the desire of computer users to more fully integrate their computational systems, the existence of heterogeneous systems, and the certainty of introducing new systems that challenge the existing paradigms. The overriding need is to develop a structure and framework that will permit heterogeneous systems to work together.

This book addresses the fundamentals of these areas. I emphasize the underlying technologies and associated issues and tradeoffs as I focus on those parameters that are important in distributed multiprocessor systems.

INTENDED USAGE

This book is intended to provide a self-contained text on distributed multiprocessing. I assume that you have a basic knowledge of programming, operating systems, and the facilities provided by low-level communications architectures. Knowledge of distributed operating systems or applications is not required, since the text introduces many of the concepts that are in common with distributed systems. Each chapter covers a different aspect of the technology and addresses popular technologies and design principles applicable to a wide variety of systems. Most chapters can be read independently.

Progressing to Distributed Multiprocessing is intended for people in universities and industry interested in computation in the heterogeneous environments. Teachers can use this book to refresh their knowledge of technologies. Systems designers and builders can use it as a source book when trying to solve problems they encounter in their work.

ORGANIZATION

The book is loosely organized in four parts: the first part covers the need for multiprocessing and distributed systems, the second part addresses the many technologies that are an integral part of understanding such systems, the third section deals with the implementation of distributed multiprocessing systems, and the fourth part examines their management.

Chapters 1 and 2 cover the evolution, need, and the behavior of distributed systems.

Chapters 3 through 11 cover the many technologies (current and expected) that have a role in building multiprocessor systems.

Chapters 12 and 13 address the implementation of these technologies in multiprocessor systems.

Chapters 14 and 15 cover the implementation of these multiprocessor systems, with an insight of what to expect in the future.

Acknowledgments

I acknowledge many debts: to my daughter Samita Singh, for keeping me focused to complete this manuscript; to the Prentice Hall production staff, for painstaking scrutiny; to the many computer science practitioners and technologists, for providing much of the critical mass; and to my friends, for their perseverance in the face of missed appointments.

I am particularly grateful to Don MacLaren and Sherri Emmons of BooksCraft, who have reviewed the book with great energy and provided me with many constructive comments and suggestions. Finally, I want to thank Mike Meehan of Prentice Hall, the anonymous reviewers, and the cohort of friends who provided me with their comments.

Dr. HARRY SINGH

Harry Singh is an educator and consultant with three decades of experience in Information Sciences. Dr. Singh has more than 18 years experience in the fields of systems architectures, communication technologies, languages, and office systems. A former professor of computer science at the University of Texas, he holds eight patents and is the author of numerous technical papers, as well as books on *Heterogeneous Internetworking; UNIX for MVS Programmers; Data Warehouse: Concepts, Technologies, and Implementations*; and *Interactive Data Warehousing via the Web,* all published by Prentice Hall PTR.

Need for Distributed Technologies

Evolution of Distributed Technologies

1.1 INTRODUCTION

The Industrial Revolution changed the Western world from a basically rural and agricultural society to an essentially urban and industrial society. Power-driven machines replaced handiwork, production rocketed, and standards of living grew, but with concomitant problems that linger nearly two centuries later.

Personal computers came of age in the 1980s and the Internet, as we know it, in the 1990s. The two changed the way we live and work. Do we have to brace for concomitant problems with the Internet Revolution? I think so. The PC revolution has made us demand *instant* delivery not only of information, but also of solutions and products for our daily use.

Information used to be the domain of management information services (MIS), or glasshouse, and now lies on every desktop. In other words, it has been distributed and there has been a shift in the computing paradigm. Distributed processing is spreading the work of program execution and data retrieval over multiple machines. It is the opposite of the philosophy of having one huge computer that serves all users simultaneously.

Not only does this distributed architecture allow us to balance the processing load optimally, but it also lets us add additional capacity easily and quickly. Instead of having to scrap existing hardware and purchase a larger machine when capacity is needed, we can just add more modules.

To ensure continued performance as we add users, our plans include dynamically distributing users among diskless hosts so that there is never any serious degradation of performance.

The distributed computing is the closely related development of client/server solutions and reflects a sweeping change in how computer systems are designed and deployed. Anyone who deals with modern computing technology—as a user, purchaser, administrator, or vendor—must understand what distributed client/server computing means and what its benefits and risks are.

This simple idea of distributing computing resources leads to powerful capabilities, extended requirements, interesting technical issues, and sophisticated solutions, which I explore and explain in this book. Distributed computing is a natural, inevitable, and beneficial step in the evolution of computing technology.

Distributed computing opens another dimension when various technologies are combined with client/server implementations. In this book, I examine the ways to combine all these technologies to solve real world problems of the future.

1.1.1 Consequences of the Digital Age

Something is happening as the twentieth century comes to a close. There is no defining moment, in the way that significant events can often mark the boundary of an era. Still a divide has been crossed. The latest wave of technology, born of the personal computer, spawned a great new ability to communicate down the street or around the globe. Indeed, the connected computers that made this possible began to be as common as other appliances in the home or the workplace.

This new information age, or the age of the Internet, has made the leap into the international consciousness and vernacular. Funny little things with *www* popped up everywhere. In homes, offices, and schools, something called *E-mail* began crowding out postage stamps. At the phone companies (which now want to charge for Internet access by the minute), there were warnings of meltdown, because people were spending more time *on-line* than people ever spent talking to each other.

Does that mean that digital age has come of age? Half a century after the invention of the transistor, the digital age has joined an established technology—mainframes and personal computers—with a new digital distribution network—a web of wires and fiber called the Internet—and cemented one of the most significant new communications mediums of the century.

1.1.2 The Fourth Wave Begins

The first wave (1946–1980): The modern computing era began in 1946 with a big machine called ENIAC. Terms such as PDP, BASIC, FORTRAN, COBOL, ARPA, UNIVAC, MOS, C, CP/M, VisiCalc, punch tape, Ethernet, microprocessor, and vacuum tubes became familiar.

The second wave (1981–1989): Arrival of the computers on the desktop, led by IBM, unleashed computing power for the masses and what we recognize as today's Internet, the global network of networks, began to take shape. Terms such as PC, TCP/IP, compiler, modem, OS, RISC, baud, WYSIWYG, MS-DOS, DRAM, Cray, RAM, ASCII, virus, byte, and mouse adorned everyday conversation.

The third wave (1990–1996): Truly speedy personal computers became widespread. Fax machines, pagers, and cellular phones became common. The World Wide Web was born. The Internet and multimedia computing enticed millions to buy home computers. Early *digital convergence* was seen as new technologies began to blend into new consumer products, such as televisions doubling as computers. This wave is also known as the Internet watershed. Terms such as router, firewall, packet, URL, WWW, Cyberspace, bandwidth, dial-up, E-mail, host, .com, online, domain, search engine, FAQ, Http://, multimedia, Java, and ActiveX became part of lunchroom conversations.

The fourth wave (1997 and beyond): With momentum established and early mass market penetration achieved, will the revolution roll on and, if so, how fast?

1.1.3 The Need for Distributed Multiprocessing

Distributed multiprocessing differs in significant ways from the types of distributed computing that have been common from the 1970s into the 1990s.

During this period, a move occurred from mainframe systems to networked personal computing and to the World Wide Web. Despite the interconnectivity of such systems, they remain largely independent. Each user runs his or her applications. Communication between them is through shared files and E-mail. In contrast, the distributed systems of the future should be characterized by a direct coupling of application programs running on multiple platforms in a networked environment.

Businesses are moving to exploit computing systems more effectively, giving rise to a new class of large-scale distributed applications, primarily based on object technologies, utilizing such new languages as Java and object brokers as ActiveX via the Internet. Object technology is a new method of application development. The functions are divided into objects. Each object contains both data and logic in a simple software entity. An object owns its information (data) and the procedures (methods) that manipulate its data. Objects can communicate with other objects and can be reused by anyone. Such systems offer highly integrated, highly reliable computing to users who may be physically separated by large distances and interacting with many computing systems. They combine large numbers of independently executing programs, varied operating systems, and heterogeneous platforms into a seamless whole.

1.1.3.1 The Challenges   The development of software for such systems often poses difficult challenges, particularly because of the need to respond dynamically to failures and recoveries. This is further complicated by the constraint that the systems behave consistently regardless of where they are accessed.

The list of settings in which distributing computing issues arise is growing rapidly. Banks and brokerages, for example, are rapidly moving to develop electronic stock and bond trading markets. Scientific computer users seek ways of sharing supercomputers over a network. So the issues involve sharing resources such as storage, databases, CPUs, and even distributed memories, over heterogeneous multiplatforms.

1.2 THE EVOLUTION

Re-engineering is not an event. It has become a way of life in computing technologies. We like to think that business drives technology for faster, cheaper, and superior products. But we have to live with the fact that technology also drives business in this competitive world.

We also have witnessed the evolution of the client/server system, from a single tier to two and three tier to multitier. This has translated into *thin* to *thick* and back to *thin client* implementations. Internet technologies point us toward *thin* client computing, but the jury is still out on the exact nature of the future implementations that will win out.

1.2.1 Systems Architectures

Keeping in step, systems architectures are evolving from a single system to host centric to network centric, and now distributed. This is depicted in Figure 1.1.

1.2.2 Hardware Architectures

Figure 1.2 portrays the evolution that is taking place in hardware systems technologies. It started with mainframes, which performed most operations centrally to minicomputers. Then PCs entered the picture for personal computing and to act as workstations. With enhancements in speed and storage and diminishing costs of personal computers, we are now moving toward multiprocessors on a distributed scale across networks.

1.2.3 Operating Systems

An operating system is a program that controls the resources of a computer system and provides its users with an interface or virtual machine that is

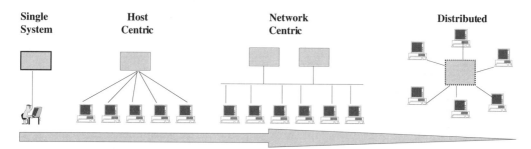

Fig. 1.1 Systems Architectures

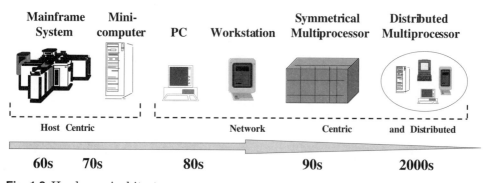

Fig. 1.2 Hardware Architectures

more convenient to use than the hardware alone. Therefore, the operating system is utilized to manage the various resources of the system.

There are two types of basic operating systems, computer operating systems and network operating systems. The operating systems, like other architectures, have undergone quite an evolutionary change. They commenced with simple instruction sets for executing applications to today's complex environments, in which they manage not only the computing resources but also networks. In the twenty-first century we will be moving from an operating system managing resources centrally—e.g., memory, storage, and central processing units (CPU)—to a distributed and shared management.

A distributed operating system is like an ordinary centralized operating system but it runs on multiple independent CPUs. The key concept is transparency, advanced by the need for such operating systems to manage distributed memories as well as storage and to run in parallel environments. Transparency is a concept that provides single-system image in regard to the distribution of its components.

1.2.4 Parallel Systems

Parallel processing is one of the most effective mechanisms for increasing performance on large systems. Parallel processing requires splitting tasks into multiple components. This can be accomplished by employing distributed multiple processing (DMP) architectures. Parallel processing (shown in Figure 1.3) is evolving from uniprocessors to symmetric multiprocessing (SMP), from massively parallel processing (MPP) to DMP, and to clustering.

1.2.5 Distributed Systems

Distributed systems used in commerce, industrial automation, and information services are among the largest and most complex systems in existence. The earliest, yet still common, form of a distributed system is a *client/server*

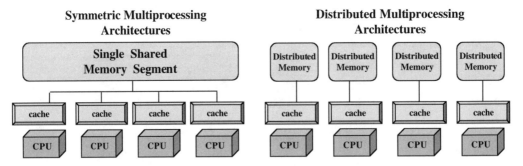

Fig. 1.3 Parallel Processing

design, in which one or more independent servers perform centralized tasks such as database maintenance. Distributed processing refers to any computers with communications between them.

While software for parallel systems executes on multiple processors on the same computer, software on distributed systems executes on two or more independent nodes, which can range in size and complexity from personal computers to supercomputers.

For a particular processor, its own resources are local, whereas the other processors and their resources are remote. A minimal distributed system may be as small as two nodes if software connectivity is present. This connectivity may be provided via local area networks (LANs), wide area networks (WANs), or the Internet. In the evolutionary spiral, the connectivity ranged from a direct connection during the IBM 3270 (dumb terminal) to the mainframe to distributed anonymous resources via the Internet today (see Figure 1.4).

1.2.6 Distributed Object-Oriented Computing

Distributed object systems are mechanisms whose intent is to allow programmers to deal with objects (packages of data and the operations that can be performed on them) on remote systems as if the objects were local. In fact, in some systems, there is absolutely no difference in programming for a local object versus a remote one. With the advent of the Internet, such systems make resources (information and services) available globally, via database information and search engine services. Object-based distributed operating systems either have been built on top of existing operating systems or built from scratch. They view the entire system and its resources in terms of objects.

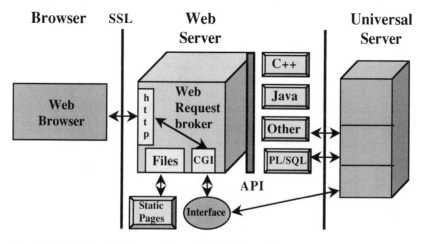

Fig. 1.4 Distributed Processing and the Internet

Distributed object-oriented systems minimize bandwidth requirements by mirroring the natural distribution of work that the programmers chose for their own work as opposed to the artificial separation of components based systems where what is communicated is the effect of some action in the system, not the cause itself. Figure 1.5 depicts a general schema of such systems.

1.2.7 Languages

The programming environments have undergone a complete evolution of languages. First there were assembly and machine languages complemented by such procedural languages as COBOL and FORTRAN. Then came the algorithmic languages, followed closely by operating system-specific and object languages. Today another revolution is in the making with scripting languages, which can meet the static and dynamic application requirements to combine text, graphics, video, audio, and the like. Some of these languages are discussed below.

Scripting languages are designed primarily for nonprogrammers who need to create simple programs or macros that extend an operating system or application. They are usually easier to learn and use than the traditional programming languages of C, C++, or Pascal, but they also tend to be proprietary, slower, and less flexible.

Netscape and Microsoft have developed separate scripting languages for the Web, such as JavaScript and VBScript. Netscape's Navigator supports only JavaScript, while Microsoft's Explorer supports both JavaScript and VBScript.

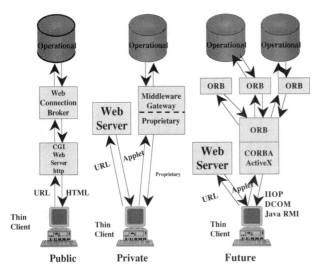

Fig. 1.5 Object-Oriented Computing

Scripts created for the Web can be used to create form pages, which validate and calculate user information before returning it to the Web server; run simple macrolike programs; and create more interactive and dynamic pages. Both JavaScript and VBScript are prevented from direct memory access or file I/O. This limitation is called *sand-boxing*, and it is designed to prevent JavaScripts and VBScripts from damaging users' files or applications. However, both JavaScripts and VBScripts can communicate with Java applets or ActiveX controls.

1.2.7.1 JavaScript JavaScript was developed by Netscape and is not directly related to Sun Microsystems programming language, Java, although they are often confused. JavaScript was originally called "LiveScript" and was renamed "JavaScript" only after Java became popular.

If a Web page contains a JavaScript, the raw hypertext markup language (HTML) of the page usually shows the script code. This allows you to view and learn from other people's JavaScripts, but it also allows other people to view and perhaps copy scripts that you have developed for your site and use them on their own sites.

1.2.7.2 VBScript VBScript is based on a subset of Microsoft's VisualBasic for Applications. The syntax for VBScript is similar to Basic. Like JavaScript, VBScripts are embedded within the HTML page and are viewable via the raw HTML.

1.2.7.3 ActiveX ActiveX is the umbrella name for Microsoft's dynamic content initiative. It consists of active controls, which are downloadable programs, and active documents, which allow a Browser (or other container) to host a file with all of its editing tools and functions available.

1.2.8 Distributed Applications

The client/server computing model is widely used in a distributed system. The model defines two separate parts of a client/server application (refer to Figure 1.6):

- ☞ The client (for example, an application running on a workstation) calls for services, such as data or processing functions.
- ☞ The server performs services on behalf of the calling client. The server can be a program, located on the same machine as the client, or it can run on a remote machine, even on a different operating system from that of the client machine.

In the client/server computing model, the client application does not have to distinguish between local and remote services. The programming complexities of network distribution are transparent to the client application,

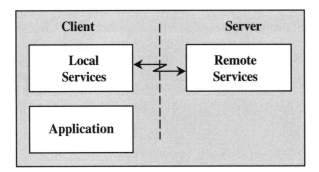

Fig. 1.6 Client/Server Computing Model

regardless of whether they are handled by the called service or the calling mechanism. Thus, the client application need not care about the location of services or the interconnection media.

The client/server model is inherently capable of providing resource sharing. A server can, for instance, provide access to data that resides on fast disks. It can improve data access further by using large cache buffers in memory.

1.2.9 The Internet

Figure 1.5 depicts the evolution of a data warehousing application over the Internet using a simple Web Browser, to a proprietary solution, to an object technology-based (Java or ActiveX, for example) standard-based distributed solution. We will examine the role of Internet in more details in later sections.

1.3 THE ISSUES FOR DISTRIBUTED TECHNOLOGIES

For many reasons, designing a distributed system is more difficult than designing a centralized system. In a centralized operating system, the operating system has complete access to information in the environment in which it is functioning. However, a distributed system must be designed with the assumption that complete information about the system environment will never be available at a given time.

In a distributed system, the resources are physically separated. There is no common clock among the multiple processors and delivery of messages may be delayed or even lost. So a distributed system does not maintain a consistent knowledge about the state of all the various components of the connected distributed systems. This lack of such a consistent state makes it much harder to design a distributed system.

Regardless of the complexities, a distributed system must be designed to provide all the advantages of a true distributed environment. The users should view the system as a centralized system that is reliable, secure, scalable, easy to use, and allows transparent access to resources. Overall system performance quality must be assured.

1.3.1 Reliability

A distributed system manages multiple instances of resources distributed over a span of geography and operating systems. Mere existence of multiple instances does not guarantee the system's reliability. Rather, the system, which manages these resources, must be designed to increase the system's reliability by taking full advantage of the multiple instances.

For higher reliability, the fault-handling mechanisms of a distributed system must be designed both to avoid faults and to tolerate a certain level of faults and to recover from faults automatically.

1.3.2 Security

For complete user trust, the various resources must be protected against unauthorized access. Enforcing security in a distributed system is more difficult than in a centralized system because of the lack of a single point of control and the use of insecure networks for data communication.

In a centralized system, all users are authorized at login time and are constantly monitored if authorized to perform operations on an accessed resource. In a distributed system, on the other hand, the client/server model is often used for requesting and providing services. This is not the simple scenario it appears to be because any client identification field in the message cannot be trusted.

1.3.3 Scalability

It is inevitable that a distributed system will grow with time since it is common to add new machines or an entire subnetwork to the system to take care of increased workload or organizational changes. Therefore, a distributed system must be able to cope with the growth of nodes and users.

1.3.4 Ease of Use

A distributed system must be easy to use, at least to the level of a central system. Flexibility is the most important ease-of-use feature. Ease of modification and enhancement also must be built into a distributed system because it incorporates a large heterogeneous mix of resources.

1.3.5 Transparency

A distributed system is primarily designed to make transparent—having a single system image to its users—the existence of multiple computers, storage devices, and locations and shared memories. Achieving transparency is a difficult task. It requires that several different sets of transparency be supported, among them name and user transparency.

1.3.5.1 Name Transparency   The name of a resource (a file or a workstation) always should be independent of physical connectivity or topology of the system despite the current location of the resource. A resource must be able to move from one location (node) to another in a distributed system, without having to change names.

1.3.5.2 User Transparency   A user should not be required to use different names to access the same resource from two different modes of the system. In a distributed system that supports user mobility, users can freely log to any machine from anywhere in the network.

1.3.6 Performance Quality

In a distributed environment, overall performance should be better than or at least equal to that of running the same application on a centralized system. To achieve this goal, the system must be designed to allow different choices under a variety of situations.

Sometimes, it may be performance enhancing to consider the transfer of data across the network in large chunks rather than as individual pages. Caching of data at client sites frequently improves overall system performance because it makes data available when it is currently needed, thus saving a large amount of computing time and network bandwidth.

1.4 GUIDE TO THE READER

Any data-processing professional will be aware of the computing industry's love-fest with object-oriented programming and the Internet. This book surveys current trends in distributed client/server applications utilizing Internet and object technologies.

Essentially, every business is beginning to implement some type of an Internet solution. May it be for a full-fledged comprehensive intranet or a simple *extranet* solution. The options and potential are limitless. Since the book addresses a wide variety of audiences in the industry, practically every enterprise, large or small, can benefit from it.

This text leads the reader, step-by-step, from the basic concepts of the technology through the most advanced. This book is not a beginner's introduction to computers, operating systems, or database technologies. This book will serve you better as a reference and a guide to facilitate learning and building successful distributed systems.

Chapter 2 introduces the fundamentals of distributed systems. The third chapter identifies the issues and concerns of distributed systems and offers some solutions. In the following chapters, I build upon these foundations. For a comprehensive enterprise solution, I also include transactional services for shared data, object technologies, and the impact of these technologies on the future of computing.

This book describes techniques necessary to answer the technological challenges and how to support an enterprise's computational needs. It provides users with information designed to:

☞ Lay the foundation for understanding distributed processing technology concepts by discussing the environments, evolution, and the problems associated with today's implementations

☞ Detail various technologies and environments that are essential for the success of distributed multiprocessing

☞ Describe techniques necessary to use these technologies to access distributed resources such as memory, databases, and processors

☞ Focus on exploiting the technologies, such as object-oriented tools, neural computing, parallel databases, standards, and the Internet

☞ Build upon the implementation development to construct effective distributed systems, to manage the distributed systems, and, finally, to access and use these systems

You will learn why you may need to enhance your current skills for effective programming or building enterprise systems and you will be introduced to new and adapted techniques with which to do so.

Broadly speaking, this book is organized into four major sections: The need, for distributed technologies, a description of these technologies, implementations of the technologies, and management of the distributed systems built upon the technologies. The book concludes with a summary of the technologies, implementations, problems, and strategies, followed by a comprehensive bibliography and glossary of terms.

1.4.1 The Audience

To function effectively as a technology developer in distributed systems, knowledge of the basic techniques available in this area has become vital. This book is written for a broad class of computer professionals, users, and decision makers. Through the technologies brought together in this book, a professional can rapidly come up to speed, learning what is known, what works and when, and how the basic techniques have already been applied in projects.

1.5 CONCLUSIONS

The purpose of a distributed file system is to allow users of physically distributed file system's to share data and storage resources by using a common system. A typical configuration is a collection of workstations and mainframes connected by a LAN. A distributed file system is usually implemented as part of the operating system of each of the connected computers. I emphasize the viewpoint of dispersed structure and decentralization of both data and control in the design of such systems. This viewpoint defines the concepts of transparency, fault tolerance, and scalability in the context of distributed file systems. I also present alternatives for the semantics of sharing and methods for providing access to remote files.

A survey of contemporary UNIX-based systems illustrates the concepts and demonstrates various implementations and design alternatives. Assessing these systems, I suggest a departure from the extending centralized file systems over a communication network is necessary to accomplish sound distributed file system design.

The book covers the naming schemes for files, the semantics describing what happens when multiple clients access a file simultaneously, and methods for accessing remote files. It also discusses issues of fault tolerance, high availability, and scalability.

Most of the trends in the distributed computing arena are identical or similar to one another. Underlying these similarities are common or shared technologies. But, because of the differences in the evolutionary spiral of different facets of these technologies, the perceptions of them may differ considerably. Two major challenges face these technologies: Merging the technologies to assure viable systems and managing the technological changes to come.

Distributed Systems

2.1 INTRODUCTION

The field of distributed computing has witnessed an explosive expansion during the last decade. As the use of distributed computing systems for large-scale computations is growing, so is the need to increase their reliability. Nevertheless, the probability of failure of an individual processing node in multinode distributed systems is not negligible. Hence, it is necessary to develop mechanisms that prevent the waste of computations performed on distributed processing nodes if one of the nodes fails, either due to a hardware transient fault (bus error or segmentation fault) or a permanent fault (power failure or communication network malfunction).

Advances in communications technology and methods of work introduced at diverse workplace environments naturally led to a greater distribution of information processing. Initially, most distributed systems were homogeneous, but now many distributed environments are heterogeneous. Therefore, the distributed systems design must focus on heterogeneous environments, treating homogeneous systems as special cases in a heterogeneous world. Key issues in distributed systems design include where specific functionality should be located within the information infrastructure.

2.2 WHAT ARE DISTRIBUTED SYSTEMS?

A distributed system is a collection of independent computers which appear to the users of the system as a single computer. Nearly all large software systems are by necessity distributed. For example, enterprisewide business systems must support multiple users running common applications across different sites.

A distributed system encompasses a variety of applications, their underlying support software, the hardware they run on, and the communication links connecting the distributed hardware. The largest and best-known distributed system is the set of computers, software, and services comprising the World Wide Web, which is so pervasive that it coexists with and connects to most other existing distributed systems. The most common distributed systems are networked client/server systems. Distributed systems share the general properties described below.

2.2.1 Resource Sharing

The most common reason for connecting a set of computers into a distributed system is to allow them to share physical and computational resources (printers, files, databases, mail services, stock quotes, and collaborative applications, for example). Distributed system components that support resource sharing play a similar role as, and are increasingly indistinguishable from, operating systems.

2.2.2 Multiple Nodes

Software for the distributed system executes on *nodes*, or multiple independent computers (not merely multiple processors on the same computer, which is the realm of *parallel computing*). These nodes can range among personal computers, high-performance workstations, file servers, mainframes, and supercomputers. Each can take the role of a *client*, which requests services by others; a *server*, which provides computation or resource access to others; or a *peer*, which does both. A distributed system may be as small as two nodes, provided software connectivity is present. This arrangement is represented in Figure 2.1.

2.2.3 Concurrency

Each of the nodes in a distributed system functions both independently and concurrently with all of the others. More than one *process* (executing program) per node and more than one *thread* (concurrently executing task) per process can act as components in a system. Most components are reactive, continuously responding to commands from users and messages from other components. Like operating systems, distributed systems are designed to avoid termination and so should always remain at least partially available.

2.2.4 Heterogeneity

The nodes participating in a system can consist of diverse computing and communication hardware. The software comprising the system can include diverse programming languages and development tools. Some heterogeneity issues can be addressed with common message formats and low-level protocols that are readily implemented across different platforms (e.g., PCs, servers, and mainframes). Others may require construction of *bridges* that translate one set of formats and protocols to another. More thorough

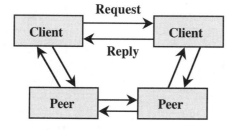

Fig. 2.1 A Small Distributed System

system integration can be attained by requiring that all nodes support a common *virtual machine* that processes platform-independent program instructions. The systems that use the Java programming language follow this approach.

2.2.5 Multiple Protocols

Most distributed message passing differs significantly from the kinds of invocations (such as procedure calls) used within the confines of sequential programs. The most basic form of distributed communication is *asynchronous*. Similar to letters mailed in a postal system, senders issue messages without relying on receipt of or reply by their recipients. Such basic distributed messages usually take much longer to reach recipients than do local invocations. They sometimes reach recipients in a different order than they were sent and they may fail to reach them at all. To avoid this, more sophisticated protocols must be constructed. These may include:

- ☞ Procedural messaging, in which senders wait for full replies
- ☞ Semisynchronous messaging, in which senders wait for an acknowledgment of message receipt before proceeding
- ☞ Transactional protocols, in which all messages in a given session or transaction are processed in an all-or-none fashion
- ☞ Callback protocols, in which receivers later issue different messages back to their senders
- ☞ Time-out protocols, in which senders only wait for replies for a certain period before proceeding
- ☞ Multicast protocols, in which senders simultaneously issue messages to a *group* of other nodes

These and other protocols are often extended and specialized to enhance reliability, security, and efficiency.

2.2.6 Fault Tolerance

A program running on a single computer is, at best, only as reliable as that computer. Most distributed systems, on the other hand, need to remain at least partially available and functional even if some of their nodes, applications, or communication links fail or misbehave. In addition to outright failures, applications may suffer from unacceptably low *quality of service* due to bandwidth shortages, network contention, software overhead, or other system limitations, so fault-tolerance requirements present some of the most central, yet difficult challenges in the construction of distributed systems.

2.2.7 Security

Only authorized users may access sensitive data or perform critical operations. Security in distributed systems is intrinsically a multilevel issue, ranging from the basic safety guarantees provided by the hardware and operating systems residing on each node; to message encryption and authentication protocols; to mechanisms supporting issues concerning privacy, appropriateness of content, and individual responsibility.

Techniques for addressing trustworthiness include using digital certificates and preventing component code performing potentially dangerous operations such as modifying disk files.

2.2.8 Message Passing

Software on separate computers communicates via structured message-passing disciplines built upon a number of networking protocols (for example, TCP/IP). These, in turn, may run on any of a number of connection technologies (for example, Ethernet and modems). The nodes in most distributed systems are *completely connected*—any node may send a message to any other node. Delivery is mediated by underlying routing algorithms and related networking support.

Messages include commands, requests for services, event notifications, multimedia data, file contents, and even entire programs. It should be noted that most multiprocessors communicate via shared memory rather than message passing and therefore are not distributed.

2.2.9 Openness

Most sequential programs are considered *closed* because their configurations never change after execution commences. Most distributed systems are, to some degree, *open*, because nodes, components, and applications can be added or changed while the system is running. This provides the extensibility necessary to accommodate expansion, and the ability to evolve and cope with the changing world in which a system resides.

Openness requires that each component obeys a certain minimal set of policies, conventions, and protocols to ensure *interoperability* among updated or added components. Historically, the most successful open systems have been those with the most minimal requirements. For example, the simplicity of the HyperText Transfer Protocol (HTTP) was a major factor in the success of the World Wide Web.

Standards organizations such as International Standards Organization (ISO) and American National Standards Institute (ANSI), along with industrial consortia such as the Object Management Group (OMG) establish the basic format and protocol standards underlying many interoperability guarantees. Individual distributed systems additionally rely on context-specific or domain-dependent policies and mechanisms.

2.2.10 Isolation

Each component is logically or physically autonomous, and it communicates with others only via structured message protocols. In addition, groups of components may be segregated for purposes of functionality, performance, or security. For example, while the connectivity of a corporate distributed system might extend to the entire Internet, its essential functionality could be segregated (often by a *firewall*) to an *intranet* operating only within the firewall. It would communicate then with other parts of the system via a restricted secure protocol.

2.2.11 Persistence

At least some data and programs are maintained on persistent media that outlast the execution of a given application. Persistence may be arranged at the level of file systems, database systems, or programming language runtime support mechanisms.

2.2.12 Decentralized Control

No single computer is necessarily responsible for configuration, management, or policy control for the system as a whole. Distributed systems are instead domains joined by protocol of autonomous agents that agree on enough common policies to provide an aggregate functionality. Some aspects of decentralization are desirable, such as fault-tolerance provisions. Others are essential because centralized control cannot accommodate the number of nodes and connections supported by contemporary systems. The tools for administering systemwide policies, however, may be restricted to particular users.

2.3 DISTRIBUTED SYSTEM FOUNDATIONS

Many distributed systems rely on a common set of algorithms and protocols to solve specific problems, including:

- Termination of a distributed computation
- Election of a leader of a group of nodes to synchronize redundant computations performed for the sake of fault tolerance
- Coordination of database transactions
- Mutually exclusive access to shared resources

More specialized algorithmic problem domains include distributed simulation, electronic commerce, distributed multimedia, digital libraries, and collaborative groupware applications. One approach to fault tolerance relies on a set of algorithms to ensure (within certain limitations) that all members of a group of nodes remain in agreement about the ordering of messages sent to the members.

2.3.1 Specifications

Distributed systems do not merely compute a single function or perform a single action. Instead, they perform a continuous stream of diverse operations. Specification of the functionality of distributed systems cannot rely solely on the use of techniques (such as those that describe inputs and outputs of sequential programs). Additionally, specifications must describe ongoing properties of the system as a whole. Most approaches rely on temporal logic or related modal logic that provides at least two forms of specification.

☞ Properties that must invariantly hold true at all times; these generally take the form of *safety* requirements, so that a given security breach cannot occur.

☞ Properties that must eventually hold true; these generally take the form of requirements that a given message will be processed.

A different approach to specification is to pose requirements in terms of abstract computational models that obey simpler, more understandable, and more formally tractable properties than do real systems, thus allowing simulation and analysis of the main properties of interest.

2.3.2 Computational Models

Distributed systems cannot be modeled adequately as Turing Machines. Unlike Turing Machines, distributed systems may be *open*, arbitrarily extensible by adding new nodes or functionality, and *reactive*, continuously responding to changing environments. One framework that encompasses most current approaches to modeling distributed systems is the notion of an abstract characterization that encompasses any object with state—where the object is stable for an infinite period of time—and the ability to send and receive messages.

Particular formalizations can be used to explore rigorously the emergent properties of distributed systems, for example those surrounding security. Refinements geared toward more practical engineering efforts include two-tiered models in which each node, process, or thread in a distributed system is modeled as an *active* object, possessing an autonomous thread of control. Active objects are in turn structured using sets of *passive* objects that conform to a given sequential model of object-oriented computation.

2.3.3 Limitations

The implementation of several desired properties of distributed systems requires that a set of nodes agree about a given predicate. Consensus plays a central role in fault tolerance, for example, in which some nodes must agree that another node has failed. Even more severe limitations apply to failures in which faulty nodes misbehave rather than halt.

2.4 DISTRIBUTED SYSTEM ENGINEERING

Distributed systems used in commerce, industrial automation, and information services are among the largest and most complex systems in existence. These systems provide essential services relied upon by society and are rapidly becoming as economically, politically, and socially important as shipping, railway, highway, and telecommunication systems have ever been. Successful system development requires adherence to sound design principles and engineering practices and reliance on an increasingly standardized set of decomposition and structuring rules that in part borrow from and extend object-oriented software design methods.

The earliest form of a distributed system was a *client/server* design, in which one or more independent servers perform such centralized tasks as database maintenance. Each client executes programs that provide user-interface and computational capabilities, but communicate via database queries with servers whenever accessing or updating shared data. An examination of the limitations of the simplest client/server system reveals development issues similar to those addressed in structured distributed programming frameworks.

2.4.1 Issues Addressed

2.4.1.1 Server Centric The communication patterns, protocols, and policies seen in pure client/server designs are sometimes sensible choices for database-centric applications, but they are by no means universally appropriate. For example, a server-centric application could not support applications deploying mobile agents (see Figure 2.2).

Solutions to these problems and limitations mainly reflect experience-driven design knowledge accrued during the historical progression from custom small-scale systems, to specialized systems such as network file systems,

Fig. 2.2 Centralized Client/Server Configuration

to enterprise-level business systems, to the global multipurpose systems currently being developed. Engineering support for many of the development practices, services, and components is increasingly provided by standardized distributed programming frameworks based upon OMG's Common Object Request Broker Architecture (CORBA), OSF DCE, Microsoft DCOM, and the Java programming language.

2.4.1.2 Fixed Nodes When there are only a few fixed nodes in a system, and each performs a single dedicated task, all communication might be performed by issuing packets to fixed Ethernet addresses or by broadcasting them on a local network.

Names and Name Servers In the most fragile systems, each node runs a single, very large program. Such software components are difficult to design, implement, and test, and even more difficult to reuse, extend, and update.

Ad Hoc Messaging A small, fixed set of nodes with dedicated functionality can communicate by sending messages of a form acceptable by recipients. This practice does not scale to systems providing many services, possibly on many nodes.

2.4.1.3 Names and Name Servers Contemporary distributed systems rely on *naming services* that maintain sets of logical names and map them to physical addresses and associated low-level protocols. The most common and familiar naming service is the Domain Naming Service (DNS), which provides a basis for the page-naming scheme used on the World Wide Web. DNS maps Internet names (for example, *www.connectinc.com*) to Internet addresses, which are then further translated to hardware-level addresses and connection protocols. Most distributed systems augment general-purpose naming systems in order to maintain mappings from the services supported by the system to the nodes, processes, and software objects that provide them. Most components are not given human-readable names, but instead are assigned arbitrary object identifiers that are used by *brokers* (mediators that perform services on behalf of other components) and related components when locating services (see Figure 2.3).

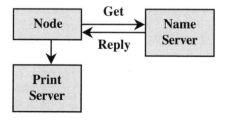

Fig. 2.3 Name Server Configuration

Naming services are usually implemented by distributed algorithms in which each node knows only a small subset of the name space, but also knows of other nodes to query when an attempted lookup fails. Distributed name spaces are structured in a hierarchical fashion that simplifies usage, stream-lines lookup algorithms, and permits federation among different name services. Name space mappings need not be restricted to nodes or objects. For example, names may be associated with groups that are accessed through channels with multiple connection points.

2.4.1.4 Interface Implementations   Interfaces are formal declarations of operations (methods) supported by implementation objects. Most distributed systems rely on a standard means of defining interfaces describing sets of ser-vices, enforced with an Interface Definition Language (IDL). Systems main-tain interface descriptions, along with bindings to available implementations, in repositories that are tied to naming services in order to provide lookup capabilities. Object interfaces are similar to classes in object-oriented pro-gramming languages. Each interface consists of a set of service declarations. Each service is declared as an object-oriented *method,* such as a *named* opera-tion that can carry arguments, results, and exceptions. Arguments and results comprise any arbitrary data, including control parameters, names or refer-ences to other components, image data, implementation code for other compo-nents, and descriptions of other interfaces.

IDLs differ from object-oriented languages in that they do not permit def-inition of programming details indicating how a declared service is imple-mented. Some IDLs also support declarations of special message-passing protocols that must be used when sending and receiving messages of the indi-cated form.

Special development tools can be used to generate code that connects declared services to implementation code written in a standard programming language, including many programming-language-level objects, methods, or modules. IDL-based tools typically generate code that enables components to be invoked via a particular Remote Procedure Call (RPC) or Remote Method Invocation (RMI or Object RPC) protocol discipline. The main difference between RPC and RMI is that an RMI message recipient is specified by an identifier that must be resolved by a broker. This is the role of the Object Request Broker (ORB) in CORBA. Most tools create *proxy* objects that locate ultimate message recipients, encode selectors and data into lower-level buffers and packets, and transport packets. At the recipient site, symmetrical dis-patch objects decode packets and invoke the desired service in the correspond-ing local component.

Some programming languages, notably Java, possess an interface con-struct that enables programmers to specify an interface, implement it, and arrange the underlying connections without the need for a separate IDL.

Together, interfaces, naming services, and the associated mechanisms and constructs make distributed system programming similar to sequential programming. Higher-level languages and tools can be used to make distributed programming constructs indistinguishable from sequential ones. A program statement itself need not reveal whether it is just a local invocation within a sequential program or a distributed invocation. This *transparency* shields developers from needing to know the location of the service, whether it has moved, or if it is replicated for the sake of fault tolerance.

Transparency simplifies usage of scripting languages whose main role is to combine sets of existing distributed components in order to build applications. However, most development languages and tools that are used to build the underlying components provide nontransparent programming abstractions. Distributed message passing may differ arbitrarily from local invocation with respect to semantics, latencies, and failure modes, so most languages keep them separate. This forces developers to deal with distribution-specific issues while providing programmatic support for more limited sense of transparency that may be desirable in particular systems.

2.4.1.5 Component Management

Systems composed of many small-granularity interfaces, classes, and objects are generally more reusable, reliable, and economical than those built using only a few custom monolithic programs. In some systems, just about any software object may be a candidate for independent use as a distributed component. This management process explains why there are many more components than there are computers in a system.

Object components are managed by services that are analogous to, but extend, virtual memory techniques that allow computers to act as if they have more memory than they do. Rather than have each node or process support a single service component, the system arranges for each component to be available when it is needed, without occupying computational resources when it is not needed. Such support can be provided as a set of services that are otherwise constructed in the same way as any other distributed component. These may include:

- ☞ *Replication*: By establishing multiple copies of a component for the sake of performance or reliability

- ☞ *Configuration*: By establishing or modifying parameters and bindings that control policies and protocols employed by one or more components (for example, those surrounding authentication and quality of service)

- ☞ *Load balancing*: By placing components on or moving components to the least busy nodes

- ☞ *Versioning*: By replacing a faulty or outdated implementation of a component with a new implementation

- ☞ *Activation*: By creating a new instance of a component in either a new process or an existing process

☞ *Deactivation*: By suspending a component and saving its state persistently for possible later reactivation

☞ *Data caching*: By saving copies of previously requested remote data and reusing them unless they have changed

☞ *Mobility*: By transferring a component from one node to another

☞ *Garbage collection*: By destroying and releasing resources of a component that is no longer being used in the system

☞ *Utilities*: By supplying general-purpose functionality needed by other components (for example, performing clock synchronization across nodes)

Nearly all aspects of object management and distributed programming entail performance engineering. The most central performance issue in distributed systems is the most obvious one: Distributed message passing can sometimes be a million times slower than local invocations. Some of this overhead remains even when using the fastest available computing and communication technologies. This observation has led to development of increasingly efficient schemes for performing each of the suboperations employed in message transmission. Performance optimizations that can be applied without compromising the integrity of system designs include:

☞ *Message aggregation*: Combining frequent small messages into less frequent larger ones.

☞ *Algorithmic improvements*: Using algorithms that are less impacted by communication latency. For example, *optimistic* techniques assume the success of rarely failing requests without waiting for verification, but they are also prepared to perform expensive rollbacks or retries upon notification of failure.

☞ *Component clustering*: Statically or dynamically enhancing locality by placing heavily communicating components (or their replicates) as close together as possible—in the same process, on the same machine, or on the same local network.

☞ *Protocol streamlining*: Using weaker but faster protocols when possible. For example, external requests can be screened by expensive authentication checks only upon entry into a system.

2.4.1.6 Architectural Styles   Even when they are based on common infrastructures, distributed systems or subsystems can have vastly different architectural styles. Systems or subsystems may be based on one or more of the following *design patterns*.

Fault-Tolerant Services   There are two main approaches to improving the fault tolerance of services: Replication and persistence. *Replication* entails cloning components and ensuring that all replicates process the same messages in the same order. If one of them fails, others should be able to continue. *Persistence* involves periodically saving the states of components so that they can be resurrected in the event of failure. Many variants involve both replication and persistence. In some techniques, invocations persistently log all actions to the primary host and then, upon failure, execute them all at once in order to achieve the correct state. Since there is no upper limit on how much replication is enough and since solutions can be relatively costly in terms of resources, performance, and system complexity, any application of fault-tolerance measures usually involves engineering tradeoffs.

Transactional Services Transactional protocols can extend the concurrency control and persistence support used in monolithic databases to the realm of distributed systems. Most transactions operate on sets of service requests that must be performed in an all-or-none fashion. For example, a bank transfer operation consists of two requests, to withdraw money from one account and to deposit it in another. These two requests should fail as a unit if any problems arise. Distributed transactions differ from their sequential counterparts mainly by virtue of employing multiphase commit protocols to deal with constituent operations performed on different nodes and interactions among failure-handling and concurrency-control techniques.

Peer Services Nearly every system includes at least some components that communicate via classic procedural request-reply mechanisms. For example, one component may handle a user's request for a particular stock quote by issuing an RPC or RMI, awaiting the result, and then displaying it to the user. However, service-based systems are by no means limited to pure client/server designs.

The successes of even the earliest distributed system components are in part responsible for the fact that relatively few existing distributed systems are structured in an ideal fashion. Nearly every system must accommodate *legacy* components, subsystems, and applications. Some old transaction-processing systems and databases would be too difficult, time consuming, or disruptive to redesign and reimplement. Some legacy software may be gracefully integrated by retrospectively defining interfaces and retrofitting structured messaging protocols.

Content-Based Processing In the World Wide Web, as well as many multimedia systems, each server has a very simple interface, often consisting only of an operation that returns the information content specified by an identifier. However, messages indicate the nature of the software needed to display or otherwise use the data. In turn, clients map this description to locally available software (for example, an image-rendering program) and use it to process the content. Associating content description (*metadata*) with messages provides the flexibility needed to deal with ever-growing media types and formats, but at the expense of possible failures when clients do not possess the software needed to handle a new content type.

Asynchronous Messages A number of *push* protocols extend the primitive asynchronous message-passing style in which components issue messages without necessarily expecting replies. This style is analogous to mail systems, as well as to radio and television broadcasting. Such protocols may involve many intermediate nodes that either route and distribute messages or enhance fault tolerance. Event-based systems are structured in a similar fashion. Perhaps the most widespread push-based system is the *Usenet* news system, which propagates postings to news servers across the Internet so that users can access local copies more quickly and conveniently. Similar protocols are used in software distribution systems that propagate program updates to all subscribers.

2.5 MULTIPROCESSOR SYSTEMS

Many types of multiprocessors are utilized today. Three multiprocessor (MP) technologies are introduced here.

☞ *Shared-Memory MP*: Figure 2.4 shows a symmetric multiprocessor configuration, also known as a shared-memory multiprocessor. It has multiple processors, each of which can address all the memory and devices. Processes running on any of the processors can see the full machine. If two or more processors access the same word in memory, the hardware keeps the caches consistent and invisible to application processes.

Comparatively, the advantage of shared-memory MPs is in their use of the same programming model as uniprocessors. As an example, most existing applications written for uniprocessor PowerPC platforms run unchanged on a symmetric multiprocessor under the control of an AIX operating system.

☞ *Shared-Nothing MP*: Figure 2.5 shows a shared-nothing multiprocessor or distributed memory configuration. All processors have their own dedi-

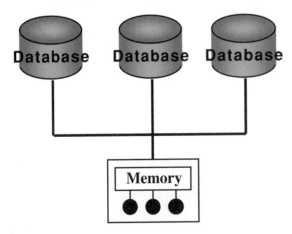

Fig. 2.4 Shared-Memory Architecture

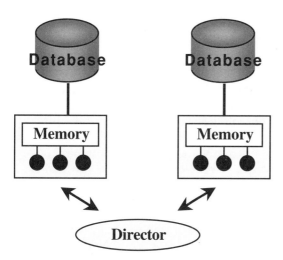

Fig. 2.5 Shared-Nothing Architecture

cated memory and disks. Uniprocessor programs must be changed to run on this configuration because they must pass messages across an interconnect in order to use the multiple processors. IBM/SP2 is an example of a shared-nothing multiprocessor that runs under AIX.

Shared-nothing MPs generally scale better than shared-memory MPs because they have no memory bus contention and no cache coherency problems among the processors. However, the changed programming model often outweighs the advantages of this type of an MP.

☞ *Shared-Disk MP*: Figure 2.6 shows a shared-disk multiprocessor configuration in which processors only share disks. Unlike the shared-memory

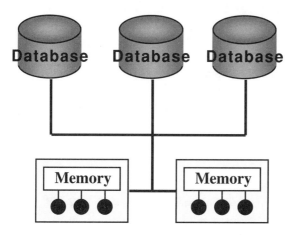

Fig. 2.6 Shared-Something Architecture

MP, each processor on a shared-disk MP has its own memory. For example, the clustered multiprocessor (CMP) portion of HACMP/6000 software allows users to configure RISC System/6000 machines in a shared-disk multiprocessor configuration.

The shared-disk MP, like the shared-nothing MP, has no memory bus contention or cache coherency problem among the processors. A centralized locking scheme controls access to the disks. This locking scheme requires a change for some applications (such as databases) and generally offsets the performance advantages of having no memory bus contention or the cache coherency problem.

To understand what is happening in the parallel database arena, we must understand symmetric multiprocessing (SMP) and massively parallel processing (MPP). The goal is to provide high performance by adding processor nodes in order to scale performance linearly. Adding processors to improve performance is not simple. The barriers of scalability stem from the following factors:

1. The overhead associated with starting processes consumes greater amounts of CPU time as the number of processes increases.
2. The processes can interfere with each other by contending for shared resources.
3. As tasks are broken down into ever smaller processes, it becomes more likely that some indivisible process will take longer to complete than others. This creates *skewness*.

Shared-disk systems can scale to many CPUs, but they become more difficult to administer as the number of CPUs increases. Scalability is also limited because setting locks to manage contention for the shared data can introduce overhead. On the other hand, clusters can tolerate node failures because the remaining nodes can take over the processing.

In addition to disks, systems can also share main memory, which is physically centralized. In addition, each processor has local cache memory. These are referred to as SMP or *tightly coupled* because they share a single operating system instance. SMP looks like a single computer with a single operating system. A database management system (DBMS) can use it with little, if any, reprogramming. However, modifications such as multithreading based on small-grained, lightweight threads can help the DBMS take better advantage of SMP.

2.5.1 MPP

Initially, the market definition of an MPP system emphasized the notion of *massive*. MPP designs offer the promise of unlimited configurations involving hundreds, if not thousands, of microprocessors (CPUs) which could be applied to application problems.

The reality is that while some MPP designs do support hundreds or thousands of CPUs, some do not. Some entry-level MPP machines have as few as 8 or 16 CPUs. Indeed, there may be a trend toward fewer processor/memory units, or nodes (P/Ms). For example, IBM's SP2 only scales up to 128 nodes while Intel, Teradata, and Tandem have already shipped machines with about 200 CPUs.

Shared-nothing architectures offer the most scalability. Each processor has its own memory, its own operating system, and its own DBMS instance, and each executes tasks on its private data stored on its own disks. The processors are connected and messages or functions are passed among them. Shipping tasks to the data, instead of data to the tasks, reduces interprocessor communications. For example, one node can request from other nodes particular rows in a table that is partitioned across multiple disks. The other nodes send the rows back to the requester, which merges them into the answer set. Thus programming, administration, and database design are intrinsically more difficult in this environment than in the SMP environment.

A potential problem in a shared-nothing system stems from the fact that a node failure renders data on that node inaccessible. Therefore, data must be replicated across multiple nodes or alternate paths provided so that it can be accessed even if one node fails. In such cases, the process can *fail-over* to another node that can access the first node's data. In addition, as with a shared disk, the interconnected processors can reside in different computers.

Even while multiprocessors and distributed computing are garnering increasing attention, a new breed of computer or computing environment is being introduced as a significant player. The multicomputer (MC)/MPP, or the clustered computing environment, is characterized by the potential of thousands of computing nodes. Typically, such an arrangement involves a high-speed interconnect with a strong need for single-system image and load leveling across a set of nodes. A single-system image provides a single interface to the user regardless of the distribution or arrangement of computing nodes. Since the MPP and MC/MPP are relatively similar systems, I refer to such systems as multiparallel or massively parallel computers (MCPs).

To avoid expensive hardware and to enhance parallelism and availability, most of the multicomputers have little or no physically shared memory and run all or part of the open-system kernel software on each node. This software must cooperate in four major areas and must do so in a largely transparent and noninvasive way. The four areas are file sharing (including devices), processes, load leveling, and interprocess communication (IPC).

The dilemma is whether to write a new distributed operating system or to leverage the standard open systems that exist today and provide distributed functionality in a modular fashion that can track other operating system developments. To date, most distributed projects claiming any form of single-system image have been the distributed operating systems.

2.5.2 SMP

During the past few years, a new definition based on the underlying system architecture has emerged. With this new definition, SMP and MPP systems can be evaluated side by side. Simply put, SMP architectures are characterized as *shared-everything*, MPP architectures as *shared-nothing*.

In an SMP system, the components—CPUs, physical memory, buses, I/O subsystem (disks and controllers), the operating system, the RDBMS, and the physical database partitions—are shared (See Figure 2.4). In an MPP system, none of these components is shared and there is only an interconnect to link the disparate nodes together. This bifurcation reflects underlying SMP and MPP architectural differences better than the terms *massive* and *nonmassive*. Another way of expressing the same point involves the terms *tightly coupled* and *loosely coupled*.

An SMP is unique in that it looks exactly the same to each processor in the system. In the past, the design of an SMP hardware platform concentrated on the following three components:

1. Memory bus architecture
2. Cache and memory management unit
3. Operating system

The proprietary design of each SMP product has made these systems unique. Their practical application is generally limited to large corporate server environments with enterprisewide database servers.

Operating system design is one of the biggest challenges in developing SMP platforms. The most common operating systems—UNIX, DOS, NetWare, OS/2, and Apple System 7—are either incapable of supporting SMP hardware or require major redesigns. In the past, UNIX has been the chosen platform for modification due to both industry-available expertise and easier portability for application designers. Unfortunately, there is no accepted standard for SMP kernels or threaded application programming interfaces (APIs). A plethora of incompatible UNIX SMP implementations has been created by NCR, Sequent, Sun, SGI, Pyramid, and others. This lack of a standard creates several disadvantages:

☞ The operating system has to be modified to support SMP hardware. To design and tune the implementations is a very complex task.

☞ Each implementation must decide whether to exploit any threading features in the OS. This requires more work and leads to more support problems due to the differences between each OS.

☞ The benefits of SMP designs will not have been exploited, limiting acceptance and utility of SMP hardware.

☞ Device drivers for each brand of operating system must be designed and developed. These separate designs are expensive and limit the availability of peripherals on each platform.

End users carry the burden of these disadvantages with exorbitant costs and poor availability of hardware and software solutions.

A solution to this problem is a standard, SMP-capable operating system. Such a standard allows a system designer to design a hardware platform to run a readily available operating system. Each implementer can support this system with standard product offerings, keeping costs to a minimum. Currently, there are only a handful of widely available operating systems that support SMP hardware.

Windows NT is the first operating system designed both to be portable and to support SMP hardware. This operating system is available for a large variety of processors. Windows NT is a fully threaded kernel with machine-specific parts isolated in the Hardware Abstraction Layer (HAL). The task for hardware vendors is further simplified by the availability of HAL components for many common architectures, which allows the system designer to target his design to run NT with a minimum of work.

With problems of hardware design and OS availability solved, SMP systems are set to become an important part of computing solutions—from the desktop to the enterprisewide servers. Relational database management system (RDBMS) products are already supporting more concurrent users with better response time than had been possible previously.

Measuring the performance of SMP systems is a complex task. Traditional industry benchmarks, such as SPECint and SPECfp, only measure single CPU performance. This does not show performance gains when using multiple processors.

Consider the SPECint92 benchmark: On a uniprocessor Pentium P5 system, it would give a result of 58; adding a second processor would not affect that result much. If you ran two or more copies of the SPECint92 benchmark concurrently, it would be much slower on a single CPU system than on the SMP system.

2.5.2.1 SMP High-Availability and Systems

Many SMP systems have one or more of the following features to improve the reliability of the system:

☞ *Hot plugable disk drives*: This feature, used in conjunction with Redundant Arrays of Inexpensive Disks (RAID) technology, allows a faulty disk drive to be replaced while the server continues to operate. No loss of data occurs and, other than a temporary reduction in I/O performance, the failure is transparent to the users.

☞ *RAID disk arrays*: Disk failure is eliminated by using fault-tolerant RAID subsystems such as RAID 1 or RAID 5. RAID technology also provides superior I/O performance.

☞ *Dual power supplies*: Even if a system is connected to an uninterruptable power supply (UPS), if an internal power supply fails, the system will halt. Load-sharing, dual power supplies eliminate this potential point of failure.

☞ *ECC memory*: The more memory resident in a system, the more likely a parity error will occur (memory failure). ECC memory allows the system to correct for such errors without failing.

☞ *Auto configuration on boot*: SMP servers are generally not fully fault tolerant. A highly available system will crash, reboot, and, during reboot, the failed processor is removed automatically from the configuration. This allows the system to continue to work with reduced performance until maintenance can be scheduled.

The distinction between fault-tolerant and high-availability systems is how they react to critical failures. A fault-tolerant system can survive any failure without the system being brought down.

2.5.2.2 SMP Applications   Applications specifically designed for SMP systems can be threaded. A database engine is a good example of an application that can be threaded. Typically, a process like a database engine consists of several logical components, such as I/O or query engines or user interfaces. Since these components or threads can run asynchronously, the database engine can be designed so each thread operates independently, only synchronizing when necessary. Once an application is threaded, the operating system can schedule the threads simultaneously on different processors.

In the past, fully threaded applications have been rare since there was no standard way to provide these features. Any vendor that needed to thread an application had to port the application separately to each SMP architecture. Windows NT gives application developers the chance to thread an application and target it at any system that runs NT. The potentially large market for NT systems makes the work of threading applications much more attractive.

SMP systems are particularly suited to supporting multiple clients in a client/server architecture. A good example of this is the database server role. Compared to a uniprocessor, SMP systems provide additional benefits in database performance and availability:

☞ *Multiple CPUs*: Existing database engines are single threaded. Even a single-threaded engine gains on an SMP system. The performance increase is the result of operating system tasks, such as networking and I/O being distributed on multiple processors, allowing the database to run with few interruptions.

☞ *Shared Resources*: In a shared resource environment, each processor executes a task on the required data, which is shipped to it. Thus, shared resource is often called data shipping. The only problem with data shipping is that it limits the computer's ability for scalability. In an SMP environment, the scaling problems are caused by interprocessor communication, and the time it takes to send code and data to each processor. The number of processors that can work efficiently is limited by the number of accesses to shared memory, the rate at which the local caches are invalidated by work on other processors, and the I/O bandwidth to memory.

Given the power of CPUs today and the speed of memory and buses, the limitations of SMP are not too great in practice. The table size and types of transactions may be more limiting than the amount of data: There have been successful implementations of databases in excess of 100GB on an SMP computer with as few as eight CPUs.

SMP implementations are improving, and the number of processors that can be supported effectively is growing as memory speeds increase and cache coherency schemes become more sophisticated. Coupled with more powerful processors, SMP hardware may suit all but the largest databases.

2.5.2.3 Clustered SMP Systems

SMP systems have proven their scalability and availability in many large enterprises. Implementers often consider MPP systems, because they perceive MPP systems to be better able to meet the performance, growth, and capacity demands of today's data-intensive applications. No one can deny the appeal of the theoretical promise of MPP systems to incrementally deliver linear speedup and linear scaleup at low cost, but reality is less clear. Proven SMP systems and clusters of SMP systems can satisfy enterprise data warehouse application needs without the drawbacks of MPP systems. In clustered SMP systems—a recent and promising variation—multiple *tightly coupled* SMP systems are linked together to form a *loosely coupled* processing complex.

Every component of an SMP system is controlled by a single executing copy of an operating system (OS) managing a shared global memory. Because memory in an SMP system is shared among the CPUs, SMP systems have a single address space and run a single copy of the OS and the application. All processes are fully symmetric in the sense that any process can execute on any processor at any time. As system loads and configurations change, tasks or processes are automatically distributed among the CPUs, providing a benefit known as dynamic load balancing.

An SMP system can support from 2 to more than 30 CPUs, producing a near linear increase in performance as CPUs are added. When additional processing power is needed, more CPUs can be installed in the system, and the OS automatically configures the new hardware. No changes to the OS, application, or data are necessary.

Current SMP machines can address tens of gigabytes (GB) of physical memory and many terabytes (TB) of storage—enough for most commercial online transaction processing (OLTP) and DSS applications. SMP systems are well suited for OLTP environments in which many users execute a common application accessing a shared RDBMS.

Systems, such as decision-support systems, that require high levels of data access and manipulation, benefit from the SMP's architectural ability to provide shared memory access to common RDBMS data structures. Eventually, contention for shared memory resources does place a limit on scaleup in shared-everything systems. However, linear speedup is no longer a function of linear scaleup. Speedup is continually being boosted by the emergence of faster CPUs, high-capacity memory, and disks which, because of cost declines, can be used in array configurations optimized for performance.

As processor speeds increase, one would imagine that adding faster processors would "speed up" an SMP design. But it is not that simple. The increased processor speed, in fact, results in shrinking the bus distances, consequently limiting the number of CPU loads that can be attached.

As speedup and scaleup demands of data-intensive applications have outstripped a single SMP system's capabilities, a logical, evolutionary approach has been taken by SMP and RDBMS vendors. Scalable hardware and software technologies are allowing shared-everything systems to be clustered for greater scaleup, speedup, and availability. Such systems share disk storage, data busses, and multiple, high-bandwidth I/O channels for high throughput levels.

Most RDBMSs allow applications on clustered nodes to share a common database. In addition, modern RDBMSs contain enhancements that allow a single database activity (a query, for example) to execute on multiple CPUs in one or more cluster-connected nodes.

In a clustered SMP configuration, each SMP node has its own copy of the OS but shares the RDBMS by sharing disks. To maintain high availability, specially designed and integrated cluster software constantly monitors the health of the system resources and directs system recovery actions in the event of a system fault. Peripherals such as tape drives are pooled together to provide a backup resource to individual system nodes.

A critically important operation in an SMP cluster is the coordination of shared resources. Clustering requires shared resource coordination via a lock manager to preserve data integrity across the RDBMS instances, disks, and tape drives. Sequent's Symmetry 5000 SE100 cluster, which supports more than a hundred processors, is an example of a clustered system providing this capability.

With clustering, scaleup is a matter of adding another node or more processors, disks, memory, or I/O bandwidth. While clustering SMP systems requires a looser coupling among the nodes, there is no need to replace hardware or rewrite applications.

Clustered SMP systems are more complex than traditional SMP systems but they offer many benefits, including an easier programming model, higher availability, automatic fail-over of hardware, system management tools, dynamic online backup, dynamic batch load balancing, and so on. A natural benefit of clustered SMP is much greater availability than MPP or SMP systems offer.

2.5.3 NUMA and COMA

In the current world of scalable distributed shared-memory machine architectures, there are two dominating architectures: The most popular is a design called cache-coherent Non-Uniform Memory Access (NUMA). The other emerging design is the Cache-Only Memory Architecture (COMA).

In a NUMA machine, the (physical) address on the memory bus of a processing node determines the home node memory location of a particular bit of data. The cache hierarchy on each processing node is constructed to replicate and hold copies of data not only from the local memory, but from the memory of remote nodes as well. A hardware coherence and directory mechanism serves to keep these cached copies consistent. While the caching helps reduce the access latency to otherwise remote memory, the total available is restricted to the size of the cache on each node. Furthermore, if data is located on a remote node then there is a case for migrating it locally. However, such migration is a costly operation involving OS synchronization between all sharing nodes.

In a COMA machine, hardware (including tag and state memory) is added to the DRAM of each processing node to convert it into a kind of cache called *attraction memory*. This additional hardware enables the disassociation of the actual data location in the machine from the physical addresses produced by the processors. Doing so enables data to be replicated and migrated automatically upon demand around the machine. This provides a very flexible platform for an application to execute upon, but at the expense of additional memory system overhead and perhaps more importantly, a complex attraction memory coherence controller implementation. By contrast, a NUMA architecture is easier to implement, but it enforces tighter constraints on the data replication an application may use and incurs a significantly higher cost of incorrect data placement and migration.

A Simple COMA machine is a hybrid hardware / software architecture in which many of the complex operations of a conventional hardware COMA have been moved into software, but with sufficient hardware retained for performance-critical operations such as data coherence.

The key realization behind Simple COMA is that the Memory Management Unit (MMU) in a commodity processor can perform much the same function as the hardware required to build the attraction memory in a contemporary COMA. In a hardware COMA, a memory reference is presented to the attraction memory system and the address is hashed and tag checked to locate (if any) corresponding data in the memory on the local node.

In the virtual memory system of a workstation, a memory reference is presented to the MMU. The MMU locates the corresponding data in the local physical memory, performing the equivalent of the COMA tag check, or page faulting if the data is not present (if there is no virtual-to-physical page mapping). The MMU, therefore, is used to make physical memory a cache of a larger virtual address space.

Since the MMU can map any virtual address to any physical address, the attraction memory built in this way is fully associative. The operating system manages the allocation and reclamation of data space, which, combined with the full associativity, enables the use of more sophisticated replacement choices, helping mitigate the overhead of software management. However, since the MMU in a commodity processor is page based, the allocation of space in such an attraction memory can only be managed at a page granularity.

Page granularity coherence is clearly unacceptable for a wide range of applications—false sharing being one of the many problems it causes. To overcome these, Simple COMA uses a hardware coherence mechanism, which involves no direct interaction with the processor and operates at a fine granularity.

2.6 FAULT-TOLERANT SYSTEMS

A fault-tolerant system should not fail because any one component fails and it should recover from multiple failures. Components are often overengineered or purposely underutilized to ensure that while performance may be affected during an outage the system will perform within predictable, acceptable bounds.

Fault resilience usually indicates that at least one of the modules within a component (a power supply in a hub for instance) is backed up with a spare. Not all modules within that component are necessarily redundant, however. The hub may have two power supplies but only one CPU. Performance of the system during an outage is therefore undefined. One fault-resilient component does not make the entire system fault tolerant.

Fault tolerance, fault resilience, and disaster recovery are intimately interrelated. You need to understand how they work together in order to design a fault-tolerant network. Simply put, the goal is to keep running no matter what, to maximize the number of failures the system can cope with, and to minimize any potential weaknesses.

Unfortunately, in the real world, there is no way to limit scope. Disasters can occur anywhere in the network, at any level in the ISO communications model—from physical layer to presentation. It can be useful, even necessary, however, to separate the problem into logical groups. For example, most corporate IS functions are divided into something like the following:

☞ Workstation support

☞ Network server support

☞ Database development, both client and server

2.7 CONCLUSIONS

We want to fully utilize a heterogeneous computing environment where different types of processing resources and interconnection technologies are used effectively and efficiently. Using distributed resources provides the potential of maximizing performance and cost effectiveness for a wide range of scientific and distributed applications.

Distributed computing environments comprising networked heterogeneous workstations are becoming the standard configuration in both engineering and scientific environments. However, the lack of a unifying parallel computing model (a parallel equivalent of a von Neuman model) means that the current parallel applications are nonportable.

2.7.1 Characteristics of Distributed Systems

Distributed systems should be designed to provide the following:

☞ Global interprocess communications

☞ Global protection

☞ Consistent process management

☞ Single set of system calls

☞ Consistent look and feel of the file system everywhere on the enterprise

☞ Same kernel on all systems

☞ Multiprocessor timesharing

☞ Tightly coupled software and hardware

☞ Multiple CPUs

☞ Single-run queue in shared memory

☞ Shared memory, allowing any process to run on any CPU

☞ File system identical to single-CPU system

☞ Design issues transparency

2.7.2 Advantages of Distributed Systems

Distributed systems have many inherent advantages, especially over centralized systems. Some applications are inherently distributed as well. In general, distributed systems:

☞ Yield higher performance

☞ Provide higher reliability

☞ Allow incremental growth

Distributed computing offers higher rates of return over individual CPUs:

- ☞ It is both feasible and easy to construct systems of a large number of CPUs connected by a high-speed network.
- ☞ It answers a need to share data scattered over these CPUs.
- ☞ It provides a way to share expensive peripherals.
- ☞ It allows one user to run a program on many different machines.

2.7.3 Disadvantages of Distributed Systems

In spite of their many advantages, distributed systems do create a few disadvantages. Some of these are:

- ☞ The need for new Operating Systems to support them
- ☞ A reliance on network communications
- ☞ The need for enhanced security
- ☞ Offer no nice classification of operating systems
- ☞ Use loosely and tightly coupled systems

Distributed Technologies

Distributed Objects and the Internet

3.1 INTRODUCTION

Over the past few years, the world has shown a growing interest in the Internet. E-mail sparked this interest and was the biggest traffic generator for several years. As the Internet grew in popularity, other tools such as file transfer protocol (ftp), gopher, and the World Wide Web emerged. Connectivity to the Internet blossomed from a few computer specialists at research institutions to include businesses, schools, and home users. At the same time, the ability to create, store, and view multimedia information became widespread.

Today, we see a proliferation of sites storing and distributing multimedia information on an ever-increasing range of topics to an exploding number of users. This section describes the technologies that provide client-based browsing and distribution via Internet resources in a wide range of media types (text, images, hypertext).

3.2 OBJECTS AND THE EVOLUTION OF THE INTERNET

At one level, the Web is considered to be a web object, although documents on the Web are quite different in many ways from objects in traditional distributed object-oriented systems. The World Wide Web exists because of object-oriented systems. Its uniqueness is the productivity of its visual environment for creating plug-and-play components. Without it, the Web would not exist in its current form.

Most organizations will not build Web-based distributed object systems, but they will deliver them. Productivity will depend on using developments for tight integration of a visual development environment with component generation facilities and seamless coupling with object/relational databases and other Internet technologies.

3.2.1 Underlying Principles

It is well understood in biological evolution that change occurs sharply at intervals separated by long periods of apparent stagnation, leading to the concept of punctuated equilibrium. Computer simulations of this phenomenon suggest that periods of equilibrium are actually periods of ongoing genetic change in an organism. The effects of that change are not apparent until several subsystems evolve in parallel to the point at which they can work together to produce a dramatic external effect.

Technological change, too, goes through periodic acceleration as a result of convergent discoveries. The pattern is the same for the adoption of eyeglasses in the eleventh century as it is for the invention of the computer in the twentieth century. Typically, it takes multiple inventions to enable a new technology and some 20 to 30 years for acceptance and adoption.

The personal computer, the mouse, the graphical user interface, the Ethernet, and the first widely used object-oriented language were all invented at Xerox in the early 1970s. The Internet was developed in the 1960s and by the mid-1970s many government agencies, universities, and research facilities were connected to what was then called *ARPAnet*. A design which led to TCP/IP was proposed by Vint Cerf and Bob Kahn in 1974 and the hypertext concept was created by Ted Nelson in the same year.

By the time these technologies had incubated for 20 years, it was evident in the 1990s that the major thrust of computer-human interaction approaching the millenium was the use of hypermedia systems to augment the human mind, much as the telescope and microscope had augmented human vision. All that remained were the triggering mutations required to cause an evolutionary explosion of distributed object-oriented, graphical, hypermedia systems on the Internet. These mutations occurred in 1993. They were the Web browser; Java, the first computer language designed for dynamic distribution of objects on the Web; and distributed objects, an approach to reengineering distributed software applications to support global renovation of corporate organizations.

3.3 DISTRIBUTED MULTIPROCESSING AND THE INTERNET

Distributed computing is the closely related development of client/server solutions and reflects a sweeping change in how computer systems are designed and deployed. Anyone who deals with modern computing technology, whether as a user, purchaser, administrator, or vendor, must understand what distributed client/server computing means and does not mean, and what its benefits and risks are. This book describes distributed multiprocessing to a broad class of computer professionals, users, and decision makers.

Very simply, client/server computing means that two parts of a single program are run by two (or more) computers. The two parts of the program are called, naturally enough, the client and the server. The server provides services to the client. This simple idea quickly leads to powerful capabilities, extended requirements, interesting technical issues, and sophisticated solutions.

Distributed computing embraces numerous products, strategies, and standards. Client/server computing is a natural, inevitable, and beneficial step in the evolution of computing technology. The advent and growth of microprocessors have brought new challenges to the enterprise. This has generated the desire in many companies to distribute their data, applications, and resources. The decentralization, cost of the microprocessors, and the growth of operating systems has caused heterogeneity of enormous proportions. But the enterprise still must be able to communicate and access the data/resources as a comprehensive system.

3.3.1 The Java Revolution

The popularity of Java has a significant impact on Smalltalk and C++ developers because Java can be viewed as a crippled Smalltalk for C++ programmers.

It avoids the complexity of C++ by introducing features that have been part of the Smalltalk environment for 20 years. More important, it can be seamlessly distributed over the World Wide Web. It is free, totally portable, runs on every major hardware platform, and is supported by every major hardware and software system.

3.3.2 Java and Production Systems

Smalltalk is currently running in many of the production, object-oriented, client/server business applications. Most of the rest are running C++. Java is running in a few of these applications today because it is not robust, performance is poor, and Java development environments are not ready for prime time. It is useful primarily for applets on Web pages and not much else. However, lack of tools, slow performance, and security restrictions have prevented deployment of these Java tools on a wider scale.

While Java has been designed to deal with the security issues posed by the Internet, it cannot effectively deal with client/server development on corporate intranets. For example, a Java applet

☞ Can communicate only with the server that distributed it to the client machine

☞ Cannot evoke an executable on a client machine

☞ Cannot write to ROM or disk on a client machine

Java's current performance and garbage collector limitations are similar to the first Smalltalk implemented in the 1970s. Nevertheless, Java compares well to other major object-oriented languages. Much of the leading compiler development is dedicated to providing good Java tools, improving Java performance, giving Java a state-of-the-art garbage collector, and generally getting Java ready for major developments. With good tools, excellent performance, and a robust environment, Java might outrank Smalltalk as a software development language.

3.3.3 Software Issues

It is not new that there is a software crisis. The news is that it is getting a lot worse:

☞ Developer productivity has dropped considerably.

☞ It costs a fortune to maintain ten billion and more lines of legacy code in the U.S. alone.

☞ Over half of the projects are over budget.

☞ Nearly one-third of new projects are canceled before completion.

Java produces no more functionality per line of code than C++, but the elimination of pointers in the language significantly reduces debugging time and eliminates memory leaks, producing more robust applications.

Yet another computer language will not solve our software productivity problems. Only component-based development with scalable, advanced environments can help. Enterprise solutions based on business object design and implementation are needed. New approaches to software development and higher levels of engineering skill are required.

3.3.4 Process Re-engineering

The global market has become an intensely competitive environment moving at an accelerating rate of change. Gradual improvements in productivity and enhancements in quality are no longer enough to maintain market leadership. Timely marketing of new products and rapid evolution of old products and applications are key success factors.

Accelerating product evolution requires reinventing the processes that bring products to market and eliminating processes that do not add value. Since modern corporations have embedded many rules and procedures for product delivery in computer systems, the software applications that run the business must undergo significant change. To gain the strategic advantages of speed and flexibility, corporations must remodel their business processes, and then rapidly translate that model into software implementations.

Business Process Re-engineering (BPR) sets the stage for continuing evolution of business processes to meet rapidly evolving requirements. Implementation of software systems that support BPR requires distributed objects that can both simulate corporate procedures and translate smoothly into software objects. Well-designed distribution object implementations can be modified easily as the business changes.

3.3.5 Reusable Components

Early adopters of object technology asserted that packaging software in object classes would allow software to realize some of the benefits as seen in IC chip fabrication. While there are many isolated projects that used object technology to achieve dramatic productivity gains during the past decade, this success has not translated into broad improvements across the software industry. Despite the promise of reusable objects, most IT organizations have realized a scant productivity improvement from object technology (OT). Failure to achieve larger productivity gains was attributed to:

☞ Data-centric, task-oriented application development

☞ Methodologies and cultures that do not promote reusability

☞ Few linkages between BPR-defined business processes and IT support initiatives

While productivity gains from object technology in recent years have been limited, some companies have been able to achieve dramatic returns on investment by bringing products to market sooner, with the flexibility necessary for rapid tuning of the products to meet changing market conditions.

Using an object-oriented development methodology yields quick time to market and good object-oriented design allows for rapid evolution of distributed objects in response to market conditions. The bottom line is that object technology is a necessary, but not a solely sufficient condition for large returns on investment. The Internet provides the first global infrastructure for rapid implementation of these capabilities.

3.4 DISTRIBUTED OBJECT ARCHITECTURE

As business models are renewed, software architectures must be transformed. A Distribution Object Architecture (DOA) is an effective solution for dynamic automation of a rapidly evolving business environment.

Dynamic change requires reuse of chunks of business functionality. A DOA must support reusable, plug-compatible business components. The two primary strategies now being used for implementing client/server systems to support reengineering of business processes are visual fourth-generation languages and classical object technology. While both of these approaches are better than traditional COBOL software development, neither provides adequate support for implementation of distribution objects.

3.4.1 Building Object Components

A group of objects is the ideal unit of reuse. These groups of objects should behave as a higher-level business process and have a clearly specified business language interface. Distributed components are encapsulated with a protocol that allows efficient communication with other objects on the network.

Consider a typical client/server application like an order entry system. This system takes a Purchase Order as input and produces a validated order as output. The internals of this component should be a black box to the external world. The resulting order is input for another subsystem or, alternatively, an exception condition is raised if the Purchase Order is not valid for processing.

To support plug-compatible reuse, a business component must be encapsulated in two directions. The external world must not know anything about component internals, and the internals must not know anything about external components, other than allowing interested objects to register for notification of specific events or exception conditions.

External databases must be encapsulated as distribution objects or reuse will not be easily achievable. There must be a database access component that causes values from any kind of database to materialize as objects inside the business component. Whether object oriented, relational, or other database access is required, a set of class libraries designed to automate this interface will result in a major savings in development.

A simple Order Entry client/server component has at least three large-grained components, one or more presentation objects, a business component that models the business process, and a database access component that shields the application developer from database access languages, database internals, and network communications.

3.4.2 Distributing Objects

System evolution will invariably distribute these objects to maximize network performance and processor utilization, and to ensure proper control, integrity, and security of information. Business re-engineering implies implementing a distributed environment where components encapsulating business functionality can be migrated to nodes on the network that allow maximum flexibility, scalability, and maintainability of a distribution object system.

Objects made up of nested components allow distribution of the components across a network. Deployment of a large-grained object may include distributing subcomponents across multiple heterogeneous computing resources in dispersed locations. Thus, an application designed on one processor is scattered across a network at runtime.

The impact of improvement in efficiency leading to greater customer satisfaction and resulting market share is far greater than any reduced costs in operations overhead or development time. It is the prime reason to use distribution object design tools.

3.4.3 RMI

Distributed systems consist of several layers:

☞ API

☞ ORB architecture

☞ Transport layer

The transport layer is the network protocol that allows one piece of a distributed system to talk to another piece. The ORB architecture is the system design that supports the distributed object mechanism. Finally, the API is what a programmer needs to know in order to build a distributed system.

Common Object Request Broker Architecture (CORBA) and RMI are two distributed object standards supported by the Object Management Group (OMG). CORBA is an architecture standard for building heterogeneous distributed systems. In other words, it supports the creation of distributed systems whose components are written in many different languages. An example of such a system might be a client/server application where the client is written in Smalltalk and the server is written COBOL. CORBA is specifically concerned with the architecture and API layers, using IDL to provide the API. CORBA can use different transport layers, such as the Internet Inter-ORB Protocol (IIOP).

RMI is an API standard for building distributed Java systems. In its current form, it uses its own proprietary architecture and transport layers, but neither is required. OMG has certified RMI using IIOP as the standard transport layer for doing distributed computing. By using IIOP as the transport layer, RMI is capable of interfacing with CORBA systems.

By using RMI in a pure Java environment, you gain the benefits of distributed garbage collection and full Java semantics. For example, CORBA cannot support distributed garbage collection since not all languages support garbage collection. In addition, because the API in CORBA uses IDL, this means that in order to build distributed systems programmers must leave the semantic context of the language in which they are developing. Java RMI enables developers to write Java code to build their distributed systems.

CORBA and RMI are not competing systems; they are complementary. Each of them suits different needs. The basic determinant is whether you require homogeneity or heterogeneity. Systems made up of components in languages other than Java demand CORBA. Systems that must be deployed partially in Java can use a hybrid of RMI and CORBA.

The hybrid solution makes sense if your delivery window is after IIOP support has been added to RMI and you need Java-to-Java distributed computing within your system, in addition to interoperability with other languages. Even in a 100% Java scenario, there is a place for CORBA.

3.4.4 Object Request Broker (ORB)

In CORBA, an ORB is the programming that acts as a broker between a client request for a service from a distributed object or component and the completion of that request. Having ORB support in a network means that a client program can request a service without knowing where the server is in a distributed network or exactly what the interface to the server program looks like. Components can find out about each other and exchange interface information as they are running.

CORBA's ORB may be thought of as strategic middleware that is more sophisticated conceptually and in its capabilities than earlier middleware, including RPCs, message-oriented middleware, database stored procedures, and peer-to-peer services.

An ORB uses the CORBA Interface Repository to find out how to locate and communicate with a requested component. When creating a component, a programmer uses either CORBA's IDL to declare its public interfaces or the compiler of the programming language translates the language statements into appropriate IDL statements. These statements are stored in the Interface

Repository as *metadata* or definitions of how a component's interface works. In brokering a client request, an ORB may provide all of these:

- ☞ *Event service*, which lets components specify events they want to be notified about.
- ☞ *Life cycle services*, which define how to create, copy, move, and delete a component.
- ☞ *Naming service*, which allows a component to find another component by name and supports existing naming systems or directories, including distributed compute environment (DCE), X.500 (a directory standard), and Sun's NIS (a naming server).
- ☞ *Transaction service*, which ensures that when a transaction is complete, changes are committed, or that, if not, database changes are restored to their pretransaction state.
- ☞ *Persistence service*, which provides the ability to store data on object databases, relational databases, and plain files.
- ☞ *Query service*, which allows a component to query a database. This service is based on the SQL3 specification and the Object Database.
- ☞ *Concurrency control service*, which allows an ORB to manage locks to data that transactions or threads may compete for.
- ☞ *Relationship service*, which creates dynamic associations between components that have not *met* before and for keeping track of these associations.
- ☞ *Externalization service*, which provides a way to get data to and from a component in a *stream*.
- ☞ *Management Group's* (ODMG) *Object Query Language* (OQL).
- ☞ *Licensing service*, which allows use of a component to be measured for purposes of compensation for use. Charging can be done by session, by node, by instance creation, or by site.

An ORB can even provide security and time services. Additional services for trading, collections, and change management are also available. The requests and replies that originate in ORBs are expressed through IIOP or other transport layer protocols.

3.4.5 IIOP

IIOP is an object-oriented protocol that makes it possible for distributed programs written in different programming languages to communicate over the Internet. IIOP is a critical part of CORBA.

Using CORBA's IIOP and related protocols, an organization can write programs that will be able to communicate with their own or other company's existing or future programs wherever they are located and without having to understand anything about the program other than its service and name.

CORBA and IIOP are competing with a similar strategy from Microsoft called the Distributed Component Object Model (DCOM). Microsoft and the Object Management Group, sponsors of CORBA, have agreed to develop software bridges between the two models so that programs designed for one can communicate with programs designed for the other.

CORBA and IIOP assume the client/server model of computing in which a client program always makes requests and a server program waits to receive requests from clients. When writing a program, you use an interface called the General Inter-ORB Protocol (GIOP). The GIOP is implemented in specialized mappings for one or more network transport layers. Undoubtedly, the most important specialized mapping of GIOP is IIOP, which passes requests or receives replies through the Internet's transport layer using the Transmission Control Protocol (TCP). Other possible transport layers could include IBM's Systems Network Architecture (SNA) and Novell's IPX.

For a client to make a request of a program somewhere in a network, it must have an address for the program. This address is known as the Interoperable Object Reference (IOR). Using IIOP, part of the address is based on the server's port number and Internet Protocol (IP) address. In the client's computer, a table can be created to map IORs to proxy names that are easier to use. The GIOP lets the program make a connection with an IOR and then send requests to it and allows servers to reply. A Common Data Representation (CDR) provides a way to encode and decode data so that it can be exchanged in a standard way.

A somewhat similar protocol, the RMI, is also becoming quite commonplace in distributed object environments.

3.5 WEB-BASED SOLUTIONS

To enhance competitiveness in an environment of accelerating change, businesses are turning to Web-based solutions for intranet client/server applications. Some potential benefits are:

- Thinner clients
- Reduced network costs
- Lower development and maintenance costs
- Simpler technology for MIS to implement
- Automated software distribution
- Transparent portability dramatically reduces complexity
- Infrastructure for distributed business object architecture

Building nontrivial client/server applications on the Web requires more than HTML programming. Current approaches are not object-oriented; common gateway interfaces (CGI) invocations must return a new screen on every interaction and context is lost. Every CGI access reopens the database, dramatically reducing performance characteristics of the application. Working around these problems requires a high level of technical skill and significant development resources not normally available to corporate MIS shops.

Current development typically is focused on an Internet-based object-oriented implementation that improves maintenance and enables reuse. C++ CGI components are used to maintain open database connection for sessions, radically improving performance. Java applets communicate with the C++ components to maintain context between screen interactions. The minimal environment needed for easy implementation of client/server applications on the Web includes:

☞ Remote method invocation across the network, dramatically simplifying programming.

☞ Java Applets or Servlets, which can initiate action (pull-and-push technology), and peer-to-peer communication is supported between applets and servlets. A simple example is the need for a servlet stock ticker that can update the browser applet.

☞ Servlet/JDBC optimization of database performance and simplification of object-to-relational table mapping.

☞ Database connections automatically held open for session and proper management of multiple simultaneous connections to the database.

3.5.1 Turning an Application into a Web Object

Software developers are in a mad rush to move their applications to the Web—to *webify* them. There are three basic steps involved in *webifying* existing applications. They are:

☞ *Webification*: Preparing programming objects for deployment on the web.

☞ *Decomposition*: Analyzing existing code to re-architect it as objects. Objects need to be well designed and well behaved, relying on a minimum of other objects for operations, but encompassing a full suite of useful functionality. A variety of re-engineering tools and methodologies are available for re-architecting the code base as libraries of reusable objects.

☞ *Componentization*: Architected web objects need to be built using as much existing code as possible. A wide variety of programming tools, such as Visual C++, are available to aid construction.

At the heart of this webifying endeavor are two competing standards for web objects: Java from Sun and ActiveX from Microsoft. Both Netscape and Microsoft are using the digital signature technology from VeriSign to identify the authors of downloadable programs. While this will not protect anyone from viruses and malicious code, it will make sure that applets and controls have not been tampered with after they are placed on the Web. If someone breaks into your company's system, you will know who did it.

Active Documents technology is a new feature that is available in Internet Explorer. Basically, Microsoft has taken the browser itself and reduced it to an empty container that ships with an HTML parsing engine inside. That container could just as easily hold a word processing, spreadsheet, or graphics engine. When Internet Explorer hits a file type it knows, it loads the appropriate engine and pops up all of the toolbars and editing functions appropriate to it. Potentially, this means users will be able to browse through all files, local or on the Internet, the same way they would browse through the Web. That is what the Active Documents technology is all about.

Both Java and ActiveX are powerful technologies allowing the deployment of sophisticated applications on the Web. Realistically, developers lack resources to pursue both paths, and must choose one of the technologies. Until Java or other technologies take better hold or unless users are likely to be working on nonmainstream platforms (UNIX, Linux, OS/2), they may be well served going with Microsoft's ActiveX initiative. Here are some important reasons why:

☞ Java applets cannot interact with any other kinds of object (such as OLE controls, SOM objects, OpenDoc servers). ActiveX objects, on the other hand, can communicate with other objects using a variety of protocols.

☞ Unlike Java, ActiveX objects can be called on a method-by-method basis within HTML pages. Java applets must be loaded and executed, in their entirety, when the HTML page containing them is loaded.

☞ Java applets cannot directly leverage critical system services (such as disk caching and communications facilities).

☞ Javascript scripts are unable to communicate, in any sophisticated way, with Java applets. Developers can use Basic scripts, on the other hand, to perform a rich set of operations with ActiveX objects.

☞ It is difficult to leverage an existing code base (such as C++ or VisualBasic applications) to create Java applets. ActiveX objects, on the other hand, can be created in a variety of languages, using existing libraries of code.

It may be true that Java applets will run on more platforms than ActiveX objects, but Microsoft encompasses Windows 95, Windows NT, and now the Macintosh platforms. This covers the vast majority of computers on the planet.

3.5.2 ActiveX and the Web

Critics of the ActiveX web objects strategy have ridiculed the neglect of safety issues. For example, an ActiveX object that a user encounters and executes in a web browser could easily erase the entire hard drive. Microsoft has begun to address some of these issues, including such initiatives as:

☞ *Windows Trust Verification*: The byte stream that comprises an object includes a proprietary authentication of the object, similar to a checksum. If someone were to modify the object (for example, decompile it and add a virus), this authentication would not match the modified object, and the object could not be loaded.

☞ *Code signing*: Certifying OCXs as safe and reliable.

3.5.3 Inside the ActiveX Platform

ActiveX is a powerful Web development paradigm with huge potential. Many pieces of the ActiveX platform are now in place, and they add up to a compelling solution for some applications—especially intranets.

Fundamentally, the ActiveX standard rests on Object Linking and Embedding (OLE) and COM, Windows development standards with years of history behind them. VBScript, the language used to program ActiveX objects on Web pages, is a dialect of Basic, a key language. The available tools used to build Web pages with ActiveX functionality owe an obvious debt to Visual Basic.

3.5.3.1 ActiveX Controls   ActiveX control is simply the new marketing term for *OLE control* (which was the new term for *OCX control*). OLE controls are only a subset of possible ActiveX controls, however, and, as a group, they are not necessarily the ones best suited for Web developers.

The problem with existing OLE controls is their typically large size. This is due both to the inherent complexity of the full OLE interfaces the controls must implement and to the fact that the Microsoft libraries used to create the controls were never optimized for size. Because any control that is not resident on the user's system must be downloaded across the Internet before it can run, controls used on Web pages need to be as small as possible. Only a few existing OLE controls fit the bill in this regard.

An ActiveX control, technically defined, is any COM object that implements Unknown, the basic OLE interface providing access to all the object's other interfaces. This makes it possible for developers to implement just a subset of the OLE interfaces needed for the task at hand, yet still be within the requirements of the specification. In essence, ActiveX controls provide a way for a programmer to create a high-level, reusable object with some type of useful generic behavior. The programmer then can pass the control along to another developer, who can use it as a building block inside any programming tool that supports ActiveX controls. (Most major Windows-based tools for C/C++, Basic, Pascal, and many other languages do.)

An ActiveX control might be anything from a push button to a fully functional spreadsheet.

3.5.3.2 ActiveX Control Pad   It takes nothing more than a text editor to create pages using VBScript and ActiveX controls. The basic ActiveX Control Pad interface is a single text-editing window that shows the full HTML source code of the page you're working on. A column on the left side of the editing window displays icons showing the position of any controls, scripts, or layouts embedded in the HTML code. The Control Pad will generate a bare HTML skeleton for new pages or let you import an existing document.

Selecting Insert ActiveX Control from ActiveX Control Pad's Edit menu or the right-click context menu brings up a list of the registered ActiveX controls on your system. Selecting a particular control brings up a modal control editor with an instance of the control displayed on a pseudoform. You can resize the control visually and set properties through a property sheet or a right-click context menu, the same way you would in Visual Basic. When you have finished setting properties and exited the form, the ActiveX Control Pad inserts the required <OBJECT> code block into your HTML page, along with the <PARAM> tags that correspond to the properties you selected. It also adds the correct 128-bit Object Class ID entry (something you would not want to do yourself!). Your control will appear in the page at the point where the Object code block was inserted in your HTML code. Once the ActiveX object has been inserted, you can add VBScript code to handle events or change properties.

3.5.3.3 ActiveX Layout Control

In addition to working with single controls, the ActiveX Control Pad also lets you create Layouts. These are collections of ActiveX controls within a container called the ActiveX Layout Control. The concept, which is somewhat analogous to a Visual Basic form, represents a big step away from HTML. Inside the Layout Control, the programmer now has precise control over the two-dimensional placement of controls including overlapping and transparency, allowing for a much more Windowslike approach to interface building.

You build layouts within the ActiveX Control Pad by selecting the Insert Layout option. This brings up a Layout control and a tabbed Toolbox containing controls you can add to that form. The Toolbox collection includes labels, text boxes, list boxes, scroll bars, command buttons, radio buttons, check boxes, tabs, and hot spot-sensitive image controls. You can also add more tabs and ActiveX controls to the Toolbox. The standard controls and the Layout control itself will be included with Internet Explorer eventually, so programmers can assume that these items will not need to be downloaded.

When your Layout is complete, save it as a text file, with an .ALX extension. In this file, the two-dimensional Layout is defined within <DIV> tabs, and the child controls are specified inside this block with <OBJECT> tags. (Note that an .ALX file can also contain VBScript procedures.) The Layout is referenced in the HTML page using a standard <OBJECT> reference, and at runtime, the controls can either be called from the local system or be downloaded from a remote server. By giving developers the ability to create complex apps with multiple controls and providing precise control over the placement of those controls, layouts represent a significant step away from the vagaries of HTML.

3.5.3.4 Weighing Pros and Cons
ActiveX is a compelling technology, but it faces an uphill battle on the Web. Support is currently limited to the Internet Explorer platform, which in turn limits you to the Windows environment. This leaves the domain of private intranets, and it is for this area that ActiveX makes the most sense right now.

Currently, ActiveX and VBScript are best suited for enhancing the client side of the application, something that Java also addresses. Using Java to put a full-featured charting engine or data grid on a Web page would be a mammoth task. Building the same page using ActiveX controls would be relatively trivial.

3.5.4 ActiveX/CORBA Harmonization

One of the most encouraging developments for building distributed object applications for the Web is the emerging synergy between Java and ActiveX strategy based on OLE/COM. It turns out to be as easy or easier to use Java for creating COM components as it is to use Visual Basic or C++. In fact, COM architects say that Java is becoming the language of choice for COM component implementation. Every ActiveX component has started to look like a Java class to a Java application and every Java class to look like an ActiveX component to a Windows application.

Java's support for garbage collection eliminates the need for reference pointer counting, which is very tedious when building COM components in C++. It also hides some of the complexity of the COM interfaces. As a result, it is possible to supply seamless integration between ActiveX and Java components. If the vendors implement products properly, it will be possible to talk to the same component via DCOM or CORBA protocols.

Most CORBA-compliant, ORB implementations enable DCOM clients to access CORBA objects on the network. This is a primitive capability compared to two-way interoperability between DCOM and CORBA: full interoperability is lacking. Users must be knowledgeable and careful when selecting CORBA middleware to ensure that required capabilities are supported.

Both Windows NT and OS/2 Warp have object-orientation facilities built into the operating system, allowing developers to write distributed applications, portions of which can reside on remote servers anywhere on the network.

DCOM and IBM's Distributed System Object Model (DSOM) basically do the same thing. They allow developers to create objects and to have other programs and objects operate on them in a binary-standard manner. The binary-standard part is significant: C++ objects, for instance, exist only for the program in which they were compiled, whereas DCOM and DSOM objects can be written in any language and can communicate with other such objects, no matter which language they were written in, even if they were written by another vendor.

Compound document systems, such as OLE and OpenDoc, are built on system object facilities, specifically DCOM and DSOM. Microsoft used to call both the object model and the compound document OLE; now, however, OLE is just the compound document API, and the object model is COM. ActiveX is basically synonymous with COM, with some facilities added for Internet work.

Many of the controls in Windows 95 and Windows NT Explorer are COM objects, and much of the OS/2 Workplace Shell is built on SOM. The advantage of this is that developers can write simple programs to use the same controls that are in the operating system and easily modify their behavior.

3.5.5 VBScript

Visual Basic Scripting Edition (VBScript) is the native scripting language of Microsoft Internet Explorer and the obvious choice for programming ActiveX-based Web pages. VBScript is a Web-adapted subset of Visual Basic for Applications (VBA). It uses Basic's familiar object-property dot notation, subs, functions, and flow-control structures, and it has the broad range of intrinsic functions that Basic programmers expect. Anyone who has programmed in a modern Basic language will feel at home in VBScript.

Like VBA, VBScript supports the Option Explicit statement to force variable declaration. But unlike VBA, VBScript is not explicitly typed, and all variables, string or numeric, are stored as Variants. Implicit data types—including integer, long, single, double, string, numeric, date, and financial—exist, but the system only infers these by the format of the data. Fortunately, there are conversion functions and functions for testing the type of a variable (VarType, IsNumeric, for example) that you will almost certainly employ for pages that implement data validation.

VBScript lacks any support for file I/O and direct memory access. This approach, which VBScript shares with Java and JavaScript, is necessary to prevent the language from becoming a vehicle for programs with subversive or destructive behavior. VBScript does not support a Debug object.

Your VBScript source code is embedded into the HTML page using <SCRIPT> tags and is typically placed in the <HEAD> section of the page. The code block is prefixed by a LANGUAGE="VBScript" statement, which tells the browser the language to execute. You should embed your code in comment tags (<!--, -->) so that it will not display in Browsers that do not support VBScript.

As tempting as it is to dive right into page construction using ActiveX controls, it is worth noting that VBScript can manipulate HTML form objects like text boxes and buttons. Even with these simple ingredients, you can build a wide range of useful functionality into the page. VBScript calls the HTML form objects by referencing the FORM NAME and the NAME property of each object within the form.

ActiveX controls offer substantially more power than HTML forms, however. Controls are added to code using <OBJECT> tags. The code specifies the object's ID, which is the object name referenced in your code, and a CLSID, which is the 128-bit globally unique identifier (GUID) for the OLE control. When an ActiveX control is called from VBScript, the system searches the Windows Registry to see if the control is present. If not, the system uses the CODEBASE attribute (specified in the <OBJECT> tag), which points to the server containing the required control. After the control is downloaded and installed through an intrinsic system service, it is ready for execution.

3.5.6 Internet Explorer

The Internet Explorer has three particularly important features for developers: It can act as a container for ActiveX controls, it can execute scripts in VBScript or JavaScript embedded in HTML documents, and it provides a Java virtual machine (VM) for executing Java programs.

The Internet Explorer's Java VM can expose itself to the developer as an ActiveX control. This allows you to launch a Java program programmatically. The Internet Explorer is also able to provide wrapper Java applets as ActiveX controls so that the applets' methods and properties are accessible to VBScript and other supported scripting languages. Internet Explorer also implements Authenticated feature, which allows control vendors to provide a digital authenticity signature for their controls and gives end users a basis on which to enable or deny the installation of controls during a download.

3.6 OBJECT-ORIENTED WEB SERVERS

The best object-oriented (OO) Web servers are those whose designs and implementation are completely object-oriented, not merely object-based APIs. Web server technology has evolved rapidly. Web servers started as simple HTML document servers, then were augmented with the CGI for invoking scripts and other processes on the server. CGI scripts (generally written in Perl), combined with HTML input forms, created the basis for very useful data access utilities and dynamic HTML documents. Developers have been very creative in applying the limited CGI interface for connecting to a wide variety of back-end systems.

Through these extensions, the Web server has evolved to become a middle layer within an n-tier (4, 5, 6, ..., n tiers) client/server architecture, connecting Web clients to other database and legacy servers.

The essential characteristic of a Web server is not that it supports CGI extensions, however, or even that it be capable of delivering static HTML and multimedia files. A Web server is recognized by a client simply by the fact that it supports the Hypertext Transfer Protocol (HTTP). Most Web server requests are received as GET or POST commands, and the results are delivered as a data stream with additional MIME-type header information. Because HTTP rides on top of TCP/IP, the language of the Internet, it is easy to add HTTP support as a front-end to almost any network system. For example, embedded systems for real-time manufacturing controls were already converting to TCP/IP network communication, and now lightweight HTTP servers are being added to these embedded systems, allowing any Web browser to query their status.

An OO Web server can be created either by adding HTTP protocol support to an existing server platform or by developing an extensible Web server using OO technologies. The best OO Web servers are those whose designs and implementation are completely object-oriented, not merely object-based APIs.

3.6.1 Extensible Web Servers

Most client/server systems are designed with a two-tier architecture—that is, a *fat client* connected to a database server. Even Java-based systems are not deviating from this approach, but they use Java Database Connectivity (JDBC) in a large client applet to connect to a database. In these systems, the Web server has the trivial role of delivering the applet to the client browser. Object-oriented Web servers are able to take a more active role in a middle tier of the architecture.

Object-oriented Web servers are often described as *extensible*, meaning that they either expose class interfaces to be implemented or provide superclasses for inheritance, or both. Application specific subclasses are loaded into the server process and become an integral part of its functionality. There is growing support for a standard *servlet* API so that new subclasses can be written that will run on many different servers.

The servlet object is primarily responsible for communicating with the client. For HTTP protocol, this communication consists of retrieving parameters from the GET and POST requests, and prepending appropriate headers onto the response. The actual work done by the servlet is performed by other objects instantiated by the servlet object. These other objects might be responsible for database or legacy system connectivity, or they might be skeletons for CORBA-based objects that are implemented on yet another server. This is where it gets interesting. Other previously written, domain-specific classes can be integrated, thus extending the Web server with application logic, business rules, or other middle-tier functionality.

3.7 TRANSACTION PROCESSING MONITORS (TPMS) FOR DISTRIBUTED ENVIRONMENTS

Strategically, *distributed TP monitors* are the most important type of middleware. In today's corporate computing environment diverse computer systems must work together in a coherent, unified fashion. Distributed TPMs provide a tangible, pragmatic solution. But, by its nature, a TPM is invisible, like all middleware. You should investigate a distributed TPM if you

☞ have downsized to client/server and introduced heterogeneous platforms connected by some form of distributed communications

☞ have inherited a legacy of mixed operating systems, DBMSs, computers, and networks

☞ need services such as security, transaction control, timing, and guaranteed delivery

☞ are building business-critical, multinode transaction applications

☞ have tried to build your own middleware and realized it is expensive, time consuming, and hard to keep current with ever-changing technologies

3.7.1 What Makes a TPM Distributed?

Anyone running a legacy system is familiar with the traditional transaction processing monitor. A TPM is a deeply proprietary piece of software capable of funneling transactions from hundreds of terminals into a single mainframe.

But the single mainframe has been replaced now by a much more complex, multivendor, distributed environment. It takes a distributed TPM to coordinate and control these heterogeneous resources and to ensure that each transaction is completed successfully. If any part of the transaction fails, the distributed TPM must restore all affected resources, no matter where they reside. Keeping distributed resources in line is beyond the traditional TPM so vendors are enhancing and repositioning their traditional TPMs to deal with the complexities of distributed systems.

3.8 MERGING DISTRIBUTED OBJECT TECHNOLOGIES

Different object models arise from differing requirements. OLE/COM provides interfaces for popular existing desktop suites and applications; Smalltalk provides a superior object-oriented application environment; C++ provides a method for object-oriented systems, infrastructures, and component-building. Important new standards like CORBA IDL provide a language- and location-neutral messaging interface for component integration. As an example, Expersoft's ORB provides the communications backbone with which these different object models can coexist as one enterprise system. Some of the types of object models employed in the enterprise are:

1. Fabricating the CORBA components out of smaller, individual objects that cooperate to form components. These individual objects may perform business rules and support logic such as graphical user interfaces (GUIs). Since they form the *plumbing* for components, they frequently have more stringent performance characteristics, such as asynchronous messages and event handlers. They are frequently written in such object-oriented languages as C++ or Smalltalk.

2. A message bus for CORBA component objects and servers. Components can be individual large-grained objects, collaborating groups of objects, or existing nonobject-oriented monolithic applications wrapped with CORBA interfaces. Also called distribution objects and Frameworks, these building blocks employ object-oriented mechanisms like inheritance and polymorphism to provide higher-level applications logic.

3. Assembling and coordinating (*scripting*) the CORBA components into desktop-centric applications. This involves connecting OLE/COM components and enterprise component (CORBA) objects. Scripting tools at this layer would also make use of tools such as Visual Basic to allow nonprogrammers and power users to build the final stages of the user applications.

The CORBA IDL specification is not an implementation model, but rather an interface and services model. It is language neutral and leaves maximum flexibility for underlying implementation details. In fact, recent attempts by some ORB vendors to build enterprises using CORBA IDL as the low-level implementation model have resulted in performance and integration concerns that have forced the customer to provide expensive, proprietary extensions to the CORBA-based ORB. This problem could be avoided by using CORBA IDL for distributed component interfaces rather than for individual C++/Smalltalk distributed objects. The goals of CORBA and other object models are examined below .

3.8.1 Goals of Component Integration

A component in CORBA is intended to behave like an object or object server to a client application, regardless of whether it is written in an object-oriented language. This component *encapsulation* of an application is done by representing it with the IDL and hiding the details of the application, and its location, from the client. In particular, the CORBA object model provides a strong separation of *interface* from *implementation*.

CORBA is oriented to the level of the component subsystem or server, rather than that of the individual object. The CORBA IDL is not pure OO technology; while it does support interface inheritance, it is more a tool for encapsulating things to make them look like objects to a client. Bindings to convert IDL to such languages as C++, Smalltalk, C (all of which are already standardized), COBOL, and ADA mean that an organization can describe application objects and services with a well-known IDL interface. It can provide this interface specification enterprisewide to software developers using many implementation languages.

The CORBA IDL component is intended to serve as an interface specification or *contract* among departments, corporations, larger applications, or entities in a system that will be smaller in number and larger in size so that they provide adequate performance with a synchronous or deferred synchronous (also called *polling*) architecture. In other words, IDL provides a standard client/server interface: A client program requests a server for information, waits until the information is obtained, and continues on to the next activity.

3.8.1.1 Environment Independence CORBA is not only language neutral (it is intended to support C++ and C), but it is also fairly object-model neutral. What this means is that even though it is an ORB model, it is flexible enough to allow nonobject-oriented modules and applications to fit into the ORB mechanism.

Nonobject-oriented pieces can exchange data with each other and with object subsystems as well. Given that the components in an enterprise might not all be object-oriented, CORBA IDL must provide descriptive features that are not tied to any language or object model.

The purpose of the ORB is actually pretty narrow in terms of enterprise application functionality: To provide an interface to remote object components and a *router* between local and remote objects and components. CORBA does not go beyond this base ORB functionality for a reason. It is envisioned that there will be many special-purpose ORBs for a variety of application needs ranging from lightweight embedded requirements to full-service corporate infrastructures.

This least common denominator does have a cost, however, in that it cannot directly exploit the features of native object-oriented languages that can enhance functionality or performance. For example, IDL interfaces do not currently provide for the transmission of full objects between components: There are no pointers as in C++, no event callbacks for asynchronous behavior, and no broadcasting/multicasting of objects to multiple receivers because these features are not common to all the languages that need access to the ORB. But they are needed for functionality and so have to be provided at some level for a working system to be built. Discussing the low-level enablers and services of distributed object systems leads naturally to the discussion about the strengths of a more generic object model for full enterprise capable applications.

3.8.1.2 Language-Specific OO Systems Extended C++ would be a good starting point to discuss a more general language-based object-oriented model for enterprise systems. The main difference between this extended C++ toolkit and the CORBA model is that the former allows for the direct manipulation of objects as remote call arguments and callbacks. Extended C++ behaves like, and uses the same idioms as, nondistributed C++.

CORBA, on the other hand, is a *looser* object model that minimizes dependencies on OO languages, so that its main goal of encapsulating existing large-grain applications is easier to achieve in a multilanguage environment. With a C++ model, objects are individually distributed, as well as used as parts of larger-grained distributed components. Of course, individual objects can come in all sizes, but they have the more flexible communication styles that enable them to be used in much larger numbers for more effective scaling and event-driven real-time notification.

3.8.1.3 Asynchronous Message-Based Communications   The design features for object systems are already well-understood: Inheritance, encapsulation, and polymorphism. These three characteristics of objects provide the central design benefit of objects, namely, reusability. Another factor in reusability is a communications model using a message-based architecture. Messaging is a lightweight communications paradigm, which allows for an object to be available for further requests and activities instead of being blocked, waiting for a server to return a result.

With asynchronous messaging, the client can be notified when the results are ready instead of waiting, or repeatedly polling, for data. The benefits of asynchronous messaging are quite evident in a large network with many objects, since the overhead from the synchronous blocking, and for client-side polling, can be quite high.

3.8.1.4 Event-Driven Capabilities for Response and Manageability   Other characteristics that fully distributed object systems have (that must be implemented in the server side of the ORB) are centered around object-level deployment and management features. In a multiplatform networked environment, systems need to migrate transparently and transport objects around the network so that client-level services can be provided independent of location. Also, migration permits services to be load-balanced or failed-over to another system, transparent to the client. Another feature is event-driven response capabilities. As they are coming from outside the system or control, messages loop. These messages can range from networks going down to inventory objects suddenly running low on an item in stock. The system needs to be able to respond to events like this, asynchronously, and in a controlled manner.

In summary, communications requirements at the component level and individual object level differ in that the latter require lightweight interobject communications that allow objects to send a message and then continue with other activities until notified when the request is ready. Events and messages are part-and-parcel of object systems, especially distributed object systems with all their complexities of network behavior. Object systems are fundamentally different from synchronous *call and wait* client/server programs in this regard, and the application of RPC-style call-and-wait communications will bog down a system with numerous objects.

Until now, the difference was that CORBA is a language-independent specification built by an OMG-industry consortium.

Most Java developers will find it more convenient to use RMI in order to employ the same programming style both to all-Java and heterogeneous systems.

3.8.2 A Way to Merge Object Models

We have seen that a distributed enterprise object model needs to contain an ORB, rather than merely be an ORB. The ORB needs to be integrated within an adequate enterprise object model. Simply stretching the ORB interface model into an implementation model causes significant performance and manageability problems. The enterprise object model itself needs to leverage actual experience and expertise in building systems for vertical applications. The ORB has been modularized to support both the different object models and the modular configuration of the engine either to include, or exclude, specific services.

3.8.2.1 A Complete CORBA Environment   A complete CORBA environment will be provided for C++ and Smalltalk developers. The CORBA compilers (for static and dynamic interfaces between client and server) will contain integrated repositories for industry standard C++ and Smalltalk ParcPlace/VisualWorks component building.

3.9 ISSUES IN DISTRIBUTED OBJECT SYSTEMS

The key to building standards-compliant distributed object systems is to use the features of the different object models when they are most appropriate, based on business requirements. Specifically, the enterprise object-oriented application should be driven by lower-level object models for the implementation details, with CORBA IDL used for interface specifications between components. At times, there will be a language mismatch between the CORBA and OO-language models, given that CORBA is designed for integration with existing client/server and legacy applications and that native approaches (like Smalltalk/C++) are designed for low-level modeling of application support and system support objects. Both models are important, and both models must be managed and merged for enterprise object systems.

3.9.1 Implementing a Message-Based Architecture

One example is the need for a low-level interobject communications approach that works well inside as well as between components. Some implementations provide an easily implemented asynchronous method call mechanism that provides good scalability for numerous low-level object communications. The misapplication of component-level IDL communication models to individual object-level communications leads to the following issues of performance and maintenance:

1. *Clientside threads*: The individual object has an over-reliance on the IDL's synchronous approach. With synchronous-method invocation the only calling style, client code needs to propagate threads (which attempt

to build async behavior on top of sync calls) to other intermediate software packages as well.

The client has to maintain and manage threads, in addition to its own applications' functionality. Threads are powerful enablers for concurrency on the server side, where they provide transparent scalability to many clients, but they should not be the primary means of concurrency on the client side, where they increase the coding burden and make integration more difficult (with add-on packages) since they must support threads as well.

2. *Interobject network coupling*: The object messaging-event paradigm is compromised somewhat by the component synchronous/deferred synchronous approach, if used for too many low-level objects. When a client object connects to another object which in turn connects to another object, a *stacking* effect results, in which the intermediate object is blocked and unavailable to other potential clients. This stacking increases behavioral coupling between objects and in fact reduces availability (reusability) for other potential clients. This can be avoided by allowing heavily used intermediate objects to send messages on and then continue with their own control loop in order to service other object requests. There have been attempts by ORB vendors to get around these problems with low-level, interobject synchronous communications, but the work-arounds are not optimal for a variety of reasons:

✗ One strategy is to simulate asynchronous callbacks with IDL *oneway* function calls to set up a double oneway connection between the client object and the server object, each managing the connection to each other. Unfortunately, now the server is no longer independent of the client and has to be aware of clientside behavior, especially if it has to manage connections to more than one client—which is generally the case. A better solution would be to allow the client to set up a callback so that it could be notified when the server data is ready, since the client and server are uncoupled in time and more independent of each other. This latter approach is frequently needed for numerous objects and is an example of asynchronous method invocation.

✗ Another uses the Dynamic Invocation Interface *deferred synchronous* method invocation style, which is useful for component clients to poll for data from a server, if they know that the waiting period will be too long for a synchronous wait. A polling approach works for a few large processes because, just like the synchronous calling style, it is dependent on how many clients will be doing it over the network. The disadvantage of polling is twofold: it may clog the network if done too much and it requires that the client go back and check for data, wasting time managing the information transaction instead of saving its CPU cycles for more useful work. Here again, the asynchronous callbacks of Extended C++ permit the client to be notified, and hence interrupted, only when its data is ready. This is very effective for a large number of distributed objects in large networks.

3. *Smart Proxies*: A caching scheme to duplicate the remote object server into local memory is another approach to dealing with synchronous calls over a network. Essentially, this tactic replicates the data from a remote object into a local object, transparent to the client, providing better performance because communication does not have to go over the network itself. Of course, this requires that an additional copy of each remote server be placed into local memory and additional connections now exist between server and smart proxy and between client and server/proxy.

3.9.2 Event Management

The need for component objects to have an event-management interface is well recognized by the CORBA standards developers, and the CORBA services-events interface has been defined. This will enable standard IDL-based APIs to send and receive applications events by client objects.

3.9.3 Transportation and Migration of Objects

Since the CORBA IDL model has to be OO-language independent, any object movement over the wire needs to convert objects to *flat* records, or opaque byte streams, and back to objects again at the receiving end. This feature must be used with care in CORBA, since there could be performance hits. A better solution to this conversion process would be to provide different access levels in one unified mechanism so that CORBA and the native object interface could map to a single object transportation engine without a performance penalty.

3.10 CONCLUSIONS

The lack of tools to simplify implementation of distributed object systems on the Internet or an intranet is a major factor inhibiting adoption of Java-based client/server applications. The lack of a robust, bug-free Java integrated development environment is a second impediment. The third major handicap to building these applications is the lack of the component-based environment required for building business object architectures.

Corporations that take advantage of object architectures will significantly shorten product cycles. Java will play a major role sometime before the year 2000. Consulting groups that use distribution objects should be able to underbid their competition significantly and deliver new systems on time and under budget. Because a distribution object architecture will allow software to change as rapidly as the underlying business processes, corporate viability will be enhanced by early implementation.

Client/Server Environments

4.1 INTRODUCTION

Client/server computing is a managerial and computational model that partitions information work to maximize efficiency and flexibility. Client/server is the combination of three major technologies: Relational database management systems (RDBMSs), networks, and client interfaces (see Figure 4.1). Each element contributes to the overall platform with very specific roles but is independent of the others in performing its functions.

Clients execute specific local tasks with local resources. Servers provide shared resources and fulfill broad tasks. Communication enables definition and completion of full work processes. Through optimal mapping of tasks to exploit each partition of this model, maximum efficiency and flexibility of work processes is achieved, especially in distributed multiprocessing environments.

This section explains how the client/server architecture is a fundamental enabling approach that provides the most flexible framework for using new technologies such as the World Wide Web in establishing distributed computing environments. The old paradigm of host-centric, time-shared computing has given way to a new client/server approach, which is message based and modular. Thus most new technologies can be viewed as simply different implementation strategies built on a client/server foundation.

Even though most people use the term client/server when talking about group computing with PCs on networks, PC network computing evolved before the client/server model started gaining acceptance in the late 1980s.

These first PC networks were based on file sharing. In file sharing, the server simply downloads or transfers files from the shared location to your desktop, where the logic and data for the job are. File sharing is simple and

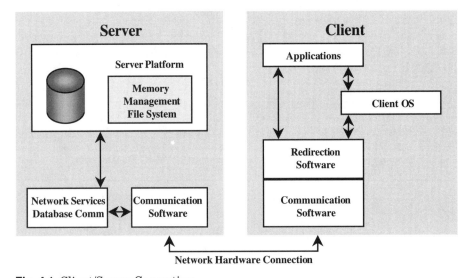

Fig. 4.1 Client/Server Computing

works as long as shared usage is low, update contention is very low, and the volume of data to be transferred is low compared with LAN capacity.

As PC LAN computing moved into the '90s two trends provided the impetus for client/server computing. The first was that as the number of first-generation PC LAN applications and their users increased, the file-sharing capacity was strained. Multiuser technology provided satisfactory performance for up to as many as a dozen simultaneous users of a shared file, but it was rare to find a successful implementation beyond that point. The second change was the emergence and then dominance of the GUI metaphor on the desktop. Very soon, GUI presentation formats, led by Windows and Mac, became mandatory for presenting information. The requirement for GUI displays meant that traditional mini or mainframe applications with their terminal displays soon looked hopelessly out of date.

The architecture and technology that evolved to answer this demand was client/server, in the guise of a two-tiered approach. By replacing the file server with a true database server, the network could respond to client requests with just the answer to a query (rather than the entire file) against a relational DBMS. One benefit of this approach is to significantly reduce network traffic. Also, with a real DBMS, true multiuser updating is now easily available to users on the PC LAN. Today, the idea of using Windows or Mac-style PCs to front-end a shared database server is familiar and widely implemented.

In a two-tier client/server architecture, RPCs or standard query languages (SQLs) are typically used to communicate between the client and server. The server is likely to have support for stored procedures and triggers. This means that the server can be programmed to implement business rules that are better suited to run on the server than the client, resulting in a much more efficient overall system.

The two-tiered client/server architecture has proven to be very effective in solving workgroup problems. *Workgroup* is loosely defined as a dozen to a hundred people interacting on a LAN. For bigger, enterprise-class problems and/or applications that are distributed over a WAN, using a two-tier approach has caused some problems.

4.1.1 Client/Server Software Infrastructure

With competing paradigms—SQL databases, TP monitors, groupware, and distributed objects—the middleware that connects clients to servers has grown dauntingly complex. Client/server is the combination of three major technologies: relational DBMS, networks, and client interface (usually GUI/PC based). Each element contributes to the overall platform with very specific roles but is independent of the others in performing its functions.

Processing is divided between the client system and the server. Each application involves two programs linked by the network: one program is a client, the other is a server. The client makes requests for services provided by the server.

The network traffic is reduced to queries to and responses from the database server rather than the entire database file being sent back and forth. Users are not limited to one type of system or platform. In a client/server environment, the workstations can be IBM-compatible PCs, Macs, UNIX workstations, or a combination of these, and can run multiple operating systems.

The division of services performed by database servers and client computers follows a natural division of labor, taking into consideration the relative strength of each resource. Since the database server automatically handles many of the difficult and complex data processing tasks, including concurrency control (locking) and transaction processing, the application's responsibility is to issue requests for data and to handle returning data.

4.1.2 Advantages of the Client/Server Environment

Client/server is an open system. The advantages of this environment include:

- ☞ *Interoperability*: Key components (client/network/server) work together.
- ☞ *Data integrity*: Entity, domain, and referential integrity are maintained on the database server.
- ☞ *Scalability*: Any of the key elements may be replaced when either the need to increase or reduce processing for that element dictates, without major impact on the other elements.
- ☞ *Accessibility*: Data may be accessed from WANs and multiple client applications.
- ☞ *Performance*: Performance may be optimized by hardware and process.
- ☞ *Security*: Data security is centralized on the server.
- ☞ *Adaptability*: New technology (e.g., multimedia, broadband networks, distributed database, pen computing) may be incorporated into the system.
- ☞ *Affordability*: Cost effectiveness is insured by using less expensive million instructions per second (MIPs) available on each platform.

Client/server is a computational architecture that involves client processes requesting service from server processes. Client/server computing uses local processing power—the power of the desktop platform. Client/server architecture allocates the application processing between a client and a server so that each component performs the tasks for which it is best suited. It is a combination of a client or front-end portion that interacts with the user, and a server or back-end portion that interacts with the shared resource. The client process contains solution-specific logic and provides the interface between the user and the rest of the application system. The server process acts as a software engine that manages shared resources such as databases, printers, modems, or high-powered processors.

The client is a process (program) that sends a message to a server process (program), requesting that the server perform a task (service). Client programs usually manage the user-interface portion of the application, validate data entered by the user, dispatch requests to server programs, and sometimes execute business logic. A server process fulfills the client request by performing the task requested. Server programs generally receive requests from client programs, execute database retrieval and updates, manage data integrity, and dispatch responses to client requests. Sometimes server programs execute common or complex business logic.

Compared with other kinds of networked computing, it is clear that the users in client/server own much more power and ease of use. Client/server computing refers to a split task that a server and a client computer share. It allows desktop computers to access very large libraries of data without drowning in the information or swamping the request for information to the file server.

However, other forms of networked computing, such as file servers or printer servers, offer the redirecting function in their client software and do not share the task as client/server does but share its resources (hard disks, printers) to users' computers. Compared with mainframe/terminals, such as the VAX environment, client/server owns its presentation interface and computing ability, unlike terminals which, unless connected with the mainframe, cannot do anything. When connected, the terminal displays incoming data on the video screen and sends keyboard input to the host computer.

Distributed data processing refers to a data processing arrangement in which the computers are decentralized—scattered in various places. Hence, processing occurs in a number of distributed locations and only semiprocessed information is communicated on data communications lines from remote points to the central computers. It requires two or more distinct processors to complete a single transaction, and the distribution of applications and business logic is spread across multiple processing platforms. Often the data used in a distributed processing environment is also distributed across platforms.

4.2 CLIENT/SERVER ARCHITECTURES

Client/server was one of the most ubiquitous phrases of the 1990s, with the trade press, advertisements, and news media filled with stories of client/ server products and solutions. The client/server concept and the closely related development of distributed computing solutions reflect a sweeping change in how computer systems are designed and deployed today.

The client/server software architecture is a versatile, message-based modular infrastructure intended to improve usability, flexibility, interoperability, and scalability as compared to a centralized, mainframe, time-sharing computing. A client is defined as a requester of services and a server is defined as the provider of services. A single machine can be both a client and a server depending on the software configuration.

As a result of the limitations of file-sharing architectures, the client/ server architecture emerged. This approach introduced a database server to replace the file server. Using a relational DBMS, user queries could be answered directly. The client/server architecture reduced network traffic by providing a query response rather than total file transfer. It improves multiuser updating through a GUI front end to a shared database. In client/server architectures, RPCs or SQL statements are typically used to communicate between the client and server.

Client/server computing embraces numerous products, strategies, and standards, and it is a natural, inevitable, and beneficial step in the evolution of computing technology.

4.2.1 Client/Server Solutions

Implementing a client/server environment requires the integration of data, applications, application development, management and control, and system- and network-operating software, all running on systems of heterogeneous origins. Organizational structures are flattening in order to empower employees to make decisions closer to the customer, to be more responsive to the customer. Personal computers provide a whole new level of computing flexibility, with simple, easily used programs. These programs are transportable, allowing businesses to react instantly to customers' needs.

To the end user, simplicity is critical to the success of client/server computing. End users need information access as easy as getting cash from an automated teller machine (ATM). Customers can get money from their bank account at any ATM across the country with just an ATM card and a password. Client/server computing means changing our information systems to support the changes of the business environment.

4.2.2 Integration of Computing Systems

Client/server computing provides the seamless integration of personal computers with host systems. This style of computing allows organizations to be responsive to their customers while maintaining the security and integrity to manage their business effectively.

Client/server computing generally refers to a computing model in which two or more computers interact in such a way that one provides services to the other. This model allows customers to access information resources and services located anywhere within the customer's information network. Customers are very interested in client/server computing because it allows them to be more responsive, as well as to effectively utilize all computing resources within their network.

Clients are typically thought of as personal computers, but a client can be a midrange system or even a mainframe. Servers are typically thought of as a midrange or mainframe system, but a server can be another personal computer on the network. Today's networks have computers for file serving, database serving, application serving, and communications serving. Each of these servers is dedicated, providing a specific service to all authorized users within a network. These servers also allow some of the processing to be handled on each user's PC and some on a centralized server.

For example, a database server uses the PC for the display (user interface) and processing (application logic) portions of an application, while the server provides the data-management portion of the application. On the other hand, an application server uses the PC for the display portion of an application, while using the server for both the processing and data management portions. In a rapidly changing business environment, client/server computing offers customers the flexibility they need to manage their business effectively.

4.2.3 Mainframe Software Architectures

With mainframe software architectures, all intelligence is within the central host computer. Users interact with the host through a terminal that captures keystrokes and sends that information to the host. Mainframe software architectures are not tied to a hardware platform. User interaction can be done using PCs and UNIX workstations. A limitation of mainframe software architectures is that they do not easily support graphical user interfaces (GUIs) or access to multiple databases from geographically dispersed sites. In the last few years, mainframes have found a new use as a server in distributed client/server architectures.

4.2.4 File-Sharing Architectures

The original PC networks were based on file-sharing architectures, in which the server downloads files from the shared location to the desktop environment. The requested user job is then run (including logic and data) in the desktop environment. File-sharing architectures work if shared usage, update contention, and the volume of data to be transferred all are low. In the 1990s, PC LAN computing changed because the capacity of the file sharing was strained as the number of online users grew and GUIs became popular (making mainframe and terminal displays appear to be out of date).

4.2.5 Two-Tier Architectures

With two-tier client/server, the user-system interface is usually located in the user's desktop environment and the DBM services are usually in the server. The server provides stored procedures and triggers. Processing management is split between the two.

The two-tier client/server architecture is a good solution for distributed computing when workgroups are limited to about a hundred people interacting on a LAN simultaneously. When the number of users exceeds a hundred, performance begins to deteriorate. This limitation is a result of the server maintaining a connection via *keep-alive* messages with each client, even when no work is being done. A second limitation of the two-tier architecture is that implementation of processing management services using vendor-proprietary database procedures restricts flexibility and choice of DBMS for applications.

Two-tier software architectures were developed in the 1980s from the file/server software architecture design. The two-tier architecture is intended to improve usability by supporting a forms-based, user-friendly interface. The two-tier architecture requires minimal operator intervention, and it is frequently used in simple nontime-critical information-processing systems. Two-tier architectures consist of three components:

1. User-system interface (such as session, text input, dialog, and display management services)
2. Processing management (such as process development, process enactment, process monitoring, and process resource services)
3. Database Management (such as data and file services)

The two-tier design allocates the user-system interface exclusively to the client. It places database management on the server and splits the processing management between client and server, creating two layers. In general, the user-system interface client invokes services from the database management server. In many two-tier designs, most of the application processing is in the client environment. The database management server usually provides the processing related to accessing data (often implemented in storing procedures). Clients commonly communicate with the server through SQL statements or a call-level interface. It should be noted that connectivity between tiers can be dynamically changed, depending upon the user's request for data and services.

As compared to the file/server software architecture (which also supports distributed systems), the two-tier architecture improves flexibility and scalability by allocating the two tiers over the computer network. It improves usability by making it easier to provide a customized user-system interface.

It is possible for a server to function as a client to a different server in a hierarchical client/server architecture. This is known as a chained two-tier architecture design.

4.2.5.1 Usage Considerations Two-tier software architectures are used extensively in nontime-critical information processing in which management and operations of the system are not complex. This design is used frequently in decision-support systems where the transaction load is light. Two-tier software architectures require minimal operator intervention, and they work well in relatively homogeneous environments with processing rules (business rules) that do not change very often.

4.2.5.2 Limitations Implementing business logic in stored procedures can limit scalability because the need for processing power grows as more application logic is moved to the database management server. Each client uses the server to execute some part of its application code, and this will ultimately reduce the number of users that can be accommodated.

The two-tier architecture limits *interoperability* by using stored procedures to implement complex processing logic (such as managing distributed database integrity) because stored procedures are normally implemented using a commercial database management system's proprietary language. This means that to change or interoperate with more than one type of database management system, applications may need to be rewritten. Moreover, database management system's proprietary languages are generally not as capable as standard programming languages in that they do not provide a robust programming environment with testing and debugging, version control, and library management capabilities.

4.2.5.3 System Administration and Configuration Two-tier architectures can be difficult to administer and maintain because when applications reside on the client, every upgrade must be delivered, installed, and tested on each client. The typical lack of uniformity in the client configurations and lack of control over subsequent configuration changes increase administrative workload.

The two-tiered architecture is not effective running batch programs. The client is typically tied up until the batch job finishes, even if the job executes on the server.

4.2.6 Three-Tier Architectures

The three-tier architecture, also referred to as the *multitier architecture*, emerged to overcome the limitations of the two-tier architecture. In the three-tier architecture, a middle tier was added between the user-system interface client environment and the database management server environment. There are a variety of ways of implementing this middle tier, such as transaction processing monitors, message servers, or application servers (refer to Figure 4.2). The middle tier can perform queuing, application execution, and database staging. For example, if the middle tier provides queuing, the client can deliver its request to the middle layer and disengage because the middle tier will access the data and return the answer to the client. In addition, the middle layer adds scheduling and prioritization for work in progress. The three-tier client/server architecture has been shown to improve performance for groups with thousands of users, and it improves flexibility when compared to the two-tier approach.

Flexibility in partitioning can be as simple as *dragging and dropping* application code modules onto different computers in some three-tier architectures. A limitation with three-tier architectures is that the development envi-

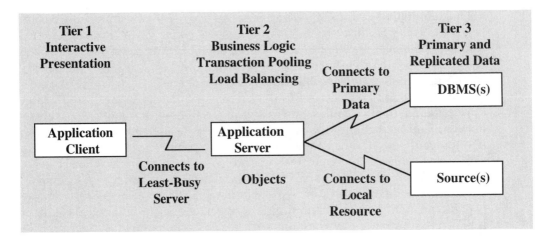

Fig. 4.2 Three-Tier Client/Server Architecture

ronment is reportedly more difficult to use than the visually oriented development of two-tier applications. Recently, mainframes have found a new use as servers in three-tier architectures.

4.2.6.1 Transaction-Processing Server   The basic three-tier architecture has a middle layer consisting of TP monitor technology. The TP monitor technology is a type of message-queuing, transaction-scheduling, and prioritization service in which the client connects to the TP monitor (middle tier) instead of the database server. The transaction is accepted by the monitor, which queues it and then takes responsibility for managing it to completion, thus freeing up the client. TP monitor technology provides the ability to update multiple DBMSs in a single transaction connectivity to a variety of data sources including flat files, nonrelational DBMS, and the mainframe.

A three-tier client/server architecture with TP monitor technology provides an environment that is considerably more scalable than a two-tier architecture with direct client-to-server connection. For systems with thousands of users, TP monitor technology (not embedded in the DBMS) is reported to be one of the most effective solutions.

4.2.6.2 Message Server   Messaging is another way to implement three-tier architectures. Messages are prioritized and processed asynchronously. Messages consist of headers containing priority information, the address, and the identification number. The message server connects to the relational DBMS and other data sources. The difference between TP monitor technology and message server is that the message server architecture focuses on intelligent messages, whereas the TP monitor environment has the intelligence in the monitor and treats transactions as dumb data packets. Messaging systems are good solutions for wireless infrastructures.

4.2.6.3 Application Server

The three-tier application server architecture allocates the main body of an application to run on a shared host rather than in the user-system interface client environment. The application server does not drive the GUIs; rather, it shares business logic, computations, and a data retrieval engine. Among the advantages application servers offer are that with less software on the client there is less security to worry about, applications are more scalable, and support and installation costs are less on a single server than when maintaining each on a desktop client.

4.2.6.4 Object Request Broker

Currently industry is working on developing standards to improve interoperability and enhancing what the common ORB will be. Developing client/server systems using technologies that support distributed objects holds great promise, as these technologies support interoperability across languages and platforms and enhance maintenance and adaptability of the system. Two prominent distributed object technologies are CORBA and COM/DCOM.

The Object Management Group (OMG) has published a standard for ORBs. These systems provide the basic object dispatch capability of routing a request from a user or an object to another object. In this way, users can build distributed object systems by piecing together objects from different vendors and letting them communicate with each other via the ORB.

This is an effective foundation for building distributed systems, but the ORB itself is only the dispatch mechanism. Other services, such as persistence, recovery, concurrency, and naming, are needed to support a full production environment. With this, users can build systems of interacting objects and take advantage of the services of an object manager, such as an object database management system (ODBMS).

4.2.7 Usage Considerations

Client/server architectures are being used throughout industry. They provide a versatile infrastructure that supports insertion of new technology more readily than earlier software designs. A number of tradeoffs must be made to select the appropriate client/server architecture. These include business strategic planning and potential growth of the number of users, costs, and the homogeneity of the current and future computational environment.

If a distributed object approach is employed, then the CORBA and/or COM/DCOM technologies should be considered.

4.2.7.1 Complementary Technologies

Complementary technologies to client/server (two-tier) architectures are computer-aided software engineering (CASE) tools because they facilitate client/server architectural development and open systems because they facilitate the development of architectures that improve scalability and flexibility.

4.3 DISTRIBUTED CLIENT/SERVER ARCHITECTURES

Distributed client/server systems serve environments with mixtures of heterogeneous computers and networks, with users and objects everywhere. Distributed Object Database Management Systems (ODBMSs) provide a mechanism for users to transparently access objects anywhere, with the efficiency of native access via caching. In addition to recovery, integrity, concurrency, and scalability, these systems provide higher-level services for management of relationships, versions, and composite objects.

The current generation of distributed client/server computing allows information and resources and users to be located anywhere, with transparent access among all of them. This is unlike virtual memory-based applications, and also unlike traditional central/server database systems. The result is effective use of computing resources wherever they may be, the ability to incrementally take advantage of additional resources, and much greater sharing and communication capabilities. A ODBMS can manage access to these objects, store them with integrity and recovery, cache them locally for performance, and provide several levels of services such as relationship management and version management.

4.3.1 The Architectures

These software architectures are based on the ORB technology, but go further than the CORBA by using shared, reusable business models (not just objects) on an enterprisewide scale.

An enterprise can build its new business applications on top of distributed business models and distributed computing technology. The applications are built from standard interfaces with *plug-and-play* components. At the core of this infrastructure is off-the-shelf, standards-based, distributed object computing, messaging communication component such as an ORB that meets CORBA standards. This messaging communication hides the following from business applications:

☞ Location and distribution of data, processes, and hosts

☞ Implementation details of networking and protocols

☞ Production environment services such as transaction management, security, messaging reliability, and persistent storage

The message communication component links the organization and connects it to computing and information resources via the organization's LAN or WAN. The message communication component forms an enterprisewide standard mechanism for accessing computing and information resources. This becomes a standard interface to heterogeneous system components.

4.3.2 Administrator and Developer Tools

One of the strengths of the traditional DBMS has been the availability of tools, both for rapid application development and for end user administration. A variety of front-end analysis and design tools allow the designer to work directly with objects.

Administrator tools have grown with the production use of ODBMS products to include interactive and programmatic interfaces. These tool capabilities include:

- ☞ Moving objects and databases
- ☞ Dumping objects and databases to text interchange format and loading back
- ☞ Detaching databases from shared environments to portable ones
- ☞ Backing up online (which, of course, must be consistent across all databases in the distributed client/server environment)
- ☞ Querying and forcing locks
- ☞ Tuning and performance and usage statistics

4.3.3 Objects, Components, and Transactions

Component-based development looks like the next big wave in software engineering. Microsoft's COM is the most widely used component model today. Generally, so far, components have been popular for building client applications, but that is about to change. Components for servers are available, and building serious server applications, whether components are involved, often requires transactions. Transactions have long been a mainstay of business computing, and today objects are too. It should not be surprising, then, that these two technologies need to be united in some way.

4.3.3.1 Understanding Transactions
Defined narrowly, a transaction can be thought of as a group of changes (to one or more databases) with the property that either all of those changes happen or none of them do. In the IBM mainframe world, for example, the venerable Customer Information Control System (CICS) is the leading example, while products like BEA's Tuxedo, NCR's TopEnd, and Transarc's Encina provide the same kinds of solutions for UNIX and Windows NT servers. Microsoft's MTS fits in this same category, although it is an NT-only solution.

An application that needs transactions very likely needs other services, too. For example, the application will probably need to scale to handle a large number of clients. TP monitors usually provide services that can improve application scalability.

4.3.3.2 Transactions and Objects A typical TP monitor provides applications with several standard API calls. The usual pattern is for an application to make a call to begin a transaction, perform the work that makes up the transaction (such as changing records in one or more databases), and end the transaction by asking the TP monitor either to commit the transaction (making the changes permanent) or abort it (rolling back the changes). Accomplishing this requires that the TP monitor work together with the database(s) in which those changes were made.

The straightforward way to make this object oriented is to express all of these interactions as method calls on appropriate objects. Rather than just calling an API function to start a transaction, for example, an application might create a new transaction object, and then, when its work is finished, invoke appropriate methods on that object to commit or abort the transaction. This is essentially what the OMG's Object Transaction Service (OTS) does. Microsoft does this, too, in OLE Transactions. OLE Transactions is broadly analogous to OMG's OTS, but the objects defined by OLE Transactions are COM objects.

A CORBA-based TP monitor typically exposes the OTS objects to clients, allowing them to invoke methods in the familiar pattern of *Begin Transaction, Do Work, Commit or Abort Transaction*. Interestingly, MTS does not do this. In fact, MTS does not even implement OLE Transactions itself. Instead, the objects are mostly implemented in the Distributed Transaction Coordinator (DTC). DTC acts as the transaction coordinator when committing or rolling back the changes made by an application. TP monitors provide services that make it easy to write scalable applications.

4.3.4 Using an ODBMS with an ORB

The OMG CORBA works well for large-grained objects in heterogeneous environments. Large grain can mean size (as in file, application program, document, spreadsheet), but more accurately refers to access time, measured in milliseconds, for interprocess communication. For such use, CORBA by itself works well. However, for environments with millions of fine-grained objects, a direct object manager, as in an ODBMS, is also necessary to manage the caching and access to these objects efficiently.

Also, such an object manager, by maintaining identity for the objects, can efficiently support relationships with referential integrity and other similar added-value services. The user can freely choose which of the objects should be made available as CORBA objects, and hence appear just as any other CORBA objects, with all the concomitant capabilities and overhead, while leaving other fine-grained objects for internal use. All of these can be managed directly and efficiently by the object manager, which caches them together—across the network—and coordinates integrity across all access. The combination gives the user the best flexibility to build systems with components from diverse vendors and, simultaneously, to take advantage of higher-level services of an object manager.

4.4 CLIENT/SERVER WITH DISTRIBUTED OBJECTS

An object in C++ or Smalltalk encapsulates code and data and can be specialized by means of inheritance, but it cannot reach across compiled-language or address-space boundaries. In contrast, distributed objects are packaged as binary components accessible to remote clients by means of method invocations. Clients do not know which language or compiler built a server object or where on the network the object physically resides. They only need to know its name and the interface it publishes.

Ultimately, we want smart client/server components that can interoperate and collaborate. For example, agents roaming the intergalactic network should be able to negotiate with other agents. In a homogeneous programming environment, that is easy. But the emerging world of software components is heterogeneous, and we need standards that set the rules of engagement among different types of components.

4.4.1 Object Management Architecture

The OMG envisions a common interconnection bus that hosts client components, core services needed by all components (including naming, persistence, events, and transactions), and common facilities for component collaboration. These may be horizontal in the case of user-interface or system-management facilities that interconnect components from different application domains. Or they may be vertical when specific to particular domains. In these vertical domains, users manipulate suites of business objects on the desktop and tap into underlying client/server webs. The OMG's architecture includes four key elements:

☞ *The ORB*: It is the object interconnection bus. Clients are insulated from the mechanisms used to communicate with, activate, or store server objects. CORBA defines the IDL and APIs that enable client/server object interaction within a specific implementation of an ORB. CORBA also specifies how ORBs from different vendors can interoperate.

☞ *Object services*: Packaged as components with IDL-specified interfaces, these extend the capabilities of the ORB. OMG has adopted the following object services: naming, event notification, persistence, life-cycle management, transactions, concurrency control, relationships, and externalization.

☞ *Common facilities*: These collections of IDL-defined components define the rules of engagement for application objects. They are categorized as horizontal and vertical. The horizontal ones address four disciplines:

user interface, information management, systems management, and task management. The user-interface services, like OLE and OpenDoc, govern on-screen activities such as in-place editing. The information-management services resemble the OLE and OpenDoc mechanisms for compound document storage and data interchange.

System-management services define interfaces used to manage, instrument, install, configure, operate, and repair distributed objects. Task management services include work flow, long transactions, agents, scripting, and rules. In the realm of vertical facilities, IDL-defined interfaces support suites of interacting objects specialized for health, retail, finance, and other domains.

☞ *Application objects*: These are components specific to end-user applications. To participate in ORB-mediated exchanges, they too must be defined using IDL. Application objects build on top of services provided by the ORB, common facilities, and object services.

CORBA provides IDL interfaces for virtually every distributed service we know today.

4.4.1.1 CORBA ORB Client   A CORBA ORB looks more complex than it is. The key is to understand that CORBA, like SQL, provides both static and dynamic interfaces.

On the client side, IDL stubs provide the static interfaces to object services. These precompiled stubs, generated by the IDL compiler, define how clients invoke corresponding services on the servers. With dynamic invocation APIs, on the other hand, you can discover a service that you want to invoke (at runtime), obtain a definition of it, issue a parameterized call to it, and receive a reply from it.

Interface repository APIs allow you to obtain and modify the descriptions of all the registered component interfaces, the methods they support, and the parameters they require. CORBA calls these descriptions method signatures. The interface repository stores, updates, and manages object-interface definitions, and programs use its APIs to access and update this information.

The ORBs provide global identifiers called *repository IDs* that uniquely and globally identify a component and its interface across multiple ORBs and repositories. The repository IDs are system-generated unique strings that enforce naming consistency across repositories and no name collisions are allowed. They are generated by means of Distributed Computing Environment (DCE) universally unique IDs (UUIDs) or by a user-supplied unique prefix attached to IDL-scoped names.

The ORB interface (used by clients and servers alike) supplies miscellaneous useful APIs. For example, there are APIs to converse between object references and strings. These calls are handy if you need to store or communicate object references.

With support for both static and dynamic client/server invocations and an interface repository, CORBA is more powerful and flexible than first-generation middleware, such as RPC. Static invocations are easy to program, fast, and self-documenting. Dynamic invocations, while harder to program, offer maximum flexibility and are essential when applications must allocate services at runtime.

4.4.1.2 CORBA ORB Server Servers cannot tell the difference between static and dynamic invocations. The same message semantics apply in both cases. The ORB locates an object adapter, transmits the parameters, and transfers control to the object implementation through the server IDL stub (also called a *skeleton*).

Static skeletons provide interfaces to each service exported by the server. These stubs, like the ones on the client, are created using an IDL compiler. A static skeleton provides hardwired support for the IDL-defined methods of a particular object class.

The dynamic skeleton interface provides a runtime binding mechanism for servers. The dynamic skeleton inspects the parameters of an incoming message to determine a target object and method. This technique is handy for building bridges between ORBs. It also can be used by interpreters and scripting languages that have to fabricate object implementations on the fly. Dynamic skeletons can receive either dynamic or static invocations from clients.

The object adapter sits atop the ORB's core communication services, accepting requests for service on behalf of the server's objects. It provides the runtime environment for instantiating server objects, passing requests to them, and assigning object IDs (object references) to them. The object adapter also registers the classes it supports and their runtime instances (objects) with the implementation repository. CORBA specifies that each ORB must support a standard adapter called the basic object adapter. Servers may, however, support more than one object adapter.

The implementation repository lists the classes a server supports, the objects that are instantiated, and their IDs. It also serves as a common place to store trace information, audit trails, security, and other administrative data.

4.4.1.3 CORBA Intergalactic ORB CORBA 1.1 was only concerned with creating portable object applications. The implementation of the ORB core was left for the developers. Components resulted that were portable but not interoperable. CORBA also tackled interoperability by specifying the IIOP—TCP/IP with CORBA-defined message exchanges that serve as a common backbone protocol. The messaging part of the backbone supports common data representations for all the OMG IDL types, interoperable object references, and common message formats and semantics optimized for ORB exchanges. Every ORB that calls itself CORBA-compliant must either speak IIOP natively or be able to bridge to it.

CORBA 2.0 specifies DCE as the first of many optional inter-ORB protocols, called Environment-Specific Inter-ORB Protocols (ESIOPs). At a semantic level, the DCE and Internet ORB implementations use the same messaging protocols. The IIOP is designed to enable out-of-the-box ORB interoperability over TCP/IP. The DCE ESIOP provides a more robust environment for mission-critical ORBs requiring advanced features, such as Kerberos security, cell and global directories, distributed time, and authenticated RPC.

CORBA 2.0 also defines how to build ORB-to-ORB bridges. When a client on one ORB calls a server on another ORB, the new dynamic skeleton interface (DSI) transmits the request to the target ORB, and then the dynamic invocation interface invokes the target object on that ORB. This dynamic technology is also well suited for building gateways to non-CORBA object busses, such as COM.

4.4.1.4 CORBA Object Services   The CORBA object services provide a unique way to build custom middleware. It is unlike anything today's conventional client/server systems offer. Component providers can use mix-in multiple inheritance to integrate their own code with the CORBA object services. Components gain persistence or transactional capability by inheriting these through IDL interfaces. OMG currently defines standards for eight object services.

☞ The persistence service provides a single interface for storing components in a variety of containers, including object databases, relational databases, and simple files.

☞ The life-cycle service defines how to create, copy, move, and delete components.

☞ The naming service enables components to locate other components. The service allows objects to be bound to existing network directories or naming contexts, including ISO's X.500, Open Software Foundation's (OSF) DCE, and Sun's Network Information Service (NIS).

☞ The transaction service provides two-phase commit coordination among recoverable components using either flat or nested program calls.

☞ The concurrency service provides a lock manager that can obtain locks on behalf of either transactions or threads.

☞ The event service allows components on the bus dynamically to register (or unregister) interest in specific events. The service defines a well-known object called an event channel that collects and distributes events among components.

☞ The relationship service provides a way to create associations (or links) between components. It also provides mechanisms for traversing the links that group these components. The service can be used to enforce referential integrity constraints and to track containment relationships and other linkages among components.

☞ The externalization service provides a standard way to stream data into and out of an object.

An intergalactic client/server requires a common interconnection bus and an environment in which smart components can collaborate.

4.4.2 CORBA Standards for Component Evolution

A common interconnection bus, the ORB hosts systemwide object services, such as naming, persistence, and transactions, and application-specific services, including user-interface technologies similar to OLE and application objects that wield all these other services.

4.4.2.1 Structure of a CORBA ORB   CORBA clients invoke services statically by way of compiled IDL stubs or on the fly by way of dynamic invocation APIs. CORBA servers route client requests to object implementations analogously by means of static skeletons or at runtime using the new dynamic skeleton interface. Clients and servers share the utility APIs of the ORB interface.

4.4.2.2 ORB-to-ORB Bridging   Logically, a client in communication with one ORB just requests a service from a server associated with another ORB. Under the covers, ORB A uses the new DSI to route the client's request across an inter-ORB bridge, and then ORB B issues a dynamic invocation to the server. According to database advocates, simple database transactions with stored procedures are all the transaction management anyone requires.

4.5 CLIENT/SERVER VERSUS WEB SERVER DEVELOPMENT

Client/server and Web-based architectures represent the current state of the art in software technology, with client/server technology being more mature. The most significant difference between the two approaches lies in their promise for the future and how each adapts to industry directions and trends.

Client/server systems cannot easily take advantage of new technologies, such as network computers (NCs), intranets, and Java for instance. Web-based applications (rendered in Java or ActiveX form) represent a retreat away from the empowering effect of desktop computing toward centralized computing. Putting aside the intangible considerations for a moment, let us look at how these approaches might fare on your particular network.

Influencing how any system will behave in production are its performance, reliability, network traffic, administrative workload, security, and load-balancing characteristics. To complicate matters further, these factors are interrelated. Additionally, the two architectural approaches are not necessarily easy to categorize. A classic client/server application is a *fat client*, usually written, for example, in Visual Basic or Delphi. It is fat because it contains presentation and business logic. The client program accesses an RDBMS, shared files on a file server, or both (see Figure 4.3).

A classic Web-based application uses a browser for data presentation, application servers for business logic, and database servers for storage. However, you could have a client/server system that off-loads some of the business logic from the client onto a series of unattended computers; the extra processing tier gives the client/server application some of the attributes of a Web-based application. Or you could have a poorly designed Web-based application with a substantial or inappropriate amount of business logic rendered in JavaScript or as a Java applet.

4.5.1 Middleware Key to Distributed Web Applications

Middleware is often defined as the plumbing that connects the pieces of a distributed application. As with clogged pipes, middleware is something most of us would prefer someone else deal with. Many tool and application server developers promise to handle the dirty work, freeing you to concentrate on the application you are building. But unless you can do everything within one tool, you still have to worry that the pipes used by one tool might not fit with those of another.

The other problem for Web development in particular is the running debate over which middleware is best for Internet or intranet development.

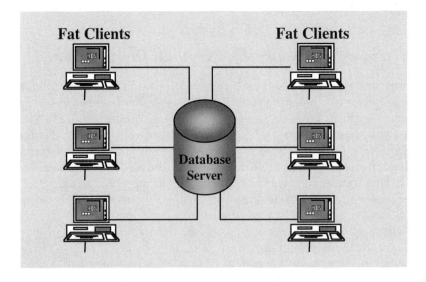

Fig. 4.3 Client/Server Architecture

The two subjects that get the most attention in this regard are distributed object computing and transactions. By their nature, Web applications are distributed and often involve components written in different languages, problems that DCOM and CORBA aim to solve.

A relatively simple Web application—for example, one that looks up a phone number in an employee directory—can use HTTP to cause the Web server to invoke a script that uses open database connectivity (ODBC) or a proprietary database driver to execute the query. The application then displays the results as an HTML page. If the network connection, the database, or the Web server fails in the middle of this process, it is a minor annoyance. But suppose you want to sell antiques over the Web, charge them to a credit card, and guarantee delivery the next day. Now your application has to record a sale, charge the credit card, enter an order with your shipping department, and update an inventory database. You will have a big problem if the application tells shipping to send the item even though the credit card charge did not go through or if the credit card was charged but the order was never entered.

IBM had solved such problems in the mainframe era with systems called IMS and CICS. CICS is alive and well and is supported on many platforms these days, including Windows NT, but the client/server era gave rise to many similar products: TP monitors (a typical middleware).

Even though database servers typically include their own transaction processing capabilities, TP monitors are a popular means of distributing workload and handling transactions that cross multiple servers.

A TP monitor ensures that all steps are completed. If the transaction is interrupted, the TP monitor will try to recover from the point at which the interruption occurred. If the transaction cannot be completed, the TP monitor rolls back the transaction, leaving the application in a consistent state—the customer does not get his or her antique unless the credit card charge goes through.

TP monitors can help make Web applications more reliable, but they were designed for relatively predictable corporate environments. By themselves, they do not solve all the problems of applications that aspire to traverse the globe.

Assuming that the application uses a basic HTML form and the HTTP protocol, the TP monitor serves requests from a Web application server. The TP monitor does not know about the Web browser and has no way to get its user into a *consistent state* of knowing whether the transaction succeeded or failed.

The application server may be able to take on that responsibility through logic created by either the vendor or the application developer. For example, it might send an E-mail notification of credit problems and try to detect duplicate transactions. Some Web applications try to recognize users who were interrupted in mid-transaction, and let them pick up where they left off.

From a Java worldview, the solution might be to download an applet that includes the necessary logic to tell the user whether the transaction was complete when the network connection was broken. The applet could then synchronize with the application server when the connection was re-established and help recover the transaction.

Some would also advocate having the applet talk directly to objects on the server using either CORBA/IIOP or RMI, rather than HTTP. Others say they do just fine using HTTP or by creating their own application-specific protocols.

Whereas traditional transaction systems are synchronous (like having a phone conversation with someone), message-oriented middleware products are asynchronous (more like sending a certified letter). Such servers guarantee that they will deliver all the messages placed in their queue to the intended recipient or notify the sender if the recipient remains inaccessible after repeated attempts. They are also adept at load balancing, dividing the queue of messages to be sent among the available servers. For this reason, messaging technology is important for large-scale systems. The trend is for database, object, transactional, and messaging middleware solutions to come together in an application server or multiprotocol middleware.

A parallel trend is to give application developers relatively easy-to-understand component interfaces to middleware services. For Microsoft-based Web developers, this might mean using Microsoft transaction server components in their active server page applications. Other transaction server developers are beginning to deliver components based on the preliminary specification for Enterprise JavaBeans, which can then be added relatively painlessly to Java applications.

The promise is that some day these technologies will be buried so far beneath the covers that you will be able to forget all of these abbreviations and acronyms. That day cannot come soon enough.

4.6 CLIENT/SERVER IN LARGE ENTERPRISE ENVIRONMENTS

In large enterprise environments, the performance of a two-tier architecture client/server usually deteriorates as the number of online users increases. This is primarily due to the connection process of the DBMS server. The DBMS maintains a thread for each client connected to the server. Even when no work is being done, the client and server exchange keep-alive messages on a continuous basis. If something happens to the connection, the client must reinitiate the session.

The data language used to implement server procedures in SQL server type DBMSs is proprietary to each vendor. Oracle, Sybase, Informix, and IBM, for example, have implemented different language extensions for these functions. Proprietary approaches are fine from a performance point of view, but are a disadvantage for users who wish to maintain flexibility and the choice of which DBMS is used with their applications.

Another problem with the two-tiered approach is that current implementations provide no flexibility. Once an application is developed it is not easy to move (split) some of the program functionality from one server to another. This would require manually regenerating procedural code.

The industry's response to limitations in the two-tier architecture has been to add a third, middle tier, between the input/output device (a PC on your desktop) and the DBMS server. This middle layer can perform a number of different functions, such as queuing, application execution, database staging, and so forth. In some of the newer three-tiered approaches, tools offer the capability to drag and drop application code modules onto different computers. The use of client/server technology with such a middle layer has been shown to offer considerably more performance and flexibility than the two-tier approach.

To illustrate one advantage of a middle layer, when the middle tier can provide queuing, the synchronous process of the two-tier approach becomes asynchronous. In other words, the client can deliver its request to the middle layer, disengage, and be assured that a proper response will be forthcoming at a later time. In addition, the middle layer adds scheduling and prioritization for the work in process.

There is no free lunch, however, and the price for this added flexibility and performance has been a development environment that is considerably more difficult to use than the visually oriented development of two-tiered applications.

4.6.1 Three-Tier with a TP Monitor

The basic middle layer is the TP monitor. You can think of a TP monitor as a kind of message queuing service. The client connects to the TP monitor instead of the database server. The transaction is accepted by the monitor, which queues it and then takes responsibility for managing it to correct completion.

TP monitors first became popular in the 1970s on mainframes. Online access to mainframes was available through one of two metaphors—time sharing or transaction processing (OLTP). Time sharing was used for program development and the computer's resources were allocated with a simple scheduling algorithm like a round robin. OLTP scheduling was more sophisticated and priority driven. TP monitors were almost always used in this environment, and the most popular of these was IBM's CICS (pronounced "kicks").

As client/server applications gained popularity over the early 1990s, the use of TP monitors dropped by the wayside. That happened principally because many of the services provided by a TP monitor were available as part of the DBMS or middleware software provided by vendors such as Sybase and Oracle. Those embedded TP services (in the DBMS) have acquired the nickname "TP Lite." The "Lite" term comes from experience that DBMS-based transaction processing works OK as long as less than a hundred clients are connected.

TP monitors ("TP Heavy") have staged a comeback because their queuing engines provide a funneling effect, reducing the number of threads a DBMS server needs to maintain. Some other key services a monitor provides are the ability to update multiple DBMSs in a single transaction; connectivity to a variety of data sources including flat files, nonrelational DBMSs, and the mainframe; the ability to attach priorities to transactions; and robust security, including Kerberos. The net result of using a three-tier client/server architecture with a TP monitor is that the resulting environment is *far* more scalable than a two-tier approach. For large (e.g., 1,000 and more users) applications, a TP monitor is an effective solution.

As you might expect, however, there is a downside to network-based TP monitors; that is, the code to implement TP monitors is usually written in a lower-level language (like COBOL), and support for TP monitors is not (yet) widely available in such popular visual toolsets as PowerBuilder or Visual Basic.

4.6.2 Three-Tier with a Messaging Server

Messaging is available from companies such as IBM, DEC, Sybase, and Oracle. A messaging server can be thought of as a kind of "second generation" TP monitor and provides the same funneling process. Messages are processed asynchronously with the appropriate priority level. And, like a TP monitor, a messaging server provides connectivity to data sources other than RDBMS.

A message is a self-contained object that carries information about what it is, where it needs to go, and what should happen when it reaches its destination. There are at least two parts to every message—the header, which contains priority, address, and ID number, and the body of the message, containing the information being sent, which can be text, images, or transactions.

A primary difference from TP monitors is that a message-server architecture is designed around intelligence in the message itself, as opposed to a TP monitor environment, which places the system intelligence in the monitor or the process logic of the application server.

In a TP monitor environment, the transactions are simply dumb packets of data. They travel over a preexisting and predefined connection to the TP monitor. The TP monitor interrogates and processes the transaction, usually submitting the request to a server tier application.

In contrast, in a message-based architecture there's intelligence in the message itself. The message server just becomes a container of messages and their stored procedures. The operations performed by the message server on the message are communications related (e.g., encrypting the message over one service and decrypting the message over another service). For the most part, messages are treated as discrete objects. The message contains all the information needed to traverse network services (network addresses, both logical and physical). Because the message contains the intelligence, the middle tier of a message-based system is more flexible than a TP monitor. For one kind of message, the middle tier may simply serve as a routing point between two kinds of network services. For another kind of message, the middle tier may execute a stored procedure or business rule as directed by the message. This abstraction of the middle tier away from the contents and behavior of the information flowing through it makes the system more portable to different environments and networks. The specifics of communicating the information are hidden underneath the messaging service.

Messaging systems are designed to be robust. By using store and forward logic, they provide message delivery after and around failures. They also provide independence from enabling technologies such as wired or wireless protocols. They do not require a persistent connection between the client and server. Because messaging systems support an emerging wireless infrastructure, they may become popular for supporting mobile and occasionally connected workers.

A typical message server architecture would look like Figure 4.4, which, of course, looks just like any of the other three-tier approaches we are going to discuss. The architecture of an application that uses messaging services will turn out to look similar to an approach that depends on distributed objects and ORBs for communication. If you are unwilling or unable to wait for the arrival of distributed object technologies to build your application (widespread popularity probably will not happen with ORBs until the next century), you can construct a reasonable clone using the messaging approaches that are now available. When distributed objects are a reality, you can migrate your application if that seems like the best move.

4.6.3 Three-Tier with an Application Server

When most people talk of three-tier architectures, they mean using an application server (see Figure 4.4). With this approach, most of the application's business logic is moved from the PC and into a common, shared host server. Basically, the PC is used for presentation services—not unlike the role that a

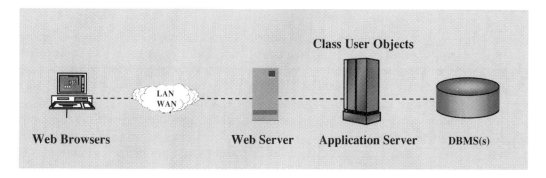

Fig. 4.4 Three-Tier Client/Server Architecture

terminal plays on a mainframe. Of course, because we are talking about a real PC here, it still has the advantages of being used for clientside applications.

The application-server approach is similar in overall concept to the X architecture that was developed at MIT in the 1980s. The goal in X is to allow host-based computing with graphical interfaces on the desktop. (I'm using "desktop" here because "server" in the X architecture refers to the graphical server that sits on the desktop and "client" refers to where the application runs—on the shared host.) The similarity between X and a three-tiered client/ server architecture with an application server is that both architectures have the goal of pulling the main body of application logic off the desktop and running it on a shared host.

The application server is also similar to a mainframe in that it does not need to worry about driving a GUI, and therefore it shares business logic, computation, and data retrieval. This server normally operates under a multi-tasking OS such as NT, OS/2, NetWare, or UNIX. As an option, these OSs can run on SMP configurations. In addition, some are available on massively parallel hardware. Therefore, the server is scalable in terms of performance. As new versions of the application software are developed and released, the installation of that software occurs on only one server rather than on hundreds or thousands of PCs.

The approach of putting business logic on a server offers a number of important advantages to the application designer:

- ☞ When less software is on the client, there is less worry about security since the important software is on a server in a more controlled environment.

- ☞ The resulting application is more scalable. For one thing, servers are far more scalable than PCs. While a server could be a single Pentium-based Compaq or Dell, it could also be a symmetric multiprocessing Sequent, with 32 or more processors, or it could be a massively parallel UNIX processor like IBM's SP2.

- ☞ To install and support software on a single server is much less costly than trying to maintain the same software on hundreds or thousands of PCs.

- ☞ With a middle application-server tier it is much easier to design the application to be DBMS independent. If you want to switch to another DBMS system, it is more achievable with reasonable effort with a single multithreaded application than with thousands of applications on PCs.

- ☞ Most new tools for implementing a three-tier application server approach offer "after the fact" application partitioning. This means that code and function modules can be reallocated to new servers after the system has been built. This offers important flexibility and performance benefits.

The major downside to an application-server approach is that the technology is much more difficult to implement than a two-tier approach.

4.6.4 Three-Tier with an ODBMS

A variation on this theme of application server is that of using an ODBMS as the middle layer. In this sense, the ODBMS acts as an accelerator or "hot cache." Data in a relational DBMS is usually stored in normalized fashion across many tables and for access by different applications and users. This generalized form of storage may prove inadequate (performancewise) for the needs of a particular application. An ODBMS can be used to retrieve the data from the common store, assemble it for efficient usage by your application, and provide a persistent store for that data as long as your application might need it. Since extended data types like video or voice are not typically supported in today's RDBMS, those data types might also be stored in the ODBMS, which could then associate the appropriate multimedia data with the data retrieved from the RDBMS.

4.6.5 Distributed Components and the Three-Tier Architecture

This brings us to distributed object computing and components. Many software pundits are predicting a future featuring the creation of application systems through assembly of software components. That kind of software approach is available today in a few proprietary object environments like NeXT's NeXTStep and ParcPlace's VisualWorks. The emergence of a broad-based industry for component-based software requires the prior emergence of industry standards for interchangeable parts.

For components to be assembled like tinker toys, they are going to have to match up in terms of connectors. So all vendors that want to create software components are going to have to agree on the software object bus. Not enough of either OLE or CORBA technology is currently available for ordinary mortals to build with.

The distributed object implementation of client/server computing is going to change the way applications are built. There should be some very interesting advantages to observe. For one, if we needed fault-tolerant computing, we could implement copies of objects onto multiple servers. That way if any servers were down, it would be possible to go to another site for service. Because distributed objects are self-contained and executable (all data and procedures are present) a systems administrator will be able to tune the performance of the network by moving those objects from overloaded hardware to underutilized computers. This approach is called tuning through drag and drop, referring to the metaphor the administrator uses on a workstation to move the components.

A distributed object architecture should also offer other benefits for application developers. For example, consider the following:

☞ The same interface can be used for building a desktop, single location application, or a fully distributed application.

☞ The application can be developed and tested locally and you'll know that it will work fine when it is distributed. You depend on the known services of an ORB for distribution.

☞ Since the application developer is dealing with an ORB for transmission services, technical concerns like queuing, timing, and protocols are not an issue for the application developer.

4.6.6 Three-Tier with a Data Warehouse

A three-tier architecture is also useful for data mining or warehouse types of applications. These applications are characterized by unanticipated browsing of historical data. The databases supporting this type of application can sometimes be huge (up to a few terabytes) and have to be structured properly for adequate performance (a few-seconds turnaround). If the system cannot provide that kind of performance, the thought process of the human analyst is disrupted and the overall purpose of the system is foiled. A production database established for multiple users typically is not in a form that can support ad hoc queries. The approach to support this browsing is to make data copies available for the browsing and to organize the data in those copies in the best supporting fashion. This typically means that the data is denormalized, summarized, and stored in a multidimensional table—all of which is very nonrelational. IT systems and operations managers usually do not want access to those tables to be on the mainframe. Unpredictable performance from ad hoc browsing can have a nasty impact on production OLTP systems, which require predictable response times.

For cost, management, security, and other reasons, it makes sense to load this data copy on its own server rather than leaving it on the mainframe. Often this server is called the online analytical processor (OLAP). In other circumstances, this server can be a symmetric or massively parallel processor running an RDBMS. Since the OLAP server is typically a UNIX- or PC-based technology, the MIPS costs are much lower than for the same cycles executed on a mainframe.

4.6.7 Three-Tier and the Future

Client/server architectures are flexible and modular. They can be evolved in a number of ways. All of the three-tier approaches I've described can be mixed and matched in various combinatorial sequences to satisfy almost any computing need. As the Internet becomes a significant factor in computing environments, client/server applications operating over it will become an important new type of distributed computing. (This is probably an understatement, since the use of Internet- and intranet-based applications will very shortly dwarf all of the distributed computing initiatives of the past.)

The Internet will extend the reach and power of client/server computing. Through its promise of widely accepted standards, it will ease and extend client/server computing. The movement in programming languages to the technology of distributed objects is going to happen at amazing speed—because of the Internet.

Client/server still remains the only architecture for taking advantage of the Internet. We'll have to add "changes in client/server computing" to death and taxes in our list of inevitability. Client/server computing is likely to remain the underpinning for most computing developments we will see over the next decade.

4.7 CONCLUSIONS

To truly understand how much of the Internet operates, including the Web, it is important to understand the concept of client/server computing. The client/server model is a form of distributed computing where one program (the client) communicates with another program (the server) for the purpose of exchanging information. The client's responsibility is usually to:

1. Handle the user interface
2. Send the request to the server
3. Translate the user's request into the desired protocol
4. Wait for the server's response
5. Translate the response into "human-readable" results
6. Present the results to the user

The server's functions include:

1. Listening for a client's query
2. Processing that query
3. Returning the results back to the client

A typical client/server interaction goes like this:

1. The user runs client software to create a query
2. The client connects to the server
3. The client sends the query to the server
4. The server analyzes the query
5. The server computes the results of the query
6. The server sends the results to the client
7. The client presents the results to the user

Flexible user-interface development is the obvious advantage of client/server computing. It is possible to create an interface that is independent of the server hosting the data. Therefore, the user interface of a client/server application can be written on a Macintosh or a PC and the server can be writ-

ten on a mainframe. Clients also could be written for DOS- or UNIX-based
computers. This allows information to be stored in a central server and dis-
seminated to different types of remote computers (servers).

Since the user interface is the responsibility of the client, the server has
more computing resources to spend on analyzing queries and disseminating
information. This is another major advantage of client/server computing; it
tends to use the strengths of divergent computing platforms to create more
powerful applications. Although its computing and storage capabilities are
dwarfed by those of the mainframe, there is no reason why a Macintosh could
not be used as a server for less-demanding applications. In short, client/server
computing provides a mechanism for disparate computers to cooperate on a
single computing task.

Use of ODBMSs brings distributed client-server computing to users, carrying them beyond the mainframelike central servers, providing access
equally to all resources, and adding the database capabilities of recovery,
integrity maintenance, concurrency, and scalability.

Additional features enable designers to build richer object systems with
relationships, versioning, and composites. Integration of object design tools
supports developers, and a wide variety of end-user administration tools provide ease and flexibility. Recent support for SQL and ODBC allow virtually all
front-end tools to immediately access the object databases, providing an easy
starting path into the world of objects and distributed computing.

Distributed Operating Systems

5.1 INTRODUCTION

The Operating System (OS) is the basic software controlling a computer. The OS coordinates and manipulates computer hardware, organizes files in storage, and limits hardware errors and the loss of data.

An OS controls the interpretation of commands from the user to the computer. Some command interpreters require that commands be typed in. Other command interpreters let the user communicate by pointing to and clicking on pictures. Beginners generally find pictorial interpreters easier, but many experienced users prefer more powerful text interpreters.

An OS is either single-tasking or multitasking. Single-tasking operating systems perform only one function at a time. Every modern OS is multitasking and can perform multiple functions simultaneously.

The operating systems commonly found on personal computers are UNIX, Macintosh OS, MS-DOS, OS/2, and Windows 95 and 98. Operating systems on large systems are dominated by MVS, AIX, Solaris, HP-UX, VM, and VMS. UNIX is popular among academic computer users, largely because the software for the Internet was first designed for UNIX. The commands in UNIX are not intuitive, however, and mastering the system is difficult.

DOS (Disk Operating System) and its successor, MS-DOS, are popular among personal computer users, although they are single-tasking because they were developed before personal computers became powerful. A multitasking variation is OS/2. Many users prefer an OS with a graphical user interface (GUI), such as Windows or the Macintosh OS, which make computer technology more accessible. However, systems with GUIs generally require faster central processing units, more memory, and higher-quality displays than other operating systems.

5.2 DISTRIBUTED OPERATING SYSTEMS

Like a conventional operating system, a distributed operating system is a collection of software components that simplifies the task of programming and supports the widest possible range of applications. On the other hand, unlike conventional operating systems, distributed operating systems are modular and extensible.

New components may be added to distributed operating systems in response to new application needs. The modularity of distributed operating systems is based on the support that they provide for communication between modules. Because they are extensible, it is not feasible to specify a fixed set of components that describe a distributed operating system.

Distributed Operating Systems extend the notion of a virtual machine over a number of interconnected computers or hosts. Note that the user/programmer still has the illusion of working on a single system. All the issues of concurrency and distribution are completely hidden by the virtual machine, and the user/programmer is not at liberty to exploit them (nor should they be hindered by them). Distributed Operating Systems are often broadly classified into two extremes:

☞ Loosely coupled systems (workstations, LAN, and servers)
☞ Tightly coupled systems (processors, memory, bus, and I/O)

Often this classification is a reflection of the reliability and performance of the communications subsystem. Frequently, shared memory systems are regarded as more tightly coupled than message-passing systems. Another way of looking at these classifications is to think of tightly coupled systems as dependent and loosely coupled systems as independent, with dependency a matter of system availability in the event of a failure of some single host. In tightly coupled systems, it is reasonable to consider shared memory (at least hierarchical cache mechanisms) as a communications mechanism. In loosely coupled systems, only message-passing can be considered.

5.2.1 The Model

This text assumes a model with distributed applications running in multiple processes in multiple computers linked by communications. The applications are supported by a programming environment and runtime system that makes many aspects of distribution in the system transparent.

Another approach to supporting applications in a distributed system is to use a distributed operating system. On every computer system, the operating system provides an interface that the programs use to obtain services, such as I/O or file sharing.

In a distributed operating system, this interface is enhanced so that a program may be run on any computer in the distributed system and access data on any other computer. The operating system provides data, execution, and location transparency, often through an extended naming scheme. The advantage of a distributed operating system is that it uses an interface below that of the application program. This means the existing programming environments can be used, the programmer can use the system with little or no extra training, and in some cases existing software can be used. The disadvantage is that a number of problems (for instance, concurrency) are left for the programmer and the user to handle. Essentially, the distributed operating system dictates the policies of distribution for all aspects of programming and the programmer cannot use the distributed functionality in an application-specific way to optimize a solution.

Another major disadvantage is that the distributed system is tied to a particular style of operating system interface. There are lots of different operating systems today to meet differing requirements (real or imaginary). There is no reason why future distributed systems will not need different operating system interfaces. Consequently, it is not possible to build a truly heterogeneous open distributed system by building it on top of an homogeneous distributed operating system.

Such a model needs to provide an application interface to the distributed system. This interface is extremely simple and is concerned with distribution only. The application may still be run on any local operating system that is appropriate.

This also includes the use of distributed operating systems, but would require any particular type of distributed operating system to interwork with other types and with nondistributed operating systems as well. The applications would see no difference. One popular implementation is the CORBA.

5.2.2 Applied Technologies

A typical distributed operating system is designed for a network of computers sharing hardware resources. In a distributed OS, a process can run on any computer in the network but all basic OS functions are more complex.

The emergence of a new generation of networks and workstations has dramatically increased the attraction of using a workstation cluster as a multiprocessor or multicomputer. The key to achieving high performance in this environment is efficient network access, because the cost of remote access dictates the granularity of parallelism that can be supported. Thus, in addition to traditional distribution mechanisms such as RPC, workstation clusters support lightweight communication paradigms for executing parallel applications.

5.2.3 Remote Memory Access

Let us review a simple communication model based on the notion of remote memory access. Applications executing on one host can perform direct memory read or write operations on user-defined remote memory regions. The model provides protected and efficient access to the network in the presence of time slicing and virtual memory.

The model separates control and data transfer, allowing either or both to be optimized. This type of a model can be supported safely and efficiently on current systems. In its simplest representation, the model allows distributed systems to be implemented efficiently by separating out data and control transfers. It also helps in implementing transport protocols as user-level libraries and in writing medium-grained scientific applications on workstation clusters.

5.2.4 Remote Memory Management

As network latencies decrease, the time to fetch a page from the memory of another node in the network becomes smaller than the time to read a page from local disk. In many cases, this allows the operating system to exploit the enormous collection of network-wide RAM to avoid or greatly reduce time-consuming disk reads.

Some algorithms have been tried to enable memory to be managed globally in the network. In such a system, one node that is heavily paging can use memory in other nodes that are lightly loaded. The scheme is to remove the globally least valuable page in order to keep the globally most valuable pages loaded in primary memory on the network. A number of such models have been implemented by modifying the virtual memory and file buffer system, demonstrating the performance advantages.

Currently, modern workstation operating systems do not provide support for efficient distributed program execution in an environment shared with sequential applications. The goal should be to provide better performance for both parallel and sequential applications. To realize this goal, the operating system must support gang scheduling of parallel programs, identify idle resources in the network, allow for process migration to support dynamic load balancing, and provide support for fast interprocess communication.

5.2.5 Virtual Memory Management

Most software-based distributed shared memory (DSM) systems rely on the operating system's virtual memory interface to detect writes to shared data. Strategies based on virtual memory page protection create two problems for a DSM system. First, writes can have high overhead since they are detected with a page fault. As a result, a page must be written many times to amortize the cost of that fault. Second, a virtual memory page is too big to serve as a unit of coherency, inducing false sharing. Mechanisms to handle false sharing can increase runtime overhead and may cause data to be unnecessarily communicated between processors.

DSM systems utilize two types of concurrency: Apparent or pseudoconcurrency and real concurrency. With the former, a single hardware processor is switched between processes by interleaving; over time this gives the illusion of concurrent execution of the processes. With the latter, multiple hardware processors are present in the machine, and the OS can schedule tasks onto the processors. Usually, there are far fewer processors than there are processes. Correctness depends not only on logical result but also on response time.

Distributed and parallel operating systems facilitate the use of geographically distributed resources. The systems' functions include supporting

☞ communication within a job or between jobs; information sharing is most significant

☞ parallel applications wishing to obtain speedup of computationally intensive tasks

☞ synchronization of activities to coordinate sharing of information

☞ distributed activities by using primitives defined within OS, such as RPC

5.3 KEY CHARACTERISTICS

In general, designing a distributed operating system is more difficult than designing a centralized operating system. In a centralized operating system, it is assumed that the operating system has access to all the components and resources in the environment in which it is functioning. In the distributed operating system, the resources are physically separated. For example, there is no common clock among the multiple processors so delivery of messages is delayed and the messages could even be lost. Because of this drawback, a distributed operating system does not have current or consistent knowledge of the state of its various components. Lack of up-to-date information makes many operations, such as resource management and synchronization of activities, much harder.

In spite of these complexities, the users of a distributed operating system should be able to view it as a virtual centralized system that is flexible, efficient, secure, reliable, and easy to use. Some of its key characteristics include distribution, name services, transparency, resource sharing, concurrency, fault tolerance, scalability, heterogeneity, security, and performance.

5.3.1 Distribution

To maintain the illusion of an unbounded data space, persistent stores eventually must be distributed. There is a tension between the conceptual ideals of orthogonal persistence and the technological realities of distribution, however, that makes their integration difficult. A spectrum of possible solutions to this difficulty balances the ease of user programming and conceptual modeling with the ease of implementation of the underlying system.

At one end of the spectrum, distribution is introduced to enhance the performance of the overall system. Ideally, as far as ease of programming is concerned, the distributed system is programmed as if it were nondistributed. All other models of distribution expose some aspect of the underlying distribution to the user. To this extent, distributed systems can be categorized by the manner in which they hide the underlying distribution mechanisms from the user so the system is perceived as a whole. This transparency has a number of dimensions.

In persistent systems, the dimensions of distribution transparency may be refined to the following:

☞ *Operation transparency*: A uniform mechanism invokes operations of both local and remote values, concealing any ensuing network-related communications.

☞ *Location transparency*: The user cannot tell the location of a value in the network from its name.

☞ *Migration transparency*: An object may be moved from node to node by the system while it maintains its identity.

☞ *Replication transparency*: An object is replicated by the system for greater availability or efficiency and the intricacies of replica consistency maintenance remain concealed.

☞ *Recovery transparency*: The semantics of any recovery mechanism is independent of the way the data it governs may be distributed.

In addition to the above and in order that the distributed stores be considered as part of one system an underlying mechanism must allow them to work in unison. This is provided by the concurrency control mechanism, which may be cooperative and controlled by synchronization or competitive and controlled by atomic transactions or in between (as in designer transactions). Thus the concurrency control ensures both synchronization and isolation across the network. Implementation of this is nontrivial and may involve systemwide semaphores and two-phase commit protocols.

Where the distribution mechanism is completely transparent the user is presented with a single large persistent space, the one-world model. This approach fits well with the concept of orthogonal persistence since all the physical properties of the data are hidden from the user, including the placement of data, replication of data, and the failure of nodes. The system is free to move, copy, and replicate data to optimize its utility and is responsible for abstracting over any failure due to distribution. Applications need no modification to operate in different distributed environments.

While the one-world model is conceptually simple, a number of technological issues make it difficult to deliver in scale. The management of very large stores involves problems that cause implementation difficulties.

5.3.2 Name Services

In client/server systems, a client process must interact with a server process whenever it requires access to a resource that it does not control—hardware, software, or data.

The nature of distributed systems requires that processes interact in order to achieve the fundamental aim of resource sharing. However, the concept of transparency requires that the communications network be hidden. The problem of hiding the distribution while enabling processes to interact is solved using a *naming service*.

At the highest level, resources are accessed via a name. At the lowest level, resources are accessed via a communications identifier. The process of mapping a resource name to the communications identifier is known as *resolution*. This may involve several translation steps before a communications identifier acceptable to the low-level network protocol is produced.

5.3.2.1 Naming Schemes and Name Space
Many schemes exist for the format (and hence syntax) of names (note these are not necessarily distinct from one another):

- ☞ Human readable names are those that users can read and recall for subsequent use. (e.g., cynthia).
- ☞ Names containing clues to a resource's location in the network. Such names conflict with the notion of location transparency.
- ☞ Names containing a reference to a resource location in a hierarchy (e.g., harry.conn.ca.us—"us" is the hierarchy's root).
- ☞ Names containing information about the permissions required to access the resource.
- ☞ Names chosen for size—short names allow compact storage.
- ☞ Names to aid computation of locating them with a data structure.
- ☞ Pure names, which carry no interpretation. These can only be resolved using a stored list of names and their mappings to communications identifiers.
- ☞ Naming schemes designed for security, protecting the resources they refer to from unauthorized access. Identifiers are chosen so that it is computationally difficult for any process that does not already hold the communications identifier to reproduce it without access to a naming service.

Names exist within a name space. A *name space* is all the possible names given a particular naming scheme. Name services translate names from one name space to another. Name spaces may be finite or infinite depending on the rules of the naming scheme. Additionally, name spaces may be structured or flat. A name that is associated with a resource is said to be *bound*.

5.3.2.2 Context   The use of a structured hierarchical naming scheme may result in the naming services database of names being separated into parts. These separate parts of the database are called contexts. A name's meaning is dependent upon its context. Thus, a name should be resolved with reference to its context.

5.3.3 Transparency

The separation of components is an inherent property of distributed systems. Separation allows truly parallel execution of programs, the containment of components from faults without disruption of the whole system, and the use of isolation to control security. It also provides the incremental growth or contraction of the system through the addition or subtraction of components.

The primary goal of a distributed operating system is to make the existence of multiple computers transparent and provide a single system image to its users. Thus, a true distributed operating system is a collection of machines connected by a communication subsystem as a virtual uniprocessor. Achieving complete transparency is a difficult task and requires the support of several different aspects of transparency as described below. Application designers simply select which transparencies they wish to assume and where in the design they are to apply.

The transparency approach can lead directly to software reuse. Selection of transparencies in the system specification can lead to the automatic incorporation of well-established implementations of the standard solutions by the system-building tools in use, such as compilers, linkers, and configuration managers. The designer expresses system requirements in the form of a simplified statement of the system required and the transparency properties that it should possess.

5.3.3.1 Access Transparency Access transparency masks differences in data representation and invocation mechanisms to enable interworking among objects. This transparency solves many of the problems of interworking among heterogeneous systems, and will generally be provided by default.

Access transparency enables local and remote information objects to be accessed using identical operations.

5.3.3.2 Access Method Transparency Access method transparency eliminates the need for coding for a database-specific access method or SQL set by allowing applications to utilize a single set of SQL for any data store.

5.3.3.3 Concurrency Transparency Concurrency transparency enables several processes to operate concurrently, using shared information objects without interference among them.

5.3.3.4 Failure Transparency Failure transparency masks from an object the failure and possible recovery of other objects (or itself) to enable fault tolerance. When this transparency is provided, the designer can work in an idealized world in which the corresponding class of failures does not occur.

Failure transparency enables the concealment of faults, allowing users and application programs to complete their tasks despite the failure of hardware or software components.

5.3.3.5 Location Transparency Location transparency enables information objects to be accessed without knowledge of their location. Location transparency masks the use of information about location in space when identifying and binding to interfaces. This transparency provides a logical view of naming, independent of actual physical location. Location transparency enables end users to access tables by name without knowledge of each table's physical location.

5.3.3.6 Migration Transparency Migration transparency masks from an object the ability of a system to change the location of that object. Migration is often used to achieve load balancing and reduce latency.

Migration transparency allows the movement of information objects within a system without affecting the operation of users or application programs.

5.3.3.7 Network Transparency   Network transparency allows users to access data across multiple networks without concern for specific protocols.

5.3.3.8 Operating System Transparency   Operating system transparency enables data to be accessed across multiple operating systems.

5.3.3.9 Performance Transparency   Performance transparency allows the systems to be reconfigured to improve performance as loads vary.

5.3.3.10 Persistence Transparency   Persistence transparency masks from an object the deactivation and reactivation of other objects (or itself). Deactivation and reactivation are often used to maintain the persistence of an object when the system is unable to provide it with processing, storage, and communication functions continuously.

5.3.3.11 Relocation Transparency   Relocation transparency masks relocation of an interface from other interfaces bound to it. Relocation allows system operation to continue even when migration or replacement of some objects creates temporary inconsistencies in the view seen by their users.

5.3.3.12 Replication Transparency   The system allows for automatic maintenance of copies of the same data (refer to Figure 5.1) at several sites transparent to the application or user. Replication transparency masks the use of a group of mutual behaviorally compatible objects to support an interface. Replication is often used to enhance performance and availability.

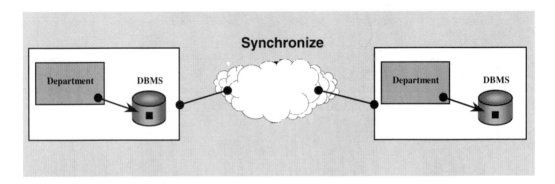

Fig. 5.1 Replication Transparency

Replication transparency enables multiple instances of information objects to be used to increase reliability and performance without knowledge of the replicas by users or application programs.

5.3.3.13 Scaling Transparency   Scaling transparency allows the systems and applications to expand in scale without alteration of the system structure or the application algorithms.

5.3.3.14 Storage Format Transparency   Storage format transparency enables information to be accessed regardless of its database or file format.

5.3.3.15 Transaction Transparency   Transaction transparency masks coordination of activities to achieve consistency among a configuration of objects.

5.3.4 Transparent Distributed Heterogeneous Computing

A heterogeneous computing environment, in which different types of processing resources and interconnection technologies are effectively and efficiently used, has the potential to maximize performance and cost effectiveness of a wide range of scientific and distributed applications.

5.3.5 Multiple Queues

Typically, multiple queues are appropriate for a variety of jobs. If homogeneous, they can be used to service parallel jobs. In a powerful server, they can be used for CPU-intensive jobs. They also can be used for jobs that need a rapid turnaround. The number of possible queue configurations will depend on the profile of the typical throughput of jobs on the system.

5.3.6 Fault Tolerance

The master scheduler is responsibile for monitoring jobs until they successfully finish. If a job fails due to problems other than an application runtime error the master scheduler will schedule the job to run again.

5.4 OBJECT-ORIENTED MODELS

Object-oriented models are involved in many aspects of computer science, including system design and programming. The essence of an object-oriented approach is that concepts, ideas, processes, data, or combinations of these are grouped together into a capsule called an object. One object supports a number of interfaces with which it communicates with other objects. In a programming analogy, an interface is like the declaration of a procedure or function.

Thus an interface can be supported by one or more actual implementations or definitions. In an object-oriented model, the implementations behind interfaces are called methods or operations.

Objects provide us with an effective way of encapsulating things so that we can use them in other parts of the model. The interface describes exactly how to use the object. Theoretically, in a true object model everything is an object. Going too far down this road enables us to describe anything recursively, however, and we end up explaining nothing. I will use the object concept to build up a model of a distributed system; the model then will show us what types of object interaction we need to support.

The reusability of objects and refinement through inheritance make systems more open, since they can support diversity, but permit enclosure of diverse systems into one. Because we use an object-oriented approach to make descriptions consistent and related, it does not mean that we must build an object-oriented distributed system. We could just as well program and use a distributed system in assembler code.

5.5 DISTRIBUTED OPERATING SYSTEMS

5.5.1 Paramecium

Paramecium is a simple, adaptable, and extendable operating system used to explore the tradeoffs between user processes and kernel boundaries. Services are provided by objects named in a per process name space. Each process may change its own name space, which boils down to installing new services, overriding or interposing existing services, and so on. Through the use of code signing a user process may put objects into the kernel address space.

This kernel uses an object-based software architecture which, together with instance naming, late binding, and explicit overrides, enables easy reconfiguration. Determining which components are allowed to reside in the kernel address space is up to a certification authority or one of its delegates. These delegates can include validation programs, correctness provers, and system administrators. The main advantage of certifications is that it can handle trust and sharing in a noncooperative environment.

Current distributed applications like E-mail, electronic news, distributed calendars, and network information browsers often have a complex structure. This is due partly to a lack of suitable support from the underlying operating system, which is often too low level. At the same time, multimedia applications, parallel programs, wide-area applications, and database systems have very different operating system demands. Although it is possible to put support for the above-mentioned systems in a single operating system kernel, this is generally undesirable from a software engineering point of view, as the resulting software may become unmanageable.

5.5.2 ChorusOS

CHORUS is a family of open microkernel-based operating system components that meet advanced distributed computing needs in areas such as telecommunications; internetworking; embedded systems; real-time, "mainframe UNIX" supercomputing; and high availability. The CHORUS/MiX multiserver implementations of UNIX allow designers to dynamically integrate part or all standard UNIX functionalities and services in the above application areas.

This operating system provides one of the most feature-rich, real-time operating systems and development environments in the industry. Its unique componentized OS architecture allows ChorusOS configurations to scale seamlessly from very embedded instances (10 Kbytes) to high-functionality transparently distributed platforms.

ChorusOS component interfaces offer an open environment for the integration of third-party system software. Multiple application programming interfaces including legacy environments can be supported simultaneously on a single hardware platform. High availability enablers, such as hot restart, make ChorusOS ideal for mission-critical embedded systems.

With its optional, fully-integrated CORBA object-oriented services, ChorusOS pushes real-time operating systems into the twenty-first century. Componentized OS architecture with replaceable system components can be selected as needed to meet memory footprint, performance, and feature requirements of the target system.

The ChorusOS architecture has been designed to provide the user with fine-grain selection of OS components. ChorusOS components are layered on top of a core executive. They can be replaced by similar components to fit particular hardware capabilities or specific application requirements. The result can be an optimal configuration. It is available on the x86, Pentium, Sun, and PowerPC platforms.

5.5.3 RTMX O/S

RTMS O/S is implemented in a demand-page, virtual memory system. RTMX O/S is extremely protective of task memory space. Tasks are protected from each other. Users are protected from run-away programs. Unlike many real time kernels, more than one developer can debug code at a time.

RTMX O/S supports a standard Berkeley fast-file system. This file system allows data transfer directly between the task's memory and the disk.

The use of Direct Memory Access (DMA) allows these high data to take place simultaneously with other activities. It provides for effortless data sharing and gateways between dissimilar system types. RTMX O/S includes standard TCP/IP, PPP, SLIP, and OSI protocol support; full BSD socket library; and a thoroughly reworked Network File System (NFS) to provide fast, transparent, reliable interprocess, intertask communication and files. It also provides a shared-memory (backplane) networking layer for closely coupled multiple CPU systems. RTMX O/S currently runs on a wide variety of popular platforms.

5.5.4 Linux

Linux is a UNIX-type operating system. It is an independent portable operating system interface for UNIX (POSIX) implementation and includes true multitasking, virtual memory, shared libraries, demand loading, proper memory management, TCP/IP networking, and other features consistent with UNIX-type systems.

5.5.5 Angel

Angel is designed as a generic parallel and distributed operating system, although it is currently targeted toward a high-speed network of PCs. This model of computing has the dual advantage of both a cheap initial cost and also a low incremental cost. By treating a network of nodes as a single shared memory machine, using distributed virtual shared memory (DVSM) techniques, Angel addresses the need for improved performance and provides a more portable and useful platform for applications.

5.5.6 Amoeba

Amoeba is a powerful microkernel-based system that turns a collection of workstations or single-board computers into a transparent distributed system. It has been in use in academia, industry, and government for many years. It runs on Sun, Intel, and Motorola processors.

The architecture separates the tasks of maintaining memory mappings and protections from the task of paging memory in and out of backing store. A per-node virtual memory manager is responsible for maintaining the mappings on the local machine while external pagers are responsible for managing backing store. A novel aspect of the architecture is the separation of the memory abstraction from the interface that provides the paging operations. The design supports flexible memory sharing, sparse address spaces, and copy-on-write mechanisms. Support for distributed shared memory and extensible stackable file systems are natural consequences of the design. The architecture is implemented and has been in use for over two years as part of an experimental operating system.

5.6 CONCLUSIONS

The emergence of a new generation of networks and workstations has dramatically increased the attractiveness of using workstation clusters as multiprocessors or multicomputers. The key to achieving high performance in this environment is efficient network access, because the cost of remote access dictates the granularity of parallelism that can be supported. Thus, in addition to traditional distribution mechanisms such as RPC, workstation clusters should support lightweight communication paradigms for executing parallel applications.

A simple communication model is based on the notion of remote memory access. Applications executing on one host can perform direct memory read or write operations on user-defined remote memory regions. The model provides protected and efficient access to the network in the presence of time-slicing and virtual memory. The model separates control and data transfer allowing either or both to be optimized. The model allows distributed systems to be implemented very efficiently by separating out data and control transfers. It also helps in implementing transport protocols as user-level libraries and in writing medium-grained scientific applications on workstation clusters.

As network latencies decrease, it becomes faster to fetch a page from the memory of another node in the network than to read a page from local disk. In many cases, this allows the operating system to exploit the now-enormous collection of networkwide RAM to avoid or greatly reduce disk reads.

Distributed DBMS

6.1 INTRODUCTION

Data/information management has always been a leading application of computers and it will play an even stronger role in the future. It supports complex information at levels defined by users, provides distributed views over worldwide networks, and is integrated with communication systems. The result is a synergy that makes electronic information management a part of everyday life, integrated into many activities.

While computers have popularly been thought of as fancy calculators, and they do serve many computational or number-crunching purposes, their widest use has been in storing, accessing, managing, and analyzing information.

The history of computing has been a steady advance from the language and communication level of the machine toward that of the user. The earliest machines required users to drop themselves to the level of the machine, to translate what they wanted done into the machine's language of 0s and 1s and the machine's operations of store, increment, load, and execute. Next, high-level languages allowed users to write mathematical statements describing operations, which were automatically translated into machine code. However, the user, or programmer, still had to translate the problem into this computer language. Fourth-generation languages (4GLs) allowed nonprogramming end users to access information without explicitly defining each step, but only provided certain built-in types of operations on predefined data types, such as tables.

The latest advance is object technology, which allows users to package code and data into units, called objects, at higher and higher levels. The user of an object does not need to know how it is implemented to invoke the object's operations, and those operations can correspond directly to the user's desired application. By combining objects into composite objects, users can build fairly complex systems.

6.1.1 Data Management

The evolution of information management parallels this programming progression, starting from low-level programs that directly read and write core memory to tape, disk tracks, and cylinders, followed by file systems that for improved performance gave higher-level views of byte arrays, records, and indices. Databases started with the same model of records and indices, adding the capability to recover from failures, to manage data integrity, and to control concurrent accesses by multiple users.

These early database models were at the level of the machine, much like the early programming languages. Later databases, such as relational ones, evolved a mechanism to perform ad hoc queries on the data, while the DBMS automatically figured out an optimized execution path, based on dynamic indices, and returned the result. Although this added a higher-level interface, just like the 4GLs, it did so at the cost of limiting the data to simple, flat tabular formats and a few predefined operations. It was up to the user to figure out how to map the application operations and data structures in order to flatten them into tables. The most recent trend in databases is to support objects directly, allowing users to define, create, modify, and share objects with the traditional database facilities for recovery, concurrency, integrity, and query.

The object trend is catching on rapidly in all aspects of computing, from GUIs and icons, such as Macintosh and Windows; to languages (C++ and Smalltalk); analysis and design tools; operating system frameworks; and databases. By avoiding the need to translate from the application domain to programming constructs, users save time in telling the computer what they want (programming) and in executing the result (runtime). They can reduce errors by reusing objects and working directly at the application level.

As tools mature and users begin to appreciate their value, more and more libraries of off-the-shelf objects are becoming commonplace. Programming today requires learning complex techniques for translating application problems to computer languages. Tomorrow it may simply be a matter of choosing pre-existing objects that can be combined to achieve the desired result. These objects may be accessible in libraries of standard, widely available objects. Today we are just beginning to see the accessibility of worldwide massive information stores via the Internet.

The result is distribution of this information among many direct users of computers—in a wide variety of professional, business, and home use—far more powerful uses of computers, far more reliable uses (because standard, tested, working components are reused), and greater access to wider varieties and amounts of such information in heterogeneous environments.

6.1.2 Distributed Storage

In the old way, a user writes a program, makes special calls to the I/O system, and saves some information. This *get/put interface* usually includes a translation of data format from the programmer's language (COBOL or FORTRAN) to the DBMS format (e.g., indexed sequential access method [ISAM] records). This translation is complicated, slow, and error prone. With the object-oriented techniques, users view their information as part of objects and simply invoke operations on the objects. The ODBMS transparently (without regard to location or platform) maintains the object persistently on disk, ensuring recoverability and concurrency management, among other capabilities. No more is there a dichotomy between the program and the data storage since these are just objects.

The result is that all programmers and all users of computers become users of DBMSs, because they are all directly using objects that are managed in secondary or tertiary storage, even though they never think about that storage or explicitly control it. Most of the processing that has traditionally been part of the application program is becoming part of the objects themselves, within the DBMS. Semantics, or meaning—including interpretation, rules of integrity, and behavior—are inherent in the object.

6.1.3 Database Management System

A database management system is one that allows storing information, sharing it among multiple users, and maintaining its integrity. The three factors driving use of a DBMS are:

☞ Databases can contain a lot of information.

☞ Recovery and data integrity keep the information safe.

☞ Simultaneous sharing of information.

A DBMS is a set of programs that manipulate and maintain the database. A true DBMS must be able to maintain many tables and cross-reference items between these tables. Because a DBMS allows data to be drawn from many database tables, it can provide such benefits as minimized data redundancy, improved data integrity, and data independence.

Database management systems use their own native internal language. Data Definition Language (DDL) statements serve to define data and establish constraints on how data can be entered or accessed. Data Modeling Language (DML) statements manipulate the data to put it into a form suitable for presentation to the user.

When the volume of information becomes quite large, some facility may be needed to manage that information, move it to and from secondary storage (such as tape or disk), and search it quickly. Similarly, when information is simultaneously used by multiple users (people and/or programs), some system is needed to coordinate their access, so they can all get to the information and modify it without destroying each other's work.

Finally, a mechanism is needed to protect information from accidental loss due to power failure or application failure. In each case, the system that performs this service is a DBMS. Each DBMS has a number of key defining characteristics.

6.1.3.1 Persistence and Recovery   Among the defining characteristics of a DBMS, persistence is the foremost, which means that the information stored in the DBMS will be there tomorrow, even after you turn off the computer. Recovery describes the ability of the DBMS to return the state of stored information to a consistent point even after failures such as power outages or application errors.

6.1.3.2 Schema Application   A DBMS must support language capabilities in at least three areas: DDL, DML, and Query (declarative access). DDL provides a mechanism for users of the DBMS to define new structures or information types. DML provides a mechanism to access instances of such information structures, including modifications. Query is a facility that enables users to state what they want and DBMS then determines how to find that information and return it to the requester. DBMSs can support DDL and DML in many host languages. Query support usually includes a query engine that examines the declaration of desired result, devises an execution plan to obtain it, optimizes that plan based on knowledge of the database (e.g., indices, which information is local or remote), and then executes it. Often these are available through graphical interfaces.

A DBMS must support sharing of information among simultaneous users. The most common mechanism is via a *transaction*, which groups a user-defined set of operations and ensures either that all or none of the operations execute. Transactions also often implement recovery mechanisms.

Various kinds of *locks* are used to control who has access to information and force other users to wait their turn. Timestamps may also be used, and different levels of concurrency are also applicable.

Many DBMSs provide additional capabilities beyond these basic functions, including distribution, which allows information to be stored in different locations. Users need not know where the information is. The DBMS finds it for them. In many environments security is an important DBMS capability. It can restrict access to information to authorized users only. Many approaches exist, such as access control lists (ACLs), which define allowed access (read and/or write) to a specified user, to a group, and to everyone else. The defense community has many levels of security, including discretionary (similar to access lists) and mandatory (similar to classification of information as top secret). In the U.S. Department of Defense (DOD), the *orange book* defines four major levels of system-enforced security, A through D, each with numbered sublevels, where A is the most secure.

6.1.3.3 Multiple Language Access

6.1.3.3 Multiple Language Access   Another popular DBMS capability is the maintenance of user-defined *integrity* constraints. If different pieces of information are dependent on each other, the DBMS can be instructed to keep them in sync, or if information has only certain allowed values, the DBMS can restrict it. Database *administration* allows the users or administrators of databases to examine, control, and adjust the behavior of the system. For example, based on usage loads, administrators might want to move some information, optimize via clustering or indexing, investigate who the biggest users are. Finally, the ability to access the same shared information from multiple languages and environments (operating systems, networks, hardware) can be an important feature.

6.2 OBJECT TECHNOLOGY REVISITED

6.2.1 Why Objects?

We are in the midst of a broad change to a new approach to software construction, a change as significant to software as the change in manufacturing from medieval crafts to modern automation. This change affects all aspects of software, from GUIs to languages to analysis and design tools to operating systems and databases. Over time, the change will bring us through the current software crisis to higher levels of quality, larger systems, and greater productivity.

Why do we need a change? It seems strange for an advanced technology such as computer science, but the approach to building software has been a very limiting, old-fashioned one. Just as the medieval craftsperson built crafts by hand—from scratch—software today is built by hand, by specialized craftspeople (software gurus). This leads to several problems.

☞ There are a limited number of such software gurus.

☞ Constructing software by hand is slow and expensive.

☞ Hand crafting leads to unavoidable imperfections, limiting quality (each new piece of software has a new set of bugs).

☞ System complexity is limited.

System compatibility is worth deeper consideration. A software architect must be able to envision all aspects and implications in the system design (e.g., if something changes in one part, what will be the effect in another part?). This effectively limits the size of the system to the size of the architect's head! This is the major limitation in how we can use computers.

Object technology holds one of the keys to breaking through this complexity barrier. Software is organized into objects—units containing both the code and the data to represent some application entity, whether it be a customer or manufacturing process or a telecom switch or satellite. Users of the object need not know how it is implemented, but only how to request its services (via its interface). In this way, system designers can build systems out of objects, with no limit, thereby breaking through the complexity barrier.

This is not new technology, but is simply well-known technology applied to software. Henry Ford, for his Model T, used standard parts, rather than manufacturing each car separately, and achieved higher production rates, lower cost, and higher quality. A computer designer today builds a computer by piecing together chips and components such as CPU, memory, and I/O devices. If the designers were to consider, at the system design level, the behavior of the electrons in the transistors of the chips, they would never finish a computer. Too often, though, in software, we're doing exactly that: Considering each bit and byte, each primitive data structure (table, queue, list), each primitive operation, and so limiting our ability to build and maintain large, complex software systems. Objects allow software designers to avoid worrying about details, to treat component software as a black box, and to build larger components.

Such modular software components can be reused. After building a railway operations system, with objects for trains and tracks and customers, Kintetsu found it could reuse many of those objects for their trucking system, and just program the differences (delta). This allows follow-on systems and enhancements to be assembled much faster.

Reusing already-working objects means higher quality, rather than chasing new bugs with new software. Changing or improving an object's internals is guaranteed not to break other software that uses the object, dramatically reducing maintenance costs. Wider varieties of users can piece together software systems out of libraries of such objects. Over time, as users absorb this new approach, and as libraries grow, we can break through the limitations of the medieval approach to software, with implications for the information management industry as far-reaching as the industrial revolution was for manufacturing.

The advantages of objects apply to all aspects of software. They were first popularized in GUIs; e.g., the icons in Windows or Macintosh are objects, each of which accepts the request to print themselves, though the code executed (the internals) is quite different for text, spreadsheets, and graphics. Object languages such as C++ and Smalltalk recently have grown tremendously, as have analysis and design tools based on objects and operating system frameworks. Where do object databases fit? First, let us examine object technology in general.

6.2.2 Object Technology

The basic idea of object technology is to form software into objects, which contain both the data and the code for an application entity. This combination is called *encapsulation,* indicating that the internal implementation of the object is not visible to its users, but rather only the well-defined external interface. This object can behave just like the real-world application entity. It is the familiar concept of modularity, with three key features: abstraction, extensibility, and reuse.

Abstraction means that the object directly represents higher-level application or real-world entities, such as an employee or a telecommunications switch, a document or sales order. Rather than forcing programmers to translate these abstract quantities down to records or tables or queues, abstraction allows direct represention of them as objects. This results in easier and more accurate modeling of the application.

Essential to object technology is *extensibility*, or the ability to add new types of objects. Instead of a fixed set of data types (tuple or set) and operations (union or join), the designer can freely define arbitrary new structures and operations to compose arbitrarily complex and sophisticated systems.

The ability to reuse objects is also essential to object systems. Instead of starting by developing everything from scratch, programmers can take pre-existing objects off the shelf and use them "as is." Often, pre-existing software does almost what one desires, but not exactly, forcing traditional programmers to copy the code and slightly modify it, resulting in new code to be maintained, to be debugged, or to be kept in sync with the original. Instead, with objects, slight changes or be made by only expressing the differences, and actually reusing the rest of the object. These object technology features benefit users with faster development, cheaper maintenance, and higher quality.

As with most new disciplines, object technology takes some time to learn. Designers must learn how to model systems in terms of interacting objects, each behaving just as it does in the real world, and forget the old approaches of shared data structures operated on by separate procedures. This is a progressive skill, and the better one develops this skill, the more effective the reuse of objects will be and the more efficient the system will be.

Over the lifetime of a software product, perhaps 80% of the cost is in maintenance. The encapsulation of objects, however, guarantees that internal implementation changes cannot affect any users of that object or any other object. This turns the common spaghetti tangle of traditional software into well-organized, separately maintainable units, dramatically reducing software maintenance costs.

Reused objects are already tested, debugged, and working. This ability to build on the past and make continual forward progress holds the potential for a major evolution in the software industry.

6.2.3 Identity

Each object is a well-defined unit, addressable uniquely and independently of all other objects. In some traditional information systems (e.g., RDBMSs) there is no such concept. Instead, there is only data. If all the data in a person's record changes, there is no sense in asking whether it is the same person. As an object, however, that question does make sense. Even if the person changes name, hair color, and social security number, he or she is the same person. It is the same object.

6.2.4 Polymorphism

Polymorphism implies that the same operation, when invoked on different objects, can result in executing different code. For example, a draw operation might be invoked the same way for a rectangle and a circle object, but they might be drawn by quite different algorithms. The choice of which code to execute is made at runtime, depending upon which object it is acting on.

A *class* collects together common characteristics of objects, not only external interfaces but also internal implementation, including data structures and method or operation code. Each *instance* of the class uses these same definitions, but with different stated values. For example, an employee *class* might define internal structures to store name, salary, department, and operations to raise the salary, fire the employee, or change departments. All of this structure and code is common to each employee object instance, though each has a different value for name and salary.

Inheritance is one mechanism of extensibility. It allows defining new classes from old. The new class may use all of the structure and code of the old, may modify or *refine* any of these, may replace any of them, and may add new ones. In this way, extensions can be made by working only on the differences and reusing the common parts. An employee object might be a subclass of a *person* object. Since the *person* already has name and age, the employee definition simply uses those and adds salary and department. System designers often use inheritance to build hierarchies and trees of classes.

Finally, *composition* is a technique used to build new object instances by connecting together other object instances. As inheritance allows building hierarchies of classes, composition allows building hierarchies of object instances. The composed objects need not necessarily be of the same class.

6.2.5 Product Assembly Object

Documents may be represented by component objects consisting of chapters, sections, figures, tables, paragraphs, words, index entries, and footnotes. Another example of objects is product assembly, such as a bicycle: The wheels, seat, frame, and pedals are all component objects, which, when connected together, form the bicycle object.

6.3 DBMSs AND THE CLIENT/SERVER MODEL

In order to serve distributed environments with mixtures of heterogeneous computers and networks, with users and objects everywhere, Distributed Object Database Management Systems (ODBMSs) have evolved to provide a mechanism for users to transparently access objects anywhere. Architectures for distributed client/server computing have evolved from the single-user, virtual memory-based approach through the first-generation client/server with the central server.

The new generation of distributed client/server combines the advantages of each of those and adds additional flexibility. Recent extensions include support for Wide Area Networks (WANs) and, via ANSI-standard SQL and ODBC implementations, the world of front-end client/server tools immediately plugs in. In addition to recovery, integrity, concurrency, and scalability, these systems provide higher-level services for management of relationships, versions, and composite objects.

6.3.1 Client/Server Models

The first generation of client/server computing arose from the background of mainframe computing and was implemented on minicomputers. It represented a first step in bringing computing from the mainframes to the fingertips of the user, but it was modeled on the old architecture. The server was a centralized system, just like a mainframe, and the clients were remote terminals accessing that central server. Although that allowed many clients to access and share the same resources and information, it took no advantage of distributed computing power, but instead kept it all centralized.

The current generation of distributed client/server computing carries that one step further. The information, resources, and users may be located anywhere, with transparent access among all of them. The result is effective use of computing resources wherever they may be, the ability to incrementally take advantage of additional resources, and much greater sharing and communication capabilities.

In the second-generation client/server, the server does not need to be centralized in one location; the server processes and information can be allocated anywhere. Similarly, the client need not be simply a remote terminal sending requests to the server, but may subsume as much of the actual processing and even storage as desired. The user decides where to draw the boundary, how much to put on the server, how much on the client, and when to adjust that allocation based on changing usage patterns.

This evolution to distributed client/server crosses three intermediate steps—the central server, server-based virtual memory, and client-based virtual memory—to the distributed server.

6.3.1.1 The Central Server Most client/server systems, among them most traditional (including relational) database systems, are based on a central server. Just like the mainframe, this server localizes in one place all the storage and processing for the system. Clients, even when built on high-powered computers, act as simple remote terminals, sending a request for processing or a query for information retrieval. This maps well to some applications, such as OLTP. For example, a simple airline reservations system has many clerks sending simple requests to one centralized repository, each requesting or releasing a seat reservation, each issuing a short query, and all sharing the same information.

All the information is isolated to the one system, where it can be controlled and managed. A large and well-designed system can manage large amounts of information. Performance is limited by the network and interprocess communication time for the clients to send requests to and receive responses from the server, but for a simple OLTP system with short high-level queries and for simple information, this can work just fine. However, for more complex applications, with interacting users and interrelated information, this architecture limits performance and scalability.

The central server does create a bottleneck (refer to Figure 6.1). All user requests go to the one server queue to be processed. Once through this queue, the processing might consist of relegation to separate computational threads, but first the request must clear the queue. As new users are added, their requests wait in the same queue, which means the user response time slows. This bottleneck limits scalability in users. As demand increases, the only solution the user has is the same as the mainframe solution, i.e., buy a bigger server. There is no flexibility to share the processing and storage among multi-

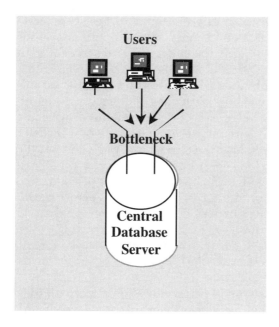

Fig. 6.1 Central Server Bottleneck

ple systems to achieve increased performance and scalability or to take advantage of new computing resources.

Similarly, the central server lacks flexibility. As server limits appear, it is natural to try to split information across multiple servers. Since the clients connect to a specific server, the client must know where the information is and often must manage interactions among separately stored information. If some of the information or processing is moved to a different server, the client application typically breaks.

The central server does provide these advantages:

☞ Effective sharing for simple information

☞ Centralized and safe administration

☞ Large information management

On the other hand, its limitations are:

☞ Insufficient performance for complex or interrelated information

☞ Bottlenecking, limiting scalability

☞ Inflexibility, with an inability to move or separate information

6.3.1.2 Server-Based Virtual Memory Systems involving complex information—having dynamic structures of varying sizes, time series data, audio, video, graphics, and interconnected information of composite objects—do not map well to central servers. Virtual memory, as a computing technique, grew up in the 1960s and 1970s, predating the client/server emergence in the 1970s and 1980s. From the point of view of complex object management, virtual memory provides useful capabilities missing in the simple server model. The virtual memory capabilities combine with the client/server model to provide the full power of managing complex objects in a distributed environment.

The early object systems were built around a single-user model, in which all of the complex structures and interconnections were laid out directly in memory. Such a model provides complete flexibility for structure, object behavior, and object relationships. For a single user, it provides fine performance, avoiding the need to send interprocess requests across networks, but rather works directly on memory images. The information can exceed physical memory by using virtual memory, supported in most operating systems up to a full gigabyte. When necessary, the information can be saved directly in the same format by storing and retrieving the virtual memory swap file as a memory-mapped file.

Virtual memory systems tend to perform well only when all the data fits into memory. As systems grow, developers run into memory size problems. Concurrent access by multiple users is also a problem. Once the information is in one user's virtual memory, it is difficult to provide access to other users. Surrendering the control of the fundamental memory and disk management to the operating system works well for prototypes and small applications. Large production environments require the ability to control page size, clustering, caching, and swapping algorithms, all across multiple machine architectures.

6.3.1.3 Client-Based Virtual Memory   Integrity problems also arise with virtual memory systems. Allowing applications to use pointers to physical locations in memory leads to integrity problems from invalid pointers. After a transaction commit, for example, such pointers are invalid (because the object may have moved to a different machine), so application use of the pointers can result in crashes or subtle data corruption. For single applications, these problems are limited to application crash and loss of session information. For a database, however, the problems are much more insidious. Shared information—corrupted—swapped out at commit time causes problems for many users, sometimes not noticed until much later, when it is impossible to repair the damage. Virtual memory has these advantages for objects:

☞ Ease of implementation
☞ Support for complex and interrelated objects
☞ Efficient complex single-user processing

It also presents some of the following problems for distributed production environments:

☞ Integrity problems leading to corrupt databases

☞ Weak concurrency support

☞ Insufficient performance scaling

6.3.1.4 Distributed Server-Based System

A typical computing environment today includes a large variety of computers, from mainframes to PCs and diverse vendors, operating systems, and networks. Users struggle to access shared information and processing resources throughout a network, but too often find that they cannot get from point A to point B. Data formats differ, access mechanisms differ, and there are no mechanisms to maintain integrity and provide concurrent access across these environments. Distributed client/ server technology meets these needs, combining the ability of the central server first-generation client/server to support integrity, concurrency, and scalability, with the virtual memory support for complex interrelated objects and added flexibility.

6.3.2 Distributed Client/Server

A distributed client/server system provides a single logical view of all objects. Users see and interact with a purely logical view of objects connected to objects, with no need to know that one object happens to currently reside on a UNIX server, another on a Windows NT, and yet another on a Mac system. When an object is accessed, by whatever mechanism, name or ID, or relationship traversal, the object manager determines where the object is and makes it accessible.

The users need not worry about how to get to the object or how it is represented physically. All operations are transparent across this single logical view, including relationship traversal, propagating methods across composite object relationships, versioning, or atomic commits. If an object is moved from one computer to another, or from one database to another, applications continue to work normally. If users run into limits on one server, they can simply add another, move some of the objects to it, and continue running.

6.3.2.1 Integrity Maintained by Safe Pointers

At the same time, as objects are accessed by a particular user, those objects are cached locally, in that user's address space, in the native format for that environment, including floating-point, byte-ordering, alignment, and compiler differences. This allows access to arbitrary structure and arbitrary behavior with direct memory performance. Access to the object is via one pointer indirection. This allows the object manager to guarantee integrity, even if the object moves—due to transaction commit—to another machine. The object manager can trap the reference at this indirection point, retrieve the object, fix the reference, and let the application continue normally. This safe pointer indirection also gives the object manager the freedom to move, cluster, and cache objects as necessary to achieve scalable performance.

To provide this support, it is necessary to support both a distributed repository and a heterogeneity mechanism. The repository allows the system to locate an object, wherever it might be, on whatever server. The heterogeneity engine allows translation between the logical view and various physical views, adjusting for differences in byte ordering, floating point, pointers, packing and alignment, word size, and compilers.

This distributed client/server environment allows sharing of objects, information, and processing among users and object databases, across heterogeneous computers and networks, at the same time providing the power of highly efficient access to arbitrary objects, providing:

- ☞ Transparent access across heterogeneous computers and networks
- ☞ Flexibility to move objects without breaking applications
- ☞ Integrity
- ☞ Scalability
- ☞ Arbitrary object structure, relationships, and behavior
- ☞ Networkwide administration and tools
- ☞ Native memory access efficiency

6.3.2.2 WAN Support via Partitions   A recent product advancement extends distributed client/server support across WANs via local autonomy through object database partitions. Administrators dynamically create and change partitions, in which all system services, including schema, repository, and locking control information, are automatically replicated. If a cross-partition network link temporarily fails, users within partitions can continue to operate, accessing all the objects resident or already cached within their partition. This provides greater availability, fault tolerance, and performance, without affecting the applications at all and without limiting the single logical view over the WAN.

Another recent advancement extends the distributed client/server object database to the world of SQL and ODBC users. Virtually all the available front-end tools can immediately access distributed object databases.

6.3.2.3 Support for SQL and ODBC   Use of ODBMSs in production now extends to production use in application areas including multimedia, CAD/CAM, aerospace, manufacturing, process control, document management, groupware, and financial systems. This brings distributed client/server computing to users today, carrying them beyond the mainframelike central servers, providing access equally to all resources and adding the database capabilities of recovery, integrity maintenance, concurrency, and scalability. Users freely choose where to store objects and where to execute objects' methods. Applications include new classes of groupware, cooperative computing, and sharing of objects, even across WANs. Recent support for SQL and ODBC allows virtually all front-end tools immediate access to the object databases, providing an easy starting path into the world of objects and distributed computing.

6.3.3 ActiveX

ActiveX software provides connectivity using Internet and Web technology, even though the user may connect only to internal networks (intranets). HTTP is the protocol used to provide data to Web browsers. ActiveX permits an application to use objects that reside on a local hard disk, a server in the next room, or a Web server anywhere in the world.

OLE provides object sharing for local or remote objects. Because ActiveX enhances OLE with Web access, ActiveX controls are now trendy and OLE custom controls (OCXs) have become passé. ActiveX controls are like low-fat OCXs: They involve fewer interfaces and load faster. ActiveX also applies to other OLE technologies. For example, OLE automation interfaces that are Internet-enabled become ActiveX automation interfaces.

The classic SQL client/server model uses remote procedure calls with proprietary network libraries. Applications use client/server protocols that operate over standard network transports such as TCP/IP, NetBIOS, and IPX/SPX.

6.3.4 SQL

Ease of programming has become as much a part of a product evaluation as the results of performance benchmarks. Because programming features affect sales, most DBMS vendors recognize the importance of programming interfaces. The recently adopted SQL Call Level Interface (CLI) provides little opportunity for product differentiation. In an era when embedded SQL and SQL CLI are standard, how is a vendor to provide unique programming features? The answer is objects.

6.3.5 OLE

OLE is an enabling technology for building shared, distributed objects. A review of certain OLE and ActiveX concepts will help you understand. The binary-level incompatibility of classes and objects created with C++, Smalltalk, and other object-oriented programming (OOP) languages caused a demand for a shared object architecture. Such an architecture would enable us to share local or remote objects among disparate programming languages and applications. OLE is based on a COM, which provides interoperability at the binary level.

OLE components encapsulate data and the methods that operate on that data. OLE includes service layers that build on COM to provide embedded objects, access to structured storage, persistent objects, drag-and-drop editing, and other capabilities. Automation interfaces permit OLE components to expose the commands and methods that cause scripts and programs to drive an application.

OLE supports transparent remoting, a process that makes objects on remote computers appear to be local. The OLE architecture includes proxies and stubs so that remote or out-of-process objects appear to be in the same address space (in-process) as the object user. The version of the COM that supports distributed component objects is DCOM. COM and DCOM use remote procedure calls to marshal data between processes and computers so that components appear to have the same word size, bit orientation, and address space.

6.3.6 SQL and OLE

Prior to the introduction of OLE, Windows client applications often used Dynamic Data Exchange (DDE) to communicate with software that provided access to SQL databases. OLE introduced automation interfaces that were easier to use and more reliable than DDE. Many independent software vendors developed Visual Basic controls (VBXs), but then rewrote their component products as OCXs and eventually as ActiveX controls.

SQL DBMS vendors noticed the demand for components and adopted OLE in clientside tools or as an object interface to their servers. Oracle Objects for OLE encapsulates the Oracle Call Interface (OCI). Oracle Objects for OLE includes a data control that replaces the Visual Basic data control for developers who prefer to connect to Oracle databases without using the access engine.

6.3.7 OLE DB

OLE DB is the data access cornerstone that uses OLE-based solutions for crafting enterprise applications. OLE DB includes software components that provide COM interfaces with C and C++ bindings. Programmers manipulate OLE DB objects by setting properties and executing methods.

An OLE DB provider is software that sends data or services to consumer applications. OLE DB providers support schemas and repositories consisting of one or more schemas. A data provider enables access to specific data (text or a database, for example) and a service provider performs a service (such as processing queries). Data providers implement a fundamental set of interfaces by which applications can use their component services and they also may implement other interfaces for transactions, ISAM access, data definition, and command processing.

OLE DB defines handles to reference entities such as rows (HROW) and result codes (HRESULT). OLE DB also defines an ERRORINFO structure and error interfaces, which support multiple error objects. It supports retrieval of metadata and schema information using techniques similar to those used for data. OLE DB supports the retrieval and storage of binary large objects (BLOBs) and OLE objects.

6.3.7.1 Transactions and the ODBC
OLE DB programmers can do commit and abort processing by using transaction interfaces. To coordinate these activities across computers, a programmer can use the Windows NT Distributed Transaction Coordinator (DTC). The DTC works with X/Open XA-compliant transaction managers and is therefore compatible with some transaction monitors. OLE DB supports coordinated transactions by exposing an ITransactionJoin interface on DBSession objects. Multiple providers can participate in coordinated transactions. OLE transactions support event notification through the use of OLE's connection point mechanism.

6.3.7.2 Security Model
Security is a concern when developing software that operates on enterprise databases. Those concerns increase if the Internet is involved—so security is a requirement for OLE data access. DCOM implements a security model for components. OLE DB complements DCOM with authentication and authorization services. OLE DB permits developers to get and set permissions based on users, objects, and groups.

6.4 OBJECT RELATIONAL DATABASE MANAGEMENT SYSTEM (ORDBMS)

ORDBMSs add new object storage capabilities to the relational systems at the core of modern information systems. These new facilities integrate management of traditional fielded data, complex objects such as time-series and geospatial data, and diverse binary media such as audio, video, images, and applets. By encapsulating methods with data structures, an ORDBMS server can execute complex analytical and data manipulation operations to search and transform complex objects.

As an evolutionary technology, the object relational (OR) approach has inherited the robust transaction- and performance-management features of its relational ancestor and the flexibility of its object-oriented cousin. Database designers can work with familiar tabular structures and DDLs while assimilating new object-management possibilities. Query and procedural languages and call interfaces in ORDBMSs are quite familiar. SQL3; vendor procedural languages; and ODBC, JDBC, and proprietary call interfaces are all extensions of RDBMS languages and interfaces.

6.4.1 Object Relational Features

Object relational databases organize information in the familiar relational tabular structures. In fact, object relational implementations subsume the relational database model. ORDBMSs are an incremental upgrade of their RDBMS predecessors, and, unlike the move to object database systems, object relational migration need not entail wholesale recoding. Just as a C++

compiler can handle C code despite its lack of classes, once you accommodate the mostly syntactic changes from SQL-92 to SQL3, an ORDBMS should support same-vendor relational schemas. Current ORDBMS implementations do have gaps, however, such as the first-release lack of replication facilities, so implementation details must be kept in mind.

The most important new object relational features are user-defined types (UDTs), user-defined functions (UDFs), and the infrastructures, such as indexing access methods and optimizer enhancements, that support them. User-defined types may be distinct, opaque (base), and row (composite).

Distinct types, also known as value types, are derived from other types but have their own domains, operations, functions, and casts: ORDBMS applications can be strongly typed, helping ensure application integrity. System-defined types are familiar: Most RDBMSs implement money, for example, as a numeric type with a defined number of decimal places. It is logical to add and subtract money values and to multiply them by scalars, but not by other money values. Money types could have a function such as growth and casts to real and string types if methods associated with those types are needed.

Opaque types are not derived from source types, so their internal structures must be defined to the DBMS along with their operations, functions, and casts. Once properly defined, an opaque type can be used as a source type for defining distinct and row types and can be used in tables.

A row type is a collection of fields of other types. One row type can include another row type nested among its fields. Handling of the constituent fields is derived from their types so the operations, functions, and casts of the row type must be defined. Collection types (sets or lists of values of a built-in or user-defined type) are another object relational innovation.

Cartridges, DataBlades, and Extenders are modules that build on the DBMS's object relational infrastructure. They consist of types, data structures, functions, and data and often include special developer interfaces or prebuilt applications.

6.4.2 Modeling

To date, ORDBMSs have had their greatest success in managing media objects and complex data such as geospatial and financial time-series data. They are frequently used in Web applications and specialized data warehouses. Advanced Web applications are notable beneficiaries of the ORDBMS's ability to integrate management of media, traditional fielded data, and templates for dynamic page generation.

Media objects include audio, video, images, and formatted and unformatted text. The data structures themselves are not very interesting; to an ORDBMS, beyond defined access methods they are undifferentiated BLOBs. What is interesting is the new possibility of creating server functions to index, search, and process stored media. For instance, some implementations include a set of data structures for medialike application (template) pages, as well as functions that process the SQL queries, variables, and procedural tags embedded in the HTML. Application pages are stored with a UDT, an opaque type called html, which has methods defined for their management and processing. The source type is just text, however; it is the methods that are interesting.

A time series, an ordered array of values indexed by a time value, is a representative complex data type. All the major object relational DBMSs have or will have one or more time. You can also build your own time-series structures and methods from the ground up. Whatever its source, the time-series type would have a name and other descriptive fields, plus one or more date-indexed vectors of values.

The object relational models include both data and processes, what information you have and what you are going to do with it. By contrast, relational databases support only limited encapsulation of operations and processes. Clearly, design methodologies and tools must now model both data and operations, a requirement that calls for approaches that cover both traditional databases and object-oriented applications and optimally would allow designers to encapsulate functions with data and generate classes or code structures external to the database. Tools should offer the ability to work with built-in types and methods and to extend the model with user-defined types and functions and modules.

6.4.2.1 Methodologies
There are many reasons for creating a model, and for using a modeling and design tool, rather than just jumping in and directly programming a database and application code. Modeling can help bridge the gaps between business physical models or concepts, database, and physical database implementations.

A logical model created with a design tool is insulated from DBMS specifics, allowing a single design to be implemented in different DBMSs. Unlike logical models, schemas are tied to specific DBMS server products. For many years, modeling tools have had both reverse- and forward-engineering capabilities.

6.4.2.2 Relational and Object Relational Modeling
Entity relationship (ER) is the traditional relational modeling approach. Information engineering (IE) is a variant with methodological and notational differences. Given the relational underpinnings of ORDBMSs, these approaches have been adapted for modeling object relational databases, but they suffer from serious conceptual modeling weaknesses and an inability to capture processes. For instance, an often-cited shortcoming of IE is a difficulty depicting business objects that are naturally modeled in unnormalized form. The usual example, simplified, is an order, a conceptual entity that IE would prefer to normalize into purchaser, product, and shopping basket entities.

6.4.2.3 Other Modeling Tools
For the future, it is worthwhile to keep an eye on other modeling tools. Database-design tools, for example, must add support

for user-defined types and functions and other object relational features in order to be used for object relational modeling.

6.5 ODBMS

Many choices are available for designing and implementing an ODBMS. Even though these choices may be hidden from the interface, they can have a significant impact on your implementations in the following areas:

- ☞ Scalability
- ☞ Interoperability
- ☞ Integrity
- ☞ Flexibility

To evaluate their architectural impact in these areas, we can categorize the various prototypes and products into three major architectural types:

- ☞ Virtual memory (with page server)
- ☞ Central server (with object server)
- ☞ Distributed client/server (with object and storage managers)

Each represents quite different choices in the design space—resulting in quite different behavior—and applicability to quite different environments.

6.5.1 Virtual Memory Server

The virtual memory (VM) choice uses a page server that maps pages directly into the virtual memory mapping scheme, allowing applications to access that memory via direct pointers and allowing virtual memory to manage the swapping. Direct pointers are physical addresses into any part of VM, within any part of the objects. Use of direct virtual memory offers several advantages:

- ☞ Ease of implementation
- ☞ Efficient single-user complex processing
- ☞ Support of complex objects and relationships

Because arbitrary memory layouts are directly supported, any structure can be implemented, including interconnection. This gives much greater flexibility than traditional database architectures for modeling complex information and executing complex algorithms, and it can result in very efficient single-user processing. Also, such a system is easy to implement because there is no object manager but rather just the reliance on the operating system's VM. The disadvantages of this architectural criterion follow from its use of VM and page server, though they are not necessarily obvious. They include:

☞ Lack of object granularity

☞ Insufficient performance scaling

☞ Weak concurrency support

☞ Integrity problems, leading to corrupt databases

This criterion gives the application direct (raw, unprotected) pointer access to the virtual memory-mapped file, so the ODBMS has no control over access at the object level. The architecture limits ODBMS granularity to the page level. If the application requires an object, for example, the ODBMS must swap in a page (often a segment) and process all the objects on that page or segment, including heterogenous transformations. If all the objects on that page or segment are used (dense usage), then there is no problem. If, however, only 5 of 2000 objects are used (sparse usage), for example, fully 400 times unneeded overhead is incurred. Further, any other object-level processing is architecturally precluded, including object-level versioning, security, and cache management.

The second disadvantage is one of performance (speed), which does not scale as the number of objects grow. Since this ODBMS relies on operating system VM, its performance will mirror that of the VM, which yields high performance when most data fits in physical memory, but much lower performance (thrashing) when the data exceeds memory and must be swapped in and out. Further, it imposes hard limits: Once the ODBMS gives out pointers to the application, they cannot be retrieved, so the ODBMS is architecturally constrained to keep those objects in VM throughout the transaction. In other words, it cannot swap objects and cannot implement a cache manager. This lack of cache management also introduces a hard architectural limit: Once the VM is full, no more objects may be accessed. In fact, VM is filled not only by objects actually used, but also by the fanout (all the objects pointed to by those objects used). At this limit, no more can be done and it simply breaks.

This criterion also has limitations in multiuser environments. Once objects are mapped into one user's VM, they are tied there by pointers, and cannot be moved into other users' VM spaces. This inherent limitation causes the same kind of thrashing when the number of users grows.

This architecture also has a fundamental integrity weakness. The pointers given out to the application become invalid when objects move, and so are invalid after transaction commit because commit implies that objects are available for other users, and so might be moved back to the server or to other users' machines. However, the application still has the pointers. Any mistaken use of pointers will either cause a crash (segment violation) or de-reference into the wrong object, resulting in subtle database corruption that might not be noticed for days, long after the information is lost. In a shared database environment, though, they corrupt the objects shared by hundreds or thousands of users.

Since this criterion exposes physical memory layouts directly, and provides access via direct pointers rather than object identifiers, some would not term this an ODBMS; instead of managing objects, it is managing virtual memory images swapped to and from disk. Terminology aside, it is a useful approach for some applications. In particular, this architecture best applies to:

☞ Single user to small group

☞ Small size (mostly fits in memory)

☞ Programmers used to single applications, not DBMS

☞ Non-mission critical prototyping

6.5.2 Central Server

The second major architectural criterion is a central server, commonly known as object server, although much of this criterion applies to centralized page servers, too. This architecture, which grew from the monolithic databases of the 1960s and the first-generation client/server databases of the 1970s, comes from the traditional database world, which followed the mainframe model, even when building on minicomputers and workstations. Like mainframes, all storage and processing occurs on the central server. The user or client is effectively a dumb remote terminal sending requests and receiving answers.

The central server offers almost the opposite of advantages and disadvantages of the above VM approach. Its advantages include:

☞ Centrally controlled administration

☞ Effective sharing for simple data and short transactions

☞ Large data management on large servers

Because all resources are localized at the central server, it is relatively easy to build administration tools to manage them and control access. Similarly, when the server has large storage, input/output, and processing power, it can handle large amounts of information, just as with mainframes. Many users may share this information effectively, as long as they require only small amounts of information at a time (to move from server to client) and their requests or transactions are short, allowing other users to access the server's resources.

The disadvantages of such an architecture are the following:

☞ Bottlenecks limit scalability

☞ Inflexibility

☞ Insufficient performance for complex and related information

This architectural model does not map well to complex information or information with many interconnections, as is often found in object applications. Such applications require the ability to move from one object to the next, invoke a complex operation, move back to the first and onto a third, and invoke another operation. Each such step involves a communication with the server, which requires milliseconds, resulting in performance that is intolerably slow. In fact, this is the primary reason that complex applications such as computer aided design (CAD), multimedia, and financial simulations rarely use traditional databases. Even when centralized, a page server, rather than an object server, can provide effective performance for such complex, interconnected information.

The central server limits scalability of multiuser performance by introducing an architectural bottleneck. All user requests must go through the single server queue. When the server executes requests by spawning new processes, the requests must wait in the queue. This means that as more users are added, the longer they must wait for each other. This problem is compounded when, as in most central server ODBMSs, the server is single threaded, so it can process only one request at a time, and all other users must wait for that request to fully complete before they can be served. It is also compounded by servers that are slow to commit, as are most traditional and ODBMS central servers when complex information changes are involved.

The common central server technology works well for simple short transactions, where only a few numbers are changed, so that logs are short. However, when many interconnected objects are changed, the logs become long and commit becomes slow. When the changes are applied to objects on other servers, the servers must send messages to each other. This is a slow process, forcing the servers to wait for each other, forcing all users to wait, limiting flexibility. Objects must be stored in the central location and query processing must be performed there too.

If objects or databases need to be moved, applications will break because they are written to connect to a specific server and database. If performance gets too slow, the only solution is to upgrade or replace the server. There is no option to spread the storage and processing.

The strengths of this approach map best to:

☞ Simple data, few relationships, simple processing
☞ Online transaction processing
☞ Environments with large central computer

It works well for transactions that are short; for data that is simple and wholly contained; and for processing that is simple and modifies a small amount of data, all of which is contained together. Other environments and applications run into the limits in flexibility, performance, and scalability.

6.5.3 Distributed Client/Server

The second-generation, or distributed, client/server approach distributes storage and processing of information among all available computers, with transparent access to all objects by all users. Users see a single logical view of connected objects and do need not know which object is on which computer.

This can work even across heterogeneous computer hardware, operating systems, networks, compilers, and languages. All database operations, including atomic commits, propagating methods, and composite objects, can be supported transparently and automatically across this single logical view. The result is flexibility, power, performance, and scalability.

Where the VM approach made sense for single-user applications processing complex information that was mostly localized into memory, the distributed client/server approach provides the same support for complex data, without the single-user or small data size limitations. Since the objects are cached locally with the client and processing can occur locally, the same performance and the same support for arbitrary structures, interconnections, and operations can be achieved as in the VM approach.

The central server approach made sense when most of the processing power was in the central computer. Today, however, the processing power of a high-end server is only 3 to 5 times that of a desktop workstation, and those workstations are growing—from 10 to 100 million instructions per second (MIPs) to yet more—so most of the corporate computing asset is spread across the desks and departments and the ODBMS can take advantage of it (see Figure 6.2) . This distributed client/server approach provides the same central server advantages for managing large amounts of information and high concurrency (high transaction rates), but adds the flexibility to move objects around, and avoids the central bottleneck.

The VM requires all queries be executed in the client, whereas the central server requires they be executed on the server. Distributed client/server,

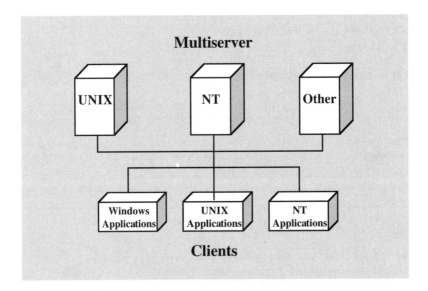

Fig. 6.2 Distributed Database Server

on the other hand, allows the user to choose whether queries should execute at the client or the server, or a designated high-performance query server.

The VM approach reveals the physical layout of objects to direct pointer access, and so it restricts applications in format and interoperability, while the central server forces the single format of the server. The distributed client/server allows shared access to objects in any format, with automatic translation between these formats. This heterogeneity supports different hardware, operating systems, and languages.

With a distributed client/server, a direct link can be built between each user and the servers. Information can flow directly between server and client. As more users are added, they do not wait for other users, unless and until they need to lock exclusively the same objects. Even then, advanced locking mechanisms such as multiple readers one writer (MROW) can allow higher concurrency, with the writing concurrent with any number of readers, each of whom sees a consistent pre-image of the object (unlike dirty read, in which partially changed information leads to inconsistencies and corruption). When multiple simultaneous writers are desired, branching versions can be used for maximum concurrency. When multiple users do need the same objects and server resources, multithreaded backends can provide a measure of concurrency and continue scalability.

To achieve high transaction rates when transactions get short, the backend servers must implement intelligent commit and recovery mechanisms. Unlike traditional ones, they are not unnecessarily slow, especially for complex modifications to interconnected information across multiple servers.

Implementation of this architecture requires at least two components not usually present in traditional systems. First, a distributed repository is required to allow the DBMS to track the location of objects, even as they dynamically move, and present a single logical view to the user. For efficiency, this repository should be implemented at each hierarchical storage level (database, container, and page); should be distributed; and should be replicated locally, with lookup information cached. Second, the DBMS must include a heterogeneity engine, capable of transforming data among all the different formats required by computer hardware, operating systems, compilers, and languages. This includes byte ordering, floating-point format, packing, padding, alignment, and compiler layout structures with pointer locations and headers. For efficiency, instead of going through a neutral intermediate format, which would require a double translation, this engine should convert directly from any format to any other, using an extensible scheme for future changes based on highly optimized primitives.

To achieve flexibility, performance, and scalability, two levels are required to implement this architecture's object cache management: An object manager, which deals with logical object-level granularity, and a storage manager, which deals with physical units of information. The storage manager can move page (or larger) units of information to and from disk and across the network, avoiding the slow performance of the object server. The object manager enables the logical view of objects, managing access at the object level.

This facilitates objects being moved without breaking applications, even to other users, because the object manager controls object-level access. Similarly, this allows objects to be swapped out, making room for new objects and for scalability in objects and size. Further, this limits overhead to the objects actually used; e.g., operations such as heterogeneity conversion need be performed only on objects used rather than entire pages or segments, which, for sparse data, can easily be 100 times faster. Finally, the object manager's object-level control allows all ODBMS functionality at the object level; e.g., instead of versioning segments or pages, versioning can work—as desired—at the logical level, on any object.

This object cache management intelligently manages the cache in the client's address space so that, just as in the VM approach, as the cache builds, performance is at native, single-user, in-memory hardware speeds. At the same time, though, it provides scalable performance for object growth by dynamically moving objects in and out of the cache. Similarly, it provides the same management of large amounts of information and transactions as the central server, but without the bottlenecks. To summarize, the advantages of the distributed client/server architecture include:

☞ Scalability in objects

☞ Scalability in users

☞ High performance for complex, interconnected information

☞ Transparent access to objects anywhere from users anywhere

☞ Heterogeneity across hardware, operating systems, languages

☞ Flexibility to dynamically move objects

☞ Networkwide administration and tools

The primary disadvantage of this architecture is the complexity in DBMS implementation. The distributed catalog, heterogeneity engine, dynamic object cache management with its object and storage manager, and the backend server optimizations for fast commit all require extra work in the ODBMS engine development. If not architected into the product initially, they are quite difficult to retrofit.

6.6 FAULT TOLERANCE WITH OBJECT DATABASES

Error handling is the key to successful programming. Fault tolerance extends that concept to unexpected errors such as failure of power, network, disk, node, system, and application. To a user of a computer information system, the difference between a toy program and a useful production tool is robustness and reliability. Reliability means that it does not often fail, and robustness means that if it does fail, it behaves reasonably.

Newer programming techniques for exception handling have helped clean up the programmer's task. They separate the major flow of the program, within which the programmer signals exceptions, causing execution to jump to another piece of code to handle that exception, and then possibly returning, possibly not. Still, techniques aside, the programming and design must be done.

Further, that approach typically handles only the errors the application or designer expects. We need to respond when the power goes out, when a node or a disk fails, a network link fails in a distributed system, or even when the application or the system has a bug. These things do happen, but most programs, even with the effort expended in exception handling, do not behave reasonably in such situations.

Any user that depends on computers is vulnerable to such loss. Another approach supplements the exception handling of the application designer by adding separate systems, hardware and/or software, to manage such failure situations. In software, the most common are built into database management systems (DBMSs), which are traditionally used when the information is critical and its integrity must be guaranteed. These systems can increase reliability, reduce the loss if there is a failure, lessen the effort required to restore from a failure, and increase availability of system and information.

Historically, most programmers did not use DBMSs, only certain types of systems were developed using DBMSs, and only specially trained DBMS programmers worked directly with the DBMS. With today's increasing demand for reliability, more and more software systems want the reliability benefits of DBMSs.

Luckily, the new breed of DBMSs (especially ODBMSs) have significantly increased the ease of use and accessibility to nonspecialist programmers. Instead of a separate DBMS language and separate DBMS data structures, which programmers must translate to and from their program data structures, ODBMSs allow users to use their native structures and operations (combined into objects) directly from the programming language, and the DBMS automatically manages them. There is no need to learn a new approach or to translate data structures. There is no need to fetch data from storage or store data back. The programmer simply uses the objects as desired.

As systems become more distributed, involving more computers, disks, and networks, the possible modes of failure multiply, and the possibilities of failure also increase. At the same time, these distributed systems can dramatically reduce the frequency of failures and their damage, both in lost information and in length of downtime.

6.6.1 Recovery and Backup

The traditional mainstay of the DBMS is recovery, which is usually based on transactions. The DBMS is supposed to ensure that everything up to the last commit is safe, no matter what might happen. Of course, it is important to choose transaction commit points for which all the information is logically consistent. Also, it is important to choose frequent enough commit points, lest too much be lost in a failure. When a transaction abort occurs, whether application- or system-initiated, the system can insert a piece of code to clean up whatever else is necessary, such as the screen graphics, notifying the user, etc.

Typical DBMS systems today guarantee such recovery for almost any system, application, and computer error. Of course, no such mechanism can be perfect. Suppose, for example, as is typically the case, the recovery implementation saves information for recovery by writing it to a disk. Admittedly, that may be rare. The disk itself could fail. Less likely, but still plausible, the operating system failure mode could erase the disk. Such *media failure* usually requires a different recovery mechanism.

Backup can provide at least some measure of recovery from media failure, because it copies the information to a second medium (disk, tape, etc.). It could copy it to more than one too. Systems typically offer both full backup and incremental backup, the latter being important for users of large databases with which it is impractical to do full backups frequently enough. Usually, these have no impact on the programmer, but are set up independently by a database administrator (DBA). In better systems, they can run with minimal impact on active users.

Of course, restoring a backup restores the state of information as of the time of the backup, losing any later changes. To restore to the most recently committed transaction, the DBA requests a roll-forward. If the DBMS wrote a log of all changes for each transaction since the last backup, and wrote it to a different disk from the one that failed (as is typical), then it can replay those transactions, applying them to the backup copy, and thereby restore the database to the state of the last transaction commit.

Transactions also have the effect of controlling concurrent use by multiple users. The result of one user's changes are not seen by another user until the first executes commit, and "simultaneous" changes are serialized so they do not overwrite each other. However, a programmer may wish to ensure recoverability and not yet expose changes to other users, reserving the option to abort later. That functionality is provided by a transaction checkpoint, available in many systems.

Some systems are also providing nested transactions, allowing the programmer to start a transaction, and within it start another child transaction. When the child transaction commits, the parent continues. This does not aid concurrency, because the results still cannot be seen by other users until the top-level transaction commits, but it can, in some implementations, achieve a recovery point, just like the checkpoints mentioned above. Also, it can be convenient to use within a subroutine or function, whose writer does not know whether the caller might have already started a transaction.

After a failure occurs, some systems require manual intervention for recovery. But for unattended systems and remote servers, it is convenient and might be critical for the system to recover automatically.

6.6.2 Distribution

In the mainframe-only world, there was typically one computer, with central control over all resources. Today, however, there are multiple computers, with multiple tiers of servers and clients. This provides better functionality and might provide better performance and easier access, but there are many more possible faults. Not only are there more computers and disks that can fail, but the communication links between them can fail, too. This presents new challenges to the DBMS for recovery and backup. If well handled, the result can be increased fault tolerance and increased availability.

Consider an application that modifies objects on multiple nodes. If a failure occurs after updating some nodes, but before completing all nodes, the collective result is an inconsistent state. A distributed DBMS automatically extends its recovery scheme to allow for such situations, ensuring that either all changes are made or that none are made. Some DBMSs provide such consistent, atomic updates, but only over predefined sets of servers or objects. This requires us to explicitly specify desired resources, such as databases. Also, it fails if the end user or DBA later desires to redistribute objects among databases and servers.

A distributed DBMS, however, provides the user a single logical view of all objects, regardless of their location, database, and server, and supports all operations, including atomic commit, within that logical view. Automatically mapping the logical view to physical views provides support for recovery of all DBMS services, with no impact to the end user, even in distributed environments. Additionally, it provides the flexibility for the end user or DBA to redistribute objects as desired, online, without affecting programs.

Another solution, especially if multiple DBMSs are used, is a third-party transaction monitor. It will execute the transaction commit in two phases, first asking each DBMS if it is prepared to commit, and if all respond affirmatively, then instructing each DBMS to commit. Each such DBMS or resource manager must be prepared, between the two phases, either to guarantee completion of commit, or to guarantee completion of abort (restoration to the previous committed state), usually via the standard X/A protocol, from X/Open, or newer versions of the same, such as the OMG Transaction Service. The programmer must write additional code to wrap all of the transactions, in each DBMS, with transaction start and transaction commit to the transaction monitor.

So far this sounds like extra overhead to achieve a comparable result for a two-phase commit, albeit in a more complicated environment. What happens if one of the nodes fails or if a network connection severs, producing a *partitioned* network? The above scheme means that all users could well be stopped and prevented from committing transactions. This leads to the next level—an even newer evolution in DBMSs.

6.6.3 Autonomous Partitions

In a network failure, the result is a partitioned network. Users and servers in different partitions cannot communicate or share changes, but it is still at least possible for users in each partition to continue to receive the services of the information system. To achieve this, the DBMS must replicate its own services within each partition. Typically, these include the schema and data dictionary, catalogs or repositories for locating servers and other resources, locking and logging information, and basic servers able to take over. In this way, the system can continue to offer the user all basic services such as creation, access, modification of information, and recovery. Such a partition then can continue to execute autonomously.

This approach can dramatically reduce risk of catastrophic failure or loss of service, and it can do so with no impact at all to the programmer. For this, the DBMS must support mapping of a logical view transparently over all servers, and the system must allow the DBA to dynamically create and modify such partitions. By creating arbitrary numbers of such autonomous partitions, each with its own replicates and servers, the DBA can achieve any desired level of fault tolerance. If a node fails in another partition, it may prevent other users from accessing information stored on that node, but at least other users will be able to continue using all other information and services. The same is true for network failures that isolate partitions. This not only allows service to continue, but does so in a way most users find understandable and reasonable. The users can still do everything, except access the inaccessible information.

6.6.4 Replication

By making copies, or replicas, of objects, the availability of access to those objects can be maintained, even under some failures. The simplest way to do so is to create a single, online, hot backup, by having the (primary) server copy every action to a secondary server. If one of the servers fails, the other can take over instantly, maintaining uninterrupted service, and this can be done with no impact to the system. Usually, however, this means increased overhead, even for read operations, because each operation must be passed to the secondary server. Integrity is at risk, too. If the network fails between the two servers, each must assume it's the only remaining server, so each will allow updates. There will be no way to resolve these updates, even after the network is restored.

A more general scheme is to allow any number of desired replicas in any number of partitions. This increases the availability to any desired level, rather than just one backup. Also, this approach can be implemented with no extra overhead for reading. In fact, a wise choice of replicas can improve read performance, by allowing the system to access a closer (in access time) replica server or a more lightly loaded server. Of course, there is extra overhead for writes, because the write locks and updates must be extended to all replicas, though this can be minimized by caching and batching such updates.

A tricky situation arises, though, when users in disconnected partitions wish to update the same objects. If each is allowed to update independently, the same integrity issue can arise. The simplest solution is to restrict updates to one user only, perhaps the *owner* of the object. Greater update availability under such network failures can be achieved by having the replica servers communicate with each other in a manner similar to voting. Then all users who have access to a majority of the servers can be safely allowed to update, without danger of integrity loss. Those in the minority must be limited to read access, but still, more than half have continued write access. For situations in which some users require special consideration, they can be given greater weight in the voting—up to infinite weight—to reproduce the *owner* scenario selectively.

6.6.5 Impacts

All these capabilities of fault tolerance in the DBMS are available today. Yet more possibilities can be envisioned. For example, the DBMS might incorporate an expert system that measures frequency of access and automatically attempts to create or modify partitions and replicas, perhaps with programmer control to avoid massive undesired restructuring.

In addition, hardware solutions include mirrored disks that automatically duplicate each write to both disks. This is much like the hot backup mentioned above, but, done in hardware, it avoids the performance problem. RAID is a generalization of this concept. Similarly, redundant processors can provide protection from processor failure, with some fail-over software system to maintain replicated operating system structures, detect failures, and switch over. Finally, redundant network connections, with intelligent network routers, can automatically work around failed communication links.

With all these, we must still design classes or types, relationships, and composites, separating information into individual objects with the granularity appropriate for replicating and sharing. Middleware may be appropriate for coordinating diverse resources such as different DBMSs. Fail-over management is appropriate for managing redundant hardware. Finally, all other resources managed by the system must be coordinated with recovery, often by registering them in the DBMS.

6.7 THE ODBMS IN DISTRIBUTED CLIENT/SERVER SCHEMAS

Two trends in today's corporate world demand distribution:

☞ Downsizing from centralized mainframe single-database environments.

☞ Wider integration, for example, connecting finance, engineering, and manufacturing information systems for enterprisewide modeling and operations optimization. The resulting environment consists of multiple databases, at the group level, department level, and corporate level, but with the need for dependencies among data in all of them.

The solution is full distribution, which provides a single logical view to objects anywhere. Users see a logical model of objects connected to objects, with atomic transactions and propagating methods, even though composite objects are split among multiple databases, each under separate administrative control, on multiple, heterogeneous platforms, operating systems, network protocols, and even languages (C, C++, Smalltalk, SQL).

Support for production environments includes multiple schemas, which may be shared among databases or private, encrypted schemas, dynamic addition of schemas, and schema evolution. Integration includes legacy databases, such as RDBMSs, in this same transparent logical view of objects, and cooperates with standards such as ODMG and the OMG CORBA. Finally, the logical view must remain valid, and applications must continue to work, as the mapping to the physical environment changes, moving objects and databases to new platforms.

6.7.1 Downsizing

The first generation of client/server technology and traditional DBMSs were designed in a very different computing environment. The computing resources were all centralized in a large, centrally-administered mainframe or minicomputer (the server). Access to these resources was from remote dumb terminals (the clients), that had almost no computing power for their own. Hence, the architectures developed for this environment kept all the data storage and all the processing on the central computer, while the clients did nothing more than send in requests.

As PCs were added, GUIs were built into the clientside, but all data storage and processing remained on the server. As more users were added, the system became slower and slower as their requests waited for one another in the central-server bottleneck.

Today's computing environment, however, is quite different. There are still powerful servers, but there are many of them, and there are also powerful desktop workstations. Since the ratio of server-to-workstation power is in the range of three to five times, the collection of desktop workstations represents the bulk of the computing power in the environment. Also, since these desktop machines are usually dedicated to a single user, rather than context switching among multiuser services, they have more of their power available for that single user.

To better suit this environment, a second generation of distributed client/server technology appeared. It allowed data storage and processing to be shared across all the servers and workstations in the environment. The result is that the user sees a single logical view of objects connected to objects even though the objects reside in different databases, on different computing hardware, operating systems, and so on. The DBMS manages a distributed catalog to allow transparent location of the object when requested by name, reference, and query.

This allows the maximum use of resources, both pre-existing and new, as they are added incrementally.

6.7.2 Integration

The other major trend in computing sounds almost the opposite of the downsizing above. Instead of separate systems for order entry, human resources, engineering project management, design, and manufacturing, corporations are demanding integration across these systems. For example, a new order might automatically initiate a project and reference assigned personnel, appropriate designs, and manufacturing.

This move toward enterprisewide integration allows greatly improved efficiency and automation, and the ability to model and analyze the entire business. To achieve this, the distributed client/server environment must allow multiple databases, multiple schemas, and heterogeneous computers. Each department or group, then, can create its own database and its own schemas and can decide who has access. Simultaneously, it can share corporatewide schemas, allowing its objects to connect to and be part of composite objects across the enterprise. Such composites can be accessed as single objects, with method invocations propagating among the component objects, even across databases and heterogeneous operating systems. This gives each local group the ability to work with its resources, to meet its goals with the level of autonomy needed, but still allows the increased efficiency of enterprisewide integration.

6.7.3 Address Space

It seems only yesterday that 32-bit VM computing provided a major advance over the previous 16- and 8-bit generations. For a single-user, single-computer, local environment, 32 bits or 4 gigabytes (GB) of VM is often enough.

That size becomes tight for large applications, however, especially when systems use a couple of the high bits, cutting it down to a GB or half a GB, and it becomes far too little when there is a need to share information across multiple users. The advent of 64-bit computers stretches this, not by a factor of 2 or 10 or 100 times, but by 4 billion times, providing ample room for growth and for support of the sharing necessary for enterprisewide integration. With an ODBMS that can support 64-bit addressing, this means 64 bits worth of objects, or millions of terra-objects, each of which can be any number of GB.

Another address space-related issue is integrity. Pointers used in VM computing become invalid when the referenced objects move, resulting in program errors. For a single-user program, this is annoying, but the user can usually restart the program and fix it with only a small amount of information loss. However, when sharing objects across multiple users, across groups, with mission-critical corporate information, pointers that are invalid (after transaction commit) would lead to database corruption. To avoid this, the object database manager can transparently insert a level of indirection in the pointer. To the application, it looks the same, but now the ODBMS manager can guarantee that the reference will be safe and correct, even across commits.

6.7.4 Flexibility

With enterprisewide sharing of objects, flexibility becomes more than a nicety. It becomes a necessity. This includes the ability to:

☞ Add and remove schemas so that groups can get the job done without requiring changes from all other groups in the organization

☞ Add new machines, with the latest price/performance, even if the hardware and operating system are different, and move some objects or databases onto those new machines, without breaking any applications

☞ Run familiar SQL- and ODBC-based front-end tools and perform online backups without affecting applications

☞ Monitor activities and locks and detach and reattach databases to the distributed environment, browse any objects in any database with any schema, and dump objects to text language and back

When the computing environment extends beyond a single location to a WAN, the distributed ODBMS can continue to support the same single logical view and the same flexibility, but it can add local autonomy as well. In that way, when a WAN link (satellite or modem) is temporarily down, each local partition can continue to operate, with the limitation, of course, that it cannot access objects across the disconnection. This is accomplished by replicating system services, schema, catalog, and locking information within each partition.

Such partitions can be created and changed dynamically by the administrator, without breaking applications or users.

6.7.5 Standards

For such a large-scale distributed computing environment to succeed in practice, it must support a variety of common tools, languages, and users, and that requires standards. The CORBA allows objects from different vendors to communicate, dispatching methods from one to the other. The Object Database Management Group's standard, ODMG, allows applications to work against any compliant ODBMS. This raises the level of services from the simple CORBA dispatch of method requests to include mission-critical database capabilities such as recovery, integrity, concurrency, and transactions, as well as include an object manager for caching and efficient support of millions of fine-grained objects. Finally, the SQL widely used standard is available, too, on some ODBMSs, allowing users, applications, and front-end tools to access object databases just as they have accessed relational and other databases.

6.8 DEPLOYING ODBMS APPLICATIONS

To produce a prototype may be less than 10% of the effort of producing a full production application. Unless your ODBMS meets your key production requirements, that prototype may never be successfully deployed. We examine here the key requirements and some examples of successfully deploying applications and their architectural implications. Production requirements should include:

☞ Reliability and integrity, including referential integrity, no danger from stale pointer corruption, and full recovery with online backup

☞ Scalability, with linear performance in objects/second even as the number of objects grows, with minimal degradation as the number of users grows

☞ Distribution and heterogeneity support, so that more platforms can be added and databases may be moved, all without affecting applications

☞ Fault tolerance, support for WANs, support for existing 4GL GUI tools

Support for standards such as ODMG allows portability to different ODBMS engines, while support for SQL and ODBC provides compatibility with existing database users, applications, and direct access from GUI 4GLs such as Visual Basic and PowerBuilder. It is important to analyze your application's functionality and map those to the needed functionality in the ODBMS. It is these key ODBMS characteristics that often determine whether you will succeed in production.

Before delving into these requirements in detail, it will help if you study the basics of object and DBMS technology, how these combine to yield an ODBMS, which applications are appropriate for an ODBMS, some examples of these applications, why they worked on an ODBMS, and what was critical to them.

6.9 WHERE OBJECT DATABASES ARE HEADED

The computer industry has grown with the need to manage information, from simple flat files; to network databases; to relational, and most recently, to ODBMSs. Each approach to information management solves a certain class of problems, so the user can choose the right tool for each job. As information management grows to support broader types of data, such as multimedia, so grow broader types of applications with more complex processing and sharing of composite objects. As object technology is used more widely for reuse and higher quality and productivity, and as applications are distributed across servers, departments, LANS, and WANs, ODBMS technology will play a progressively larger role.

6.9.1 Why Databases?

Information can be managed with a variety of tools. Sometimes it is fine to store information in simple, flat files. Other uses include personal information management, which is slightly more sophisticated. A simple contacts manager might allow, for example, sorting or searching your business contacts by name or company. When is it appropriate to use a database management system? The answer is much the same for traditional software and for object technology. Databases make sense for large scale applications and mission-critical environments, where integrity and flexibility are required.

If your application will grow to manipulate many objects (millions, billions, trillions, etc.), support is needed to manage all those objects, to keep track of where they are, to locate them efficiently, and to move them in and out of memory efficiently and on demand. The support for this is provided in a DBMS.

Similarly, if many users simultaneously share objects, support is needed to provide such access to ensure that simultaneous users do not destroy each other's work and to maintain and coordinate the sharing. Again, the DBMS helps.

Finally, there are mission-critical environments in which it is unacceptable to lose objects or to lose the integrity of the information. DBMSs provide recovery and transaction mechanisms to guarantee integrity. Also, in such environments it is often necessary to have the flexibility to change the environment; to move objects, databases, or users; and to change the logical model (schema, types, classes) or the physical model (storage hierarchy, clustering, indexing) without interrupting applications, let alone requiring the rewriting of applications. This, too, is supported by a DBMS.

Any of these capabilities is a good reason for choosing a DBMS. However, the same could be said for traditional databases, so where do object databases differ?

6.9.2 Why Object Databases?

The aphorism tells us: If you have only a hammer, then everything looks like a nail. But you would have difficulty driving a screw with that hammer. We might even say, if all you have is an RDBMS, the whole world looks like a table. Rather than rely on an aphorism we will be better off analyzing what problem we have and then choosing the best tool to address it. Object databases provide a tool, not necessarily for all tasks, but a good one for certain tasks. The user's challenge is to identify which of those tasks will benefit most from an ODBMS. The identifying characteristics of a good-fit application are:

☞ Use of objects

  ✗ Easier and faster, no need to translate

  ✗ Same object in design, implementation, and so on

☞ New kinds of information

  ✗ Complex structure and behavior

  ✗ Interconnected networks of objects

☞ Shared distributed objects

  ✗ Objects, users, databases anywhere

  ✗ Heterogeneous platforms, networks, languages

First, if you choose to employ objects, for reasons described above (quality, complexity management, and productivity), then it can often be easier and faster to use an object database rather than translating from application objects down to records or tables and back. In fact, you can use the same objects in analysis, design, implementation language, query, framework, GUI, and database. This results in faster application building, more reliability, and fewer system errors.

The second category is what drove the early users (in engineering, manufacturing, multimedia). They were managing information that just would not fit into simple records and tables, and often had to build their own custom files to get the functionality and performance they required. To contrast, if your information consists of short, fixed-length, simple data that fits nicely into tables (name, address, bank account balance), then it will fit nicely into relational databases and they will work fine. However, if your data contains nested structure, dynamically varying size, user-defined arbitrary structure (images, audio, video, time-series data, etc.), then squeezing them into tables can be very difficult, time consuming for the programmer, and slow at runtime. In an ODBMS, each such user-defined structure is directly an object, managed as-is by the database. Similarly, if your operations are simple, short, and work on localized data, traditional DBMSs do well, while an ODBMS does well for operations that span many objects and even many databases, complex operations, user-defined arbitrary operations, etc.

The other side of this category is based on the relationships in your information. Again, to contrast, in an RDBMS, relationships are managed by the user creating foreign keys, and then, at runtime, asking the system to discover the relationships dynamically by scanning two (or more) tables and comparing foreign keys, until it finds a match. This process, called a *join*, is the weak point of relational technology. More than two or three levels of joins is a red flag to look for a better solution.

In an ODBMS, the user simply declares the relationship, and the ODBMS automatically generates the methods to manage it and to dynamically create, delete, traverse relationships. Traversal is direct, with no need for scanning and comparing or even looking up an index, which can make it orders-of-magnitude faster. All this applies to bidirectional relationships with referential integrity, many-to-many relationships, and cross-database relationships. The more relationships you need to manage, the more you will benefit from an ODBMS.

The third category is whether the application is deployed in a distributed environment. To contrast, again, traditional database systems (including RDBMSs and some ODBMSs) are built around a central server. Everything happens on the server, including data buffering, operations, joins, projects, and selections, etc. The user simply sends in a request and gets back an answer. Although many of these systems were built in the 1970s and 1980s, this is in fact the same mainframe architecture of the 1960s; i.e., the central server might as well be a mainframe computer and the user might as well be a dumb terminal.

Today, however, with desktop workstations that have computing power of 30 to 50% that of servers, most of the power is spread across the desktops. So more and more applications are deployed in a distributed environment, in which objects may be spread across many workstations, servers, mainframes, etc., with users everywhere accessing objects everywhere. An ODBMS can support this by using object identity to locate objects automatically, on whichever server they are, and transparently passing them to users—already converted—into the native format for that user. This can work transparently across diverse hardware, operating systems, networks, compilers, languages, front-end 4GL, query and report tools, and it can continue to work as objects are dynamically moved.

The more distribution you have, the more benefit you get from an ODBMS. A simple example can help to illustrate the difference between an ODBMS and an RDBMS for an application with complex, structured information. Consider the problem of modeling a car and storing it in the garage at the end of the day. As usual, the ODBMS supports the application objects directly, so it will have an object for the car, an object for the garage, one operation to store, and that's the end. In an RDBMS, though, all information must be flattened (normalized), into tables, with each type in its own table. In this example, that means disassembling the car, storing the gears in one table, pistons in another, wheels in another, etc. In the morning, before driving to work, you must reassemble the car.

This may sound silly, but it is common to see users writing stacks of code to translate from complex application entities down to flat records or tables. That translation code presents three problems:

☞ It is expensive to write. You'd prefer having your programmers writing applications.

☞ It is error-prone. Even if bug-free, one application might disassemble one way while another reassembles another—and integrity is lost.

☞ It is slow. At runtime all that disassembling and reassembling takes a lot of time.

In the ODBMS, the car is an object, and the piston is an object, and the ODBMS understands their relationship. You may ask for the car or for the piston and invoke operations at each level, which makes it easy for the user. The ODBMS need not dynamically rebuild higher-level structures from flat data, because it stores and understands that structure, making it much faster. This explains the classes of applications that benefit most from ODBMSs, and some of the benefits, but what are the issues in ODBMS use in production applications?

6.9.3 ODBMS Issues

All ODBMSs support storing and sharing objects, with an interface to the object that allows combining and invoking operations. However, there are big differences when it comes to deploying mission-critical applications on ODBMSs. These fall into four categories:

☞ Integrity

☞ Scalability

☞ Reliability

☞ Flexibility

To illustrate the first, consider ODBMS support for caching. Unlike server-centered DBMSs, most ODBMSs actually move referenced objects into the application's address space, which has both a good and a bad side. The good side is performance. Operations across address spaces take milliseconds, while operations within an address space take tenths of microseconds (on an 8 MIPs machine, even less on newer machines), so you get fully 15,000 times faster access. Complex applications often have 10 to 100 times better performance from such caching and relationship management. On the bad side, however, an application with a bug can damage a cached object and corrupt the database. So, a key issue for the ODBMS is what it does to prevent such corruption.

Most systems give the application a direct pointer into the objects. Eventually, such pointers become invalid; they are always invalid after a commit, because commit means, semantically, that the object can move to other users. If the programmer is perfect, no problem. If she or he ever uses the pointer at the wrong time, however, it will either crash or worse, de-reference into the middle of some other object and corrupt the database.

A better approach uses one level of indirection to insulate the user and guarantee integrity. To the user, this looks exactly the same, but underneath, transparently, the ODBMS adds one extra pointer de-reference. Then wherever the object moves—even after commit, when it is moved to another workstation—the ODBMS can automatically fix up the pointer (re-cache the object if necessary) and execution continues normally. The cost of an extra pointer de-reference is unnoticeable in most applications, while the benefit is that all references are good, and no corruption occurs because of bad references.

This indirection also gives the ODBMS the ability to swap objects, which is a key for scalability. The prototype that works well with 10 objects may collapse when put into production with 10 million objects, so it is necessary to provide scalable performance. The indirection allows an intelligent cache management strategy that swaps out old, unused objects, making room for new objects, so performance can continue to unlimited size. In fact, where most scale exponentially, some systems have been measured to scale linearly.

Scalability in users also varies. Systems built around clientside-only functionality tend to bog down quickly with only a handful of users. Systems built around serverside-only functionality (traditional DBMSs and OLTP systems) can do very well for simple short transactions, but suffer from a server bottleneck. All requests must pass through the same server queue, so the more users you add, the longer they wait at that queue.

A distributed client/server architecture can spread functionality across client and server to avoid such a bottleneck. The server can move clusters of objects at a time for high performance, support multithreading and simultaneous communication links to each client, so there is no waiting until object conflicts arise, in which case the usual locking keeps everything safe. The clientside object manager supports the indirection for integrity, the intelligent cache management for scalability in size.

A separate logical view over all the distributed databases allows transparent and dynamic server reconfiguration, so even as server capacity is reached, administrators can simply add new servers and spread objects across them. The result is scalability in clients (due to direct communication links and no bottlenecks) and also in servers (due to distributed ability to add servers and spread objects across new servers).

Another mission-critical need, in the area of reliability, is fault tolerance. It is great to be able to access objects transparently in Los Angeles or Paris, but what happens when the satellite link between them goes down? Support for redundant replicates of system structures—including the object catalog, schema, and locking information—can enable users in Tokyo and in Los Angeles to continue to work, even though they cannot access new objects at the other site until the satellite link is restored. Additionally, user object replicates can allow even object access, with update correlation performed according to rules chosen by users when the link is re-established. In fact, increasing the number of such system and user replicates allows any desired level of tolerance of failures in networks, hardware, and software.

A last example of a production issue is flexibility. When an application is deployed, it is very difficult to predict what will happen, but one prediction is sure—change will occur. No matter how good the designer was, there will be a need to change object types and logical models, and to do so while maintaining compatibility between old and new applications. Support for schema evolution is critical. Beyond these schema, without bringing down databases or applications there will be a need to change the physical model; reconfigure clients and server; move objects and databases; change indices; and gather statistics for load balancing, import/export, incremental backups, etc.

Over time, new users will want new applications and new ODBC-based tools such as PowerBuilder and Visual Basic, in a variety of languages—C, C++, Smalltalk, SQL—running on a variety of computer platforms. The key to production success is allowing all these users and tools to share the same objects, spread across all the different platforms.

6.9.4 The Future

What trends are occurring, how can we expect them to influence information management, and what role will ODBMSs play? While it is always difficult to predict the future, certain trends have already begun, and we can extrapolate them. These include:

- ☞ Downsizing and moving to distributed systems
- ☞ Wider Integration
- ☞ More complex information, linked to communication
- ☞ More complex applications

In each of these areas ODBMSs are likely to play a key role. Also, as the use of ODBMSs expands, there will be new ways in which the ODBMSs will be called upon to grow:

- ☞ Standards
- ☞ Tool support and integration
- ☞ Security

Traditionally, users have found themselves locked into mainframe computers, with single-vendor solutions for hardware and software. The lack of competition limited the capabilities and resulted in high prices, so users are moving from centralized mainframes to networks of workstations and servers, with open operating systems (UNIX or Windows) that support a variety of hardware and software. The competition gives the users more choices for functionality and fair market pricing, but raises new issues in databases.

The mainframe databases (Codasyl/Network, ISAM files) do not work well in a distributed, open environment. The RDBMSs, though newer and available on open servers, still do everything on the server, just like mainframes, wasting all the workstation computing power and limiting information spread and transparent access to it. This is where the distributed capabilities of ODBMSs can add value. As more users downsize and reevaluate their information management needs, it becomes attractive to skip directly from the network generation to the object generation in order to get the full functionality and compatibility with object tools, high performance on complex data, and support for distribution.

6.9.5 Multiserver Clients

Such clients place greater demands on the ODBMS. They're already sensitive to the importance of standards, because they make the difference between the vendor exclusivity of the mainframe world and the competition of the open world. Although ODBMSs began with proprietary interfaces, the vendors recognized the importance of standards and banded together in the ODMG to publish a single standard interface that they all could support.

Early ODBMS users were sophisticated technologists who had no fear of diving into the intricacies of C++ and ODBMSs, but future users will demand easier interfaces and more tools for higher productivity. In line with the move to open systems, they'll demand that tools be open too, rather than tied to single vendors. ODBMSs have begun to move in this direction. Some now support SQL, leveraging existing user training and programs and even Open Database Connectivity (ODBC), which allows off-the-shelf plug-and-play with most of the standard 4GLs, GUI tools, report generators, and form generators.

Some third-party object tool vendors have begun to integrate with the leading ODBMSs, and the availability of the ODMG standard is accelerating this.

One area in which ODBMSs have been weak is security. Broader use will demand more sophisticated models of security to support objects, object clusters, and composite objects distributed across networks of computers and models yet to be determined.

In addition to downsizing, there is a trend toward wider integration. At first this may sound contradictory, but networking and the demand for efficiency to compete is leading users to connect once disparate systems.

Instead of separate databases for personnel, finance, manufacturing, order-entry, etc., companies today want all these systems interrelated. The incoming order will automatically communicate to the manufacturing database to schedule the products. Users can model the entire enterprise to finely tune and optimize their business. Each department wants to control its own database, determine access, schema, etc., but still share corporatewide schemas for information sharing and dependencies.

The ability to handle complex cross-database structures such as composite objects and to work across multiple servers, databases, schemas, and interfaces makes the ODBMS the ideal basis for such systems. Finally, as the demands of consumers grow, as technology evolves, applications of computers and systems will continue to become more and more complex. They will support more complex information, more relationships and dependencies, and more complex operations. All of this means that, as time goes on, more applications will move from the domain of traditional databases to that of ODBMSs.

6.10 THE ROLE OF OPEN DATABASE CONNECTIVITY (ODBC)

In an effort to standardize an interface to DBMSs, Microsoft created ODBC, based on the X/Open definitions of SQL CLI. ODBC is an API in which application developers can code their programs using ODBC function calls, and each DBMS vendor can provide an ODBC driver for its DBMS. An application written for the ODBC API can be used to access any DBMS, given the appropriate ODBC drivers.

6.10.1 Many Vendors, One ODBC Solution

ODBC now provides a universal data access interface. ODBC alleviates the need to learn multiple APIs. Application developers can allow an application to concurrently access, view, and modify data from multiple diverse databases. ODBC is a specification to which developers write either:

☞ An ODBC-enabled front-end or client desktop application, also known as an ODBC client. This is the application that the computer-user sees on the computer screen.

☞ An ODBC driver for a back-end or server. The ODBC driver resides between the ODBC client and the DBMS; it is loaded on the front-end computer.

To use ODBC, the following three components are required:

1. ODBC client: An ODBC-enabled front-end (also called ODBC client); examples include Microsoft Access or ODBC-enabled applications from other vendors (such as Lotus).

2. ODBC driver: An ODBC driver for the ODBC server. Any ODBC client can access any DBMS for which there is an ODBC driver.

3. DBMS server: A back-end or server DBMS; examples include SQL Server, Oracle, AS/400, Access, or any DBMS for which an ODBC driver exists.

6.10.2 ODBC over a Network

Some DBMS vendors provide a transport mechanism for client applications to access the database server over a network. MiniSQL is built around a network paradigm, as the database engine is a daemon accessed locally via a UNIX domain socket or remotely via a TCP socket. Oracle provides developers with SQL*Net, a set of libraries to facilitate data transfers over a TCP/IP network.

A three-tier architecture can be used to develop ODBC clients in a TCP/IP network. The client application is written to the ODBC specifications and compiled with the ODBC and DBMS transport libraries. The client binary is now equipped to communicate with a DBMS server remotely and the source code is portable among other DBMSs.

6.11 CONCLUSIONS

Information has become the medium of business, of professions, even of entertainment, with intelligent agents automatically tracking changes users are interested in, sorting and caching locally desired information, and sharing changes and desired changes with others.

Object databases provide the following benefits:

☞ Integrity, recovery

☞ Scalability in objects (size)

☞ Scalability in users (concurrency)

☞ Distribution

☞ Features (versioning, relationships)

Applications with simple data, simple operations, short transactions, and an environment of remote terminals accessing a central server can continue to do well with traditional databases, including RDBMSs. However, applications with

☞ Object usage (same object in design, language, GUI, DB)

☞ Complex and/or highly interconnected information

☞ Distributed, heterogeneous environments

require ODBMSs to obtain the functionality and performance desired.

Users with such applications are found in a wide variety of industries and vertical markets, in areas including telecommunications, multimedia, manufacturing, financial analysis, and document management. These applications often cooperate with traditional database applications and can share legacy information in several ways. Successful deployment of such applications over the past couple of years has included real-time, 24-hour/day fault-tolerant environments, databases over tens of gigabytes, and shared users over thousands of gigabytes for mission-critical production.

To achieve such successful production, a variety of features can help, including relationships, object versioning, and support of ODBC GUI tools. Often the critical determinants are production requirements such as performance scalability in users and objects, integrity, recovery, and flexibility to adjust to changing demands in computer systems, languages, and schemas.

Three primary architectures have been used to develop ODBMSs, each with its own area of best applicability. The first is based on the virtual memory techniques of the 1960s, and works well for mostly single-user, small-data-size applications, with arbitrary complexity of structure and interconnection. The second is based on the central server or first-generation client/server technology of the 1970s and 1980s. It works best for simple data and operations, restricted multiuser concurrency limited to the server, but with large data management capacity. The last is distributed or second-generation client/server, which allows objects and databases anywhere on the network to be accessed transparently by users anywhere with processing anywhere, the same high performance of virtual memory on complex objects, and the same management of large numbers of objects as the central server, but offering better scalability in users and more flexibility. This is provided by dynamic cache management based on a more complex combination of object and storage manager, the former offering the object granularity of an object server, while the latter offers the performance of a page server.

Your key to success in production, then, is to identify your key requirements, focus on them, and build a solution that satisfies those needs.

The everyday world will be as much changed by this growth in information management as it was by the industrial revolution. That revolution changed the world from manual labor, agriculture, and crafts, to one in which most of us are involved in manufacturing and use manufactured goods. This revolution will change the world to one in which most of us are involved in processing information, and information will become the basic stuff of our daily lives—work and play.

From the future looking back, it will seem strange that only a few could use computers, because everyone will be using them in almost all aspects of work and play. It will seem strange that it used to take a cadre of specialists months or longer to get the computers to do what they wanted, because everyone will be doing it themselves, directly, instantly. It will seem strange that users spent time trying to find what they wanted, hiring services to locate desired information, shopping, traveling, mailing, and waiting, because information will be at everyone's fingertips, updated instantly, accessed directly. It will seem strange that users spent time copying data and figuring out where to store the copies, as users will simply process information as they like—without regard to where it is or where it goes—because it is dynamically and transparently available, automatically replicated and reconfigured as needed for use in the office or on the beach.

Distributed File Systems

7.1 INTRODUCTION

A file system is a subsystem of an operating system whose purpose is to provide long-term storage, and it is an integral part of any computing infrastructure. The file system provides a mechanism (a scheme) that enables users to access data stored in a computer. A file system maps easily understandable names to a data group on physical devices which are usually organized in some kind of hierarchy. Users utilize the file system to create, delete, read from, write to, rename, or edit files. Programmers can use the same file system to open, close, read from, or write to files.

A distributed file system is a basic component of distributed operating systems. Any self-contained computer has a file system, be it a hard disk, optical drive, or floppy drive. A distributed file system, however, is a file system whose clients, servers, and storage devices are dispersed among the machines of a distributed system. A distributed system can be thought of as a network of computers, loosely coupled together, for the purpose of working together in common tasks. A distributed file system allows programmers and users to access files on other computers in the same way they access files on their own computer.

7.1.1 Goals and Design Issues of a Distributed File System

A well-designed distributed system must meet a number of characteristics:

1. *Transparency*: A distributed file system (DFS) must have some degree of transparency to facilitate both ease of use and security. The system must interfere as little as possible with the interface the user is accustomed to. The best DFSs have almost no (local) user interface, and thus the user sees no difference between accessing a local file and a remote file.

2. *Operating system independence*: A positive property of DFSs is that their files can be accessed from a number of different platforms. For example, network file system (NFS) clients exist for Macintosh, Windows, OS/2, Windows NT, and most varieties of UNIX.

3. *Efficiency*: Distributed file systems, due to the fact that a large percentage of activity on a computer system consists of file accesses, must be efficient. This efficiency generally needs to be targeted at certain areas. For example, in any file system, the following tend to hold true:

   ✗ Life expectancy of an average file is very short.

   ✗ Reads are much more frequent than writes (about five to one).

   ✗ Usually, one user reads and writes. Sometimes one user writes and many users read, but very rarely do many users read and write, simultaneously.

   ✗ File sizes are strongly skewed. That is, file sizes are much more common on the order of 10 kilobytes (K) than on the order of 100K, and even more so than 1000K.

4. *Robustness*: A DFS must be fault tolerant and be able to efficiently handle errors. Some of the problems that might frequently occur include:

✗ *Concurrent accesses*: More than one user may try to write different information to the same file at the same time.

✗ *Consistency*: If the client copies files from the server, then one of these files on the server is modified, the client now has a *stale* copy of the file. Consistency and concurrent access go hand in hand; if the client overwrites the copy on the server a problem of concurrent access occurs.

5. *Scalability*: Essentially, scalability means how many users the DFS needs to cater to. The scalability of different DFSs varies. For example, some DFSs are scalable on the order of thousands while others are only scalable on the order of tens. The following issues must be considered:

✗ Kind of enterprise using the DFS

✗ Numbers of computers connected to the DFS

✗ System security requirements (more users generally means less security)

6. *Performance*: The type of machines that house the actual data of a DFS must be able to support the kind of usage load that is expected. For example, a DFS that needs to be scalable to at least 1000 users should not be served from a small Intel processor, which might be sufficient if no more than 30 users are expected.

7. *Replication vs. downed volumes*: If a file server volume goes down, the part of the file system on that server cannot be accessed. This is often handled by replication: Every part of the file system is stored on at least two separate machines.

8. *Administration*: Another of the many tradeoffs of a DFS is that of administration. Most of the other design goals of a DFS can be implemented easily, but they make the DFS difficult to maintain. If the organization can afford to pay several people to administer the DFS, then ease of administration is not an issue. If only one or two people are working on it in their spare time, however, then it is reasonable to expect that ease of administration should be one of the major design issues, even at the cost of other features.

7.1.2 Major Types of Distributed File Systems

There are two widely implemented distributed file systems: Network file system (NFS) and remote file sharing (RFS) system. Both of these operate over the network and allow users to share files. The latter also allows users to share devices. A single machine can support NFS and RFS simultaneously.

The NFS allows the sharing of file systems and directories, and provides a common login environment regardless of the network machine on which you login. It is a service that is designed to be machine independent and transparent to the user. An NFS uses remote procedure calls (RPCs) through the external data representation protocol (XDR) to communicate between machines. The user does not have to know any of the details. When things are working properly local and remote file systems will appear as one big local file system to the user.

The major functions of NFSs are mount/export directories from/to other computers, on/off your local network, so that they can be accessed as if they were local. An NFS client can mount files systems from more than one NFS server. These mounts are done through the Ethernet. The NFS server does not maintain state information about its client's open files; this must be done by the client. The server program is small and efficient, while the client program has to do most of the work. The NFS supports diskless workstation booting and auto-mounting, and it allows you to mount NFS directories on top of each other.

The RFS system enables workstations to share files over a network. Workstations can act as clients of servers. The RFS provides access to files and directories without the user having to know where the resource is located. A name server is used to register resource names, so the client machine does not need to know where the resources are. Resources are moved simply by a change of entries in the name-server registry.

An RFS allows users to mount special directories so that they can share devices (e.g., tape drives) residing on other machines. RFS is a stateful protocol, where the server maintains state information of local resources. The server knows what each client is doing to its files at all times. The server can detect client crashes, so cache consistency is guaranteed. There is a large variety of distributed file system implementations, but I will concentrate discussion on the following:

☞ LAN file systems

☞ NFSs

☞ Andrew File Systems (AFSs)

☞ DFSs

☞ RFSs

7.2 LAN FILE SYSTEMS

When people talk about network file systems, they are typically referring to LAN file systems. These local area network file systems include products such as:

☞ Novell Netware

☞ Apple Filing Protocol (AFP)

☞ Banyan Vines

☞ LANTastic

These file systems evolved in a truly local area networked environment. The typical environment was a small number of personal computers with a few servers at a single location. Security features were simple or nonexistent because the network was not accessible to anyone except the people with physical access to the system. The network was never shared. When security features were provided in these products, their design typically was based on a work-group model.

These LAN file systems tend to have limited application as internetworked file systems because of shortcomings in all three areas mentioned above. The basic transport protocol these systems use is not that used by WANs. Each vendor designed its own proprietary transport protocol (e.g., Novell's IPX).

The solution to this problem that allows LAN file systems to use Internet connectivity is a technique called *tunneling*. Tunneling allows two or more LANs to be connected using virtual point-to-point connections across the internetwork. The server's proprietary packets are encapsulated in a packet that can be used on the Internet and forwarded across the Internet to another server, which removes the Internet headers and places the packet on a local LAN.

Tunneling can be done with most local area networks. A large number of servers linked together with tunneling forms a wide area file system made up of multiple, geographically distributed file servers.

Even with the tunneling ability, the configuration and management of the clients and servers must be coordinated. It is hard to imagine, for example, that all of the users in the world would be willing to participate in a large Novell network with accounts and configuration managed by a central authority. The system administration and security do not scale to internetwork sizes.

These Internet links must be set up explicitly for each pair of servers because the Novell IPX protocol relies on *broadcast* packets. IP does not support true broadcast packets. (If it did, it would probably be unusable as an internetworking protocol.) When server 134.15.114.2 receives a broadcast packet on the IPX network, it must send the packet through each IP tunnel to the remote server, which rebroadcasts the packet on its respective local IPX networks.

An important aspect of these LAN file systems is that individual clients typically do not exchange data across the internetwork. Data from one workstation is routed to its local server which forwards it to a remote server across the net, which might forward the request to yet another server.

7.3 NETWORK FILE SYSTEMS

The NFS is probably the most prominent network service using RPC. It allows users to access files on remote hosts in exactly the same way a user would access local files. This is made possible by a mixture of kernel functionality on the client side (using the remote file system) and an NFS server on the server side (providing the file data). This file access is completely transparent to the client and works across a variety of server and host architectures.

The NFS is a common network file system, running on a large number of different systems. There is even an NFS server for PCs, so that a UNIX system can act as a file server for a PC system. NFS is a stateless service. There is no open or close mechanism for files, because each access message is self-contained. Any host can act as a server and any host can be a client of any server. At boot time a system advises which directories it is exporting. At boot time (or at any other time) a remote file system can be mounted into the local file system. References to the local file are translated into references to the remote file. This is done within the NFS by returning a *file handle* to the client when it mounts a remote file system. This handle contains—among other things—the *inode* on the remote machine of the directory that it is exporting. UNIX maintains an intricate system of file pointers, known as inodes. *Inode* is also known as index node: This maintains the location of the physical file and the directory. When access to the remote directory is required, its inode is already available.

7.3.1 How NFS Works

A client may request a directory be mounted from a remote host on a local directory in the same way it can mount a physical device. The syntax used to specify the remote directory is different, however.

When a user accesses a file over NFS, the kernel places an RPC call to the NFS daemon (nfsd) on the server machine. This call takes the file handle, the name of the file to be accessed, and the user and group id as parameters. These are used to determine access rights to the specified file. In order to prevent unauthorized users from reading or modifying files, user and group ids must be the same on both hosts.

In most implementations, the NFS functionality of both client and server are implemented as kernel-level daemons that are started from user space at system boot. These are the NFS daemon on the server host and the block I/O daemon (*biod*) running on the client host. To improve throughput, the *biod* performs asynchronous I/O using read ahead and write behind. More than one nfsd usually runs concurrently.

The NFS implementation of server is a little different in that the client code is tightly integrated in the virtual file system (VFS) layer of the kernel and does not require additional control through the *biod*. On the other hand, the server code runs entirely in user space, so that running several copies of the server at the same time is almost impossible because of the synchronization issues this would involve.

7.3.1.1 Preparing NFS   Before NFS can be used, be it as server or client, the kernel must compile with NFS. Newer kernels have a simple interface on the

proc file system for this—the */proc/filesystems* file—which can display using *cat*. Proc is a directory name where file names and their addresses are kept.

If *nfs* is missing from this list, then the kernel must be compiled with NFS enabled. The easiest way to find out whether the kernel has NFS support enabled is to try to mount an NFS file system. If this mount attempt fails with an error message saying *fs* type *nfs* is not supported by the kernel, the kernel with NFS must be enabled.

7.3.1.2 Mounting an NFS Volume

NFS volumes are mounted in the same way file systems are usually mounted. You invoke mount using the following syntax: *nfs_volume* is given as *remote_host:remote_dir*. Because this notation is unique to NFS file systems, you can leave out the *-t nfs* option.

Any system can be used as either a client or server or both with simple configuration changes. To configure a system as a server, the system administrator indicates the areas of the disks that are to be accessible to the network-attached clients. The configuration of the data exported from the server is typically stored in the file */etc/exports*.

Different portions of the disk can be exported with different access controls. The *mount* command associates a network file system with a local path. It is not necessary for the local name to be the same as the remote name. Network mounts that the system administrator wants to occur at system restart time are typically placed in a file such as */etc/fstab*. Once the mount has completed successfully, the data can be accessed on the client system as if it were a local disk.

You can specify a number of additional options upon mounting an NFS volume. These may be given either following the *-o* switch on the command line or in the options field of the */etc/fstab* entry for the volume. In both cases, multiple options are separated from each other by commas. Options specified on the command line always override those given in the *fstab* file. In the absence of an *fstab* entry, NFS mount invocations look a lot uglier.

Whenever the client sends a request to the NFS server, it expects the operation to finish after a given interval (specified in the time-out option). If no confirmation is received within this time, a so-called minor time-out occurs, and the operation is retried with the time-out interval doubled. After reaching a maximum time-out of 60 seconds, a major time-out occurs.

Usually, the mounted daemon will keep track of which directories have been mounted by what hosts. This information can be displayed using the *showmount* command, which is also included in the NFS server package.

7.3.1.3 Exporting Files

When files are exported on an NFS server, the administrator designates which clients can mount specific directory trees located on the server. The type of access may also be given for exported files.

For NFS, the */etc/exports* file contains entries for directories that can be exported to NFS clients. Each line of the */etc/exports* file has the following format:

directory -options[,options]...

Directory is the pathname of a directory or a file system. *Options* allow a variety of security-related options to be specified. It is important that a system administrator be aware of default access that is allowed if certain options are not specified. It is also important that the system administrator be aware of the implications of the use of particular options.

Files should be exported only to clients that need them. Having a line in the */etc/exports* file of the */usr* format is strongly discouraged because the */usr* directory is being exported to all systems on the network. The *access=client[:client]...* option should be used so that mount access is given only to each client listed. The client field can either be a hostname or a netgroup. For remote mounts, the information in a netgroup is used to restrict access to a group of machines. The following example exports the */usr* directory to clientA and clientB. All other systems are denied permission to mount these files.

/usr -access=clientA:clientB

Shared files, such as system files, should be exported read-only and owned by root. This helps prevent system files from being modified. It should be noted that the default is for directories to be exported read-write. The following command exports */usr/bin* read-only to the clientA, clientB, clientC, and clientD systems.

/usr/bin -ro,-access=clientA:clientB:clientC:clientD

Files should not be exported with the *root=client[:client]...* option. This option gives root access for root users from specified clients. If a client is impersonated, then an unauthorized user could modify files on the server.

When feasible, only the minimal subdirectory tree should be exported. For example, if access is needed only for */usr/bin*, it should be exported instead of */usr*. It is not possible to export either a parent directory or a subdirectory of an exported directory that is within the same file system. For example, it would be illegal to export both */usr* and */usr/local* if both directories resided on the same disk partition. As a result, sometimes it is necessary to give access to more files for more clients than is desired.

The *showmount* command can be used to print all directories that are exported for either a local system or a remote system. Systems that do not export directories to specific clients are particularly vulnerable because the output of the *showmount* command will reveal that any client on the network can mount the directory. If a system is using the */etc/hosts* facility, the */etc/exports* file can contain aliases for host names.

Using aliases for client names will prevent *showmount* from revealing which clients have permission to mount specific directories. It is advisable for administrators to regularly inspect the file that gives permission for directories to be exported to verify that entries have not been modified.

7.3.2 NFS Design and Architecture

NFS is designed to give users high performance and transparent access to server file systems on global networks. Some of the most important design principles are summarized here:

☞ *Transparent access*: Users and applications can access remote files as if they were local. They are not required to know whether the files reside on the local disk or on remote servers.

☞ *Statelessness*: NFS operates in a stateless manner using RPCs built on top of an external data representation (XDR) protocol. The RPC protocol enables version and authentication parameters to be exchanged for security over the network.

When an NFS client mounts the file system, the server examines the mount request to be sure that the client is authorized, then issues a magic cookie to the client for use in later accesses. The *magic cookie* keeps the server stateless since no record of authenticated clients needs to be kept. Unmounting and remounting an NFS file system changes its magic cookie. The magic cookie persists across reboots provided the client does not boot as a single user or play with the file system. Once the client has the magic cookie, it uses RPC to make file requests. Because the server is stateless, it is the responsibility of the client to ensure that it has received acknowledgments of write requests before deleting its copy of data.

☞ *Portability*: NFS is machine and operating system independent. This allows it to be ported easily to multiple OSs and hardware platforms from PCs to mainframes.

☞ *Fast recovery from failure*: NFS is designed to recover quickly from system failures and network problems, causing minimal disruption of service to users.

☞ *Network protocol independent*: NFS has the flexibility to run on multiple transport protocols instead of being restricted to just one. This allows it to utilize existing protocols that emerge in the future.

☞ *Performance*: NFS is designed for high performance so that users can access remote files as quickly as they can access local files.

☞ *Security*: The NFS architecture enables the utilization of multiple security mechanisms. This enables system administrators to choose the security mechanism that is appropriate for their distributed file sharing environment instead of being restricted to one solution. This also allows NFS to utilize new security mechanisms in the future. A server can also be a client with respect to file systems it has mounted over the network; however, its clients cannot directly access those file systems. The client must mount the file system directly from the server on which the file system resides.

These features are implemented within the NFS client/server framework, which reduces costs by enabling heterogeneous resource sharing across the global enterprise.

7.3.3 NFS Implementation

NFS was initially designed and is still primarily used as a LAN file system. NFS has an advantage over the other LAN file systems because it uses IP as its transport protocol, making tunneling unnecessary as NFS traffic can be routed directly across the IP-based internetworks. Using IP for the NFS protocol allows NFS clients to communicate with NFS servers directly across the Internet without having to pass through intermediate servers.

NFS is well integrated into most UNIX-based systems. On these, NFS is delivered as part of the base operating system. Some UNIX systems automatically install and configure NFS for a client/server network. (Many users of UNIX are using NFS without being aware of it.)

While NFS is well integrated and easy to use, it has problems scaling into an internetworked file system because it was designed as a LAN. These problems are in the area of data security, data protocols, and system administration.

7.3.4 NFS Security

NFS security is a simple extension of the UNIX file system security. In UNIX, each file is owned by a single user. The file system tracks the ownership of a file based on an integer number called the user identification number (UID). Although this number is often displayed as a symbolic name, it is stored internally as a number. This mapping between the internal UID number and symbolic name is typically stored in the file /etc/passwd on UNIX systems.

When systemA exports a file to systemB, the UID numbers on systemB are used to control the access to the files stored on systemA. On most UNIX systems, the root system administrator can set its UID to any number, allowing the system administrator of a client system to access any file across NFS that has been exported for read-write access to the system. Exporting data through NFS allowing read-write access to a system that cannot be trusted is a potential security hole. In an internetworked environment, it is dangerous to trust the administrator of a remote system.

The security configuration of NFS for multiple systems can be coordinated centrally using the Network Information Services (NIS). An earlier version of NIS was called *yellow pages* (YP). NIS allows multiple systems to share a common security configuration. Unfortunately, NIS requires cooperation among all the systems in a network to trust a central security authority.

While NFS does not have sufficient security to operate in a general internetworked environment using read-write data, it can be effective in an enterprisewide environment where a central security authority may be less a problem.

Even though the NFS protocols are based on IP transport protocol, NFS data protocols are not well suited for internetworked environments. A number of messages must be exchanged between the client and the server each time a file is accessed or a block of data is read. Because so many packets are exchanged between the client and the server, the longer latencies of an internetworked environment can significantly impact the perceived response time of an NFS file system. The following features will help you understand the security implementations for NFS.

7.3.4.1 File Permissions File permissions indicate what kind of access is granted to users on a system. There are three types of permission (the ability to read, write, or execute) and there are three categories of users (the file's owner, users who are in the file's group, and everybody else on the system, with the exception of the superuser). When using NFS, and when using the underlying RPC protocol, unauthorized users can obtain unintended access to files.

It should be noted that the semantics of using commands that change the permissions mode of a file, the owner of a file, or the group ownership of a file differ slightly when using NFS from those of a local file system. Often with distributed file systems, caching is used to increase performance. If caching is used, then the effects of changing the permissions mode of a file, the owner of a file, or the group ownership of a file may not occur immediately on the remote file system.

7.3.4.2 Threats to NFS Many threats are associated with using NFS. Because of the inherent security problems, NFS should not be run on a secure gateway. Threats associated with using NFS include:

☞ If a directory is exported with no access list specified, any system on the network is capable of accessing the exported files.

☞ If a directory is exported with root access given to specified clients, anyone with superuser privileges on one of the clients can modify files on the server owned by root.

An NFS server grants file access to users on clients that have user and group ID mappings that correspond to the server (i.e., a user on a client who has a user ID of 100 can access on the server files that are owned by user ID100 and have the proper read, write, or execute permission bits for owner set). This is a threat because it is easy for one user to impersonate another, especially if the user has superuser privileges on the client.

A client can be impersonated, especially if it is a system that is turned off regularly. To reference files, NFS uses file handles that are relatively easy to guess because file handles consist of a file system id and inode number. It is possible to make it more difficult to guess a valid file handle by using a program to randomize the inode of each file.

As is often the case, NFS may be distributed with no security features enabled.

7.3.4.3 Protecting Against Impersonation Using NFS   One way of minimizing the risk of user impersonation is to export a user's files only to that user's personal computer or workstation. Very often in current network environments, each client system is the exclusive domain of a single user. This type of environment promotes better security since each NFS client is accessed by one user only and only that user's files need be exported to that user's system. Any other files needed by a user can be exported read-only to that user's system. Once an NFS client is able to mount more than one user's files, it becomes possible for the superuser to impersonate any user on that NFS client and there is no easy way to protect against such impersonation.

If an NFS client is a workstation, then a user is authenticated and associated with a user id by logging onto the workstation. If an NFS client is a personal computer, then the NFS client implementation on the personal computer provides a way for the PC user to be associated with a user id so that access control can take place on the NFS server.

The PC user's authentication and association with a user id is sometimes implemented with a daemon called pcnfsd. This daemon can run on a server that does not need to be NFS. The PC user is able to designate not only NFS servers from which files are mounted but also the server running pcnfsd, which authenticates the user to the NFS servers. Herein lies the possibility of a PC user assuming the identity of another user. Again, the importance of only exporting a user's files to that user's system is illustrated.

It is possible to impersonate an NFS client in the same manner as impersonating an *r* command trusted host. As in the case of the *r* commands, a significant danger here occurs when a legitimate NFS client is disabled, disconnected from the network, or turned off. It is common practice to power off a PC at the end of the day. If it is an NFS client this presents an impersonation possibility. Server administrators should be aware that almost all client implementations of NFS on PCs also support the *r* commands and are, therefore, potential *r* command trusted hosts.

A daemon, which could be a shell script, runs on the NFS server and monitors (perhaps by simply using ping to determine the status) the "health" of each NFS client. When a client does not respond, that client's files on the server are unexported, thus denying access. When the client comes back on line and is authenticated, its files are exported once again.

If the NFS client is a PC and user authentication is by means of the pcnfsd daemon, the pcnfsd can be modified (the source is available) to export the user's files when the user is authenticated and receives the user id. If the NFS client is a workstation, a client command for pcnfsd could be readily implemented on the workstation or the user could log into the NFS server to run a command which exports its files.

7.3.5 Internetworking with NFS

NFS has been used with some success to provide publicly readable information on the Internet. In a sense, the largest problem for true internetworked file systems is one of security. For an internetworked file system to be acceptable, the security must have the following attributes:

☞ The security must not require central administration.

☞ Each administrative organization must be able to completely control its own security configuration. The security administrators cannot be required to trust any services that are not under the complete control of the organization.

☞ The security must scale to millions of users without any changes in architecture.

☞ The security must be robust enough that it can withstand hacker attacks.

7.3.6 NFS Benefits

NFS offers a number of advantages:

☞ Data accessed by all users can be kept on a central host, with clients mounting this directory at boot time. For example, you can keep all user accounts on one host, and have all hosts on your network mount /*home* from that host. If installed alongside NIS, users then can log into any system and still work on one set of files.

☞ Data consuming large amounts of disk space may be kept on a single host. For example, all files and programs could be kept and maintained in one place.

☞ Administrative data may be kept on a single host.

7.4 ANDREW FILE SYSTEM (AFS)

An AFS is a location-independent file system that uses a local cache to reduce the workload and increase the performance of a distributed computing environment. A first request for data to a server from a workstation is satisfied by the server and placed in a local cache. A second request for the same data is satisfied from the local cache.

AFS is the first true distributed file system. AFS provides full file-system semantics transparently across an internetwork. Unlike NFS, AFS security is based on individual users rather than on systems and system administrators.

AFS works on a BSD 4.3 UNIX with TCP/IP as the underlying network communications protocol. Each workstation on the system requires a hard disk and works like a regular UNIX workstation. Several principles in the design of AFSs can be stated:

☞ Caching files can save considerable network bandwidth because they are likely to be used again.

☞ Workstations have enough processing power that it is wise to use them instead of server processing power whenever possible.

☞ Minimize the dependency on as much of the system as possible as part of the requirement for changes.

☞ Perform work in batches when possible.

☞ Exploit usage properties.

There are two distinct parts to the AFS file system: the *local file system* and the *shared file system*. The local file system can be set up differently from workstation to workstation but the shared file system has a universal look since it looks the same from all workstations. Regardless of which workstation a user logs on to, it sees the same directory tree. The shared file system is mounted on each workstation. Directories and files under it may be located over several file servers.

For frequently used files, symbolic links can be formed between files in the local file system and the shared file system. Read-only replicas can be made of files that are frequently read but rarely modified. AFS provides both location transparency and independence.

An AFS name space has a similar look and feel to a traditional UNIX tree. All commands traverse the tree and that which is related to files works in the same way, albeit more slowly, when accessing the shared files.

An AFS cell is an administrative entity such as a department or group. Multiple cells can be attached together to build a shared tree that spans multiple sites. They have a */file1/<cellname>/filepath* format. For example, in */file1/connect.com/common/etc/newprogs/* the connect.com component is the cell name. A local filename also can be mapped to it: */etc/newprogs/* -> */file1/connect.com /common/etc/newprogs/*.

A volume is a collection of files that are managed together to allow ease of movement: */usr/bob1* or */usr/sys3/syrett*.

File identifiers (*fids*) are global naming IDs for files on the AFS. This 96-bit global ID contains the following fields:

☞ *Volume number*: Uniquely identifies a single volume in the system.

☞ *Vnode number*: Identifies a file within a volume. It is analogous to inodes in the UNIX file system. This number can be reused by a new file if the old file has been deleted.

☞ *Unique number*: In a distributed system, old *fids* can still float around. As such, the unique number was created for reuse of Vnode numbers.

7.4.1 History of AFS

The AFS was developed at Carnegie Mellon University in 1984. The idea was to provide a campuswide file system for home directories that would run effectively using a limited-bandwidth campus backbone network.

The AFS has become a standard in both the scientific community and the commercial world. AFS accommodates a large number of workstations (in thousands), with a substantial fraction in use at the same time. Actual implementations may vary in range, however.

7.4.2 AFS Architecture

When a user logs into a client system and begins to access the data, AFS copies the user data from the server disks to local client disks. Further reads and writes access the copy of the data stored on the local disk. Using local disks minimizes the number of accesses to the data that have to travel across the network. This local caching of the data also allows a single server to support many more clients because many data accesses never need to contact the server at all.

The AFS file system allows data from many different security domains to be integrated into a single distributed file system. Unlike NFS, AFS does not require a single point of control for security. The AFS file system is broken into security domains called *cells*. Each cell can consist of one or more servers. Within a cell, the security configuration is controlled by the administrator of the cell. Each client system can access data on as many cells as they have access. A client may choose to associate itself with one particular cell as its default cell.

7.4.2.1 Configuring an AFS Server/Client   Typically, AFS servers are dedicated systems which do not allow general user access. One problem with setting up an AFS client is that AFS does not come preinstalled on many operating systems. When you are setting up an AFS client, you must configure the client with a list of the cells that will be accessed by the client. This configuration is typically done in a file such as */usr/vice/etc/cellserv*.

When a cell has more than one server, the client will attempt to contact the other servers when contact is lost for one of the servers in the cell. *Cellserv* controls which cells appear as part of the client file system hierarchy and the names that are used by those cells. File names in AFS typically start with the path */afs/* followed by the cell name. In addition, the client sets their default cell using the file named */usr/vice/etc/thiscell*.

Even though a client is associated with a cell by default (similar to a client associating with a particular NIS domain in NFS), the security relationship between the AFS client and server can be either very tight or very loose.

7.4.3 AFS Security

An account is required for a user to access read-write data on the servers making up a cell. The account name, number, and password of the server may be different from the account name, number, and password on the client system. In addition, a single user may have accounts in several cells. There is no need to coordinate the user names, numbers, or passwords between cells. Each cell can create or delete users independently.

7.4.3.1 Basic Access   In the simplest case, when a user logs in, it has no access to any nonpublic AFS data on any cell. For each cell the user wants to access, it must provide authentication for that cell using the *klog* command. In the following example, the user logs into a client system and then *klogs* into several cells.

> login: kamal
>
> Password: <- Local client password
>
> You have new mail.
>
> Coming in as vt100
>
> % klog severanc -cell hidata.com
>
> Password: <- hidata.com cell password
>
> % klog msuacc -cell transarc.com
>
> Password: <- transarc.com password
>
> %

At this point, the user can access the data that belongs to it in the cells hidata.com and transarc.com. Without the *klog* commands, the servers would not allow access to the data in those cells. With these *klog* commands and proper passwords, the servers allows access to data from any network-connected client.

The *tokens* command shows which cells the user currently has authenticated:

> % tokens
>
> Tokens held by the Cache Manager:
>
> User's (AFS ID 103) tokens for afs@hidata.com [Expires Sep 3 11:12]
>
> User's (AFS ID 993) tokens for afs@transarc.com [Expires Sep 2 14:16]
>
> %

An AFS token is a security key used to insure that the proper user is accessing the data. In addition to the token, a time stamp is also transmitted to the server. Both the token and time stamp are encrypted before they are sent to the server. This way an intruder cannot copy a message from the network and "replay" it at a later time because the time stamp in the copied message would be incorrect and the message would be rejected. These security tokens are only valid for a certain length of time (typically 25 hours).

The client stores the authentication token for each cell and uses the appropriate authentication token when communicating with each cell.

7.4.3.2 Typical Access
Typically, when a client is configured, the user will have a local cell which it uses regularly. It would be inconvenient to have to *klog* every time the user logs in to the client system, so the system can be configured to perform the *klog* automatically as part of the standard login process. In this case, the account name on the client must match the account name on the local AFS server. At login, users type their client/server account name, followed by their server password. If the server password is correct, then the user is both logged in and authenticated for the local cell automatically.

Once the user has logged in and been authenticated to the local server, additional cells can be authenticated manually using *klog*. When the client is configured in this fashion it behaves much more like a traditional UNIX system.

While the tight integration of the client and server is convenient, using the server password to log into the client presents a disadvantage in that the security administrator can change a user's server password and gain access to the client system. The local server administrator is one of the least likely persons to attempt to break into a client system. Sites with high security requirements can configure their clients to have separate login passwords from their AFS passwords (as in the previous example).

7.4.4 AFS Protocols

The AFS data protocols use IP so that AFS packets can be routed directly over many internetworks. There are many features of the higher-level protocols of AFS that make it a much better system than NFS for a distributed file system in an internetworked environment. These features include:

☞ File-oriented transfers with variable block data sizes
☞ Server tracking of client-cached data
☞ Client caching of directories
☞ Distributed administration and security

In most networked file systems, data is transferred across the network whenever an application reads the data or opens a file. In AFS, when an application on a client system opens a file, AFS copies a relatively large portion of the file from the server to the local client disk. Further reads and writes of the data are done using the local disk rather than the server. It is quite common to get many complete files into the client cache and not require any network traffic for simple operations. If a file is modified, the changes are sent back to the server when the file is closed or when the local cache fills up.

To maintain file consistency, the AFS server maintains a list of which files each client has cached. For example, if one host opened a file and read it completely, it would be completely stored in the client cache (assuming a reasonable size). Once the file is closed, the file remains in the local cache until the client runs out of space. However, if another client wants to open the file for a write, the server will "call back" the first client and instruct it to discard the cached copy of the file. In this way, a client can keep data cached for a long time and be assured that unless it has been notified by the server, the cached copy is correct.

Given that most data on a typical server is not being modified continuously from many clients, this caching technique with server callback results in a smaller network bandwidth when a client has a cache of reasonable size. A good example is when "home directory" data is used regularly on a single workstation day after day and is accessed from no other systems. After some time, nearly all of the active data will be resident in the local cache of the workstation. Because the data can be accessed locally, network accesses will be minimized and the file access effectively gives the same performance as a locally attached disk.

Experiments have been performed with modified versions of AFS in which a portable workstation connected to a network accesses all of the data in a directory, loading it into the cache on the workstation. Then the workstation is disconnected from the network and the data is used, modified, and edited with the cached versions having no network connection at all. At some later time, the portable workstation is reconnected to the network and any file updates are sent back to the server.

7.4.5 AFS Implementation

All file requests made by applications running on the client are checked and all the open and close file calls are trapped. The open and close system calls perform different functions internally but return the same values as that of a UNIX open and close file system call. Because the applications need not know the physical location (the *pathname* is needed) to open or close a file, accessing files in AFS is the same as in a single-user UNIX file system.

Furthermore, the read and write system calls remain the same and perform reading and writing on the local copies of files. Local files are treated in a manner similar to that in UNIX. For shared files, the list of files in a local cache (i.e., */cache*) is checked. Each file has a token to indicate if it is the latest updated copy (valid) or not (invalid). If it is valid, it returns the file descriptor to the calling application.

If the file is invalid and not located in the cache, it sends a request to download the file into */cache*. It transfers a copy of the file and a [*1callback* *promise*] to the workstation. It puts the copy of the file into /*cache* and returns the file descriptor to the calling application.

If the file is invalid but located in the cache, it compares the time stamps of the local files with the server copy. If the local copy is outdated, it performs the same actions as it would if there were no local copy of the file (i.e., download file and get callback promise). Such a situation would occur if the workstation was rebooted or if there was a system crash.

All reading and writing of shared files is done on the cached copies, such as in /*cache*. It traps file close system calls and closes the local copy of the file. If the file has been updated, it sends a copy to the server that is the custodian of the file. It then replaces the old copy of the file and sends a callback to all other clients holding callback promises on the file. On receiving the callback message, all the clients would invalidate their local copies of that file. Also, volume migration is atomic: When a copy is made, it is set in the file system as read-only. This allows for the easy implementation of replicated servers.

As in any distributed system, security is of prime consideration in the design. In AFS all traffic between workstations and servers is encrypted. Access to directories is controlled through ACLs while access to files is protected by the UNIX rwx bits. ACLs provide the additional functionality of defining negative rights. The current implementations of AFS use the Kerberos authentication system, a widely employed network security service, to provide ACLs for file access as well.

AFS was originally implemented with the notable assumption that files would have an average size of 10K with infrequent access, and AFS did not take into account that there might be many database files in the AFS. With the advent of large distributed file systems, the commercial environment has a much larger choice of operating environments. Therefore, studies are being done in the areas relating to file accesses over different environments before a good generic solution can be specified.

7.4.6 AFS Administration

In a worldwide file system with thousands of servers, each administered by a different organization, with hundreds of thousands of clients, system administration is a crucial issue.

The most important system administration feature in AFS is that the physical location of data is transparent to the user and the client configuration. Each cell has a server called the *volume location* server. When a client wants to open a portion of AFS space, it contacts the volume location server and the volume location server tells the client on which server and which disk on that server the data is stored.

The advantage of this feature is that data can be moved transparently among servers within the same cell. Data can be moved from one physical disk to another even while it is being accessed by clients.

AFS allows the system administration to add new servers, add new disks, or reorganize existing disks and servers with no impact on the client configuration or users.

7.4.7 Benefits of AFS

AFS has several advantages over other networked file systems such as:

☞ *Scalability*: AFS can easily scale to a few hundred thousand users.

☞ *Security*: By using the Kerberos security technology, AFS operates in a relatively insecure network environment without compromising data.

☞ *Access Control Lists*: AFS allows great flexibility in who can read and write data. Eventually, school classes will be able to create hand-in areas that will allow students to hand in their data securely to a folder stored in AFS.

☞ *Mobility*: AFS is designed to deal with "mobile" users. Data follows you to any workstation you sit down at. You may access AFS from your home in the morning, from the office at noon, from a library at 3 P.M., and from a lab in the evening. AFS detects your location and moves your data to be as close as possible.

☞ *Caching*: When you access data from one location more than once, it is cached on the local AFS gateway or AFS client, reducing the load on the network backbone.

7.4.8 Shortcomings of AFS

AFS security cannot permit access to a file directly to an individual user of a different cell. Each user needs an account on each cell in order to access secured data. While AFS security has some limitations, it is sufficient to provide a reasonably secure environment for an internetworked file system.

Because AFS was designed for an internetworked environment, some applications are better suited for a LAN-based network file system. These are applications that have one or both of the following features:

☞ Multiple clients simultaneously writing data in a single file

☞ Multiple clients reading large files randomly

Because of its caching techniques, AFS works best when only one client has write access to a file. While this is seldom a problem with user home-directory data, it is a problem with database applications.

Database applications also generate a lot of small read operations on a large file. AFS often transfers too much information to the cache for these small reads. In addition, this data will seldom be reused so the additional step of copying it onto a cache disk is unnecessary. For LAN-wide database applications, a network file system like NFS or Novell is preferable to AFS.

An internetwork-wide database application with access to read-write data is a difficult problem that remains to be solved. It is unrealistic to expect that an effective solution for an internetwork file system would also work for solving the problems in an internetwork database system.

7.5 OSF DISTRIBUTED COMPUTING ENVIRONMENT (OSF-DCE)

A distributed computing environment is one that facilitates the flow of information from its storage location to users without exposing the system's complexity to the administrator, the end user, or the application developer. The DCE is a layer of software that resides between a computer's operating system and application programs. Masking the physical complexity of the heterogeneous networked environment, it enables an application to be segmented and executed on the system best suited for each segment.

The fundamental unit in a DCE is the cell, consisting of servers and clients. In a DCE, clients within the cell can access data and applications from servers within or outside the cell regardless of geographic location, operating system, or network protocol. The cell is usually administered as a discrete entity containing each of the fundamental DCE components.

7.5.1 Fundamental Concepts (DCE/DFS/OFS)

DCE was a joint development directed by an industry consortium, the Open Software Foundation (OSF). It was planned to include everything needed for the implementation of distributed systems. This includes a thread library, because DCE programs are multithreaded; a name service; a security service; a distributed file service; a distributed time service; and an RPC protocol. All of these components are tightly integrated. Figure 7.1 shows DCE's basic architecture.

A DCE cell is a set of computers sharing such basic DCE services as naming and security. This comprises common administration, common user definitions, and, due to the security component, a certain amount of mutual trust.

All DCE components are multithreaded, and because not all operating systems provide kernel threads, DCE comes with its own POSIX-compliant thread implementation. Implementers may use kernel threads instead, if the operating system has them, or at least base their threads on kernel threads.

If the plain DCE thread library is used, threads are implemented inside of normal processes. Thread scheduling is done by the process itself, and it is done without any assistance from the kernel.

The DCE security service is built around Kerberos. Some operating system vendors provide an integrated login facility, which means a user is supplied with a Kerberos ticket at login time, and from then on no further

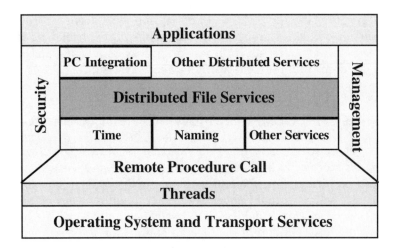

Fig. 7.1 The Architecture of DCE

password checks are necessary, at least as long as the user does not try to log into a computer outside of the cell.

The time service is not mandatory, and if a site uses a different vehicle to enforce a common notion of time, DCE can use that. In any case, there has to be common timing, as some services, most notably security, rely on time stamps.

The distributed file service (DFS) is based on Transarc's AFS. In contrast to NFS in which users may mount any network file system anywhere on their local machines, DFS presents itself on all attached computers in exactly the same way. Thus in contrast to NFS a given file on a network file system is identified by the same path on all client computers. This fits well with the vision behind DCE, the vision that users do not work with distinct computers but with the cell as a whole.

It makes migrating users between workstations easy, and it simplifies the user's mental model of the network. Supported by a reasonably modern local file system, DFS file sets can be migrated or saved without disturbance of ongoing work and without risk of inconsistencies. DFS is stateful, works with large local caches, and is based on a sophisticated token exchange mechanism.

DCE naming is a bit complicated, as there are at least two name services in each DCE installation: A local one, the cell directory service (CDS), and a global one. The global directory service (GDS) is used only for the interconnection of DCE cells—precisely for one cell to find the other.

The CDS is employed throughout the cell for server lookups, not only for user-written services but also for DCE's own services. The CDS name space is structured like a UNIX file system. Indeed, it was designed for integration with the name space of a network file system and even with the file system locally attached to a computer. Hence users of DCE and its distributed file system are able to address every object in the cell through a name that looks like a file name.

In practice, at least currently, the implementations still lack full integration with UNIX and Windows. From a user's point of view, I would wish for an *ls* command that could operate on the whole name space, not only on file systems. An integrated *chmod* command could be used to change access control lists in CDS.

In the implementation of several of these networked file systems, the developers created a number of general distributed computing tools including:

☞ RPCs

☞ Distributed security

☞ Accurate distributed time services

☞ Multithreaded application support

When a file is requested in DCE, it is first looked for in the local cache. If it is not there, a DFS is queried for its location. Then it may be copied down to the cache and accessed from there. The consistency mechanism uses a token. The server keeps track of tokens that have been issued, so it is not stateless.

The token is issued to a process that wants to write to a file. Only one token can be issued per file, so this allows only one writer at a time although any number of readers are allowed. The token can be revoked by the server at any time. In doing so, before revoking permission, it may retrieve the modified file from the process that currently has it.

DCE uses a global name space, with a root /....The network is divided into cells. Files exist on the file system within a cell, so that its location is transparent and independent.

Vendors can use the code to build applications that are DCE-compliant on any platform or OS. Currently DCE software is available for a number of platforms, including many varieties of UNIX, VMS, MVS, OS2, Windows 95, Macintosh, and Windows NT. A DCE's fundamental services include:

☞ RPCs

☞ Thread services

☞ Distributed directory services

☞ Security services

☞ Distributed time services

☞ Distributed file services

7.5.2 RPCs

An RPC allows individual procedures in an application to run on a computer somewhere else on the network, distributing application execution. RPC presentation services mask the differences between data representation on different machines, allowing programs to work across heterogeneous systems. RPC's network protocol independence and tight integration with the directory service insulates end users and programmers from the computing environment's details. RPC also integrates with the security service.

7.5.3 Thread Services

Threads support concurrent programming, allowing programs to execute multiple procedures simultaneously on one or more processors anywhere on the network on any client or server that supports OSF threads.

7.5.4 Directory Service

The distributed directory service provides a single naming model throughout the DCE, allowing users to address remote resources without knowing their location in the network. The directory service supports X.500 functionality through standard APIs and is transport independent. The directory service also supports transparent data replication, maximizing availability and data integrity. The directory itself can be replicated across several servers in the distributed environment to provide redundancy in case of equipment failure.

7.5.5 Security Service

The security service provides authentication, authorization, and user account management. Authentication is based on the Kerberos security model, which validates the identity of a user on the network. The user names and passwords are secured through encryption. The security service uses ACL to authorize access to data in the DFS. ACLs can be used to grant or deny access to files or directories based on user id or group membership. The sole repository for user account information in the DCE is the user registry. Replication of the registry allows for high availability.

7.5.6 Distributed Time Service (DTS)

DTS synchronizes each computer's clock in the DCE. This service is critical to the proper functioning of each of the four fundamental services above.

7.5.7 DFS

The distributed file system is an application that uses the fundamental services to enable access to file sets to any DCE client regardless of the client's server operating system or file structure.

DFS appears to the end user as a local resource although its constituent file sets may reside anywhere on the network. DFS is a log-based file system that facilitates recovery after server failures. Administrators can replicate file sets across the network to provide high availability and reliability. Security is provided through ACLs.

7.5.8 Benefits of DCE

DCE provides transparent services to the end user, simplifying the distributed environment by hiding the underlying complexities of operating systems, platforms, file systems, and network protocols. Some other benefits are:

☞ High availability through caching and replication

☞ Single-user account store simplifies management through a standard interface

☞ Network protocol, OS, and platform independence

☞ Interoperates with other standards such as NFS, DNS, NTP, and X.500

☞ Provides a broad range of services that enable vendors to develop standards-based distributed environments and applications

7.5.9 Drawbacks of DCE

DCE has many fundamental flaws:

☞ Not widely implemented

☞ Minimally supported on some operating systems

☞ All components must be implemented for DCE to work properly

7.6 OSF DISTRIBUTED FILE SYSTEM (OSF-DFS)

DFS is based on AFS with a few added extensions. The primary improvement of DFS over AFS is the use of the standardized distributed computing services. DFS also has improved security over AFS, adding finer grain security, cross-cell authentication, and data encryption.

7.6.1 DCE/DFS in Distributed Multiprocessing

The ability to distribute large, complex problems across heterogeneous computing environments is critical in solving today's most challenging problems. By distributing problems across several systems, users can apply each machine to do what it does best, ensuring that they are getting the most from every resource on the network.

DFS client service supports caching of data and uses a token mechanism to synchronize concurrent file access by multiple users. These capabilities enable high performance and data integrity and allow the systems to interoperate with other DFS servers on the network.

Threads support creating and managing multiple sequential flows of execution within a single process in a computer. In a multithreaded application, the multiple flows of execution can carry out concurrent processing of different parts of the application. Threads allow developers to exploit the parallelism inherent in a distributed computing environment.

7.6.2 Managing Internet User Access

Every browser user who wants to access a URL that is provided by DFS plug-in features has to authenticate with DCE security. A valid user name and password combination has to be entered into the dialog box that pops up on the Web browser. A null response in this DCE authentication dialog (when the user enters nothing or blanks) will be rejected. Unauthenticated access to DFS plug-in is not permitted, even if DFS itself is open to some unauthenticated access. Managing user access involves setting up users within the DCE registry and the groups and the organization to which those users belong.

7.6.3 User Administration

A number of utility programs can be used for adding and modifying the DCE registry. Original DCE implementations are usually included by the *rgy_edit* command. These facilities are also available through the DCE control program dcecp.

7.6.4 Using DCE/DFS on the Web

The DCE is a secure, enterprisewide middleware environment. Its strengths lie in a robust and scalable architecture which brings together all parts of an organization under a common, secure interaction environment. Interoperability spans from desktop to mainframe, interconnecting all within an enterprise intranet.

The World Wide Web has had an enormous impact on the way we share information both within an organization and, more traditionally, between organizations. In the past, this has often relied upon a relaxed security model but as more organizations open their intranets to external visitors, more emphasis is being placed on strong security policies and mechanisms. Firewalls have played a part in this revolution. They restrict access to a network by limiting access and providing auditing facilities to track problems.

A key product linking the semistructured information accessed through the Web with the more formally structured information in the DCE space is DFS plug-in technology. It links the secure world of DCE and DFS to the Web Servers. Full DCE security semantics are available to the Web browser as mediated by the Web server plug-in.

7.6.4.1 Native DFS Exploitation on the Browser Side
DCE's DFS is a robust, secure, and scalable solution to information access both within an enterprise and, through secure intercell links, to clients external to the enterprise. It abstracts location information from naming, allowing files to be moved, and possibly replicated, without concern to client access. Individuals can offer sets of files to the DCE environment through appropriate access control specification in combination with intercell agreements between cells (or enterprises).

DFS file access control requires clients to authenticate with the DFS plug-in before accessing documents stored within DFS. The same access controls are used in authenticated Web document access and natively within a DFS client/server environment. The Web document space can now be completely distributed, providing robust access through the use of DFS replication and DCE security. The browser can be anywhere in the world without knowledge of DCE or DFS.

A simpler solution to accessing documents in the DFS file space is to limit client browsers to the intranet/cell space. We assume that the local browser host includes a DCE and DFS runtime environment. A user authenticates with DCE and then invokes its local browser under this authenticated user environment. If DFS documents are accessed as local files, a similar DFS document space as was accessed through the DFS plug-in at the server is available to the user.

No Web server is involved in the document retrieval if direct file access is performed. This has the benefit of one less piece of software being maintained, but, at the same time, no logging, event triggers, or document access statistics are available.

The subsequent document access stays within the local DFS file space. Obviously, this solution only makes sense for browsers with access to DCE/DFS and either in the enterprise DCE cell or linked to it through a trusted cell. Security is identical to DFS file access security from any other application and requires no intermediary such as DFS plug-ins to translate.

Direct file access through DFS is probably not an adequate solution for large-scale Webs due to its requirements for relative links (or absolute file links) and the lack of tracing and logging facilities. But it might be an ideal solution for department-wide Web exploitation in which individuals want to selectively share information with others. Provided the document or file links are set up accordingly, this can also be used in conjunction with NFS to DFS gateways, eliminating the requirement for local DCE and DFS code on the browser host.

7.6.4.2 Browser-side Plug-Ins
Browser plug-ins are designed to extend the browser by providing additional functionality and compatibility. Plug-ins are available for Web browsers—for example, Netscape Navigator—across a range of application areas, such as:

☞ Multimedia viewers including audio, video, and support

☞ Applications such as games and information managers

☞ Utility functions such as object imbedding and compression/decompression

Plug-ins form a close relationship with the browser. They come in the form of loadable modules which are instantiated as needed. The browser recognizes a special HTML tag, which includes a number of attributes. Most important of these is a Multipurpose Internet Mail Extension (MIME) attribute that specifies the variety of information included in the embedded data. The browser is created recognizing a set of available plug-ins and their supported MIME types.

Initially, a plug-in is allocated a piece of screen real estate for which it is responsible. The plug-in and the browser communicate via a well-defined API that both brings data to the plug-in and sends it to the browser. Key elements in this relationship are events and streams. *Events* include mouse events and link into the availability of stream data. Plug-ins must be extremely careful with any synchronous activity as they can easily block other plug-ins as well as the browser itself. Currently, no plug-in technology is available that integrates DCE or DFS security with a Web browser.

The DCE plug-in module concept is searching for alternative methods to link the browser to DCE. One alternative might be to implement DCE-compatible Java classes directly, but this option can be ruled out rather quickly. The current security restrictions applied to Java applets limit how many network connections an applet can make and to whom the connections can be made. Direct DCE access would require access to several hosts providing the Cell Directory Service, the Security Service, and the DCE application server itself. In addition, the DCE protocol is complex and large. Java classes supporting the full protocol would be too large for useful network transport.

A plug-in module is a complex piece of code. The C-language API is written with primitive data manipulation in mind, such as video and audio support. To provide a generic DCE plug-in library would require a significant piece of work to support the dynamic RPC. Currently, the DCE runtime API may not generally support dynamic specification and execution of RPC calls to interfaces that are unknown at compile time. An application-specific DCE plug-in module is more feasible but again would be a large piece of work. It would not only require DCE interaction calls but also a user interface, or at least user interaction, to support the application.

7.7 RFS

RFS is a distributed file system provided with most UNIX System-V-based systems. Unlike NFS, which provides a generic file system, RFS provides an exact copy of a UNIX file system. Another difference between NFS and RFS is that RFS groups hosts into domains for facilitating the mounting of file systems. For the most part, security threats associated with NFS are also associated with RFS.

7.7.1 Connect Security

Before attempting to mount remote resources, the local system must first set up a connection to the server. For many systems, *rfadmin* is the RFS verification command used to restrict access to a given set of machines. This command specifies a password which must be entered before a system is allowed to connect to a server. If a password has not been provided for a system, the system still is allowed to connect to the server without a password check. This poses a threat of unintended access, especially if precautions were not taken when exporting files.

7.7.1.1 Mount Security
When a connection is established between a system and a server the system may mount any file systems that the server has exported. For System V, Release 4 version, of RFS, *share* is used to export file systems. Appropriate options should be specified for *share* so that unintended access is not granted for resources.

7.7.1.2 User and Group Mapping
As a method of controlling access to resources, a system administrator is able to create user and group id mappings by editing the files *uid*.rules and *gid*.rules. These files allow global and host-specific rules to be specified. Service may be denied if user and group mappings are set up in such a way that users are not able to access their own files. On the other hand, poorly defined user and group mappings may allow unintended access to resources.

7.7.1.3 Regular UNIX File Permissions
UNIX file permissions that are improperly set can allow unintended access for local users of a system. Unintended access can occur when files are exported with improperly set file permissions.

7.7.2 Improving the Security of RFS

RFS facilitates the sharing of files. Unless precautions are taken when using RFS, unintended access may be granted for shared resources. This is especially true for file systems that are not exported with options specified to control access. There are a variety of ways to make RFS more secure. Commands used pertain to the System V, Release 4 version, of RFS.

When starting RFS, issue the command *rfstart -v*. This command tells RFS to deny connection requests from any system that has not been given a password via the RFS verification procedure. Connection requests will also be denied to any system that specifies an incorrect password. This connection security feature of RFS makes it more difficult for clients to be impersonated.

Use the *-access* option on all *share* commands. Hosts not included in the access list will not be permitted to mount the resource. Shared files, such as system files, should be exported read-only and owned by the root. This helps to prevent system files from being modified. For exported file systems, use UNIX file permissions to control access to shared resources, such as

☞ Implement user-id and group-id mappings. This deters user impersonation attacks. The *idload* command can be used to display current user and group mappings in effect.

☞ Do not allow untrusted systems to mount file systems with root access enabled.

☞ The *dfshares* command can be used to display a list of all resources in the domain that are available for mounting via RFS. The *dfmounts* command can be used to display a list of remote hosts that have resources mounted from a server. These commands can be used to assist in monitoring RFS security.

7.8 INTERNET FILE SYSTEMS: WEBNFS

Since NFS servers traditionally run on UNIX, and SMB servers on Intel server hardware, WebNFS may enjoy an initial hardware scalability advantage. Huge UNIX RISC servers with a large number of CPUs are readily available and finding Intel PCs with more than four or eight processors is rare.

User Authentication Security is not a concern if your goal is open, public, read-only volumes like a replacement for an anonymous FTP site. However, when opening your file server so that you have read-write access to corporate files via the Internet, you would expect security to be well-considered in the WebNFS and CIFS protocols. Unfortunately, it is not. WebNFS lets administrators define who can read and/or write but authenticating incoming people securely is problematic.

Apparently, the authentication challenge is too great for WebNFS. Like NFS, it leaves the process of user authentication to someone else. The NFS protocol has no notion of passwords. You can control which hosts the server speaks to, based on IP address. Nevertheless, the lack of an authentication mechanism in the NFS protocol itself gives rise to the popular NFS rule of "export volumes only to trusted hosts."

Implementations prior to Windows NT could not handle this sophisticated mechanism. NetBIOS name services and the Network Neighborhood browsing scheme are also security worries, since they can be coaxed to divulge relevant host and user name information to intruders.

WebNFS servers are stateless, so they are not required to store any persistent information about what their clients are doing. All state information in

WebNFS (and NFS) is the client's business. Advocates for state in the server argue that it bestows good fault tolerance and less complicated server failover schemes. If the server crashes and then reboots, clients simply continue where they left off.

7.9 THE INTERNET AND DFSS

Most of the network services—including the Web and FTP—allow the sharing of data with others on the Internet in a read-only fashion or read-write with very simple security controls. In addition to accessing the data across the network, the user must use a special client program such as FTP.

Networked and internetworked file systems allow data from a remote system to be read and written across a network using the same interface as data that is stored on the local system. A networked file system makes the fact that the data must be accessed across a network transparent to the user.

The difference between a networked file system and an internetworked file system is the type of interconnection between clients and servers. Typically, the interconnection for a networked file system is a LAN and it covers a limited geographic area. The interconnection for an internetworked file system is a Metro Area Network (MAN), Wide Area Network (WAN), or the Internet.

With an effective distributed file system you could begin working on a demonstration using a desktop workstation in one location; transfer the data to a floppy disk; get on a plane and continue working on the demonstration on a laptop computer; and, when you land at your destination, perform the demonstration with customer equipment. Using an effective internetworked file system, it would not be necessary to use a floppy disk or explicitly transfer any data over a modem or network. Another advantage of a worldwide distributed file system is the ease of exchanging data with other users.

While these seem like fanciful concepts, existing internetworked systems allow these types of operations across worldwide networks. There are many networked file systems, ranging from very simple to very complex, but to be a true internetworked file system, the following problems must be addressed:

☞ The data transport protocol must be able to use a wide-area network protocol (e.g., TCP/IP, OSI TP4, X.25).

☞ The management and security of the file system must be distributed and scale to millions of users and millions of servers.

☞ The system must have robust security and be protected from hacker attacks.

7.10 CONCLUSIONS

The purpose of a distributed file system is to allow users to share data and storage resources, despite their dispersed structure and the decentralization of both data and control, by using a common system. A typical configuration is a collection of workstations and mainframes connected by a LAN. A distributed file system is usually implemented as part of the operating system of each of the connected computers.

The principle of distributed operation is fundamental for a fault-tolerant and scalable distributed file system design. To accomplish sound distributed file system design, it is necessary to depart from the design of extended centralized file systems over a communication network.

Many different technologies can be used to create wide-area networked file systems. The challenges of building a true distributed file system are very difficult. The AFS file system is an example of the potential of a distributed file system, but improvements need to be made. Distributed file systems and distributed computing are still evolving and, over the next several years, the DFS technologies should advance the quality and usability of distributed multiprocessing systems.

With the advent of large distributed file systems, the commercial environment has a much larger choice of operating environments. However, much more study is needed in the areas relating to file access over different heterogeneous environments before a good generic solution will be apparent.

Distributed Shared Data and Transactions

8.1 INTRODUCTION

With the increased use and popularity of client/server, data warehousing, and distributed computing, businesses need ways to manage not only large amounts of data, but geographically dispersed data that may also be stored in different systems, even different DBMSs. This section describes scenarios in which data sharing can be applied effectively to these new distributed data computing requirements. I also discuss design features required to make data movement accurate, dependable, and productive.

8.1.1 Industry Trends

Historically, large data processing establishment used centralized databases to serve the primary needs of complex organizations. The reasons for this approach included the proper utilization of powerful computing resources, centralized control, security, reliability, and adherence to standards. With the advent of inexpensive yet powerful computer systems, the trend today is to *move the data to the users* through distributed data processing and the use of data warehouses. One of the key questions for IT organizations around the world is how to deliver and replenish the data at these independent data stores, which are often dissimilar, while keeping them in sync. The problem of managing and controling information moving around the enterprise is one that all companies need to address to ensure that their decisions are based on timely and accurate data.

8.1.2 Sharing Data over Networks

With the increasing sharing of data over private or public networks, the possibility of global shared data space appears inevitable. Currently, intranets glue together the corporate shared data space within which information exchange takes place. In the global data space, the intranet concept has to be extended to the Internet. Before that can occur, two significant issues have to be addressed:

1. Speed at which data can be obtained in the current Internet and intranet infrastructure
2. Shared data space, whether files or managed objects, requires a strong security framework in terms of authentication, confidentiality, data integrity, and policy-defined access control on the objects

The issue of limited data speed in the Internet is governed by current economic constraints. However, over time these limits will surely but steadily be removed with increased connectivity options (fiber, wireless, cable, and/or satellite). Where the shared data space is private and more controlled (i.e., the sources of data belong to the same organization), the connection media is owned and therefore economic limitations are fewer. In that case, the bandwidth issue is not dictated by the width of the data pipe but by the ability of the infrastructure to move from modest to large data objects at high data rates efficiently.

The issue of sharing involves defining a global name space and creating a secure infrastructure for data access. Global name spaces can be local data repositories or file systems deciding on a unique location-independent naming system (somewhat similar to a URL naming scheme) or a scheme that maps a local file (assuming the shared object is a file) name into a global one. (This latter is not difficult since mapping a local file name to a global name can always be defined once the global naming scheme is agreed upon.) A secure infrastructure for data access requires the following:

☞ If data is cached at a site close to the user (for performance reasons, as is done today by most Web servers), then the access to the data must also be governed by the same access control defined by the data manager of the original data.

☞ The data producer, the data user, and the manager may be distinct entities. This allows from small to large systems to be data producers, since the data manager has to provide real-time access control.

☞ Data should be stored in encrypted form. Authentication, key storage, and authorization need to be accomplished using a public key system. This is necessary for this approach to be scalable to the many users that might request the same data object.

☞ The encryption has to be done at the source (the producer server) and the decryption at the destination server (where it is used). This implies there can be neither insecurity of the data while it is stored nor inefficiency in encrypting-decrypting—once for the storage and again for the network. The encryption and decryption must be done at the line rate of the media.

☞ Every user must be authenticated by a data or file manager, a proxy owner that could be different from the creator of the data.

Besides evolving data rate issues, the fundamentals of a secure distributed data infrastructure have to be realized for a global information network to be feasible.

8.2 Data Sharing in Enterprise Operations

Typically, an enterprise's organizational structure consists of human resources, procurement, finance, marketing, and operations. These functional business areas have different information requirements and, therefore, often use a variety of vertical applications, back office suites, and Enterprise Resource Planning (ERP) solutions.

A challenge for most enterprises is to share and distribute information among the many applications and within and outside corporate headquarters.

Multidirectional information sharing, and the ability to reconcile information within a decentralized environment, is needed to effectively provide users with data that supports the business process. The critical business issues are:

☞ Developing an enterprise information architecture that integrates information among the functional areas across the enterprise

☞ Allowing branches and remote sites to operate as autonomous business units, while bridging the information flow across the enterprise

For example, a manufacturer of athletic clothing is in the process of implementing an ERP solution. The back office suite at headquarters is not integrated with any retail applications nor does it share information with the manufacturing logistics program. Information about orders, billings, payments, inventory, and shipping resides in different applications and on a variety of DBMSs. The company needs a data distribution solution in which data from the various database sources is shared, synchronized, and managed from any global site, without bottlenecking resources.

8.2.1 Customer Information Management

To provide comprehensive customer service, an enterprise must manage the distribution of customer information used in Help Desk, sales force automation, and customer maintenance applications, while linking direct mail to telemarketing, order entry to order fulfillment, and warranty to service maintenance information. Most organizations employ a corporate Help Desk to track, monitor, and respond to customer calls. But most find it difficult to forecast the number of call center staff needed at any given time to respond adequately to the workload, while maintaining service quality levels. The reason is that information from the Help Desk application is not distributed to the individuals who forecast resource loads.

The process of selling products or services is information- and labor-intensive. Customer case histories and inquiries from the Help Desk need to be passed on to the sales force and, in some organizations, need to be integrated with the sales force automation applications.

Customer information management is a high-volume, high-availability service. This level of service requires current and accurate information about customer accounts and field and service operations. In some industries, customer service representatives must have instant and transparent access to information residing on multiple networks and databases. The critical business issues are:

☞ Exchanging information between corporate Help Desks and field service representatives, from customers to their sales representatives, and from branch offices back to corporate headquarters

☞ Optimizing customer data to identify customer patterns, profiles, and field operation requirements

For example, an aircraft supplier has recently restructured its sales and marketing departments, reduced the company's sales force by 50%, and eliminated the sales support department. The sales staff is now responsible for servicing a large number of customers and monitoring inventory both at home and in the field.

The sales staff needs to access information that resides in three different databases: The corporate sales and marketing database is in Oracle, the order entry and inventory systems are in Sybase, and the customer profile entries are in Informix. To better support its sales staff, the company considered purchasing additional hardware for its branch offices, but it was constrained by limited resources. The solution for this company is a scalable approach to distributing, sharing, and synchronizing information from its existing three databases so that sales representatives, field service, and branch offices can access accurate customer and sales information regardless of where the information is stored.

8.2.2 Data Warehousing

Data warehousing is becoming very popular as more organizations realize the answers to their business problems are often hidden in multiple corporate databases. The data warehousing approach in supporting complex data analysis is to separate (logically and/or physically) the daily operational data processing requirements (inventory control, accounts payable, purchasing, etc.) from decision support data.

The reason many organizations are attempting to implement a data warehouse is directly related to the following tactical issues not addressed by relational databases:

☞ Operational data is not always stored in a format suitable for planning and decision support.

☞ Operational and transactional data often resides in dissimilar platforms.

☞ Operational databases are updated continuously by online transaction processing (OLTP) applications.

☞ Decision-support queries usually interfere with system performance and operational use of the data.

The challenge for data warehouse implementations (as shown in Figure 8.1) is in populating the warehouse and data marts. The current data warehousing model assumes that as OLTP data accumulates in operational databases, it is periodically extracted, filtered, restructured, and loaded into a dedicated warehouse server that is accessible for decision support. This is achieved by either batch downloading and periodically refreshing tables—replicating only the changes between the OLTP and the data warehouse server—or by flexibly accumulating and transmitting different types of data along natural business cycles (daily, weekly, monthly). The critical business issues are:

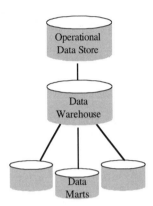

Fig. 8.1 Data Warehousing

☞ Maintaining the volumes of data from current and historical databases, while maximizing user access to that data

☞ Populating the data warehouse with current, meaningful information for decision-support queries

As an example, a well-known corporation comprising 12 distributed centers and multiple hospitals and outpatient clinics, received additional budget to establish a new hospital. In the past, establishing a new hospital cost much time to analyze data from the various other hospital facilities' patient records to determine the facility requirements and patient options for the new hospital.

The corporation used a computer operations group to set technology standards for all facilities. Each hospital remained autonomous as a business unit, however, and if a hospital thrived, it employed its own MIS team to research and implement new systems. This made the task of analyzing data from all corporate systems difficult. The corporation's computer operations group investigated data warehousing in order to establish a central repository for data used only for analyzing trends, profiling patients, facility usage, etc. The corporation identified the data it needed, and the hospitals and facilities identified the applications storing the data. All that remained was to identify the method by which the data warehouse would be populated, maintained, and kept current for analysis by the corporate MIS.

8.2.3 Internet/Intranet

While the Internet eliminates geographical, cultural, and industry boundaries, the intranet—coupled with firewalls—enables enterprises to secure applications and critical corporate information and still allow users access to the Internet through the Web.

The Internet offers a universal access method that is independent of any specific operating system, relies on a common network, and is readable by a growing number of applications. The Web introduces a single entry point into resources within and outside an enterprise. As users become experienced Web users, the expectation level for data accessibility increases. Web users believe they can dive into information regardless of its form, structure, or where it resides, including accessing data from a legacy system.

Distributing, synchronizing, and maintaining currency among the various applications, platforms, and Web servers accelerates the development of data replication and data search utilities. Data replication seems to be the solution for updating data and applications residing on Web servers and for transporting transactions from the Internet server to an organization's internal system for final processing (as shown in Figure 8.2). The critical business issues are:

☞ Developing business rules that segregate user applications from the transaction-processing applications while maintaining interaction and currency between the two

☞ Developing an Internet strategy that addresses the design of a directory schema, the synchronization of data on all Web servers, and the translation of data from different applications

For example, a software company in the U.S., with distributors and branch offices worldwide, publishes marketing data on the Internet. The company identified other services, including online merchandising, that it could provide its customers via the Web. The strategy is to migrate slowly, beginning with online customer service programs, and eventually publish a catalog

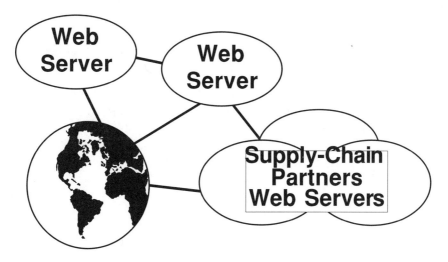

Fig. 8.2 Internet/Intranet

of products that can be purchased online and downloaded by customers. Currently its customer service inquiry database resides on a Connect's OneServer while product update bulletins are in an Oracle database. The database has data tables the company does not wish to make available to customers. To separate this data, it has established another physical Web server on a Microsoft NT.

Now that the company provides its customers with more Web services, it wants to use the information captured from customers searching the Web site and from customer responses to the data it supplied on the Web. Data from the Web Server needs to be copied back to the original source—OneServer and Oracle—and it needs to be copied to a separate corporate marketing database (Oracle) giving corporate marketing current data to analyze customer requirements.

8.3 BASICS

Since data sharing involves distribution across any boundaries, network communication becomes pivotal to any enterprise. Communication is performed by sending a message from one transaction to another. The communication is asynchronous, i.e., there is no waiting involved at either end.

The message is an instance of the predefined type message, to which additional information can be added by creating subtypes with the necessary attributes. Some databases already provide functions to:

☞ Create and send a message to a specified transaction. The message cannot be copied locally in the sender transaction.

☞ Test for the existence of messages to the current transaction. This is a nondestructive test; no message is actually read.

☞ Receive the first message in the incoming mailbox of the current transaction. The message will be removed from the mailbox and become a readable entity.

These are the basic operations that must be supported by the database. More advanced communication can be built using these. We might also have provided communication between clients, which could give us more functionality. However, the message system here is not intended to be more than a simple facility for sending some information from one transaction to another and is relatively simple to provide.

8.3.1 Middleware and Messaging

Middleware is the "glue" that holds together very disparate applications and data sources. It acts as a sort of liaison between various systems and applications, facilitating communications between components of distributed systems. With the advent of the Internet and distributed computing, middleware is becoming increasingly important. It is used to:

☞ Host robust business logic

☞ Balance distribution of processing

☞ Provide complex and rapid data access

☞ Manage persistent state and session

☞ Provide guaranteed and reliable processing

☞ Integrate heterogeneous computing resources

For the purpose of this discussion, middleware can be segmented into six functional areas: TP monitors, message-oriented middleware, ORBs, data access, transaction servers, and application servers.

8.3.1.1 TP Monitors   This software provides distributed transaction monitoring, management, load balancing, and fail-over across multiple data sources.

8.3.1.2 Message-Oriented Middleware (MOM)   MOM software provides asynchronous communications and guaranteed delivery of messages or events between applications across the LAN/WAN. It is often used to integrate disparate applications together through publish/subscribe, message queue, and/or data transformation.

8.3.1.3 Object Request Brokers   An ORB provides an infrastructure that facilitates cross-platform communication between and among distributed objects and client applets. ORB is defined in the CORBA specification.

8.3.1.4 Data Access   Products in this category provide efficient and rapid access to heterogeneous data sources from relational and hierarchical to object.

8.3.1.5 Transaction Servers   Transaction servers combine the features from TP monitors and ORBs, which support object-based distributed transactions.

8.3.1.6 Application Servers   Application servers are used to host nonvisual business logic in the middle tier of a multitier application environment.

8.3.2 Message Type

The generic message type does not include much information. Three pieces of information are provided by the database when the message is created: The sender ID, receiver ID, and a time stamp. Of course, not every receiver will be interested in the time, but in general we cannot know what the receiver would be interested in.

Messages should not be proper database entities, as they are of a more volatile, short-lived nature. However, instead of inventing a totally new paradigm in order to store the information in the message, it is more convenient to use entities. That way, pre-existing methods can be used to access them and standard subtyping or relationships to other entities can be used to add more information.

Messages should be considered private to the transaction's subdatabase, which means that they have no semantics except within that transaction while it is active, so they should not be propagated automatically to subtransactions or propagated to the parent transaction after commit, as other entities are. Otherwise, they would be treated as other entities in the database. Messages that have been sent to a transaction remain hidden for the transaction until formally received through the Receive operation.

The From attribute identifying the sender obviously is needed, as the receiver will want to know where the message comes from, so putting it inside the message is natural. Likewise, the time stamp might be useful, and is a very general kind of information, so it is natural to include it in the message.

The receiver may seem superfluous, as the receiving transaction should know its own identity. Including both sender and receiver in the message provides a way to automatically forward messages sent to a transaction. The To attribute identifies the original addressee, which may be different from the actual recipient. In order to make this possible, we should have the receiver attribute available from the start.

The user (application) would almost certainly want to subtype the message, in order to add more specific information. This information can be freely manipulated, so it is possible to modify this informational part of the message after it has been received.

8.3.3 Network

Everything starts with those cables behind your desk and in the walls. We will look at the considerations that apply to fault tolerance in terms of the components that make up a structured cable system.

Leverage your standard wiring to locate specialized devices. If you have any devices not on the LAN which require special wiring, try to put them on the LAN. For example, instead of running special wiring to standalone modems, use a modem pool. This improves reliability for those devices, and streamlines moves and changes. It also makes them a shared resource. If a device cannot be made into a LAN service, at least try to use the same cable for it that you are using for the LAN.

8.3.3.1 Hubs   The best physical wiring plan is useless unless it is connected to an equally well-considered hub deployment. Hubs play several important roles in ensuring a fault-tolerant network:

☞   Hubs prevent errors from a device from impacting the rest of the network. You need to design your network as a series of defenses against the problems created by the devices on it. Hubs are your first line of defense. All your hubs should be manageable and, ideally, should support RMON, so you know what's happening at that first line. RMON is a remote monitoring tool for management of the network.

☞ Hubs can be fault resilient. However, no matter how robust, a hub is a single point of failure. If it crashes, everyone connected to it is down. There are three ways to minimize this:

✗ Connect every workstation with dual cable to separate hubs on separate segments.

✗ Use small stackable hubs to keep the number of devices connected to a hub small, perhaps between 16 and 32.

✗ Stripe users in each department across multiple hubs.

All the hub management features in the world will not make a difference, however, unless you enable and monitor them. Given today's client workstation environment, it is not always practical to insist on active monitoring of every client.

The ability to centrally diagnose problems means that you can solve them earlier and minimize transient outages. Today's networks generate thorny, difficult-to-analyze distributed problems. A hub that supports RMON, and therefore supports the remote capture of LAN packets for analysis by a network management system or protocol analyzer, is certainly better than no visibility to the segment at all.

8.3.3.2 Routers and Protocols Routers mean protocols, and protocols need consistency to succeed. As a practical matter, it is impossible to support all the protocols everybody might want on your network—much less your backbone or WAN—and still provide the same level of support. Various protocols have differing levels of resilience. The goal of fault-tolerant networking should be to eliminate unsupported protocols at the outset and to create uniform local and backbone protocols. For TCP/IP, this means a single Internet address scheme systemwide. For IPX, it means a central assignment of network numbers. For source-route bridging, it means central assignment of ring numbers.

Routers must be consistently configured. For example, if IPX broadcasts are filtered, all routers should be filtered the same way. The router is your second line of defense, so use it to defend the backbone and WAN against outages by blocking inconvenient protocols such as NETBIOS, AppleTalk, and IPX broadcasts.

Consistency applies to the hardware as well. When selecting routers, consider the features that apply to fault resilience, online software reconfiguration, and hardware service. The router should support major changes to its configuration without requiring an outage.

Deploying routers raises several considerations. Cabling and hubs cascade data into the routers. Depending how you have striped the users across the hubs, remember to stripe LAN segments across the routers. For example, make sure that a single router outage cannot take out an entire section of a building. If you deploy two LAN segments to each desktop, make sure that each of those segments terminates in a different router.

8.3.3.3 Backbones For fault-tolerant facilities, you need a reliable, self-healing backbone. The factors involved in local backbone design are:

☞ *Isolation* means dedicating a LAN segment exclusively to communications among routers. Only routers or equivalent switches can participate in these links; end-user segments, servers, and gateways are deliberately excluded.

☞ *Alternate path* means providing at least two links. For example, the primary local backbone may be an FDDI ring, while an Ethernet or Ring segment provides an alternate. If a link failure occurs, the alternate provides backup.

☞ *Robust media* means overengineering. FDDI is a mainstream solution because each FDDI ring actually comprises two separate rings. The protocol allows traffic to deflect to the backup ring to bypass failures. Even with a robust link between the routers, a second backup is advisable.

Some situations call for a more aggressive stand-in approach. Specialized fail-over schemes may allow routers to share a single address. When the primary router fails, the backup router can step in. This does not require the use of specialized discovery protocols.

If we designed the local backbone correctly we should not have any problems with the data carrier on our WAN. Correct deployment of routing tables isolates traffic and filters miscellaneous broadcasts.

8.3.3.4 Wide Area Links No site is self-contained. Wide area links are the outer layer of the organization's backbone. We can apply the same principles to them as we did with the local backbone.

8.3.3.5 Servers You can approach server availability in two ways: lost data or lost time. The approach to take is make it right, and then make it fast.

Step one is to make your servers fault resilient. Be careful with the distinction between fault tolerant and fault resilient, however. Very few servers have no single point of failure. Other pertinent features to look for in a fault-tolerant system are:

☞ Hardware-based re-boot and power on/off for remote support of hung servers.

☞ OS support for changes in configuration and drivers without requiring a re-boot.

☞ Remote management of everything.

☞ An uninterrupted power supply (UPS) interface for a graceful shutdown in the event of a major power outage.

☞ Hot-swappable drives, both RAID and otherwise.

☞ Realistic backup and restore. Make the system usable during backups and restores.

☞ Prevent lost data by recording it simultaneously to multiple media with either disk mirroring or RAID.

Time is the next problem to tackle. If a server fails, your data may be safe, but can you get the standby server up in time? Test to see how long it takes to load a cold, supposedly identical, standby. If you are shocked to see how long it takes, experiment with additional tape drives, extra disks, and more memory to see if the time can be reduced. A cold standby can be an effective alternative if you have the time. If you do not have the time, there are two alternatives to hot standbys:

☞ *Applications-based redundancy*: Applications-level routines designed to protect data integrity, such as two-phase commit or various data replication processes. DBMSs that support two-phase commit typically are more robust when it comes to recovery and ensuring no data is lost.

☞ *Peripheral switching*: Places an intelligent switch on the SCSI chain between the server and the disk farm (typically a RAID device). This is a logical extension of the matrix switches used for years in large mainframe shops to move huge numbers of peripherals from one mainframe channel to another.

A typical example of peripheral switching would unfold like this: Two RAID devices are connected to the switch along with two servers. One server is primary, the other an active backup. Each server owns one of the RAID devices. In the standby server, a background application runs and periodically polls the primary, performing small disk reads to ensure operation. If the test fails, it waits a predetermined period to retry. After a second failure it signals the switch to move the failed server's RAID device to the secondary. The secondary then mounts the volumes and starts the appropriate applications.

Finally, do not forget about strategic server deployment. Following the cascading redundancy in the cabling, hub, and router deployment, a few configuration issues remain:

☞ All servers should have at least two NIC cards.

☞ Each of those segments should connect to separate interfaces on different routers.

☞ Those interfaces should be connected to two different LAN segments.

8.3.3.6 Application Developers and Third-Party Applications You cannot
exempt applications on either the client or server from their responsibility in

keeping things running. Application testing should be a part of your failure simulations. At a minimum, look for the following features in applications:

☞ Hot standby or alternate servers

☞ Intelligent resumption of broken connections

☞ Support for two-phase commit or data replication

☞ Processing that continues when parts of the network are down

In addition to maximizing the stability of the software environment, we should encourage developers to assume that failures will happen. Development staff should consider automatic detection of failures and automatic logons to alternative servers. Such actions can minimize the effects of an outage. Deal with these questions before the application is developed and deployed. The majority of client/server applications simply die if they cannot find their server.

8.3.3.7 Network Management   In one sense, network management does not have a large role in fault-tolerance design. As we have seen, surviving a failure depends on every link of the chain—client, cabling, hub, router, server, and application. It is too automatic a process for network management. Avoidance of outages requires management of the network—clients, servers, and network components alike.

8.4 Requirements for Information Sharing

A common concern in data distribution operations is how flexible the system is in identifying network nodes, routing patterns, and data tables, and then in reconfiguring the model as new applications or databases are added to the network. In the enterprise model framework, the data is registered and then mapped to nodes and routing paths. All of the enterprise nodes are linked in order to present the DBA with a single view and a single place in which any model changes are made as the network changes. Having a single map of the data flows in an enterprise simplifies the process of configuring heterogeneous DBMSs, platforms, and applications.

8.4.1 Maintainability

A central control point is critical in maintaining complex data distribution architectures. Because the data models are mapped to business rules and registered in the enterprise model, modifications become more manageable, and all processes, regardless of where they are executed, are maintained from the central control. Application upgrades or additions, changes in data definitions or form, and relationship changes between data tables are logically presented in the model using simple and methodical processes to integrate these modifications into the architecture.

8.4.2 Extensibility

The enterprise model must have the technological underpinnings that support the major platforms and can easily expand capabilities to include more powerful versions as they become available. And, while it is critical to include legacy data into the enterprise model, it is also essential to have a way to add data from systems that are no longer in the mainstream. A developer's toolkit that provides the data distribution rules to which special legacy data structures can be mapped is essential. This aligns with the extensibility of an architecture by not limiting support to a few chosen databases.

8.4.3 Scalability

Departments and branch sites in an enterprise need to have options of selecting the method by which data is distributed to others. An enterprise model relies on a control point to manage all processes and provides the framework from which multiple distribution methods can be supported and executed. This framework maintains a consistent method by which data is registered, mapped, routed, and distributed in the environment, regardless of the distribution method selected.

8.4.4 Interoperability

In a data distribution architecture, interoperability is the capability that enables different DBMS applications and platforms to coexist and be recognized by the enterprise model. It is also the capability that gives users the choice of the transport mechanism best suited for their data structures. Departments and sites can select any distribution method, knowing that once the data rules have been mapped, all distribution methods use the same rules and the same tools to perform operations.

8.4.5 Shared Data Access

In some cases, we want transactions to be able to write data for others to see, before committing. We could have some form of pre-commit, but a better solution probably is to have some form of data explicitly shared between ongoing transactions.

A simple way to implement a form of shared data is to start an auxiliary transaction specifically for storing these shared data. Any access to the shared data can be done by connecting to this *sharing* transaction, accessing the data with normal reads or writes, and then disconnecting again.

Since only one client at a time may be connected to any transaction, we automatically get the required access control. We will have an envelope around access to the shared data, and the sharing transaction thus works as a kind of semaphore.

The sharing transaction could be at the same hierarchical level as the transactions that want to share, assuming they are siblings. Another alternative is to let it be parent transaction of all of them, so that commits are propagated into it. The latter may require an extra level in the hierarchy, as we do not want to use the real parent transaction for this purpose. Of course, the sharing transaction might also be totally separated, or there might even be more than one, with the shared data distributed among them.

One potential problem involves which ambition to use when a transaction updates the shared data: its *local ambition* or that of the parent. Writing with the local transaction can be achieved by starting a subtransaction of the sharing transaction and then committing that when the work is done.

We must also consider alternatives to where sharing is defined. We have at least these possibilities:

☞ Individual objects may be defined as shared objects. A decision may have to be made about where they reside, unless they are to be globally shared.

☞ We may have special shared types, for which all instances are automatically shared.

☞ The sharing may be context-dependent. Each transaction, or set of cooperating transactions, defines locally which objects to share and where they shall reside.

8.4.6 Updating Shared Data

Consider the case in which many processors are spinning on a data element and a processor writes that data. With a write invalidate protocol, when the processor modifies the data all the shared copies of the data are invalidated.

Hence, data accessed in this fashion involves both a large latency to make the modification and contention at the memory module when the spinning processors obtain a new copy. With this control, software can temporarily bypass the hardware coherence, modifying shared data and multicasting it to the affected network caches without first invalidating the shared copies. In particular, the system software interacts with the hardware to:

☞ Obtain the routing mask of network caches at stations caching the data.

☞ Lock the cache line to ensure that additional stations are not granted access to it.

☞ Modify the state of the cache line in the secondary cache to dirty.

☞ Modify the contents of the cache line in the secondary cache.

☞ Multicast the cache lines using the routing mask obtained earlier. When the updates arrive at a network cache, the network cache invalidates any copies in local secondary caches. When the update arrives at memory, the cache line is unlocked.

8.5 REPLICATION

The traditional way to move data to decentralized sites is through scripts written to read the centralized database, select a subset of the data, extract the data, move the data extract(s) to the decentralized system, and merge the data into the decentralized database. These processes were often scheduled to run without human intervention during off hours.

The early to mid-1980s were when differences between distributed requests and transactions and their remote counterparts were discovered. Client/server platforms with database gateways were positioned to resolve these differences and to provide more users with access to corporate information. While client/server platforms served more users and minimized the performance problems inherent in distributed computing, they created another problem—maintaining data consistency in a decentralized heterogeneous database environment.

The replication of data introduces a new set of data movement technologies. Data replication detects a change made to data, captures the data component that changes, and applies the data change on other databases to synchronize the enterprisewide data. Data replication eliminates writing SQL scripts to move data and enables users to schedule when processes should begin.

8.5.1 Enterprise Information Sharing

As more organizations rely on data replication to ensure that users have information that is accurate and timely, management of the data-movement processes becomes a key issue. Data replication must be designed within the framework for an enterprise information-sharing system that distributes, manages, and maintains data across the enterprise. This infrastructure provides a scalable, manageable, and maintainable approach to distributing information through the enterprise.

8.5.2 Applications of Replication

All transactions committed against one database can be instantaneously replicated onto one or more databases, including those off-site. This functionality can be achieved without any changes to the applications. It is also possible to have two databases constantly mirroring each other so that either can replace both upon failure.

8.5.3 Load Balancing

If an application requires real-time response (as in an event-logging application), one database can take care of all data acquisition. A replicated copy can be used to handle all query load without slowing or locking data on the data acquisition server. A lock-free historical read feature is also useful for these applications.

8.5.4 Message Delivery

Since a transaction can have a circulation list, committing a replicated transaction can be considered to be sending a logged message with guaranteed delivery to the replicating server or servers.

8.5.5 Transactions

Each transaction is associated with the server where it is committed and is tagged with an account and an optional circulation list. This information goes into the committing server's log and is transmitted to interested servers immediately or it can be replayed later from the log.

In order to receive replication feed, a server subscribes to the account of a particular server. The subscriber receives those transactions that are tagged with the subscribed account unless the transaction's circulation list further excludes the subscriber. The mechanism of accounts and circulation lists allows the application to control what data is sent where.

Transactions within a given account of a given server are sequentially numbered, allowing synchronization of the original and replicated copies. The account is associated with a transaction for purposes of replication control only, and it does not affect storage of data inside the server.

Different accounts might be kept in separate logs. This allows keeping a trail of logs of varying length for different transactions. For instance, there might be a lifetime log of configuration information while the log of other database transactions might be only a week long.

The replication server is a separate process that accepts log entries from its master database and rebroadcasts them to subscribing replicators. When a process comes up, it automatically connects to all its replication sources. It automatically synchronizes with the relevant replication feed from each source. It is possible to determine which transactions have been missed by a node that has been down by comparing the transaction numbers on the source and replication accounts.

Replication can take place under application control. Special SQL statements allow explicitly disconnecting and synchronizing given accounts from given servers. Each server has system tables specifying which accounts of which servers it replicates, so that replication can be configured using SQL.

8.5.6 Applications of Replication

Data replication can be beneficial at every level of computing, but today it is primarily used in mission-critical applications. Larger and more distributed computing environments, particularly organizations processing high-volume transaction loads, can leverage data replication for a variety of benefits. Having a reliable data replication function is imperative to ensure accurate results and offer IT managers solutions that provide:

☞ *Reliable load balancing*: Faced with ever-rising volumes of daily transactions and stored data and called upon to serve growing user communities at far-flung sites in increasingly complex distributed environments, IT managers rely on load-balanced databases replicated to multiple hardware platforms.

In an organization with numerous locations (a hotel chain booking rooms at a central reservation system and at each hotel simultaneously, for example), sales managers must have a comprehensive inventory count at the central location and site-specific information at each off-site location.

The need to push selected data updates to remote sites and from those sites back to the central database requires the creation of a complex bidirectional system of data replication and distribution. In single-direction applications, such as a server-centric dissemination of pricing updates from a retail headquarters to remote store sites, read-only data is replicated and pushed from the central database to the appropriate remote locations. Efficient load balancing is a key component in any distributed network.

☞ *High availability*: By maintaining duplicated data on distributed databases, IT managers also protect the availability of critical enterprise information, even in the event of network failures. Strategies such as asynchronous hot standby servers and other robust mechanisms can be applied to ensure that all databases in a distributed network are secure, synchronized, and operational.

☞ *Centralized maintenance*: In many common data distribution situations, such as the dissemination of pricing changes or updates to a tax table, a revision generated at a central site must be duplicated and forwarded to numerous remote locations. To minimize the demands on personnel and system resources, IT managers need replication technologies capable of automatically propagating and delivering these routine, but important, data updates.

☞ *Ease of configuration*: Managers want replication solutions that can be quickly and easily configured and managed.

To gain these important benefits, DBMS vendors have developed successive generations of increasingly sophisticated and capable data replication technologies. It is worthwhile to analyze the relative advantages and limitations of the three most commonly used replication models.

8.5.6.1 Application-Based Model   Under the old sort/merge/forward method of data replication, IT departments were forced to devote enormous volumes of both human and system resources to the never-ending task of keeping multiple databases in sync. But with the proliferation of users, data, and sites, the costs and risks of this antiquated technique forced the development of more efficient replication strategies.

One of the first alternative systems to be developed was application-based replication, in which all replication logic was incorporated in application utility libraries. These utilities instructed the application to run predetermined library routines, which would apply the updates to the engine for placement in a queue, and the queue then would follow programmed instructions to populate the remote sites. Similar application-based techniques were used at each remote site to replicate and push information from the site to the central database.

Application-based replication delivers decent speed and exceptional code-driven configuration flexibility, but because it originates with the application, it imposes costly burdens on all future database development.

Every application that affects the database must be written to account for this same replication logic, and any deviation results in a serious loss of synchronization. In all but standalone or read-only applications, application-based methods are now quickly being replaced by more efficient and capable replication technologies.

8.5.6.2 Trigger-Based Model

In a trigger-based replication system, modifications to the data activate triggering mechanisms embedded within the database itself. These triggers activate replication-specific code which then performs the replication process. Trigger-based replication is far more manageable than application-based systems, because triggers are independent of the application code and can be created and tied to any database insert, update, delete, or select operation.

Because trigger-based replication evolved from generic database triggers and because this capture process occurs simultaneously within the same unit of work as the user transaction, trigger-based techniques are hindered by a number of performance- and administration-related shortcomings. Because many DBMS vendors do not release their internal log formats, trigger-based replication allows third-party vendors to provide heterogeneous replication solutions.

8.5.6.3 Log-Based Model

The most recent and by far the most sophisticated information duplication strategy is known as log-based, or engine-based, data replication. In this innovative model, all replication functionality is incorporated directly into the database engine. Log-based systems operate as part of the normal database logging process and, therefore, place very little additional overhead on the system. By utilizing the existing transaction log as a natural location to capture changes to the source data, those modifications can be detected and propagated efficiently and automatically.

After a rigorous evaluation of trigger-based and existing log-based strategies, Informix developed a continuous data replication system built on a log-based transaction capture and distribution mechanism incorporated as a direct function of the database engine. By integrating replication with the DBMS, this powerful new system delivers fast, flexible, and highly manageable replication performance.

8.6 TRANSACTIONS

Replicated servers are wrapped up in *metaservers*, so that the replication is transparent. However, this leads to the need to map any transaction to the metaserver into a transaction or set of transactions to the servers within. These are called *nested transactions*. The idea is generalized in most distributed system platforms, which provides a way of creating hierarchically structured servers built out of other servers.

The idea is to get the same gain for a distributed system that hierarchical modularization gains for single programs. As a consequence, the fault/failure models must reflect the nesting of services, and some care is needed to make sure that a system built out of nested servers has at least as much fault tolerance as a monolithic one.

Handling concurrent operations without damaging the consistency of shared data is a major problem that concerns designers of database management systems. In most large-scale commercial systems, this problem is solved with well-tested concurrency control algorithms that restrict user access. These algorithms' guarantee of data consistency, however, remains unproven.

One model for proving concurrency control is known as *serializability* theory. This model can guarantee data consistency if any interleaved execution of data access gives the same results as separate serial executions, but it does not work for systems with nested transactions. A new paradigm known as *operational abstraction* attempts to extend serializability theory to handle transactions that invoke subtransactions to arbitrary levels of nesting.

The paradigm states that under suitable conditions, when the results of subtransactions can be shown as serialized, the subtransactions can be replaced in further proofs with their parent transaction. Proving this paradigm requires constructing a formal model of nested transaction systems, a rigorous definition of serializability, and a set of tools and techniques for proving the serializability of computations.

8.6.0.1 Software Process as Nested Transaction Each process encapsulated in a transaction executes as an atomic entity. A process is atomic in the sense that it has only one objective and it cannot terminate before it reaches this objective. However, the atomism is virtual in the sense that, at the opposite of traditional transactions, the execution of a transaction can exchange intermediate results with other transactions, provided these exchanges verify the protocol rules.

Corresponding to the structure of a software process, a transaction encapsulating a process that breaks down into subprocesses will invoke subtransactions, with each subtransaction encapsulating a subprocess. Thus, a process executes as a nested transaction. A transaction can transfer data between databases by means of check-out, check-in, upward-commit, and refresh activities.

8.6.0.2 Synchronization   Synchronization of concurrent operations on the same resource is ensured by a lock mechanism. A lock is characterized by an external mode and an internal mode. To simplify, we suppose here a transaction can check out an object either to read it or to write it (in mode R or W, respectively). The external mode of a lock controls synchronization of accesses between a transaction and all transactions that are not enclosed or nested (either directly or transitively) to it.

The internal mode of a lock controls synchronization of accesses between all transactions which are nested (either directly or transitively) to it. The external mode of a lock defines the maximum usage a transaction can make of an object, and the internal mode of a lock defines its current usage. The internal mode cannot override the external mode.

A transaction that wants to check out an object from a database has to establish a lock on the object. When a transaction establishes a lock on an object, the external mode of this lock becomes the internal mode of the lock in the context of the ancestor transaction that is the owner of the database from which the object is checked out. When a transaction terminates (the process it encapsulates has reached its objective), its locks are inherited by its enclosing transaction. The internal modes of these locks are released.

8.6.0.3 Conflicts and Negotiations   Rather than impose a process to wait when a read/write or write/write conflict is detected, negotiations are initiated between the users associated with the processes in conflict. The conclusion of a negotiation can be:

☞ In the case of a read/write conflict to make the object, which creates the conflict, an intermediate result of the process which writes it

☞ In the case of a write/write conflict to give a copy of the object, which creates the conflict, to each process and to define a merging procedure to merge the modifications of the two processes when they terminate

8.6.1 Failures

There are three classes of failure in a distributed transaction system:

☞ The transaction service, including the communications channel, can fail.

☞ The client can fail.

☞ The stable storage can fail. Stable storage refers to storage, such as on disk or tape that persists after a power outage. While the storage medium may suffer such failures as physical damage, these are normally much more rare than a power loss.

If the client fails, it will be either during the transaction or after commitment. In the first case, the service simply undoes the transaction. If the transaction service fails, the client and server can wait for recovery and retry, or independently assume failure, and wait to issue aborts/undoes. If the stable storage fails, more reliable hardware is needed.

8.7 FAULT-TOLERANT NETWORKING

Rock climbing and building fault-tolerant systems have a lot in common. All the gear in the world does not make a mountaineer safe. All the hardware and software you can buy will not make your systems and data free from downtime.

When you climb hills, your life is constantly at stake until you are back down. The minute you lose sight of that fact, all the ropes, chocks, harnesses, and training are worthless. It is similar with networked systems. If you do not respect the data flowing through the net and your servers as if every transaction represents your life, your designs, implementations, and procedures will ultimately be ineffective.

The designer of a fault-tolerant system must guide management and users through the selection, purchase, and implementation of a fault-tolerant network.

8.7.1 Basic Concepts

Distinguishing fault tolerance from fault resilience can be tricky. As with performance claims, vendors have a way of misleading buyers. Fault tolerance is the stronger term, indicating that every component in the chain supporting the system has redundant features or is duplicated.

Fault tolerance means the system will not fail because any one component fails. The system also should provide recovery from multiple failures. Components are often overengineered or purposely underutilized to ensure that while performance may be affected during an outage the system will perform within predictable, acceptable bounds.

While fault-tolerant LANs are impossible without fault-resilient components, a system cannot truly be fault tolerant if there is no way to re-establish it in the event of disaster. You need a disaster-recovery, or business-resumption, plan to address the types of outages in your environment. It should specify a step-by-step plan for each IT group. It should address the fault-tolerant capabilities of specific sites or subsystems and include test rehearsals of mock disasters and recoveries on a regular basis.

8.7.2 Management Involvement

Prior to decision-making time, it is necessary to lay out alternative designs and component selections in order to educate management.

Management will usually jump right to the bottom line when presented with alternatives, so considerable skill is required to present information that combines graduated cost with graduated design complexity and graduated exposure to failure.

Any plan for network fault resilience should be a part of an organization's disaster recovery plan. Management should state its goals for all operations, staff, and systems. At a minimum, management should set expectations for costs of outages; escalating penalties for length of outages; and the hierarchy of importance of different activities, from key operations to support functions (e.g., the assembly line versus human resources).

Because managers often find it difficult to devote adequate time to understanding issues that do not contribute directly to the bottom line it is important to underscore the cost of downtime.

It is not worth rushing headlong into designing a fault-tolerant network unless all parties agree on the implications that downtime has for the operation. Assuming there is a consensus on the real cost of downtime, the designer can begin to craft a plan of action.

8.7.2.1 Service-Level Agreement That plan should start with a service-level agreement, which is simply a contract between the corporation and the IT department formalizing the relationship on a customer-supplier basis.

At the outset, note that fault tolerance is not simply a response to failure. It involves an ongoing cycle of planning, design, daily monitoring, long-term trends, and regular reevaluation. All assumptions and forecasts should be included as part of the plan and updated as necessary.

If this sounds like a lot of effort, it is. But the IT business is about excellence in customer service—the only real difference between you and the competition. It makes sense to apply a certain amount of rigor to the process. Organizational determination is essential to providing fault tolerance. The responsibility for avoiding failures, recovering from them, and providing backup and restoration falls entirely on IT's shoulders. No vendor can relieve you of this responsibility.

Measurement of progress against the plan should not be cast in terms of how long a particular switch or server has been up. Tracking individual components and subsystems is obviously important, but it cannot be reflected in terms of customer service. Rather, progress should reflect the ability of the system to meet the users' expectations as documented in the service-level agreement.

8.7.2.2 Conforming to the Service-Level Agreement The first step in ensuring the long-term quality of the effort is to determine which statistics will be tracked. A plan to track conformance to the service-level agreement should include:

☞ Recommended methods and tools

☞ Change control

☞ Configuration management

☞ Daily and long-term statistics

☞ Documentation plan

Be practical about how much data to store in your statistics database. A summary of statistics, if done with foresight, may be sufficient. Plan on keeping it to a reasonable size. Break it into sections that can be managed independently by different groups.

8.7.2.3 Scope Unfortunately, there is no way to limit scope. Disasters can occur anywhere in the network, at any level in the ISO communications model—from physical layer to presentation. It can be useful, even necessary, however, to separate the problem solving into logical groups. For example, most corporate IT staff are divided into something like the following support groups:

☞ Workstation

☞ Network

☞ Server

☞ Database

☞ Development, both client and server

In addition planning and operations functions are shared across all groups.

In the following sections we will address the issues and responsibilities regarding fault tolerance as they apply to those groups. Emphasis will be placed on network considerations.

8.7.3 Design Strategy

The principles that guide the design of practical fault-tolerant networks are simply put:

☞ Design and implement all important components in a fully redundant fashion with the capacity to continue processing in the event of failure.

☞ Use fault-resilient components to minimize component failure.

☞ Deploy network nodes in a matrix topology with robust recovery. Do not depend on a single point of failure link.

☞ Insist on industry standards for all components in order to ensure protection of investment and interoperability.

☞ Instrument all components so they can be managed.

8.7.3.1 Client Workstations   Who cares if one client crashes? The workstation support staff bears the brunt of the calls from these users. Too often, these problems are ignored by the rest of the support team. If the network, servers, and databases are all up, workstation outages may be ignored. Numerically, though, these outages are by far the most frequent. They are insidious because they are distant from the support staff, hard to debug, and difficult to track. The client desktop also has a way of aging and altering itself over time. Unless rigor and control are applied, the number of desktop outages is always on the increase.

8.7.3.2 Statistics—from the Client's Viewpoint   On one project several years ago, a study was commenced to develop a communications gateway for a Hotel Property Management System that resided at the end of a low-speed leased line in each hotel. The remote gateway was central to all transactions that happened at the site. Uptime and response time were imperative. Therefore, it was decided to add code to the gateway that recorded response time, all reboots, and any line or protocol errors.

All of these were collected and reported to examine statistics on a daily basis, deal effectively with trouble calls, document actual versus planned uptime, and engage in general problem solving. The key point here is that all of the uptime and performance statistics were recorded from the client's point of view.

8.7.3.3 Gain Control of the Desktop   Most client failures are software related. This is not the time to take a free-market attitude about the software that users install. If uptime is an issue, the responsibility for desktops should be centralized. This is not to say that IT is a dictator about approved for-purchase lists, but IT should establish burn-in and certification processes. Burn-in processes are the physical testing procedures each piece of software should be put through before it is supported on the network. A burn-in process ensures that there will be no negative impact from adding the software.

Certification process is an organizational procedure for determining which software will be allowed on the network. A certification process should include:

☞ Classification of supported desktops, each with its own capacity, performance, and redundancy characteristics. For example:

  ✗ Power User
  ✗ Executive workstation
  ✗ Secretarial
  ✗ Analyst
  ✗ Clerical

☞ Establishment of a support matrix for the given classes of desktop. As an example, the analyst workstations may support:

✗ OS version W

✗ Spreadsheet X

✗ Word processor Y

✗ In-house developed applications A, B, and C

✗ Third-party vertical applications D, E, and F

✗ Middleware and drivers

✗ Set of network interface cards

Once desktops have been classified and a matrix of supported software established, we can move to the burn-in stage. For every mission-critical application certified for use on any client, the development and quality assurance teams should develop a regression test script (a manual or automated process to exercise the software and record the results). This can be as simple as a set of instructions to follow as transactions are entered against a test database. More significant applications will require the use of scripting software.

Fault tolerance is impossible without full control over the upgrades made to the system and its components. The certification and burn-in of any component, hardware or software, should include the changes to design, development and testing, integration, and final installation.

Ideally, the same configuration rules and processes should apply during development and production to all the different units in the company dealing with the software. For example, the reports and data generated by the developers should be available to the testing team, and they should be in the same formats. Everybody involved should have access to and be able to understand the regression test scripts, the version control tools, the project management software performance statistics, etc. This provides clear traceability and coherence of all documentation and hardware and software components.

Understanding and control over the certification process should be clearly mentioned in the service-level agreement.

8.7.3.4 Preventive Measures Here are two specific steps for eliminating client outages. These provide essentially the same level of redundancy usually reserved for servers. They can be enormously expensive to install and maintain, but if the stakes are high, both should be considered.

1. Use an uninterruptable power supply for client machines. Contact an engineer to discuss providing conditioned and backed-up power services to all workstations. In critical areas, such as hospital medical equipment, this is already done.

2. Install dual network interface cards (NICs) in each workstation. Make sure that each NIC is connected to a separate LAN segment. The installation process for this varies depending on operating system. Ensure that the client can simultaneously communicate on both segments. In the case of a LAN failure, the client can communicate on the remaining NIC.

(This does little good, however, if the process for determining failure causes the machine to crash or forces the user to re-logon or re-boot.)

Finally, do not overlook the obvious. Have spares available to replace blown monitors, systems, and keyboards. All critical peripherals should be networked devices under central control. (For example, if a modem for dial-out is critical for a given job function, place it on the network and physically locate it in the computer room where the fault-tolerant LAN and redundant local exchange carrier's service people can get at it.) Get a real backup scheme. Forget about diskettes. Investigate backup software systems, make a selection, make the backup network based, use off-site storage and backup, and then test it all. And make sure that all users know their responsibilities, whether that means not introducing uncertified software or not storing their data outside the backup scheme.

8.7.4 Adaptive and Fault-Tolerant Routing Algorithms

In highly parallel machines, a collection of computing nodes works in concert to solve large application problems. The nodes communicate data and coordinate their efforts by sending and receiving messages through a routing network. Consequently, the achieved performance of such machines depends critically on that of their routing networks.

Most multicomputers use deterministic routing because of its simplicity. Such deterministic routing algorithms do not make effective use of the network's physical channels because they assign only a single path to each source and destination. If those channels are congested, the traffic between that source and destination is delayed, despite the presence of uncongested alternative paths.

Adaptive routing allows paths to be chosen dynamically, using network status information. Thus it offers the potential for making better use of network resources. However, though adaptive routing increases routing freedom, potentially improving performance, it also increases the cost of preventing deadlock. This cost can reduce network clock speed, overwhelming the benefits of adaptive routing. Two independent algorithms—compressionless routing and planar-adaptive routing—have been developed. Both of these are deadlock-free at minimal overheads.

8.7.4.1 Compressionless Routing
Compressionless Routing (CR) is an adaptive routing framework that supports both adaptive and fault-tolerant routing while eliminating much of the software overhead for buffer management and retransmission. It uses fine-grained flow control and the back pressure of wormhole routing to communicate routing status and error conditions to network interfaces. The network interface uses the information to detect potential deadlock situations and network faults and avoid or recover from them, eliminating the need for costly network protocol layers.

The advantages of CR include deadlock-free adaptive routing with no virtual channels (any topology), simple router implementations, end-to-end flow control in hardware, and order-preserving message transmission. Fault-tolerant CR (FCR) extends CR, providing end-to-end fault-tolerant delivery with the following advantages:

☞ Tolerance of transient faults while maintaining data integrity (nonstop fault tolerance)

☞ Tolerance of permanent faults and applicability to a wide variety of network topologies

☞ Elimination of software buffering for reliability

8.7.4.2 Planar-Adaptive Routing Planar-adaptive routing (PAR) combines elements of dimension-order and adaptive routing to produce a network with limited adaptivity. Carefully structuring routing freedom dramatically reduces the requirements for deadlock prevention. Planar-adaptive networks are deadlock-free for networks with only two virtual channels for each physical channel. In addition, planar-adaptive routing can be extended to support in-order packet delivery and adaptive, unordered packet delivery simultaneously. The designated in-order traffic is delivered in sequence, while the other packets arrive in unspecified order.

8.8 CONCURRENCY CONTROL

In order for multiple transactions to operate concurrently on a shared database, a protocol must be adopted to coordinate their activities. Such a protocol—called a concurrency control algorithm—aims at ensuring a consistent state of the database system, while allowing the maximum possible concurrency among transactions.

Traditional concurrency control algorithms can be broadly classified as either pessimistic or optimistic. Pessimistic concurrency control (PCC) algorithms avoid any concurrent execution of transactions as soon as conflicts that might result in future inconsistencies are detected. On the contrary, optimistic concurrency control (OCC) algorithms allow such transactions to proceed at the risk of having to restart them in case these suspected inconsistencies materialize.

For conventional database management systems with limited resources, performance studies of concurrency control methods have concluded that PCC locking protocols perform better than OCC techniques. The main reason for this good performance is that PCC's blocking-based conflict-resolution policy results in resource conservation, whereas OCC with its restart-based conflict-resolution policy wastes more resources. For Real-Time DataBase Systems (RTDBS), where transactions execute under strict timing constraints, maximum concurrency (or throughput) ceases to be an expressive measure of performance. Rather, the number of transactions completed before their set deadlines becomes the decisive performance measure. Most real-time concurrency control schemes are based on two-phase locking (2PL), which is a PCC strategy.

Despite its widespread use in commercial systems, 2PL has some properties—such as the possibility of deadlocks and long and unpredictable blocking times—that reduce its appeal for real-time environments in which the primary performance criterion is meeting time constraints and not just preserving consistency requirements. A recent evaluation of the behavior of both PCC and OCC schemes in a real-time environment concluded that for a RTDBS with firm deadlines (where late transactions are immediately discarded) OCC outperforms PCC, especially when resource contention is low.

However, a disadvantage of OCC is that when a conflict is detected, the transaction being validated is always the one to be aborted, without respect to transactions' priorities or deadlines. An even more serious problem of classical OCC is that transaction conflicts are not detected until the validation phase, when it may be too late to restart. PCC 2PL algorithms do not suffer from this problem because they detect potential conflicts as they occur. They suffer, however, from the possibility of unnecessarily missing deadlines as a result of unbounded waiting caused by blocking.

8.8.1 Transaction Concurrency Control

The concurrency of transactions executing on atomic data types can be enhanced through the use of semantic information about operations defined on these types. Commutativity of operations has been exploited to provide enhanced concurrency while avoiding cascading aborts. A property known as recoverability can be used to decrease the delay involved in processing non-commuting operations while still avoiding cascading aborts.

When an invoked operation is recoverable with respect to an uncommitted operation, the invoked operation can be executed by forcing a commit dependency between the invoked operation and the uncommitted operation. The transaction invoking the operation will not have to wait for the uncommitted operation to abort or commit. Further, this commit dependency only affects the order in which the operations should commit. If both commit and either operation aborts, the other can still commit, thus avoiding cascading aborts.

To ensure the serializability of transactions, the recoverability relationship must be acyclic. Simulation studies indicate that using recoverability, the turnaround time of transactions can be reduced. Concurrency is enhanced even when resource constraints are taken into consideration. The magnitude of enhancement is dependent on the resource contention: The lower the resource contention, the higher the improvement.

In general, the improvement in transaction throughput is dependent on transaction loads and the commutativity and recoverability properties of operations on shared objects. As an extension to this work, the notion of recoverability is used in multilevel concurrency control protocols for complex information systems.

The problems of real-time system scheduling involve not only guaranteeing schedulability but also ensuring that shared data will not be corrupted. Maintaining shared data consistency has long been studied in database systems. The versioning technique of concurrency control can be implemented with simple and predictable low-overhead algorithms and data structures.

In a memory management system, two different locks can be acquired for each physically addressable unit. One of these locks is maintained by the physically addressable unit (i.e., the physically addressable unit has a locked attribute). The other lock is maintained by a lock manager, which is a part of the original memory object cache that the physically addressable unit is allocated to. These locks introduce several concurrency control problems. They are inefficient because two locks are required. They are also complicated because the programmers of the virtual memory management system must be careful to avoid deadlocks. In addition, the original memory objects did not have concurrency control to ensure integrity and consistency in a multiprocessing environment.

The revised virtual memory management system addresses these concurrency control problems. It requires each memory object to have a lock manager. A revised memory object cache no longer has its own lock manager; it uses the lock manager of its memory object. Shared between a memory object and its memory object cache, a single lock manager allows the two objects to cooperate better with each other to maintain mutual consistency. Good cooperation is essential since a method in one of these objects frequently will need to invoke methods in the other to accomplish its task. For example, a memory object cache servicing a page fault may need to read data from its memory object.

The original lock associated with each physically addressable unit has also been removed. The purpose of this lock was to prevent a physically addressable unit from being selected for replacement. In the revised virtual memory management system, this lock is no longer required. Once a physically addressable unit is allocated to a memory object cache, the physically addressable unit belongs to the memory object cache. Hence, the memory object cache controls whether the physically addressable unit is eligible for replacement.

The single lock manager in the revised virtual memory management system significantly reduces the complexity of programming the system to eliminate deadlocks and concurrency control problems.

8.8.2 I/O Methods

The original MemoryObject class has two I/O methods: The read and write methods. These methods read and write to the memory object directly. With the integration of file system caching, these methods are no longer sufficient. At least two sets of I/O methods are required. The first set of I/O methods does I/O directly from and to memory objects like the original read and write methods.

In the revised virtual memory management system, the original read and write methods of the MemoryObject class have been renamed rawRead and rawWrite. The rawRead and rawWrite methods do I/O directly from and to memory objects, and then, new read and write methods are defined. If a memory object is cached, these methods invoke the cacheRead and cacheWrite methods of the memory object's memory object cache. If a memory object is not cached, these methods invoke the memory object's rawRead and rawWrite methods.

8.8.3 Distributed File System Architecture

Each host has a single host memory manager. The host memory manager manages the allocation of main memory on the host. It distributes cache memory to each cached file on the host. The memory allocated to each file is managed by the file's file cache. In other words, the host memory manager distributes available cache memory to the file caches.

When the host is about to run out of memory, the host memory manager will ask some or all of the file caches to return some of the memory allocated to them. Different hosts can have different host memory managers implementing different main memory allocation policies. These policies determine how main memory is distributed to the various file caches on the host. One possible policy is to allocate memory to each file cache in proportion to the frequency of new memory allocation requests from the file cache.

Another possible policy is to allocate equal amount of memory to each file cache on the host. Each cached file on a host has a file cache. The file cache has attributes and contains modules that determine how data from the file is cached in main memory, the transfer policy used to move data in and out of main memory, and the cache replacement policy. The cache unit size is an attribute of the file cache. It is equivalent to the block size in other distributed file systems. Data transfers take place in sizes that are multiples of the cache unit size. A large cache unit size forces large transfers.

The cache memory manager manages memory that has been allocated by the host memory manager to the file cache. If necessary, it interacts with the host memory manager to obtain more memory for the cache and to return allocated memory to the host memory manager. It allocates and frees memory in multiples of the cache unit size. In addition, the cache memory manager keeps track of which part of the file is cached and where it is cached in main memory.

The migration policy module defines the cache replacement and transfer policies. The transfer policy determines when and how data from the file is transferred in and out of the file cache. Prefetch strategies are a part of the transfer policy. Possible prefetch strategies include fetch on-demand, prefetch next unit, and prefetch all on initial access. Write strategies, such as write-through, delayed-write, and write-on-close, are also a part of the transfer policy. Different migration policy modules implement differing transfer and replacement policies. For example, a migration policy module optimized for large sequential file accesses might implement the MRU cache replacement policy and the prefetch next unit strategy.

Although each file cache has its own migration policy module, global cache replacement policies can be supported because multiple migration policy modules can collaborate to define a global policy. For example, a global LRU cache replacement policy can be implemented by attaching the same type of migration policy modules to all file caches on the host.

These modules cooperate to determine which unit is the least recently used unit in their file caches. The optional secondary cache allows data from a file to be cached in tertiary storage on behalf of the file cache. It allows a tertiary storage system to act like a backing store for the file cache.

Different types of secondary caches support different types of tertiary storage systems. Multiple secondary caches may be stacked to mirror the memory hierarchy of the host. The secondary cache allows the file system caching service to exploit the memory hierarchy of a host. A file cache only has to attach the appropriate secondary caches to itself to use the available tertiary storage systems on the host for caching. A good implementation of the architecture should allow secondary caches to be attached or detached at any time. For efficiency, it also should allow the file cache to page data directly from the file into main memory without copying the data into the secondary caches first.

As an example of how this architecture is extended to work in a distributed system, a client invokes the server to open a file residing on a CD-ROM in the server. First, the server opens the file by creating an in-memory representative for the file. Then, the server attaches a file cache to the file. The file cache allows data from the file to be cached in main memory. In addition, the server attaches a secondary cache to the file cache.

This particular secondary cache allows the server to cache the file's data in a disk that is faster than the CD-ROM. This capability enables faster subsequent client access to the contents of the CD-ROM resident file. The secondary cache is optional and is used primarily to improve performance.

The migration policy module of the file cache on the server determines how the file's data is transferred from the CD-ROM into the server's main memory and into the disk cache. One such module might copy the entire file into the disk cache on initial access. A different migration policy module might bypass the disk cache and page data directly into the server's memory on demand. It will write to the disk cache only when it has to page data out to free memory. After the server has opened the file successfully, it sends a reply message containing a token that represents the file to the client.

When the client receives the reply from the server, it encapsulates the returned token in the remote file, which represents the CD-ROM resident file on the client. Then, the client attaches a file cache to the remote file so that it can cache remote file data in its main memory. The client also attaches a secondary cache to the file cache. This particular secondary cache allows the client to cache remote file data in a local disk, which increases the amount of memory on the client that can be used to cache data from remote files.

The client file cache's migration policy module determines how data from the remote file is transferred from the server into the client's main memory and into the client's disk cache.

This architecture is flexible because each file can have a different caching strategy. In addition, the caching strategy used on the server need not be the same as the caching strategy used on the client. It is customizable because the application and the distributed operating system can mix and match components and modules of different types to define caching strategies that best suit the needs of the distributed computing environment. It is also extensible: New components that implement new policies can be added easily. It can exploit host, network, and application file access characteristics with customized caching strategies. For example, the architecture can address network latency problems with large cache unit sizes, client disk caching, and suitable prefetch strategies.

8.8.4 Strategies

The first strategy is to permit remote access to the methods of a persistent object. It allows a remote client to invoke the methods of a persistent object using an RPC-like scheme. For example, a remote client can invoke the add and remove methods of a memory object dictionary on a server to manipulate the dictionary. This strategy has a straightforward implementation—a proxy object is used on each client to represent a persistent object.

Major advantages of this strategy are that it preserves the exact semantics of the Choices file and does not require additional concurrency control support from the distributed file system. A disadvantage is that network latency, parameter marshaling, and server contention can make it inefficient. The server on which a persistent object resides may become a bottleneck since the server is required to handle every method invocation. This strategy also does not permit client caching.

The second strategy is to permit remote access to the persistent storage of a Choices file. This is also accomplished through the use of proxy objects. In this case, a proxy object, known as a remote memory object, is used on each client to represent a persistent memory object. A client can access the persistent storage of a persistent memory object by invoking the I/O methods of the remote memory object.

Alternatively, it can memory-map the remote memory object and access the persistent storage using memory reads and writes. A remote memory object is just like any other memory object. It can be cached by attaching a memory object cache to itself. This allows a client to cache data from a persistent memory object that resides on a remote server. In other words, client caching of a file is activated by attaching a memory object cache to a remote memory object.

The main advantage of this second strategy is that it permits client caching. However, the second strategy also introduces additional cache coherence and concurrency control problems when a file is cached by more than one client. There are many ways to address these problems.

8.9 CONCLUSIONS

Distributed database capabilities are a necessity rather than a luxury. The continued growth of smaller local systems means more data locations and a greater need for users to access data from multiple varying systems. Corporate growth, acquisitions, and reorganizations require businesses to adapt without losing existing processes and functionality.

Distributed Shared Memory

9.1 INTRODUCTION

Distributed computing environments comprising networked heterogeneous workstations are becoming the standard configuration in both engineering and scientific environments. However, the lack of a unifying parallel computing model means that the current parallel applications are nonportable.

Shared memory is an attractive programming model for designing parallel and distributed applications. In the past decade, a popular research topic has been the design of systems to provide the shared memory abstraction on physically distributed memory machines. This abstraction is commonly known as Distributed Shared Memory (DSM). DSM has been implemented both in software, to provide the shared memory programming model on networks of workstations, and in hardware using cache consistency protocols to support shared memory across physically distributed main memories.

9.1.1 Need for DSM

DSM is a resource management component of a distributed operating system that implements the shared memory model in distributed systems, which have no physically shared memory. The shared memory model (as shown in Figure 9.1) provides a virtual address space that is shared among all computers in a distributed system.

In DSM, data is accessed from a shared address space similar to the way that virtual memory is accessed. Data moves between secondary and main memory, and between the distributed main memories of different nodes. Ownership of pages in memory starts out in some predefined state but changes

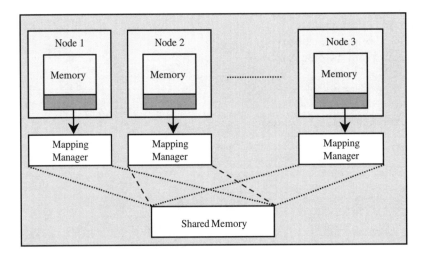

Fig. 9.1 Shared Memory Model

during the course of normal operation. Ownership changes take place when data moves from one node to another due to an access by a particular process.

9.1.2 Advantages of DSM

Some of the advantages of DSM include:

☞ Allowing operating systems to hide data movement and provide a simpler abstraction for sharing data. Programmers do not need to worry about memory transfers between machines, especially when using the message-passing model.

☞ Allowing the passing of complex structures by reference, simplifying algorithm development for distributed applications.

☞ Taking advantage of moving the entire page containing the data referenced rather than just the piece of data.

☞ Costing less to build than multiprocessor systems. DSM can be implemented using normal hardware and do not require anything complex to connect the shared memory to the processors.

☞ Allowing larger memory sizes to be available to programs by combining all physical memory of all nodes. This large memory will not incur disk latency due to swapping as it would in traditional distributed systems.

☞ Permitting an unlimited number of nodes to be used unlike multiprocessor systems, in which main memory is accessed via a common bus, thus limiting the size of the multiprocessor system.

Two ways nodes can be informed of who owns what page are:

1. *Invalidation* is a method that nullifies a page when a process asks for write access to that page and becomes its new owner. The next time another process tries to read or write to a copy of the page it thought it had, the page will not be available and the process will have to re-request access to that page.

2. *Broadcasting* automatically updates all copies of a memory page when a process writes to it. This is also called *write-update*. This method is a lot less efficient and more difficult to implement than invalidation because a new value has to be sent instead of an invalidation message.

9.1.3 Purpose of DSM

Shared memory machines are composed of a set of processors accessing a single memory. The main advantage of these machines lies in their easy programming because there are no communications between processors. However, contentions and collisions prevent applications from being scalable and most shared memory machines are limited to a small number of processors.

Distributed memory systems, on the contrary, can integrate a large number of processors. The communication mode normally used is message-passing, which allows important speedup. However its programming remains difficult since end users have to take into charge all communication operations.

In this context, by allowing the programmer to share memory objects without being in charge of their management, DSMs provide a trade-off between the easy programming of shared memory machines and the efficiency and scalability of distributed memory systems.

A DSM is a mechanism allowing end users to access shared data without taking into charge interprocess communications. In other words, the goal of a DSM system is to make interprocess communications transparent to end users. Both hardware and software implementations have been proposed in the literature. From a programming point of view, two approaches have been proposed.

1. Shared virtual memory systems are similar to the well-known concept of paged virtual memory implemented on monoprocessor systems, where all distributed memories are virtually merged together into a single systemwide address space.

2. Distributed shared memory shares objects (i.e., variables with access functions). The user only has to define which data objects are to be shared. The management of the shared objects (creation, access, modification) can be assumed by the DSM system.

In both cases, implementing a DSM system implies addressing problems of data location, data access, sharing, and locking of data for memory coherence.

The purpose of DSM is to implement—above a distributed memory architecture—a programming model allowing a transparent manipulation of shared data. In practice, a DSM system commonly handles all the communications and maintains data coherence. Though various DSM systems have been proposed, few of them efficiently and scalably deal with massively parallel multiprocessors.

Some implementations allow processes to share distributed objects. A hierarchical organization of the processes (into groups and subgroups based on the shared data they address) permits a high degree of scalability. This organization can be defined using compilation directives or dynamically generated at runtime.

9.2 A DSM SERVER

Shared memory multiprocessors are becoming increasingly available, and with them, a faster way to program applications and system services via the use of shared memory. Currently, the major limitation in using shared memory is that it is not extensible to the network, and therefore is not suited for building distributed applications and services. Uses of a DSM facility include operating system services such as file systems and process migration, distributed databases, parallel languages (Ada or Multilisp, for example) and systems for parallel and distributed programming.

More motivation for employing a DSM facility comes from the increasing interest that hardware designers show in nonshared memory multiprocessors. Some implementations, for instance, use fiber optic links. This reduces the end-to-end time to send a 1K data packet from the tens of milliseconds range of the current Ethernet to the tens of microseconds range of the fiber. Fast communication makes DSM an appealing complement to message-passing.

The virtual memory system allows the user to create memory objects that are managed by user-defined processes or external pagers. An external pager is a process responsible for providing data in response to requests for page faults (page in) and backing storage for page cleaning (page out). This is precisely the function of the in-kernel disk pager. The only difference is that the user-specified pager task can manage the data in more creative ways than the designer of the in-kernel pager may have envisioned.

A typical server provides unrestricted sharing of read-write memory between tasks running either on the same machine or on different machines. In any case, all processors have direct access to common physical memory (architectures with Uniform Memory Access [UMA] time or Non-Uniform Memory Access [NUMA] time) and the server provides a flexible management of shared memory. In the second case, processors do not have a way to access common memory (architectures with No Remote Memory Access [NORMA]) and the server provides it in software, migrating and replicating virtual memory pages between processors as needed.

To understand the properties of a DSM facility, the performance characteristics of the server itself and of some application programs have to be evaluated. To measure the effects of different page management policies in the server, a number of algorithms are implemented and evaluated, including a new distributed algorithm that outperforms centralized ones. Some of the features of these algorithms include supporting machines with differing page sizes, heterogeneous processors, and fault tolerance.

The algorithm's service page faults on multiple machines by migrating pages that must be shared, scheduling conflicting or overlapping requests appropriately, tagging and translating memory pages across incompatible processors, and keeping a duplicate copy in case of machine crashes.

The studies with application programs can be designed under the assumption that the amount of information that is communicated in each synchronization operation is the key factor.

9.2.1 Shared Memory Within a Machine

The first goal of the server is to provide sharing of read-write memory between tasks allocated on the same machine. This overcomes the standard memory inheritance mechanism constraint that the shared memory must have been allocated by a common ancestor (e.g., Mach System), as well as a security check in the implementation of the UNIX system call that deallocates all of the task's address space.

The server provides the user with a call to create memory objects—logical pieces of memory that are identified by ports. A memory object can be used by a thread in a call to the vm_map() kernel primitive, which maps a portion of the object into the task's address space at some virtual address. Note that since a port can be transmitted only in a message, memory objects are entities protected by the kernel. Note also that access to ports can be transmitted over the network and, therefore, the vm_map() primitive allows for networked shared memory.

The thread can access the memory normally, and the kernel delegates the paging duties to the user-level memory manager (external pager) responsible for the memory object. This is done via an asynchronous message protocol between the pager and the kernel. The external pager interface allows pagers to control the management of main memory by the kernel, so that main memory effectively acts as a common cache for memory objects.

The various operations have the flavor of cache control functions. For example, when a thread first accesses a page, it takes a page fault and the kernel sends to the pager a memory_object_data_request() message to request the missing page, which is similar to a cache miss. The server provides the page in a memory_object_data_provided() message. Other messages allow a pager to request a page flush or to specify the caching and copy policies for the object.

9.2.2 An Algorithm

The shared memory server can be structured in an object-oriented fashion, so that it is possible to have memory objects with different behaviors. When a memory object is mapped by tasks on multiple machines, the pager needs to manage multiple copies of memory pages in a coherent way. The various management policies for memory objects are provided by different implementations of a common set of operations.

An implementation is called a *fault scheduler* in the following, because the goal of the module is to schedule read and write faults on different kernels in the best way, just like ordinary schedulers schedule the execution order of various threads. One of the many reasons for this choice is to allow experimentation with various algorithms and heuristics. At object creation time, a user can choose which scheduling policy will be applied to the new object, or it can rely on the default one. All the algorithms I describe maintain strict memory coherence on the objects they manage. There is no stale data because at any given time each page exists in only one version.

A simple scheduler can provide centralized memory objects of single page size. There is only one pager task for each memory object, but different objects might be allocated to different pager tasks to reduce service contention. Since this scheduler is location transparent, the location of a pager task is also transparent to the client kernels.

Ownership of a page is transferred among kernels on demand. The owner of the page is the kernel that currently has write access to the page. When no kernel has write access to a page, the scheduler itself is the owner and multiple kernels are allowed to have read-only copies of the page. The simple scheduler's algorithm is an automaton with four per-page states, which correspond to the four conditions in which a page can be:

☞ *Read*: This is the initial state. When there are no writers, there may be readers with a copy. The server has a valid copy.

☞ *Write*: When there is one writer, there are no readers and no one is queued waiting. The server does not have a valid copy.

☞ *ReadWait*: When there is one writer, some readers are waiting. The server does not have a valid copy and has asked the current owner to return the page to the server.

☞ *WriteWait*: When there is one writer, some writers are queued waiting and readers may be waiting. The server does not have a valid copy and has asked the current owner to return the page to the server.

Transitions between states are driven by the requests that are made by client kernels. In practice, not all requests make sense in all states. For instance, a kernel will not page-out a page that has not been modified. Since security issues have not been addressed directly in the server, it is assumed that other servers (for example, a name service integrated with an authentication service) will do the necessary verifications before handing a memory object port to a user. An object then might have different ports associated with it—one for read-only access and one for read-write access.

Note that it is possible to prevent a user from impersonating a kernel by having a secure server handle the object's port directly, and never allowing unsecure tasks direct access to the port. The server accepts four input message types (requests), which the scheduler handles in three procedures, for example:

☞ *read_fault()*: A kernel requests read access to a page (memory_object_data_request).

☞ *write_fault()*: A kernel requests write access to a page and either needs a fresh copy of the page (memory_object_data_request) or does not (memory_object_data_unlock).

☞ *pageout()*: A kernel flushes out the page to the server (memory_object_data_write and memory_object_lock_completed).

These three functions do all the necessary work. A pseudocode description of how they operate on a page is shown here.

Example 1

```
read_fault(page, kernel)
  switch ( page->state ) {
  case Read:
    memory_object_data_provided(kernel)
    break
  case Write:
    page->state = ReadWait
    memory_object_lock_request(page->owner,FLUSH(page), ow
    break
  default: /* just enqueue */
  }
set_add(page->readers, kernel)
```

It can be assumed that all procedures keep the page locked and that messages are processed in the order of arrival. This pseudocode will be used again later to describe the distributed algorithm. The remaining procedures are either for initialization, termination, or recovery from kernel crashes. The pseudocode indicates that writers are queued in FIFO order, while readers do not need to be ordered.

Writers take precedence over readers. Other, perhaps more complicated, policies might be needed. It is possible, for example, to introduce a simple test to prevent writers from causing starvation of readers. If we ignored fault-tolerance issues, the algorithms would differ only in a minor way (e.g., the server could dispose of a page once it is sent to a writer). This and other optimizations can be applied when the server runs without the (local) support of a permanent storage server, which is the case of a diskless workstation.

An example will help clarify the following discussion. Since all the tasks on one machine use the same copy of the memory object's pages (cached copy, possibly mapped into the various address spaces with different protections), we can pretend there is a single task per machine.

Assume that a thread makes a read access to a page. The page is not in the cache, hence the kernel sends a memory_object_data_request() message to the pager. If the page is in a Read state (the initial state), the server immediately sends the page in a memory_object_data_provided() message, with read-only protection. If the thread makes a subsequent write access, the kernel sends a memory_object_data_unlock() message to request a protection upgrade that will be granted in a memory_object_lock_request() message, unless the page has changed state in the meantime. If the page is not in a Read state, the kernel's request is queued and the current writer may be asked to page-out the page via a memory_object_lock_request() message. When the page is paged out, the page-out procedure dequeues the next write access request and satisfies it, or satisfies all read requests at once.

Example 2

```
write_fault(page, kernel)
  switch ( page->state ) {
  case Read:
```

```
                    set_remove( page->readers, kernel)
                    forall( readers )
(1)                   memory_object_lock_request( reader, FLUSH(page)
                    page->readers = empty_set
(2)                 page->state = Write
                    page->owner = kernel
                    if (needs_data)
                      memory_object_data_provided( page->owner )
                    else
                      memory_object_data_unlock( page->owner )
                    break
                  case Write:
                    memory_object_lock_request( page->owner, FLUSH(page), o
                    /* fall through */
                  case WriteWait:
                  case ReadWait:
                    page->state = WriteWait
                    enqueue( kernel, page->writers )
                  }
                  pageout (page, kernel, data)
(3)               switch( page->state ) {
                  case Read:
                    return /* never happens */
                  case Write:
                    save(data) /* true pageout */
                    page->state = Read
                    page->owner = owner_self
                    break
                  case WriteWait:
(4)               save(data)
                  page->owner = dequeue( page->writers )
                  memory_object_data_provided( page->owner)
                  if (!page->writers)
                    if (page->readers)
                      page->state = ReadWait
                    else
                      page->state = Write
                  if (page->readers || page->writers) {
                  deschedule_myself()
                  memory_object_lock_request( page->owner, FLUSH(
(5)               }
                    break;
                  case ReadWait:
                    save(data)
                    forall(readers)
                      memory_object_data_provided(reader)
                    page->state = Read
(6)                 page->owner = owner_self
                  }
```

9.2.2.1 Multiple Page Sizes

The simple scheduler described above can be used only by machines with the same page size—an unpleasant restriction. Moreover, in some implementations, the size of a virtual page can be changed and set even on a per-machine basis. Transforming a scheduler of single-page size into a scheduler of multiple-page size is not immediate. The multiple-page-size scheduler uses an arbitrary page size (scheduler page size) internally and solves the problem by two means:

☞ For requests smaller than the scheduler page size, the request is rounded up to the scheduler page size.

☞ For requests larger than the scheduler page size, the request is fulfilled by multiple scheduler pages (shipped all at once) after appropriate synchronization.

Synchronization is accomplished via a queueing mechanism. It is needed to avoid both false contention and descheduling of kernels until absolutely necessary and to satisfy requests as quickly as possible while maintaining fairness. When the scheduler receives a request from a kernel, it may take one of the following actions:

1. Satisfy the request immediately.
2. Deschedule some writers and queue the request.
3. Simply queue the request.

The first action occurs when there are no writers on any of the data that the kernel requests. For a read request, the scheduler can simply add the kernel to the set of readers of each scheduler page; if the request is a write request, the scheduler deschedules all readers of any scheduler page in the writer's request range before scheduling the writer.

In the second case, the scheduler finds that there are writers on some of the requested data, but none of them have been descheduled yet. The scheduler deschedules the writers and the request is queued.

In the third case, the scheduler finds descheduled writers on some of the requested data, indicating that other requests are already waiting for those scheduler pages. In this case, the scheduler does not deschedule the rest of the writers because the requesting kernel is not yet ready to use their pages; the request is simply queued.

When a descheduled writer sends a confirmation (a memory-_object_lock_completed() message), the scheduler finds the request that was awaiting it. If the confirmation was the last one that the request was waiting for, the scheduler satisfies the request (as in case 1 above) and checks to see if there are any more requests that might be satisfied as well.

The data structures used for queueing readers and writers allow most operations to occur in constant time, while some (such as determining whether an incoming request can be immediately satisfied) take time proportional to the number of scheduler pages in the request. Each waiting client is represented by a record containing the identity of the requestor, a reference counter, and a pointer to a linked list of requests that follow. The reference counter is used to test quickly if the request can be satisfied.

When a request follows other requests, the counter represents the number of requests pointing to it; otherwise it is used to represent the number of outstanding descheduling acknowledgments. For each scheduler page, a pointer to the request is waiting for an acknowledgment from the writer of the page, and a pointer to the last request is waiting for the page. These pointers are set to nil if no such request exists.

9.2.3 Heterogeneous Processors

Parallel programs that use a DSM facility should not be constrained to run on a uniform set of processors. Such a constraint is undesirable because as the number of machines available at a given site increases an increased variation in their types typically occurs as well.

Unfortunately, interfacing heterogeneous processors not only creates the problem of potentially different page sizes, but also raises the issue of different machine representations of data objects. This problem goes beyond the byte order problem, since different processors are free to assign any meaning to any given sequence of bits. A clear example is the case of floating-point numbers.

A more difficult set of problems arises from software data types. Modern programming languages allow higher-level types to be built on top of hardware types (for instance, in composing record structures with diverse component types). Quite often, the language definition does not specify how these types should be mapped to the hardware types, and the compiler is free to define this mapping as appropriate.

A well-known consequence is that different fields of a record in the C language may be allocated at various offsets by different compilers, sometimes even among compilers for the same machine architecture. Some languages also use types that do not have any correspondent hardware type. Lisp systems, for instance, often use runtime data tags to mark a collection of bits as the representative of a data type. Only a few processors implement a form of data tagging in hardware.

Solving the heterogeneity problem is difficult because it requires that the server have knowledge of the application's data types. This leads to undesirably close links with the application's runtime system and programming language. On the other hand, the problem can be separated in two subproblems: Hardware data types (e.g., integers), and software data types (e.g., C records).

A general-purpose server solves the problems for the first class of types, and can be extended to cope with the second class of types. The server assigns a type tag to each segment of a paging object and makes the appropriate translation (if necessary) when sending data from that segment to a kernel.

The interface with the application program is defined by the memory_object_tag_data() RPC from the client to the pager which assigns a type tag to a segment. Typically, this operation is used by a dynamic memory allocator to fragment shared memory in typed segments, with each segment containing only data of the given type. Although different types cannot be mixed in a structure, one can always resort to a level of indirection, building records that only contain pointers to data.

Example 3

```
extern char
  *tmalloc( type_tag, num_elements )
enum { t_int8, t_int16, t_int32, t_float32, ... } type_tag;
unsigned long int num_elements;

#define malloc_short(n) (short*)tmalloc( t_int16, n)
...
```

All type tags and machine types must be known to the server in advance, hence each server can deal with a limited set of machine and data types. The server refuses type tags or machine types that it does not know how to handle.

This limitation is not very restrictive: Because the server is a user-level process it can be modified quite easily to account for new data or machine types. A dynamic solution requires the use of runtime type descriptors, which the server uses for data translation. This approach solves the problem of software data types as well. It is certainly possible to extend the server in this way.

Some approaches to the implementation of shared libraries require the use of a dynamic linker. Dynamic linking could be done using lazy-evaluation, only linking those pages of code that are accessed by the program when they are faulted in. A similar case arises with a secure program loader, which must check that the executable image has not been tampered with. A distributed object system might also use similar techniques while mapping objects into the program's address space.

9.2.4 A Distributed Algorithm

The motivations for a distributed algorithm are manyfold. When many kernels share many memory objects serviced by the same pager the availability of each object decreases, because the pager becomes the bottleneck where all requests pile up. A centralized server is a solution that does not scale up.

Even when few kernels are involved, the location of the server is important because local and remote messages might have very different costs. A distributed solution that can allocate any number of servers on any number of machines is more useful. In this way, the sharing of memory between tasks located on the same multiprocessor is decoupled from unrelated events on other machines.

A careful analysis of the external pager protocol also reveals one inefficiency: Transferring ownership of a page from one kernel to another requires four messages (requesting the page, obtaining it, receiving the end-of-transfer message, shipping it to the right kernel), while only two messages are strictly needed (request the page transfer, ship it from one kernel to the other). Rather than modify the external pager interface to handle this case, a distributed paging server can be implemented to exploit this and various other opportunities for reducing network traffic.

The approach is to treat each remote server like another kernel and apply the algorithm of the centralized case. You may wish to go back to Examples 1, 2, and 3 and review the algorithm, substituting the word "kernel" with "client," which now means either a kernel or (more likely) a fellow server. A pager will now accept a memory_object_lock_request() message just like a Mach kernel does and treat it as a fault notification, invoking read_fault() or write_fault() as appropriate. A memory_object_data_provided() message is handled by the pageout() procedure.

Note that the notion of the "owner" that each pager has does not need to be exact at all times. It is quite possible, actually highly desirable, that a pager be able to ask a second pager to transfer a page directly to a third one who needs it, without handling the page directly. This is called *forwarding*.

Implementing forwarding of a misdirected page fault message requires relatively simple changes to the centralized algorithm, as shown in Example 4.

Example 4

```
(1)  memory_object_lock_request( reader, FLUSH(page),
         is_server(page->owner) ? kernel : owner_self)
(2)  if (page->owner != owner_self) {
         memory_object_lock_request(page->owner, WRITE_FAULT(pa
           enqueue(page->writers, kernel)
           page->state = WriteWait
         return
     }
(3)  if (kernel != page->owner && !hinted(page))
           page->owner = kernel
     hinted(page) = FALSE
(4)  if (!page->writers) {
           page->owner = owner_self
           goto ReadWait
     }
(5)  if (is_server(page->owner))
           page_state = WriteWait /* pretend */
(6)  if (!is_server(kernel))
           page->owner = owner_self
```

A pager creates a local copy of a memory object when a user asks for it. The initial state of all pages in this case is the Write state, and the owner is the pager from which the object has been copied. Of course, no real copy is actually done. Note that it is possible to copy from another copy and that the pager does not need to have complete knowledge of all the kernels involved. The handling of read faults does not change.

While handling write faults, at line (1) all readers are informed of who the new owner is, if it is a different pager. At line (2), a check is added to see whether the true owner actually is another pager. If so, the fault is queued and the state of the page modified accordingly.

In the pageout() procedure at line (3) it is necessary to handle the case where the pager has incorrect information about the true owner. Note that the pager might have received a hint about who will eventually become the owner because it forwarded a write fault.

At line (5) it is necessary to handle the case when a page is given to a server queued for writing, while other readers are waiting. The immediate request to have the page back pretends that there are writers queued anyway, to prevent the race that would otherwise occur. Line (4) jumps to the correct code in case the last writer has actually been serviced. Line (6) handles the fact that if the pager only receives read-only access to the page it does not become the owner of the page.

Two new procedures, described in Example 5, are used to check whether a page fault must be forwarded and to handle invalidations of read-only pages. A memory_object_lock_request() message is handled first by the page_fault() procedure, which forwards it if necessary. The fault is not forwarded if the pager has ownership of the page or if the pager has already asked the current owner for write access to the page (state WriteWait), or the pager has (state Read) or is about to have (state ReadWait) a read-only copy of the page and the fault is a read fault.

In other words, a fault is only forwarded to another server when the pager has no current interest in the page. An invalidation of a read-only page is generated at lines (1) and (7) if the reader is a server and is handled in the invalidate_page() procedure. This is the only new message type needed.

Forwarding creates problems for a closed form analysis, since the effects of forwarding both page locations (page faults) and invalidations (page flush) are difficult to model. In actual use, one typically sees only the two extreme cases:

1. Pages that are frequently accessed in write mode by many parties
2. Pages that are accessed infrequently, most likely in read mode

Even if a page is accessed infrequently, it is hard to generate a faulting sequence that produces many forwarding messages. Infrequently accessed pages do not affect performance. The bottlenecks derive very easily from the opposite case. Depending on the boundary conditions, the expected number of remote messages required to service an N-party page fault for the distributed pager is $3N-4$ initially, and $2N-1$ or $2N$ at steady state.

To get the total number of messages in the distributed scheduler, one must add a total of $2N-2$ local messages between pagers and the kernels they service. For comparison, any centralized algorithm that maintains strict memory coherence must use at least $4N$ remote messages and no local messages. In the case of the simple scheduler, this figure is $5N$ messages. Since the cost of local messages is often much less than the cost of remote messages, the distributed pager clearly outperforms the centralized one. Performance evaluations confirm this.

Example 5

```
    invalidate_page(page, owner)
      if (page->state != Read)
        return /* sanity check */
      forall (readers)
(7)     memory_object_lock_request(reader, FLUSH(page), owner)
      page->state = Write;
      page->owner = owner;
    page_fault( page, who, fault_type)
      if ((page->owner == owner_self) ||
        !is_server(page->owner) ||
        (page->state == WriteWait) ||
        ((fault_type == READ) && (page->state != Write))) {
          if (fault_type == READ) read_fault(page, who)
          else write_fault(page, who)
          return
      }
      /* Forward */
      send_page_fault(owner,who,page)
      if (fault_type == WRITE) {
        page->owner = who
        hinted(page) = TRUE
      }
```

When a thread first maps a memory object in its address space, the kernel contacts the server but does not require it to send any data yet. Only when a thread touches a memory location within the address range where the object is mapped is a fault generated. The faulting thread is stopped, and a message is sent to the pager to request data to service the fault.

When the scheduling algorithm in the server has the necessary data available, the page is sent to the kernel that maps it for the faulting thread, which then can continue execution. In case the page is not immediately available at the server, a message is sent to the kernel that currently owns the page, asking to page it out to the server. In the case of the distributed algorithm, this may imply some more processing because the kernel is actually another server.

It is interesting to consider one example that shows the effect of forwarding page faults among distributed servers. Assume that N servers (each one serving one or more kernels) take repeated page faults on the same page, which is the hotspot case (as depicted in Example 6) that makes DSM perform the worst. Initially, all servers refer to the memory object's pages from the same one (say server 1). Therefore N–1 requests are sent to server 1.

The server first services its local fault(s), then ships the page to server 2, which becomes (in the opinion of server 1) the new owner. The next fault request is forwarded by server 1 to server 2, the next to server 3, and so on, to server N–1. When all faults have been forwarded and served, the situation is such that servers 1, N–1, and N all know that the page is located at server N, while every other server i believes the page is at server i+1.

When all servers take the next page fault, only two requests are sent to the owner, and any other request i is queued at server i+1, waiting for i+1 itself to be served first.

Example 6

```
          -------------------------------------------------- →
    S1 S2 -> S3 -> S4 -> ... Sn-1 -> SN
    |                         ∧
```

Studies show that in a write-hotspot the system oscillates between two configurations of this type, never entering the initial state again. A worst case could surface: An isolated page fault could trigger a number of forwarding messages. This number is N–2, since always at least two servers know exactly where the page is: the owner and the one who sent the page to it.

In this example, this would happen if server S2 alone takes a fault after the first N faults are served. After a worst-case fault, all servers know exactly where the page is, and therefore the system goes back to the initial state.

9.2.5 Fault Tolerance

A network memory server must be prepared to handle machine crashes and network partitioning without deadlocking. Once a crash has been detected, the server must either make user programs aware of the problem (for example, signaling a memory error) or attempt to recover from the problem. Whichever action the server takes will not provide application-level fault tolerance since the crash could leave memory inconsistent from the application's point of view. This happens, for instance, when a kernel crashes and a shared memory lock is held by a thread running on that processor.

The centralized schedulers provide a mechanism for surviving kernel crashes whereby memory availability is preserved despite a failure of the current owner of a page. This avoids the alternative of making the whole object permanently unavailable. Assuming the current writer crashes (or for any reason is not capable of communicating with the server any more), the server reverts to the latest copy it has of the page, which is the one that was sent to the writer when it asked for write permission.

Failure of a kernel only needs to be detected when the server needs a page back from it. The overhead of a fault-tolerance guard, therefore, is quite limited when heavily used.

9.2.6 Performance Evaluation

The performance of the server can be evaluated a number of ways. Fundamental are the average times to service a fault, in cases of single-machine and multimachine applications. These are affected by the various special features of the server. The comparison of the centralized and distributed cases, using ad hoc programs that exercise the hotspot behavior, show that:

1. The distributed algorithm is more efficient than the centralized one.

2. None of the special features has an unacceptable impact on performance.

The major bottleneck in the tested configuration (e.g., token ring workstations) is the network latency, which accounts for almost all of the elapsed times.

9.2.6.1 Basic Performance Hits The most common use of the server is in sharing memory within a single machine. A page-out operation requires two receive messages and the deallocation of data, which is not a system call but an RPC to the kernel and involves two messages. Deallocation of memory is done by a separate thread, which means that the latency of the server must be used. Since system time is by far the dominant factor in all cases, schedulers do not show significant differences in the handling of local faults.

Memory use is an important factor for characterizing the performance of a program. The server allocates memory only when a kernel demands it and then replaces each page as it is paged out by a kernel. This not only reduces the memory usage for a large and sparse object, but also removes from the critical path the copying of data (just switch a pointer) and the deallocation of memory (two messages), which can be done in batches. To quantify these improvements, the hotspot cycle time for the distributed case for the simple scheduler was reduced by this strategy, including memory deallocations. Memory deallocation can be devoted to a separate thread, which also reduces the fault time. Memory saving depends on the actual use and is very effective for some applications.

9.2.6.2 The Algorithm's Performance Hits The multiple-page-size scheduler adds some overhead to the fault times, primarily because more server pages might be needed to cover a kernel's page fault. In most cases, a small range of page sizes will be used, but even with an unlikely ratio maximum/ minimum page size of eight, the overhead over the basic fault times is very small. If necessary, however, the algorithm can be tuned further for larger page-size ranges.

The average number of messages per fault is the most important figure: For example, on average, each server handles 4.1 messages per fault. Half these messages are received and half sent. On average, 2.1 messages are local (interactions with the local kernel) and 2.0 are remote (interactions with other servers).

The studies also indicate that the distributed algorithm makes the page available in a fair fashion, in the sense that among homogeneous processors the page is made available for an equal amount of time to all kernels. If processors of different speed are used, the time during which a page is available does not change (it is bound by the network latency). So, using a processor twice as fast as UNIX workstations exactly doubles the number of operations in the user programs.

For the heterogeneity problem, only those machine types that are more or less implied by the definition of the C language may be chosen for implementation, which means integers of various sizes and floating-point numbers. Many other data types map obviously onto these types.

Assuming that the server's (multi) processor has spare cycles, it is possible to eliminate the type conversion overhead at the expense of increased memory usage. The server can keep multiple copies of each segment, one per machine type, and pretranslate it when a page is received. Translation is done in parallel by a separate thread, which works in a pipelined fashion with the main thread that services faults.

In centralized servers, each time a page is sent to a kernel, the indicated overhead is paid as added time for executing the memory_object_data_provided() operation. This means that both read and write faults are affected, for machines that are not of the same general type as the object's creator. There is no overhead for protection faults for identical or compatible machines. Note, however, that in some configurations the overhead of byte-swapping and floating-point conversion sum up. In the worst case of a centralized server, swapping is required both before and after the floating-point conversion.

Again, the distributed server performs much better since translation is merged in the page replication process. The server that receives a page from another server that is machine-incompatible translates it before forwarding it to the Mach kernel. In this case, only one translation is ever required, and read or write faults do not require translation at all when the server has a valid local copy of the page.

9.2.6.3 Application Programs   Intuitively, the performance gain from the use of memory-sharing techniques comes from the large amounts of information that can be transferred with no cost between parallel activities in each synchronization operation. On a uniprocessor, below a certain threshold, the integration of scheduling and data transfer provided by a kernel optimized for message-passing is apparent and wins over the simple busy-waiting scheme of spin-locks.

The effect must be visible in the networked case, where spin-locks are more expensive. In the networked shared memory case, all the tasks running on the same machine produce a single load on the pager, and the advantage of one of them obtaining a page that will then be used by other tasks is not apparent. One important factor affecting the performance of an application that uses dynamically managed shared memory is the memory allocation algorithm used.

9.3 SHARED MEMORY CONSISTENCY MODELS

Parallel systems that support the shared memory abstraction are becoming widely accepted in many areas of computing. Writing correct and efficient programs for such systems requires a formal specification of memory semantics, called a memory consistency model. The *sequential consistency* greatly restricts the use of many performance optimizations commonly used by uniprocessor hardware and compiler designers, reducing the benefit of using a multiprocessor. To alleviate this problem, many current multiprocessors support more *relaxed consistency* models. Unfortunately, the models supported by various systems differ from each other in subtle yet important ways. Furthermore, precisely defining the semantics of each model often leads to complex specifications that are difficult to understand for many users and builders of computer systems.

Structure and granularity affect both network collaboration and efficiency and complexity in memory management. Coherence semantics can be difficult in achieving exactly the same semantics as on a uniprocessor machine with one private memory. But if semantics are released or weak, they do not provide this property, thus requiring the programmer to perform an action in order to update their memories, or they may leave it to a compiler. Scalability is another issue that adds complexity.

The problems are in the areas of data location and access, such as replication schemes. The coherence protocols are an issue in the design of this type of system (without which it degenerates to a distributed unshared memory). Two such protocols are Write-invalidate and Write-update, which do what their names suggest.

9.3.1 Release Consistency

Remote memory accesses experience long latencies in large shared-memory multiprocessors, and they are one of the most serious impediments to good parallel program performance. Relaxed consistency models can help reduce the cost of memory accesses by masking the latency of write operations. Relaxed consistency requires that memory be consistent only at certain synchronization events and thus allows a protocol to buffer, merge, and pipeline write requests as long as it respects the consistency constraints specified in the model.

Release consistency is the most widely accepted instance of relaxed consistency model. Under release consistency each memory access is classified as an ordinary access, an acquire, or a release. A release indicates that the processor is completing an operation on which other processors may depend and all of the releasing processor's previous writes must be made visible to any processor that performs a subsequent acquire. An acquire indicates that the processor is beginning an operation that may depend on some other processor. Writes by processors that have performed previous release operations must now be made locally visible.

This definition of release consistency provides a coherence protocol designer considerable flexibility as to when to make writes by a processor visible to other processors. The processor stalls only if its write buffer overflows or if it reaches a release operation and some of its previous transactions have yet to be completed. This approach attempts to mask the latency of writes by allowing them to take place in the background of regular computation.

Release consistency is a widely accepted memory model for distributed shared memory systems. Eager release consistency represents the state of the art in release-consistent protocols for hardware-coherent multiprocessors, while lazy release consistency provides better performance for distributed shared-memory software. Several of the optimizations performed by lazy protocols have the potential to improve the performance of hardware-coherent multiprocessors as well, but so far their complexity has precluded a hardware implementation.

With the advent of programmable protocol processors it may become possible to use them after all. Here we evaluate a lazy release-consistent protocol suitable for machines with dedicated protocol processors. This protocol admits multiple concurrent writers, sends write notices concurrent with computation, and delays invalidations until acquire operations. We could also consider a lazier protocol that delays sending write notices until release operations, but it is unable to recoup its high synchronization overhead. This represents a qualitative shift from the DSM world, where lazier protocols always yield performance improvements. We can conclude that machines with flexible hardware support for coherence should use protocols based on lazy release consistency, but in a less aggressively lazy form than is appropriate for DSM.

9.3.2 Sequential Consistency

The gap between *sequential consistency* (SC) and *release consistency* (RC) depends on the cache write policy and the complexity of the cache-coherence protocol implementation. In most cases, release consistency significantly outperforms sequential consistency, but the use of a write-back primary cache and a more complex cache-coherence protocol nearly equalizes the performance of the two models. The existing techniques, which require on-chip hardware modifications, only enhance the performance of release consistency to a small extent.

9.3.3 Memory Latencies

Long memory latencies remain a significant impediment to achieving the full performance potential of shared-memory systems. The memory consistency model of a shared-memory system determines the extent to which memory operations may be overlapped or reordered for better performance. Studies show that the release consistency model significantly outperforms the conceptually simpler model of sequential consistency.

Current- and next-generation high-performance microprocessors exploit increased levels of instruction-level parallelism, using aggressive techniques such as multiple issue, dynamic scheduling, speculative execution, and nonblocking reads. For such processors, hardware prefetching and speculative loads enhance the performance of both sequential consistency and release consistency.

For earlier processors with blocking reads, the decision to support a relaxed consistency model did not have to be made at processor design time, since writes can be made nonblocking by simply providing an early acknowledgment from an external memory controller. Nonblocking reads, however, bring in a value needed by other instructions and must be integrated into the processor design. Thus, the consistency model now has a larger impact on processor design, further increasing the importance of understanding the benefits of relaxed consistency on current processors.

The difference between RC and SC performance depends primarily on whether the first-level cache is write-through or write-back and on the complexity of the cache-coherence protocol. With the base protocol, which is fairly aggressive and represents many current implementations, RC consistently outperforms SC. With write-through primary caches, RC achieves twice the speedup over the best SC for two of the six applications, and over one and a half the speedup for two others. With write-back primary caches, the speedups are less dramatic, but still fairly large (one and a half or more for three applications). With a more aggressive, but more complex, cache-coherence protocol, optimized SC achieves a comparable performance to RC for two applications, but a significant gap remains for others.

RC sees little benefit from the two techniques because these optimizations conservatively assume that after an acquire all operations in program order depend on that acquire. In many cases, however, an acquire is followed by operations that are independent of it but that may be interspersed with other dependent operations.

9.3.4 Current Implementation Examples of Consistency Models

SC, the most intuitive memory consistency model, guarantees that memory operations appear to execute in program order. RC distinguishes between data operations and acquire and release synchronization operations. The primary relaxation that RC provides over SC is that data operations of a processor can be reordered with respect to each other. The primary constraint imposed by RC is that data operations must appear to await the completion of previous (by program order) acquire operations. Simple implementations of the two models achieve these constraints by prohibiting a memory operation from entering the memory system until all previous operations for which it must appear to wait have completed.

The two optimizations for consistency models are hardware prefetching and speculative loads. These techniques take effect whenever the constraints of a consistency model could restrict the issue of a memory operation. Both techniques exploit the instruction look-ahead window in an aggressive processor. Similar techniques are used in a number of systems, including the HP PA-8000, the Intel Pentium Pro, and the MIPS R10000.

The prefetch technique issues a hardware-controlled nonbinding prefetch for a decoded memory operation in the instruction window as soon as its address is available and if the operation cannot be issued otherwise. Prefetch allows an SC system to obtain remote data for reads while a regular memory operation is pending. Prefetch allows an RC system to prefetch reads beyond acquire operations. Because processors typically implement precise exceptions, stores cannot issue to the memory system until reaching the head of the instruction window. The prefetching technique allows both consistency models to issue exclusive prefetches for such stores.

Speculative load execution goes a step beyond prefetching by using the value of a load as soon as that value becomes available (typically through the prefetches discussed above). The technique preserves correctness by requiring that any data that is speculatively loaded remain visible to the coherence mechanism. This is achieved by using additional on-chip hardware in the form of a speculative load buffer.

The speculative load buffer must communicate with the cache, tracking any invalidation, update, or cache replacement operations on cache lines that have had loads issued speculatively to them. If such a message reaches the speculative load buffer, the unit must interface with the processor's window of active instructions and reissue the speculated load and roll back all subsequent processor operations. The MIPS R10000 supports this rollback mechanism by stopping an incorrectly speculated load when it seeks to retire from the processor's instruction window; at that time, the hardware reissues the load and flushes the rest of the instruction window.

9.3.4.1 Base Processor

To exploit instruction-level parallelism, the base processor model employs such widely used techniques as multiple instruction issue, dynamic (out-of-order) scheduling, register renaming, speculative execution, and nonblocking reads. The processor exploits parallelism by examining a large window of instructions at a time, and it executes the instructions that are not dependent on the completion of any previous incomplete instructions. This allows instructions to issue and complete out of program order. Except for stores in the RC models, an instruction retires when it is complete and when all preceding instructions (by program order) have retired. A store in RC retires when its address and value are resolved and when all previous instructions have retired. To guarantee precise interrupts, stores are not issued into the memory system until they reach the head of the instruction window.

The base processor model directly supports the simple implementation of release consistency. Variations on the base processor and memory system include a sequentially consistent processor model, and support for hardware-controlled nonbinding prefetching and speculative load execution.

To implement hardware prefetching, prefetch requests are issued to the cache level appropriate for the corresponding demand fetch. Thus, write prefetches with the write-back write-allocate primary cache and all read prefetches go to the primary cache. Write prefetches with the write-through non-write-allocate primary cache only fetch into the secondary cache. Bringing these to the primary cache would defeat the purpose of a nonwrite-allocate cache.

9.3.4.2 Performance Metrics

Execution times are divided into various components, namely CPU time and stall time due to reads, writes, locks, flags, and barriers. With parallel processors, however, each instruction potentially can overlap its execution with both previous and following instructions. Hence, it is difficult to assign stall time to specific instructions. A cycle is counted part of busy time if the maximum number of instructions possible is retired. Otherwise, that cycle is charged to the stall time component corresponding to the first instruction that could not retire in that cycle.

Effectively, the statistics for individual stall components represent the cumulative time instructions in each class stall at the top of the instruction window before retiring. If an instruction retires without having spent any time at the top of the instruction window, it is considered to have fully overlapped with previous instructions. These detailed statistics offer insight into the nature of the various applications and identify the portions of the computation overlapped by various optimizations. For purposes of comparing various implementations, however, the total execution time is the primary performance metric.

9.3.5 Message-Driven Relaxed Consistency

If distributed memory machines allow very high performance, their programming remains esoteric for most of the end users are accustomed to classical monoprocessor programming. Shared-memory parallel computers are easier to program but are badly adapted to applications generating many memory accesses.

The purpose of DSM systems is to implement, above a distributed memory architecture, a programming model allowing a transparent manipulation of shared data. In practice, a DSM system commonly has to handle all the communications and maintain data coherence.

Though various DSM systems have been proposed, few of them allow efficient and scalable operations with massively parallel multiprocessors. This model allows processes to share distributed objects. A hierarchical organization (into groups and subgroups based on the shared data they address) of the processes permits a high degree of scalability. This organization either can be defined using compilation directives or dynamically generated at runtime.

9.3.6 Relaxed Consistency Models

In distributed shared-memory systems, the overhead of check-pointing and rollback recovery is increased by the need to handle rollback propagation.

Unsynchronized check-pointing eliminates coordination overhead, but it is costly in the number of checkpoints that are needed to ensure that the ordering of memory accesses does not violate sequential consistency. Under relaxed consistency models, only accesses to synchronization variables need to be strongly typed.

Relaxed-memory consistency models have recently been developed to tolerate memory access latency in both hardware and software distributed-memory systems. In recoverable shared-memory multiprocessors, relaxed consistency has the added benefit of reducing the number of checkpoints needed to avoid rollback propagation. Maintaining strict consistency restricts performance and increases the number of required checkpoints.

New algorithms have been developed that take advantage of relaxed consistency to reduce the performance overhead of check-pointing. Relaxed-memory consistency allows copies of data to be inconsistent between synchronizations and to use a lazy approach to enforce consistency only when absolutely necessary. This scheme reduces the number of communication events. The simulations show a fivefold-to-tenfold decrease in check-pointing overhead over previous techniques that require sequential consistency.

9.4 Distributed Processing in Decision Support Systems

High-performance decision support systems using parallel processing require distributed processing to overcome the limitations imposed by single processor systems. However, when moving from local to distributed programming, the conventional method of intertask communication by message passing poses major problems.

9.4.1 Message Passing

Message passing forces the programmer to deal with problems (multiple message sources, destinations, transmission protocols, formats) that can grow quite complex in rapidly evolving distributed systems, especially if there is no software layer translating the programmer's communication requests into the lower-level communication requests. A general solution to the problem of providing transparent communication links can be provided by using shared memory. Shared memory gives the programmer a shared address space linking separate processes, separating coding requirements from the complexity of the data transfer.

Distributed shared memory represents shared memory when applied to separate CPU systems where true shared memory cannot be supported. However, inherent problems associated with loosely coupled systems have resulted in few widely accepted DSM implementations.

9.4.2 X11-Based Distributed Shared Memory

X11-based distributed shared memory (XDSM) can be constructed on the basis of various library modules used for creating GUIs, user language code interfacing, and GUI message generation. At the center of an X11 client there is an infinite loop checking the input event queue for incoming information. X11 I/O events are extracted and processed by XDSM library code on the basis of whether they are intended for the X11 GUI toolkit or are control-area X11 property change events required by the control module. Reception of relevant property change events causes the configuration and control module to instruct the data access module to copy XDSM control data to a local copy of the control area.

Using the XDSM, the following functionality can be provided for an application suite:

1. Definition of shared data areas, with user monitoring and control of the shared data provided by an interactive GUI

2. Shared or exclusive access to global data

3. Task coordination and control, including automatic task startup and local task control

4. Distributed error handling and recovery achieved by maintaining shadow copies of the shared data and by error handlers

9.5 CASE STUDIES

DSM, in these days of increasingly networked computers, is widely recognized as a simple construct upon which to build inexpensive parallel processing systems.

It is widely accepted today in supercomputing that workstation farms are more economical than supercomputers because workstation networks often are already available and interconnected. DSM software permits the machines to be used like supercomputers.

9.5.1 Multitasking

Multitasking is usually accomplished either in a simple portable cooperative scheme or with OS multitasking services. There is no physical memory protection to prevent one task from crashing the OS. Instead, each task has its own stacks and user variables but all memory is shared and available to all tasks. Each task must have a certain amount of local memory for its stacks and local user variables, however. In a traditional multitasker, the word PAUSE would switch control from one task to another, simplifying task synchronization.

In a computer that provides memory protection in hardware, the OS often provides services to limit the memory that a program or task can access.

Any access to memory through protected memory hardware or through memory access services from an OS can provide error traps for attempts to access protected memory. Certain tasks and programs may be able to run with access to only one section of memory, but many others will need a certain amount of memory to be available to more than one program or task.

In the protected-mode OS, the shared memory is logically separated by memory protection hardware or OS services. Often only a small amount of memory need be global or shared. This is a form of parallelism as tasks may logically execute in parallel even though they are still physically time sharing the CPU. If task2 and task3 are copies of the same task which is operating on different data, they could share the same memory for code, but would still require a local (protected) memory for stacks and user variables.

Multiprocessors do not really have *central* processors; instead they have multiple processors. The processors on these machines can be tightly or loosely coupled. Tightly coupled machines use memory that is physically shared so that at least part of the memory available to a processor is also available to other processors.

The advantage of the tightly coupled design is that memory is physically shared so access may be very fast. For example, the Cray II memory interface has four sections of memory that may be accessed simultaneously. So only when processors access a region that another processor is using is bus arbitration needed. The disadvantages of the tightly coupled design are its high cost and the physical constraints on the hardware interconnect at the memory access level.

Most memory is shared and each task has some local memory. The memory in each of the machines is physically separate, but shared memory can easily be simulated in software using the network. The DSM is just a portion of memory on each machine that is identical on all machines. DSM must be written to via an OS service, which will update all of the memories on the network so that all computers have their own copy of this global shared memory.

9.5.2 Components for Distributed Control

With shared memory management, we have two software components (see Figure 9.2) that share the memory programming paradigm and the message-based communication paradigm. Thus, the programmer can choose the more adequate model depending on the application. These components are the core of the software library for distributed system programming as they offer communication means at the application level.

There are many algorithms in this domain. They differ from each other in their internal features, their complexity, and their behavior in a fault situation, but they share a common point as there is a notion of controller. A controller makes an interface between the network and the application level. It implements the distributed control with the other controllers which are run by the participating nodes of the network.

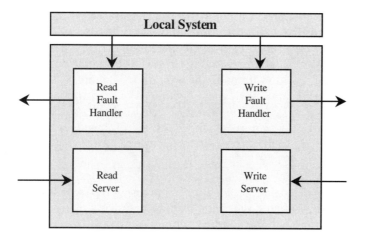

Fig. 9.2 DSM Components

9.6 CONCLUSIONS

DSM has been used to facilitate the distributed implementation of a decision-support system for monitoring and controlling water distribution networks.

We examined a user-level memory server for a Machtype system and the algorithms it uses for dealing with issues like heterogeneity, multiple page sizes, distributed service, and fault tolerance. The server has shown good performance and the distributed algorithm is effective in reducing communication over the (potentially slow) communication medium. The application programs are dominated by the network latency, but in some cases are still optimal.

The amount of data exchanged between synchronization points is the main point of consideration when deciding between using distributed shared memory and message-passing in a parallel application.

Besides final user applications (e.g., scientific applications, window managers, etc.), a number of operating system utilities can be built with shared memory, now that it is available for networks. I/O between processes can be modeled as the transfer of ownership of a shared memory buffer. In this way, a process (the producer) can allocate a buffer, fill it with data, and notify the other process (consumer) that the buffer is available by queuing it, especially for a circular queue. Supporting distributed databases with distributed shared memory is now simplified.

We can assume that all parallel languages that have a shared memory model can port on a distributed shared memory system, although they still require some tuning to obtain the best performance.

Adopting a lazy consistency protocol on hardware-coherent multiprocessors can provide substantial performance gains over the eager alternative for a variety of applications. For systems with programmable protocol processors, the lazy protocol requires only minimal additional hardware cost (basically storage space) with respect to eager release consistency. We examined two variants of lazy release consistency and noticed that delaying coherence transactions on hardware-based systems helps only up to a point.

Delaying invalidations until a synchronization acquire point is almost always beneficial, but delaying the posting of write notices until a synchronization release point tends to move background coherence operations into the critical path of the application, resulting in unacceptable synchronization overhead.

As miss latencies and cache sizes increase, the performance gap between lazy and eager release consistency increases as well. As program locality increases, the performance advantage of lazy protocols decreases: A direct result of the decrease in coherence transactions required.

Both the message-passing and DSM have advantages and disadvantages in distributed parallel programming. Messages carrying explicit causality annotations are exchanged to trigger memory coherency actions. By adding annotations to standard message-based protocols, it is easy to construct efficient implementations of common synchronization and communication mechanisms. Because these are user-level messages, the set of available primitives is extended easily with language- or application-specific mechanisms.

This chapter also described the design, implementation, and performance evaluation of virtual shared servers. These provide unrestricted sharing of read-write memory between tasks running on strongly coupled or loosely coupled architectures and a mixture of the two. A number of memory coherency algorithms have been implemented and evaluated in the industry and have outperformed centralized ones.

Distributed System Security

10.1 INTRODUCTION

A computer can be considered secure if it and its software can be depended upon. This does not mean that it is absolutely impenetrable to crackers, viruses, and other forms of unauthorized entry. The only computer that is absolutely secure is unplugged. Security is a responsibility shared between the organization that owns the system, the system administrator, anyone who uses the system, and anyone who walks into the room where the system is.

It is up to the organization that owns the system to set security policies, including who has physical access to the machines, who receives accounts on them, how security infractions are dealt with, and plans for dealing with emergencies. It is the responsibility of the users to adhere to the policies that have been established and not do things, like sharing passwords, that will compromise security. Users must agree to this set of responsibilities before they can use their account. The responsibility for installing and maintaining a secure system falls to the system administrator.

Enterprises are increasingly dependent on the use of IT systems to support their business operations. As the technology of IT systems is improving the architectures of the IT systems are changing to reflect the organization and operations of the enterprises they support. The IT system resources are increasingly distributed throughout the enterprise and the demands for interoperability and interconnectivity of IT systems within and between enterprises are increasing.

In order to survive, an enterprise is responsible for the safe custody and maintenance of its assets. These assets are both tangible and intangible. The greatest intangible asset is generally the information on which the enterprise relies to manage and conduct its business. In fact, its business may be the provision of information.

The operations of an enterprise involve interactions between security domains, between its own subdomains and between its own security domain and the security domains of other enterprises. Similarly, in distributed environments, an IT system may be broken down into a set of security subdomains. To meet these needs, the sponsor and the domain security services must:

☞ Verify a user's authorization to access the domain's services, requiring authentication of the user's identity.

☞ Mediate and record the user's access to the activities and elements of the security domain. This includes mediation of access to the security services and security information.

☞ Protect the integrity and confidentiality of the activities and elements of the domain, including segregating the domain's elements and activities from other domains' activities and elements.

10.1.1 Physical Security

Security can be roughly divided into four areas of concern: physical, accounts, networks, and file systems. Physical security is the first line of defense. All the network, file system, and account security in the world will do little good if someone walks off with the computer. Physical security includes:

☞ Limiting access to system components

☞ Inhibiting theft and vandalism

☞ Controlling the environment

☞ Restricting access to backups

Making the building and/or room where the computer is kept secure is the first step in preventing vandalism and theft. Vandalism is frequently done to exposed system components, like networking cables, rather than to the main system. Exposed cables can also be vulnerable to tapping and eavesdropping.

10.1.1.1 Types and Risk Assessment Several types of security are needed for accounts, networks, and file systems.

☞ *Privacy and isolation*: Ensuring that information is protected so that people who are not authorized by the owner of the information cannot access it

☞ *Data integrity*: Protecting data from unauthorized alteration or deletion, including files, programs, accounting records, backup tapes, documentation, and file modification times

☞ *Availability*: Making sure that services are not corrupted, degraded, or crashed

☞ *Consistency*: Ensuring that the system behaves as expected.

☞ *Audits*: Protecting the integrity of the system by closely monitoring the changes that take place

Depending on who owns the system and how it is used, some types of security may be more important than others. Assessing risks on a particular system involves understanding the potential risks while taking into account the operating system environment and the needs of users. Having a clear idea of what needs to be protected and how to prioritize those needs is the key to reducing risks.

10.1.1.2 Passwords Passwords are the first internal line of defense in a system because break-ins are frequently the result of poorly chosen passwords. UNIX does not store the password anywhere on the system. When a password is set, UNIX stores a value generated by taking the password that was typed in and using it to encrypt a block of zeros. When a user logs in /bin/login takes the password the user types in and uses it to encrypt another block of zeros. This is then compared with the stored block of zeros. If the two match, the user is permitted to log in. The algorithm that UNIX uses for encryption is based on the Data Encryption Standard (DES).

Even encrypted passwords are not secure if kept in a world-readable file like /etc/passwd. /etc/passwd needs to be world-readable for a number of reasons, including the users' ability to change their own passwords. So passwords are stored in /etc/shadow which is readable only by the root. Even this does not make passwords absolutely secure—it just makes them harder to get to.

From a security point of view, /etc/passwd is one of the most important files on a system. If unauthorized users can alter that file they can change any user's password or make themselves root by changing their UID to 0. The /etc/ group file can also be crucial. By gaining access to the right group an intruder can gain write privileges to /etc/passwd.

Password aging can be used to force users to change their passwords regularly. But due to the minimum lifespan field, it can also prevent them from changing them if they know that someone else has obtained the password for their account. On the other hand, forcing users to change passwords means if an intruder does obtain a password for a user's account, the password will only be good for a limited time. Password aging can also be added to individual accounts.

10.1.1.3 Permissions   The names of files in a directory are not stored in the files themselves. They are stored in the directory. So any user with read permission for a directory can look in and see which files are there. If users have execute permission only for a directory they can use any file in that directory, as long as they know the name of the file. Execute permission combined with read permission can be used to modify a file. Users with these permissions can copy any file they know the name of and the copy will belong to them because they created it.

10.1.1.4 Login Options   UNIX allows options to be set that determine the way the system deals with logins. A large number of failed login attempts, particularly on the same account, can indicate that someone was trying to break in to the system. Under older UNIX "flavors" login options were kept in /etc/config/login.options. This may not prevent an intruder from gaining access to the system, but it can make the process more time consuming and leave a record of it.

A security option for temporary accounts or accounts set up for a specific purpose is the restricted shell, rsh. Care must be taken not to confuse this with the remote shell command *rsh*. When a restricted shell starts it executes the commands found in $HOME/.profile. Once this is done the user cannot:

☞ Use command names with slashes

☞ Change the current directory

☞ Change the value of the PATH environmental variable

☞ Redirect output with > or >>

It is also possible to prevent a restricted shell from being used over the network. This entails having the shell script issue the *tty* command to make sure the user is attached to the physical terminal and not to a network port. Setting up a restricted account involves creating a special directory containing only programs that the restricted shell may run and making a user account with rsh as the login shell.

10.1.2 Network Security

In general, networks are vulnerable to eavesdropping, especially in distributed environments. This is due partially to the fact that many network applications transmit sensitive information, such as passwords and UIDs, when requesting services. Security risks can be reduced by encrypting the information and/or using an authentication program. One of the more popular authentication programs is Kerberos (discussed in section 10.5). It uses DES cryptology to send sensitive information over open networks and is an addition that can be used with any network protocol.

Another important factor in network security is controlling network access. The /etc/hosts.equiv, .rhosts and /etc/passwd files control whether access is given to rlogin, rcp, and rsh. /etc/hosts.equiv contains a list of hosts that are trusted or considered equivalent to that machine. Some systems use /etc/hosts.allow and /etc/hosts.deny rather than a single /etc/hosts.equiv file. The .rhosts file holds a list of hosts that are permitted access to a specific user account.

When a request is received, /etc/hosts.equiv is checked to see if the host is listed. Then /etc/passwd is checked to see if the desired account is listed. If the host and account are listed, access is granted without prompting the user for a password.

A root login bypasses the /etc/hosts.equiv file completely and uses only /.rhosts. This means that anyone who has access to the machine with /.rhosts privileges can log in as anyone on the system. Once again, no password is needed. A user could log in as root and become root on any system that has that machine's name in its /.rhosts file. This can have interesting results. Users can also set up an .rhosts file in their home directory to allow another user access to their accounts.

TCP wrappers log and control Internet access to tftp, ftp, telnet, remote shells, rlogin, finger, exec, and talk. Access restrictions can be set individually for each service. Each remote access is logged including the name of the service, whether the connection was accepted or rejected, the name of the remote host, and a date/time stamp. This additional protection can serve as a deterrent for intruders, while the log information can make break-ins easier to trace.

Another security consideration is the way ftp is set up. There are two options for building ftp—restricted and anonymous. Restricted ftp accounts allow limited access to files. When a client requests services, the server sends a *chroot* system call to prevent the client from moving outside the part of the file system where the ftp home directory is. A password is required to use a restricted account. Because the password is transmitted over the network it is vulnerable to interception.

Restricted accounts must be listed in the /etc/ftpusers file, followed by the word "restricted." /etc/ftpusers can also be used to list the names of non-trusted users, who cannot use ftp to access any files. It is a good idea to put the names of accounts that do not belong to human users in this file.

Anonymous ftp is a special type of restricted account that does not require a password. It may be set up without a listing in /etc/ftpusers. Instead an account named ftp must be created and all the files available via anonymous ftp must be put in that account's home directory.

Usenet uses UNIX-to-UNIX copy (UUCP) to transfer messages. UUCP can be used for:

☞ Sending mail back and forth between remote systems

☞ Transferring files back and forth between UNIX systems

☞ Remotely executing commands

UUCP comes with almost every version of UNIX. Because it runs over standard serial cables it requires no special hardware. Although the prevalence of networking has overtaken some of its functions, UUCP is still widely used. It utilizes batching to transfer data, which can lower the cost of networking.

Basically, UUCP consists of two programs: uucp and uux. The uucp program enables the transfer of files between UNIX systems, while uux allows commands to be executed on remote systems. When UUCP contacts a remote system it receives the login: and password: prompts, logs into a special account, and uses another copy of uucico as its shell.

10.2 SECURITY THREATS

From the perspective of users and owners, the threats to information and information processing systems are usually categorized under the following main headings:

☞ Unauthorized use of resources

☞ Unauthorized disclosure

☞ Denial of service

☞ Unauthorized modification

☞ Repudiation

10.2.1 Basic Threats

Even at this level of definition it is impossible to clearly separate each area of threat. The realization of a threat in one area often increases the risks of other types of threat occurring.

10.2.1.1 Unauthorized Use of Resources   The unauthorized use of system resources includes the theft of hardware and software, as well as the unauthorized use of information systems and the services they provide. Apart from physical theft, the most common concern here is masquerade, the unauthorized impersonation of an authorized user or other entity by discovering and using their authentication credentials.

The threat of masquerade is not limited to users, malfeasant systems and services may attempt to impersonate authorized systems and services. The unauthorized use of information system resources and services may result in unauthorized disclosure, modification, and denial of service to use the information resources.

10.2.1.2 Unauthorized Disclosure   The unauthorized disclosure of information may damage the interests of a nation, organization, or individual. Concerns over the confidentiality and privacy of information vary. At one end are government and defense concerns over the disclosure of national and allied classified information. For most enterprises, the need is to keep business information confidential. From the point of view of individuals, the primary need is for privacy. This last need is variously addressed in data privacy legislation and similar obligations on the holders of personal data.

It is important to note that certain classes of system management and configuration information, especially that which is relevant to security, constitutes sensitive information that should not be disclosed without authority.

10.2.1.3 Denial of Service   Denial of service covers actions and events that prevent information processing systems from providing agreed levels of service to authorized users. Denial of service threats range over the environmental acts of nature and man—such as fires, floods, or bombs—to more targeted threats, such as the accidental or intentional swamping of an electronic mail service with a large volume of unwanted messages.

The results of denial of service can be catastrophic loss down to a temporary suspension of a service. But even the latter could have a significant impact on the business of an enterprise. Imagine the impact, for example, of the suspension, for a few active trading hours in the stock and bond market, of an organization's IT-based trading services.

10.2.1.4 Unauthorized Modification   The unauthorized modification of information and information processing resources and services can prejudice the business of nations, organizations, and individuals. The concern is in maintaining the integrity of information. The threat is to the procedures and processes that ensure a business's sensitive and critical information not be introduced, changed, or removed in an unauthorized manner. Some examples include the modification of sales and purchase orders, funds transfers, electronic mail, or military signals information with the intention of defrauding or confusing.

10.2.1.5 Repudiation   This category of threat covers many forms of denial of accountability or responsibility. It includes the denial that a message was sent or received by the sender or receiver. When such messages are relied on for the conduct of business or some other endeavor, such a denial could damage the interests of one or both parties involved.

10.2.2 Vulnerabilities

Security vulnerabilities describe the weaknesses in the construction, functionality, and operation of information systems that expose them to the accidental or intentional realization of security threats. The intentional exploitation of information system security vulnerabilities is a kind of attack. The methods of attack vary according to the nature and functionality of the system and its components as well as to the objectives and skill of the attacker.

10.2.2.1 Unauthorized Modification   Unauthorized modification presents two areas of concern and vulnerability:

1. *System software and hardware modification*: Absence of or poor system configuration management facilitates the introduction of unauthorized software and hardware components. Such components may accidentally or intentionally contain malfeasant functionality that damages the integrity of the system. The common forms of malfeasant software are:

    ✗ Virus software with the capability of propagating itself and often carrying a payload designed to perform some malicious act.

    ✗ Trojan horse components that partially or fully emulate security-relevant software components in order to capture and relay sensitive information.

    ✗ Security- and business-relevant software components containing trapdoor functionality that permits those who know about it to bypass some part of its normal functioning. This category includes the wide range of flaws and undocumented features common to much software.

    ✗ Software components designed to perpetrate some malicious or fraudulent act either at some specific time or when signalled to do so. These are sometimes referred to as logic bombs. They may be inserted as part of a virus or be specifically engineered, usually by someone with detailed knowledge of the target system.

2. *Unapproved hardware*: Unapproved or unchecked hardware containing hardware and firmware features and functionality that allow existing security mechanisms to be bypassed.

3. *Data modification*: The preservation of the integrity of enterprise sensitive and critical information is usually based on the concept of well-formed transactions. Such well-formed transaction models specify the stages in the life cycle of each type of enterprise information; otherwise it results in information corruption.

For each stage, whether it be information creation, modification, transmission, or destruction, the well-formed transaction model should capture and define the authorizations and cross checks required in order to perform the stage.

10.2.2.2 Transmission Information communicated over networks can be intercepted and modified as it passes through the weakly defended or uncontrolled links, routers, and nodes. The classic example is the modification—upwards—of the financial amount field of an authorized message requesting a credit to the attacker's account.

Messages, perhaps previously intercepted and modified, are introduced into the communication traffic either as part of a masquerade or fraud attack or just to damage the integrity and availability of the communication services.

10.2.2.3 Storage The integrity of stored data can be accidentally or intentionally compromised in a number of different ways. Many of these result from poor access control regimes governing who has access to what stored information and what tools and utilities can be used to access the information, such as:

☞ For transmitted data, specific stored data item values can be changed in order to support a fraud attack or to facilitate the operations of the attacker in some other way

☞ Localized or generalized corruption of stored data may be either immediately obvious or only discovered after some time; the latter is more insidious as it could be copied into the entire backup archive

☞ The unauthorized removal of sensitive stored data

☞ The unauthorized introduction or replacement of sensitive information

10.2.2.4 Modification of System Data The system and security administration data, and the services used to set this system data, determine the current operational configuration of the system. If not adequately protected, this data is susceptible to all of the attacks already described.

There is a wide range of options available to the attacker as to how to exploit vulnerabilities in this area. Some are reasonably direct, obvious, and detectable, but others are more subtle, insidious, and less easily detected. Some examples are:

1. *User account modification*: Unauthorized access to user account or profile data and services can be used to:

   ✗ Increase or decrease the privileges and authorizations assigned

   ✗ Discover and use redundant user accounts

   ✗ Remove active user accounts

2. *Communication configuration modification*: Unauthorized access here can be used to create or modify communication addressing and routing parameters at different levels of communication service in order to open up new channels and even redirect communications.

3. *Changing clocks*: An increasing number of security mechanisms are dependent on correct time synchronization. An attacker who manages to falsify the system clock(s) may well succeed in defeating these mechanisms.

4. *System service modification*: More generally, inadequately controlled access to system administration and management services can be exploited by an attacker to perform disclosure, modification, and denial of service acts.

10.2.2.5 Unauthorized Disclosure   There are a variety of ways in which the confidentiality and privacy of information within information systems can be compromised. The vulnerabilities to unauthorized disclosure threats occur in the following areas:

1. *Transmission*: Sensitive information transmitted over LANs and, particularly over WANs is liable to eavesdropping in the layered communication services and networks. The term "sniffer" describes a software component designed for eavesdropping. Typically, a sniffer is placed at a strategic point in the communications services. From there it can observe and report sensitive transmitted information, such as user ids and passwords.

2. *Traffic analysis*: In certain cases, the frequency, volume, origin, and destination of messages is considered confidential information. An attacker may discover such information through the analysis of communication traffic flow.

3. *Storage*: Information, as variously stored, can be subject to unauthorized copying, deploying any of the many IT techniques and tools for reading and producing copies of stored information. A sometimes overlooked vulnerability arises in the tendency within all levels of information system services to make transient copies of information as it is processed and transmitted. These copies often take the form of large internal buffers or temporary files occupying reusable garbage space. Thus an attacker may use the electronic equivalent to garbage collection and analysis.

4. *Processing*: Attackers may introduce their own versions of regularly used tools and application components. These can be designed to capture and

relay the sensitive information they process. Computers, terminals, and electronic communication equipment, if not adequately shielded, radiate electromagnetic signals which can be picked up at distances varying according to the strength of the signal. With the appropriate equipment, the displayed, the processed, or transmitted information can be reconstructed.

10.2.2.6 Unauthorized Use of Resources
In the widest context, unauthorized use includes the theft of hardware and software resources. Weaknesses in the control of access to these resources can lead to disclosure, modification, repudiation, and denial of service attacks. The converse is also true; in particular, disclosure and modification vulnerabilities can facilitate unauthorized use attacks.

10.2.2.7 Denial of Service
Information system vulnerabilities to denial of service and availability threats abound. They include areas of obvious concern such as:

☞ Continuous power supply and communications links dependency

☞ System hardware component reliability

☞ System software component reliability

Establishing disaster strategies and plans and the regular making and securing of backup copies of sensitive information are widely practiced.

10.2.2.8 Repudiation
Repudiation attacks are predicated on the existence of some measures for making users and other entities accountable for their business- or security-sensitive actions. There are two general mechanisms:

1. *Audit logging*: Recording each action and the identity of the responsible entity in an audit trail
2. *Sealing and signing*: Binding the identity of the responsible entity to information produced by the action

An example of the latter is the binding of digital signatures to electronic mail messages. In both cases, additional information such as location, context, and time is usually recorded.

10.2.2.9 Lack of Awareness and Utility
To put things in perspective, the most common vulnerabilities currently arise from the lack of awareness of information system security concerns, needs, and practices by the users and owners. There is often a failure to clearly assign responsibility for information security to users and administrators.

A lack of *awareness* means not knowing in sufficient time that a system has been attacked or that its security has been compromised. This vulnerability occurs because measures for detecting and reporting attempted or successful attacks are inadequate. A lack of *utility* occurs despite strong security measures if these are difficult to use or manage.

Should the security behavior of the system appear to impede normal operational efficiency, then users will be encouraged to find ways round the system's security. The effectiveness and utility of system and security management are currently one of the greatest areas of vulnerability within distributed systems. Lack of facilities that allow large, heterogeneous distributed systems to be easily managed almost guarantee that they will be riddled with vulnerabilities.

10.2.2.10 Assessment of Threats, Vulnerabilities, and Risks   Security threat and risk assessment is an iterative process applied at each level: enterprise, information system, information subsystem, and IT services. The assessment steps are:

1. Identify what has to be protected against which threats.
2. Determine the vulnerabilities to these threats.
3. Estimate the risks of these vulnerabilities being exploited.
4. Where the risks are unacceptable, identify a set of countermeasures to the threats with the aim of reducing the vulnerabilities and associated risks to acceptable levels.

Information system security concerns (risk-weighted threats and vulnerabilities) vary from one enterprise to another. Protection profiles should be used to generalize these concerns. From the general, they should be interpreted and adapted to the context of the particular enterprise.

10.2.3 Common Security Threats

A *backdoor*, also known as a *trapdoor*, is a privileged entry point into the system. Generally, a backdoor is a way to get around permissions and gain superuser status. Programmers use them to monitor and test programs. They also provide an access point if problems need to be fixed.

Backdoors are usually removed before the program is shipped to the customer, but not always. They can also provide an entry point into the system if the root password is lost or corrupted. Without a root password, there is no way to use privileged commands that are necessary to repair or replace the password file. The problem with backdoors is that anyone who finds them can use them. In the case of a corrupt or lost root password, the system can be brought down and restarted in single-user mode.

10.2.3.1 Trojan Horses and Search Paths   A *Trojan horse* is a piece of code that hides inside another program and performs a concealed function. Trojan horses can be used to hide another sort of bug, such as a virus, bomb, bacteria, or worm. Another common type of Trojan horse mimics a normal login but records the password that the user types. The program then exits and returns the user to the real login screen.

Even stricter precautions should be taken with the root search path. It is a good idea to use only absolute pathnames rather than relative ones. It is also recommended that no directories in the root path be writable by anyone other than root and that the current directory not be placed in the path at all.

10.2.3.2 Viruses A *virus* is a piece of code that inserts itself into another program and modifies it. A virus is not an independent program; it depends on the program it modifies and executes only when that program runs. It then reproduces and infects other programs. A virus can infect any place where data is stored by altering or destroying the data. Software is available that will scan for and destroy the more than three hundred known computer viruses.

10.2.3.3 Bacteria *Bacteria*, also known as *rabbits*, are programs that do not directly damage the system. Instead, they replicate themselves until they monopolize the CPU, memory, or disk space. This constitutes a denial of service attack.

10.2.3.4 Bombs A *bomb* is actually a type of Trojan horse that can be used to release a virus or bacteria. Bombs work by causing an unauthorized action at a specified date or time or when a particular condition occurs. There are two types of bombs: logic and time. Logic bombs are set to go off when a particular event occurs. Time bombs go off at a specified time, date, or after a set amount of time elapses.

10.2.3.5 Salami *Salamis* cut away tiny pieces of data. They can be particularly dangerous as the damage they do is small and can be attributed to some truncation of the system. It is possible for a salami to do a great deal of damage before it is found.

10.2.3.6 Worms *Worms* are independent programs designed to move from system to system over a network. They reproduce by copying themselves from one computer to another. Although they do not destroy data or modify other programs, they can tie up system resources as they reproduce. They can also be used to carry viruses, bacteria, or bombs. Protection against worms is the same as protection against other types of break-ins. If a user can break into a system, then so can a worm program.

An increased awareness of the need for computer security came as the result of the 1988 Great Internet Worm. This was a program that moved from computer to computer, across the network, through a backdoor in Sendmail. It was stopped because a flaw in its code caused it to behave like bacteria on some systems.

10.2.4 Internet-Based Security Threats

Just a few years ago, damages from rogue computer code could be kept to a minimum by taking a few relatively simple, straightforward precautions. But, thanks largely to the Internet and collaborative work applications, IT managers today face a more formidable challenge.

Back in the good old days, viruses were the main problem. Today, they continue to be a major problem, but companies also face other threats. Specifically, corporate data can potentially be corrupted or destroyed by malicious Java applets or ActiveX objects.

Macro tools within applications such as Word and Excel and scripting languages such as Visual Basic and JavaScript let novice hackers wreak havoc on corporate networks—even if they do not know how to write code. And the file-sharing and replication mechanisms of the Internet and groupware are creating new ways to spread dangerous programs.

10.3 COUNTERMEASURES

To meet an enterprise's information security objectives an integrated set of security countermeasures need to be deployed, operated, and maintained across the enterprise (nonsystem) and system domains. Security countermeasures prevent, deter, detect, and limit the realization of identified threats.

Based on the assessment of security threat, vulnerability, and risk, security objectives can be defined and a set of security countermeasures devised. The type, strength, and deployment of these countermeasures is based on what is considered necessary to counter the identified range of security threats and vulnerabilities in all of an enterprise's domains.

Security countermeasures, or measures, encompass security strategies, procedures, and mechanisms. Procedures define the human actions to be followed in order to prevent, limit, and handle security threatening events and activities. In the case of information systems, security mechanisms are automated procedures within the information system.

The effective counter to each threat is usually achieved through a combination of measures. For each information system security domain, the principal information concerns, objectives, and rules are specified in the domain's security policy. The security procedures associated with the domain and the mechanisms implemented within the domain are the vehicles for enforcing the security policy. The countermeasures can be grouped under these categories:

- ☞ Authentication
- ☞ Authorization and access control
- ☞ Accountability and audit
- ☞ Availability

☞ Administration and management

☞ Assurance

10.3.1 Authentication

To counter unauthorized use through masquerade, identification and authentication mechanisms are required at the points of access to the information systems and the services they provide. Their purpose is to establish that the identity of entity requesting service is as claimed. These measures often need to support mutual authentication to counter masquerade by either party.

The basic authentication strategy is to use either secret information or information that cannot be forged. This is shared by the requesting entity and the identification and authentication mechanisms, possibly on both sides. Examples include passwords, secret information held on tokens or smart cards, and biometric information (fingerprints, retinal scans, etc.) unique to each user.

These mechanisms are mainly dependent on cryptography. The identity of each entity is used by other security mechanisms when making security-relevant decisions and performing operations for the entity.

10.3.2 Authorization and Access Control

Authorization and access control techniques are used to counter unauthorized modification and disclosure threats. A range of authorization and access control strategies and measures can be combined to form an access control regime. This ensures that only those entities (known as initiators) with the necessary authorizations are allowed to access sensitive information and information system resources and services (known as targets). These access control measures can individually or in combination meet organization and individual needs to preserve the confidentiality, integrity, and availability of sensitive information and information processing resources.

The level of application (granularity) of authorization and access control measures varies considerably. The access-controlled targets range over systems, services, programs, devices, files, documents, memory segments, communication channels of various forms, records, data fields, and even data fields by content. Initiators can be systems, users, devices, processes, and other instances of active executables. Access control measures are composed of four distinct techniques.

10.3.2.1 Physical This is the simplest technique in that it is based on the physical separation of information processing resources—essentially stand-alone systems—but it is inconsistent with distributed system objectives.

10.3.2.2 Temporal Temporal separation techniques operate at different levels. At the coarsest level of granularity, an information processing system is only used to process sensitivity at any one time and is totally purged before being used again. When applied at a finer level of granularity to targets, such as transient files, buffers, and memory address space, this technique counters disclosure through garbage collection and similar attacks. As such, it is known as the object-reuse measure.

10.3.2.3 Cryptographic   Cryptographic separation and protection techniques are used extensively in information system security solutions. Cryptographic mechanisms range in type, application, performance, and strength of protection. Principal types are based on symmetric and asymmetric algorithms. In the former, the same key is used to encrypt and decrypt information. In the latter case, different keys are used for these operations. The terms *private* key and *public/private* key encryption are often used to denote each type. Cryptographic mechanisms are used within authentication, accountability, and audit to protect the integrity and confidentiality of information in storage and transmission.

10.3.2.4 Logical   Protection and separation techniques of this type are based on a combination of hardware and software functionality to create separation environments and properties at different layers within an information system. At the lower levels, the operating system, usually through the use of specific hardware features, separates and protects itself from the vagaries of higher-level functionality. At varying levels of strength, it provides separation of the different services and resources the system includes, such as devices, directories, and files. It also separates and protects the higher functional components from each other by establishing a multiprocessing environment, controlling the mapping of memory to each process, and mediating the ways processes can communicate with each other.

These operating system protection and separation features are fundamental to the implementation of any reasonably robust system. Based on their sound implementation at the operating system level, logical separation and protection techniques are used where required within higher-level functional components. Authorization and access control strategies include:

☞ *Capability-based strategies*: Capabilities (authorizations) are assigned to each initiator. These determine what functionality is available to that initiator through each service invoked by the initiator. Capabilities are often used to control which initiator may override or bypass the normal functional behavior of a service or system.

☞ *Discretionary access control (DAC) strategies*: (Alternatively known as the access control list [ACL] strategy). These, typically, though not exclusively, are based on the UNIX access control mechanisms for files, devices, etc. Authorizations take the form of the individual entity and group identifiers an initiator is allowed to adopt. The initiator which owns a target—and any other initiator given the permission to do so— assigns to other initiators (individual entities and groups) permission to perform specific operations, such as read, write, and execute, on the target. "Discretionary" reflects the fact that the owner of the target who decides who else can access the target. DAC is the most commonly used strategy.

☞ *Mandatory access control strategies*: (Alternatively known as label-based or information-flow strategies). With these, system mechanisms are assigned responsibility for making access control decisions. These strategies originated in the government and military worlds. They were devised to protect the confidentiality of nationally classified information, though they are adaptable in other areas. Here authorizations assigned to initiators take the form of clearances. These in government and military application include components for hierarchically organized attributes (Top-Secret, Secret, Confidential, Restricted, Unclassified) and categories that usually identify specific projects and topics. Sometimes a third component, caveats, is added. Caveats are often used to distinguish clearances on the basis of nationality. Targets are assigned classification labels based on the same component structure and attribute values used for clearances.

Essentially, these strategies require the creation and maintenance of classification-labeled information processing, communication, and storage compartments. The strategies specify the rules governing access to and information flow between compartments based on comparisons between the relevant clearances and classification labels. Although these strategies generally have been specified to protect information confidentiality, others have been devised to meet integrity and confidentiality objectives.

To provide solutions to confidentiality and integrity protection requirements, authorization and access control mechanisms may be constructed from a combination of the techniques and strategies outlined above. Thus, a particular access control policy may be enforced by mechanisms based on the DAC strategy using both cryptographic and logical separation techniques.

Typically, capability and DAC strategies are combined. The integrity-focused measures based on and implementing the well-formed transaction modeling approach are usually engineered within the appropriate services. However, they are dependent on lower-level implementation of capability and DAC mechanisms to ensure protection of the services themselves.

Finally, to avoid the risks of assigning too many authorizations and responsibilities to any single entity (user), the separation of duties strategy can be used. The range of security-sensitive responsibilities and duties are separated into distinct roles (entity types). The authorizations allowed to any one role then are limited to only those required to perform the duties assigned to that role. Closely associated with this approach is the application of "n-person" rules. Here, two or more initiators have to collaborate in order to combine their authorizations to perform a sensitive operation.

10.3.3 Accountability and Audit

Audit and accountability addresses repudiation and awareness concerns. Mechanisms are established to record and, where appropriate, report the occurrence of all actions and events that are considered to be business- and security-sensitive or threatening.

For each action, the identity of the initiating entity and/or performing entity, together with other pertinent descriptors of the action (e.g., date and time), are recorded in a manner such that they cannot be subsequently changed or contradicted. Records of security sensitive actions and usage must be regularly analyzed. Similarly, mechanisms are required to ensure that business-sensitive actions are available to support the resolution of legal or contractual disputes.

For each security-threatening event, which may be associated with an action, an alarm is raised and reported to a designated authority. The speed with which the alarm is raised is determined by the severity of the event. Ideally, the reporting of the alarm should give as much time as possible to those responsible for limiting the potential damage. Audit and accountability strategies include:

10.3.3.1 Audit Logging   These are mechanisms for detecting security-relevant actions and events, wherever they occur, and recording them in a protected audit trail. What qualifies as a security-relevant event is determined by tuneable audit selection criteria. Examples of these selection criteria include type of entity performing the event, sensitivity of the action and/or information being processed, location, and time of day (allowing for higher level of recording beyond normal working hours).

10.3.3.2 Audit Analysis and Archiving   These are measures for analyzing the audit trails produced and generating useful reports on security-relevant usage and activity. The audit trails need to be securely archived in order to allow for subsequent analysis.

10.3.3.3 Alarm Detection and Reporting   Because not all the security-threatening events may be detectable by audit detection mechanisms, this is often closely coupled with audit action and event logging. The alarms are reported over one or more robust communication services to designated user interfaces.

10.3.3.4 Signing and Sealing   Audit logging has severe limitations in countering repudiation of business-sensitive actions performed by entities in outside security domains, particularly if the domains reside in different enterprises. Trust and mutual recognition have to be established by each domain in the audit mechanisms used by the other. Signing and sealing mechanisms based on cryptographic techniques provide a better solution.

For each business-sensitive transaction, the relevant information is cryptographically signed and sealed using a key (digital signature). The key is one which in some way can be proven to bind the initiating entity to the transaction. To overcome the remaining mutual trust issues, trusted third parties are used to establish and maintain an adequate level of trust in the digital signatures used. As for audit, nonrepudiation through signing and sealing needs to be accompanied by mechanisms that allow a proof of signature to be produced sometime after the event—in some cases, as much as several years later.

10.3.4 Availability

Information system security availability concerns and solutions merge with those of high availability and safety critical system engineering. Availability concerns are generally addressed by strategies and techniques for:

☞ Prevention

☞ Detection

☞ Duplication and redundancy

☞ Recovery and fall back

Of specific security interest are the principles of:

1. *Fail secure*: Devising and implementing measures that, when they fail, do not leave the system or service in an insecure state.

2. *Recover secure*: Establishing measures which ensure that, following a failure, the recovery procedures return the system or service to a secure operational state before it is made available for use.

10.3.4.1 Administration and Management   In general, good system and security administration is necessary to counter a lack of responsibility and control threats. Weakness in these areas currently presents some of the greatest threats to information system security.

There is a fuzzy boundary between system and security management. Like any other IT service, system security services and mechanisms have management and control requirements for:

☞ Operating control

☞ Reporting events and states

☞ Collecting and analyzing utilization and performance statistics

☞ Maintaining consistent propagation of configuration parameters and equivalent information

The first objective is to provide administration facilities that support these service management and control operations within distributed systems. Close behind this is the need to counter insecurity through complexity and confusion. The management facilities need to be easy to use and consistent in their user interfaces and in the views they present of the managed system. The more rigorous security management strategies and measures:

☞ Assign only those capabilities necessary to each role

☞ Apply n-person controls to the use of specified security critical management operations

☞ Separate system and security management duties into clearly defined management roles

Generally, system and security management facilities need to be protected and separated through the use of access control mechanisms.

10.3.5 Assurance

Any delegation of responsibility for the enforcement of security to the information system must be based on a measure of confidence in the correct and continuing working of the security relevant measures and functionality.

There is much debate on how to rate, measure, and achieve confidence (assurance). The government and military worlds have spent considerable effort over the years in devising first national and now international schemes for specifying and evaluating system security assurance. The costs associated with achieving the higher levels of assurance specified by these schemes may be beyond the budgets of the major commercial markets.

10.4 DISTRIBUTED SECURITY ARCHITECTURE

Three basic types of system architectures need to be supported: standalone, interconnected, and distributed.

A standalone system comprises a single platform domain that supports a set of applications, or service domains. The platform domain and its applications are under the control of a single administrative authority. This authority establishes the trust relationships within the system by configuring security attributes on software installation. Specific capabilities, for example, may be assigned to an application or security enforcing service elements within an application. The attributes on the elements of the platform (i.e., on its processes, files, and intercommunications channels) may have been preset, or they are set using trusted utilities and trusted management services.

The platform domain then enforces security policy with respect to those elements and the security attributes assigned to them. All applications trust the platform domain to maintain the association of the principal's security attributes (security context) with the chain of execution. Thus, the security attributes are made available, through platform services, to the relevant security-enforcing services in order to ensure that the security policy is enforced on all operations performed on behalf of the principal.

The platform maintains the segregation of service domains—their data resources. It maintains the integrity and confidentiality of their contents.

10.4.1 Interconnected System

When two systems are connected, each system remains responsible for its own security services. An interconnection policy needs to be established, defining how and when the systems can communicate and the nature of those interactions. Each system needs to be configured such that the security information it contains supports the formation of operational interrelationships between the two systems. A communications channel provides the means by which elements in one system may be accessible to the other.

Each system remains responsible for the authentication of users of its services. Hence, a principal is required to authenticate itself separately to each system it wishes to use. This involves providing a set of security information meaningful to the system accessed.

The communications channel needs to protect the data transmitted through it. Thus, it must segregate data resources and protect the integrity and confidentiality of their contents. Only rarely can this be achieved by physical means alone. Often cryptographic measures are used to provide the basic protection required. On a large scale, the interconnected system architecture is representative of many interenterprise system cases.

10.4.2 Distributed Systems

A distributed system is a set of interconnected systems that place mutual trust in certain security services that are shared by or are common to the systems, such as authentication and security attribute services. In order to do so, security information needs to be propagated throughout the distributed system in a reliable way.

In a standalone system, the platform is trusted to maintain the association of security attributes with a chain of execution. But in a distributed system, the association of security attributes is more complex. The security information needs to be propagated in such a way that the attributes are protected from threats within the communications system. In addition, security services must be deployed within the distributed processing support functional area. These are assigned the responsibility of propagating the security context associated with a chain of execution as it passes from one platform domain to another.

10.4.2.1 Authentication   The authentication requirements support and provide:

☞ Services and functions for securely storing authentication credentials, binding the authentication credentials to each chain of execution and, where necessary, transmitting authentication credentials over distributed systems. These services support a variety of mechanisms.

☞ The authentication of principals (users and other entity types) within distributed systems. The authentication services support a variety of mechanisms and devices (challenge and response, passwords, smart cards, biometric devices).

☞ Support for the authentication of such objects as messages.

10.4.2.2 Authorization and Access Control   The authorization requirements support and provide:

☞ The assignment and modification of access control information for initiators and targets.

☞ Authorization state services that maintain the current state of operational access-control information being used by initiators.

☞ Services and functions for securely storing access-control information, attaching access-control information to initiators and targets, binding the access-control information to each chain of execution, and, where necessary, securely transmitting access-control information over distributed systems. These services are required to support a variety of mechanisms.

☞ Access-control services to be used in the protection of the confidentiality and integrity of information in storage and transmission. These services support mechanisms based on cryptographic and logical separation and protection techniques.

☞ Access-control decision functions (ACDF), which make decisions as to whether a requested access action should be allowed. The decision is based on the access-control information associated with the action, target, and initiator in accordance with the access rules derived from a system security policy.

☞ Access-control enforcement functions (ACEF), which mediate all system security policy that defines access actions on targets and enforces the decisions made by the ACDF.

10.4.2.3 Accountability and Audit   Accountability includes nonrepudiation requirements, such as:

☞ Services and functions for the detection, recording, analysis, and archiving of security relevant audit events. All security services are required to detect security-relevant events that occur within their boundaries.

☞ Services and functions for the detection and reporting of security alarm events.

☞ Services and functions for setting audit and alarm detection, analysis, and reporting criteria in portable audit record formats.

☞ Services and functions for binding the initiator's id or credentials with some information through the use of signing and sealing mechanisms. The services support both automatic and voluntary application of such a signature. Automatic application applies the information resulting from an action performed by the initiator.

☞ The automatic application of signature is determined by customized selection criteria based on the identity of the initiator, the type of action, and the sensitivity of the information produced.

☞ Services for checking the digital signature.

10.4.2.4 Availability and Administration The general requirement is to ensure that, following failure, systems and their security services recover to a secure state. Security-relevant administration requirements derive from the need to manage each of the security services.

10.5 KERBEROS: THE PROTOCOL FOR AUTHENTICATING USERS

Kerberos is a network authentication protocol. It is designed to provide strong authentication for client/server applications by using secret-key cryptography. Kerberos is an independently developed protocol for authenticating users; that is, ensuring that users (defined as either a person or a computer program) are who they claim they are (i.e., are authentic). Kerberos provides authentication only—not authorization.

The Internet is an insecure place. Many of the protocols used in the Internet do not provide any security. Tools to *sniff* passwords off the network are in common use by systems crackers. Thus, applications that send an unencrypted password over the network are extremely vulnerable. Some client/server applications rely on the client program to be honest about the identity of users. Other applications rely on the client to restrict its activities to those it is allowed to do, with no other enforcement by the server.

Some sites attempt to use firewalls to solve their network security problems. Unfortunately, firewalls assume that the bad guys are on the outside, which is often a bad assumption; insiders carry out most of the damaging incidents of computer crime. Firewalls also have a significant disadvantage in that they restrict how users can use the Internet. In many places, these restrictions are simply unrealistic and unacceptable.

Kerberos was created as a solution to these network security problems. The Kerberos protocol uses strong cryptography so that a client can prove its identity to a server (and vice versa) across an insecure network connection. After a client and server have used Kerberos to prove their identity, they can encrypt all of their communications to assure privacy and data integrity as they go about their business.

10.5.1 Is Kerberos Necessary?

Current password schemes were developed in the days when users logged into a remote host via a serial or other direct link to the host. The password was kept physically secure because the serial cable was connected directly between the local terminal or computer and the remote host the user was attempting to access. Thus, it was generally not possible for a password to be compromised by an unknown third party.

Nowadays, many systems exchange data over shared networks, whose transmissions can be seen by any host on the network. Thus, passwords transmitted over network communication channels are no longer physically secure and can be easily stolen. Additionally, each host on the network must rely upon every other host on the network having securely authenticated all its users even though the local host has no control over those hosts. If any one of these hosts is compromised, all service requests originating from that host become suspect.

Kerberos was developed to overcome the insecurity of passwords used over computer network channels and the need to rely upon the security of multiple hosts.

10.5.2 How Kerberos Ensures System Security

The security of Kerberos relies solely upon the security of the Kerberos server itself, not on the security of the principals (clients or servers) involved in the service transaction or their hosts. Because the secret keys of the principals are not normally transmitted over the network channel, they cannot be compromised within a reasonable probability. Even if the secret key is required to be transmitted over the network during Kerberos administrative functions (i.e., changing the secret keys between a principal and the Kerberos server), it is encrypted in a temporary session key.

The private key of a human user is generated on the local host by encryption of the user's password, which the user enters at the beginning of a work session. This password is retained only long enough to generate the private key and is then deleted from the local host. In this way, the password is never transmitted and its exposure is limited.

In order to avoid having the user re-enter a password each time a service ticket is desired (i.e., each time a program is run on a remote host); the user is granted a *ticket-granting ticket* (TGT) upon Kerberos login. This ticket is cached during the work session and allows user-initiated service requests to automatically obtain their own session tickets on behalf of the user. Typically, the TGT expires in eight hours, although this is site-dependent. Similar to a hand stamp used by amusement parks, the TGT allows a user/service to enter and exit as many times, and as often, as desired.

Almost all of the operation of Kerberos authentication is hidden from the user. Generally, the only action required from the user is to login with the Kerberos server at the beginning of a work session, which automatically retrieves the user's TGT. The only other action required by the user is to destroy any tickets in the user's cache upon logout or to login again if the user's ticket has expired.

10.5.3 Assumptions Kerberos Makes

Kerberos makes some assumptions about its environment. It assumes that users do not make poor choices for passwords. If a user selects a password like *password* or *nothing*, then an attacker who intercepts a few encrypted messages will be able to mount a dictionary attack, trying password after password to see if it decrypts messages correctly. Success means that the user's password has been guessed and that the attacker can now impersonate the user to any verifier.

Similarly, Kerberos assumes that the workstations or machines are more or less secure and that only the network connections are vulnerable to compromise. In other words, Kerberos assumes that there is no way for attackers to position themselves between the user and the client in order to obtain the password.

10.5.4 How Kerberos Works

Kerberos relies upon a trusted third-party host, known as the Kerberos server, which maintains a list of secret (*private*) keys to all users of the Kerberos authentication system. These users are termed *principals*, whether they are human users or computer programs.

When a computer providing a service (the *server*) needs to authenticate another principal desiring to use that service (the *client*), it expects the client to present a *ticket* for that session. This ticket is cleverly constructed in such a way that only the authenticated client could provide an acceptable ticket. This ticket contains information about who received the ticket and the time it was granted. This prevents someone from stealing, tampering with, or forging the ticket or from using the ticket after its expiration. This ticket also contains a temporary session key that both the client and server are granted by the Kerberos server and can be used to encrypt any messages passed between the two parties.

Both the user and the service are required to have keys registered. The user's key is derived from a password that the user chooses; the service key is a randomly selected key (since no user is required to type in a password). For the purposes of this explanation, imagine that messages are written on paper (instead of being electronic), and are encrypted by being locked in a strongbox. In this box world, making a physical key and registering a copy of the key initializes principals.

10.5.5 The Ticket-Granting Server

There is a subtle problem with the above exchange. It is used every time a user wants to contact a service. But notice that the user then has to enter in a password each time. The obvious way around this is to cache the key derived from the password. But caching the key is dangerous. With a copy of this key, an attacker could impersonate the user at any time (until the password is next changed).

Kerberos solves this problem by introducing a new agent, called the *ticket-granting server* (TGS). The TGS is logically distinct from the administrator, although they may reside on the same physical machine. (They are often referred to collectively as the *Key Distribution Center* [KDC]). Before accessing any regular service, the user requests a ticket to contact the TGS, just as if it were any other service.

After receiving the TGT, any time that the user wishes to contact a service, the user requests a ticket not from the administrator, but from the TGS. Furthermore, the reply is encrypted not with the user's secret key, but with the session key that the administrator provided for use with the TGS. Inside that reply is the new session key for use with the regular service.

This process is like that followed when you visit some workplaces. You show your regular ID to get a guest ID for the workplace. When you want to enter various rooms in the workplace, instead of showing your regular ID over and over again, which might make it vulnerable to being dropped or stolen, you show your guest ID. The guest ID is only valid for a short time, so if it were stolen, you could get it invalidated and be issued a new one quickly and easily, something that you couldn't do if your regular ID were lost.

Of course, there is a difference. In this analogy, an agency such as the Department of Motor Vehicles issues you your regular driver's ID and the workplace issues the guest ID. These are logically and physically distinct entities. On the other hand, in the TGT exchange, the administrator and the TGS are logically distinct but generally are physically identical (the same process).

The advantage this provides is that while passwords usually remain valid for months at a time, the TGT is good only for a fairly short period, typically eight hours. Afterwards, the TGT is not usable by anyone, including the user or any attacker. This TGT, as well as any tickets that you obtain using it, are stored in the *credentials cache*. There are a number of commands that you can use to manipulate your own credentials cache. Credentials refer to both the ticket and the session key in conjunction. However, you will often see the terms *ticket cache* and *credentials cache* used more or less interchangeably.

10.5.6 Cross-Realm Authentication

So far, we have considered the case where there is a single administrator and a single TGS, which may or may not reside on the same machine. As long as the number of requests is small, this is not a problem. But as the network grows, the number of requests grows with it, and the administrator/TGS becomes a bottleneck in the authentication process. In other words, this system does not scale, which is bad for a distributed system such as Kerberos.

Therefore, it is often advantageous to divide the network into realms. These divisions are often made on organizational boundaries, although they need not be. Each realm has its own administrator and its own TGS. Cross-realm authentication allows users in one realm to access services in another. First, it is necessary for the user's realm to register a remote TGS (RTGS) in the service's realm. Recall that when the TGS was added, an additional exchange was added to the protocol. Here, yet another exchange is added:

1. The user contacts the administrator to access the TGS.
2. The user contacts the TGS to access the RTGS.
3. The user contacts the RTGS to access the actual service.

10.6 SECURE SOCKETS LAYER

Secure Sockets Layer (SSL) is an industry standard that makes substantial use of public-key technology. SSL is widely deployed on the intranet, as well as over the public Internet, in the form of SSL-capable servers and clients from such vendors as Netscape, Microsoft, IBM, Connect, and Open Market. Public-domain products such as Apache-SSL are available too. SSL provides three fundamental security services, all of which use public-key techniques. Table 10.1 displays these.

☞ *Message integrity*: Ensures that SSL session traffic does not change en route to its final destination. If the Internet is going to be a viable platform for electronic commerce, vandals cannot tamper with message contents as they travel between clients and servers. SSL uses a combination of a shared secret and special mathematical functions called hash functions to provide the message integrity service.

☞ *Mutual authentication*: Process in which the server convinces the client of its identity and (optionally) the client convinces the server of its identity. These identities are coded in the form of public-key certificates, and the certificates are exchanged during the SSL handshake.

☞ *Message privacy*: Achieved through a combination of public-key and symmetric-key encryption. All traffic between an SSL server and client is encrypted using a key and an encryption algorithm negotiated during the SSL handshake described below. Encryption thwarts eavesdroppers who can capture a TCP/IP session by using devices such as IP packet sniffers. Even though packet sniffers can still capture the traffic between a server and client, the encryption makes it impractical for them to read the message.

Table 10.1 SSL Services

Service	Underlying Technology	Protection Against
Message integrity	Message authentication codes (keyed hash functions)	Vandals
Mutual authentication	X.509 certificates	Impostors
Message privacy	Encryption	Eavesdroppers

To demonstrate that the entity presenting the certificate is the legitimate certificate owner (rather than some impostor), SSL requires that the certificate presenter digitally sign data exchanged during the handshake. The exchanged handshake data includes the entire certificate. The entities sign protocol data (which includes their certificates) to prove that they are the legitimate owner of the certificate. This prevents someone from masquerading as you by presenting your certificate. The certificate itself does not authenticate. The combination of the certificate and the correct private key does.

10.6.1 The SSL Handshake

SSL is designed to make its security services as transparent as possible to the end user. Typically, users click a link or a button on a page that connects to an SSL-capable server. A typical SSL-capable Web server accepts SSL connection requests on a port different from the standard HTTP requests.

When the client connects to this port, it initiates a handshake that establishes the SSL session. After the handshake finishes, communication is encrypted and message integrity checks are performed until the SSL session expires. SSL creates a session during which the handshake needs to happen only once. Performing an SSL handshake for every HTTP connection would result in poor performance. The following high-level events take place during an SSL handshake:

1. The client and server exchange X.509 certificates to prove their identity. This exchange might include an entire certificate chain, up to some root certificate. Certificates are verified by checking validity dates and verifying that the certificate bears the signature of a trusted certificate authority.

2. The client randomly generates a set of keys that will be used for encryption and calculating MACs. The keys are encrypted using the server's public key and are securely communicated to the server. Separate keys are used for communications from client to server and server to client for a total of four keys.

3. A message encryption algorithm (for encryption) and hash function (for integrity) are negotiated. In SSL implementation, the client presents a list of all the algorithms it supports, and the server selects the strongest cipher available. Server administrators may turn particular ciphers on and off.

10.6.2 The Intranets

One of the chief benefits of using open protocols such as SSL and secure/Multipurpose Internet Mail Extensions (S/MIME) is that systems scale from the intranet to the Internet. Although proprietary systems such as Lotus Notes, Microsoft Exchange, and Novell GroupWise offer integrated security and directory services for communications and collaboration, they do so in a way that does not scale to the Internet. The result is a jumble of gateways and other translation services that force rich, proprietary data into a lowest common denominator, such as a 7-bit ASCII text transported over Simple Mail Transfer Protocol (SMTP) in the clear.

When open standards such as SSL and S/MIME are adopted, the same systems, administrators, trainers, support personnel, and applications may be used for secure, robust communications throughout the intranet and over the public Internet as well. There is no loss of fidelity in E-mail messages, no fumbling with different attachment mechanisms, and no loss of security services. For example, the same X.509 certificate technology that authenticates users to internal servers can also authenticate users to external services such as news feeds, stock quotes, and others on the public Internet. The same security protocol, SSL, can be used to encrypt and provide message integrity services, inside and outside the firewall, for remote banking and other electronic commerce applications. And the same secure-message standard, S/MIME, enables secure interoffice E-mail as well as secure intercompany E-mail with global partners, customers, press, and analysts.

10.7 CRYPTOGRAPHY

Cryptography is a surprisingly general technology that provides the foundation for each of the security challenges listed above. Data communications channels are often insecure, subjecting messages transmitted over the channels to passive and active threats. With a passive threat, an intruder intercepts messages to view the data. This intrusion is also known as "eavesdropping." With an active threat, the intruder modifies the intercepted messages. Cryptography is an effective tool for protecting messages against the active and passive threats inherent in data communications.

Cryptography is the science of mapping readable text, called *plaintext*, into an unreadable format, called *ciphertext*, and vice versa. The mapping process is a sequence of mathematical computations. The computations affect the appearance of the data, without changing its meaning.

To protect a message, an originator transforms a plaintext message into ciphertext. This process is called encryption or encipherment. The ciphertext is transmitted over the data communications channel. If the message is intercepted, the intruder has access to the unintelligible ciphertext only. Upon receipt, the recipient transforms the ciphertext into its original plaintext format. This process is called decryption or decipherment.

The mathematical operations used to map between plaintext and ciphertext are identified by cryptographic algorithms. Cryptographic algorithms require the text to be mapped and, at a minimum, require some value that controls the mapping process. This value is called a key. Given the same text and the same algorithm, different keys produce different mappings.

Cryptographic algorithms need not be kept secret. The success of cryptography is attributed to the difficulty of inverting an algorithm. In other words, the number of mappings from which plaintext can be transformed into ciphertext is so great that it is impractical to find the correct mapping without the key. For example, the National Institute of Standards and Technology Data Encryption Standard (NIST DES) uses a 56-bit key. A user with the correct key can easily decrypt a message, whereas a user without the key would need to attempt random keys from a set of over 72 quadrillion possible values.

Cryptography is used to provide authentication, integrity, nonrepudiation, and secrecy. Authentication allows the recipient of a message to validate its origin and it prevents an imposter from masquerading as the sender of the message. Integrity assures the recipient that the message was not modified en route. Note that the integrity service allows the recipient to detect message modification, but not to prevent it. There are two types of nonrepudiation service: one with proof of origin provides the recipient assurance of the identity of the sender; another with proof of delivery provides the sender assurance of message delivery. Secrecy, also known as confidentiality, prevents disclosure of the message to unauthorized users.

Cryptography comprises a family of technologies that include the following:

☞ *Encryption* transforms data into an unreadable form to ensure privacy. Internet communications are like sending postcards—anyone who is interested can read a particular message; encryption offers the digital equivalent of a sealed envelope.

☞ *Decryption* is the reverse of encryption. It transforms encrypted data back into the original intelligible form.

☞ *Digital signatures* bind a document to the possessor of a particular key and are the digital equivalent of paper signatures.

☞ *Signature verification* is the inverse of a digital signature. It verifies that a particular signature is valid.

☞ *Authentication* identifies an entity, such as an individual, a machine on the network, or an organization.

There are two kinds of cryptosystems: Symmetric and asymmetric. Symmetric cryptosystems use the same key (the secret key) to encrypt and decrypt a message, while asymmetric cryptosystems use one key (the public key) to encrypt a message and a different key (the private key) to decrypt it. Asymmetric cryptosystems are also called public-key cryptosystems.

Symmetric cryptosystems present the problem of transporting the secret key from the sender to the recipient securely and in a tamperproof fashion. If you could send the secret key securely, you wouldn't need the symmetric cryptosystem in the first place because you would simply use that same secure channel to send your message. Frequently, trusted couriers are used as a solution to this problem. Another, more efficient and reliable solution is a public-key cryptosystem, such as Remote Security Architecture (RSA), which is used in the popular security tool Pretty Good Protocol (PGP).

10.7.1 Symmetric Key Cryptography

Symmetric key cryptography is characterized by the use of a single key to perform both the encrypting and decrypting of data. Since the algorithms are public knowledge, security is determined by the level of protection afforded the key (i.e., ensuring that the key is known only to the parties involved in the communication). If kept secret, secrecy and authentication services are both provided. Secrecy is provided because, if the message is intercepted, the intruder cannot transform the ciphertext into its plaintext format. Assuming that only two users know the key, authentication is provided because only a user with the key can generate ciphertext that a recipient can transform into meaningful plaintext.

The secrecy of the key does not ensure the integrity of the message. To provide this service, a cryptographic checksum, called a message authentication code (MAC), is appended to the message. A MAC is a hashed representation of a message, and it has the following characteristics:

☞ It is much smaller (typically) than the message generating it.

☞ It is impractical to compute the message that generated it.

☞ It is impractical to find another message generating the same MAC.

The MAC is computed by the message originator as a function of the message being transmitted and the secret key. Upon receipt, the MAC is computed in a similar fashion by the message recipient. If the MAC computed by the recipient matches the MAC appended to the message, the recipient is assured that the message was not modified.

The primary disadvantage of symmetric cryptography is the difficulty of distributing the secret keys. A key cannot be transmitted securely over data channels unless it is encrypted. Encrypting the key, however, requires another key. At some point, a plaintext key needs to be exchanged between communicating partners. One solution is to distribute the key manually (e.g., by registered mail). Manual distribution, however, is costly, time consuming, and prone to errors. There are two automated ways of distributing secret keys: The Diffie/Hellman key exchange, which I discuss in section 10.7.3., and the American National Standards Institute (ANSI) standard X9.17, which I discuss in section 10.7.4.

10.7.2 Asymmetric Key Cryptography

Asymmetric (public-key) cryptography differs from conventional cryptography in that key material is bound to a single user. The key material is divided into two components:

☞ A private key, to which only the user has access

☞ A public key, which may be published or distributed on request

Each key generates a function used to transform text. Naturally, the private key generates a private transformation function, and the public key generates a public transformation function. The functions are inversely related; i.e., if one function is used to encrypt a message, the other is used to decrypt the message. The order in which the transformation functions are invoked is irrelevant.

Note that since the key material is used to generate the transformation functions, the terms private key and public key not only reference the key values, but also the transformation functions. For example, the phrase, "the message is encrypted using the message recipient's public key," means that the recipient's public key transformation function is invoked using the recipient's public-key value and the message as inputs, and a ciphertext representation of the message is generated as output.

The advantage of a public-key system is that two users can communicate securely without exchanging secret keys. For example, assume an originator needs to send a message to a recipient, and secrecy is required for the message. The originator encrypts the message using the recipient's public key. Only the recipient's private key can be used to decrypt the message. This is due to the computational infeasibility of inverting the public-key transformation function. In other words, without the recipient's private key, it is computationally infeasible for the interceptor to transform the ciphertext into its original plaintext. Note that with a public-key system, while the secrecy of the public key is not important (in fact, it is intended to be "public"), the integrity of the public key and the ability to bind a public key to its owner is crucial to its proper functioning.

One disadvantage of a public-key system is that it is inefficient compared to its conventional counterpart. The mathematical computations used to encrypt data require more time and, depending on the algorithm, the ciphertext may be much larger than the plaintext. Thus, public-key cryptography to encrypt large messages is presently impractical.

A second disadvantage of a public-key system is that an encrypted message can only be sent to a single recipient. Because a recipient's public key must be used to encrypt the message, sending to a list of recipients is not feasible using a public-key approach.

Although public-key cryptography, by itself, is inefficient for providing message secrecy, it is well suited for providing authentication, integrity, and nonrepudiation services. All these services are realized by digital signatures.

10.7.2.1 Digital Signatures   A digital signature is a cryptographic checksum computed as a function of a message and a user's private key. A digital signature is different from a hand-written signature, in that hand-written signatures are constant, regardless of the document being signed. A user's digital signature varies with the data. For example, if a user signs five different messages, five different signatures are generated. Each signature, however, can be authenticated for the signing user.

Due to the inefficiency of public-key cryptography, a user often signs a condensed version of a message—called a message digest—rather than the message itself. Message digests are generated by hash functions.

A hash function is a keyless transformation function that, given a variably-sized message as input, produces a fixed-sized representation of the message as output (the message digest). A hash function may condense a 1MB message into a 128- or 160-bit digest, for example.

For a hash function to be considered secure, it must meet two requirements. The hash function must be one-way and collisionless. One-way means that given a digest and the hash function, it is computationally infeasible to find the message that produced the digest. Collisionless means that it is not possible to find two messages that hash to the same digest. If a hash function meets these requirements, signing a message digest provides the same security services as signing the message itself.

The following example describes the digital signature process. It assumes two users have agreed upon a hash function and a signature algorithm for the signature verification process. For clarity, message secrecy is not included in the example.

An originator needs to send a signed message to a recipient. The originator performs the following procedure:

☞ Generates a digest for the message
☞ Computes a digital signature as a function of the digest and the originator's private key
☞ Transmits the message and the signature to the recipient

Upon receiving the message, the recipient performs the following procedure:

☞ Generates a digest for the received message
☞ Uses this digest, the originator's public key, and the received signature as input to a signature verification process

If the signature is verified, the following services are provided. First, the recipient is assured that the message was not modified. If even one bit of the original message was changed, the digest generated using the received message would cause the signature verification process to fail. Second, the recipient is assured that the originator sent the message. Public-key transformation functions are one-way (i.e., not forgeable); therefore, only a signature generated by the originator's private key can be validated using the originator's public key.

In addition to integrity and authentication, digital signatures provide nonrepudiation with proof of origin. Nonrepudiation with proof of origin is similar to but stronger than authentication, because the proof can be demonstrated to a third party. To provide authentication and nonrepudiation with proof of origin using a digital signature, a message originator signs a message (or digest) using the private key bound to the originator. Since only the originator can access the private key, the signature is unforgeable evidence that the originator generated the message.

In contrast, nonrepudiation with proof of origin cannot be provided inherently in a conventional cryptosystem. Since both parties involved in a communication share a secret key, both parties can deny sending a message, claiming that the other party is the message originator.

In addition to the nonrepudiation with proof of origin service, public-key cryptography has another advantage over conventional cryptography. The keys exchanged in a public-key system need not be kept secret. Thus, key distribution with a public-key system is simpler than a private-key system.

10.7.2.2 Public-Key Distribution

Users of a public-key system must access the public keys of other users. One means of distributing public keys is by certificates. A certificate is a public document containing information identifying a user, the user's public key, a time period during which the certificate is valid, and other information. Certificates are typically issued, managed, and signed by a central issuing authority, a certification authority (CA).

One method by which certificates can be distributed is described in the following example. User A and User B register with a CA. During the registration process, the users provide their public-key information to the CA. The CA, in turn, provides each user with the following information:

☞ A signed certificate containing the user's public key
☞ The public key information of the CA

The users store their certificates in a public directory (e.g., the X.500 Directory). At some future time, User A (the originator) sends a signed message to User B (the recipient). The message is signed using the originator's private key. Upon receipt, the recipient queries the public directory to obtain the originator's public-key certificate. The recipient first uses the CA's public key to validate the certificate's signature, and then verifies the originator's message signature using the public key contained in the certificate. One advantage of this scheme is that since public information is being transmitted, insecure data channels may be used for the communication. The digital signatures assure the integrity and authenticity of the information.

10.7.3 Public-Key Cryptography

Symmetric-key or secret-key cryptography uses the same key to encrypt and decrypt messages. This is a familiar real-world phenomenon: We use the same key to unlock and lock our car doors, for instance. The problem with symmetric-key cryptography is having the sender and receiver agree on a secret key without anyone else finding out.

Public-key cryptography was invented in 1976 by Whitfield Diffie and Martin Hellman to solve precisely this problem. With public-key cryptography, each person gets a pair of keys, a public key and a private key. Each person's public key is published, while the private key is kept secret. When A wants to send B a secure message, A encrypts it using B's public key. When B gets the message, B decrypts it using his private key. The sender and receiver no longer have to share secret information before they can communicate securely.

In practice, both symmetric-key and public-key techniques are used in popular security protocols, such as SSL and S/MIME, because symmetric-key algorithms tend to be much faster than public-key algorithms. Let us visit A and B again. They want to communicate securely, but they also want to communicate quickly. Here is the sequence:

1. A generates a random number (key) that will be used for encrypting A's message to B.

2. A encrypts the random number with B's public key.

3. B decrypts the random number with his private key. Now B has a secret shared only with A that they can use to encrypt and decrypt messages to each other.

In reality, most security protocols are much more complicated than this, but this three-step process gives you an idea of the fundamentals.

10.7.3.1 Using Public-Key Cryptography

Public-key systems are inefficient for encrypting large messages. The secret keys used in conventional cryptography are characteristically small. If conventional secret keys are viewed as a kind of message, the encrypting of these keys using a public-key algorithm would not place an unnecessary burden on the processing of a computer system. Thus, the joint use of conventional and public-key cryptography can be used to provide authentication, integrity, and secrecy in an efficient manner. The following example illustrates this idea. Note that, for simplicity, the example does not include the distribution of the public-key certificates.

An originator needs to send a signed, confidential message to a recipient. The originator first computes a digital signature as a function of the originator's private key and a digest of the plaintext message. Second, the originator generates a conventional secret key, and uses this key to transform the plaintext into ciphertext. Third, the originator encrypts the secret key using the recipient's public key. The originator finally appends the encrypted secret key and the digital signature to the ciphertext and transmits the information to the recipient.

Upon receipt, the secret key is decrypted using the recipient's private key. The secret key is then used to decrypt the ciphertext. Once the plaintext is obtained, the recipient validates the message signature as a function of the signature and the originator's public key. Secrecy is guaranteed because only the recipient's private key can be used to decrypt the secret key needed to decrypt the message. Integrity is guaranteed because the digital signature was generated using a digest of the original plaintext message. Finally, authentication is achieved, because the digital signature provides unforgeable evidence that the plaintext message was generated by the originator.

This scheme addresses the two disadvantages of a public-key system: performance and the inability to send a message to multiple recipients. Performance degradation is minimized, because a conventional algorithm (e.g., DES) is used to encrypt the message. Only the encrypting of the secret key (e.g., the DES key) requires a public-key algorithm. If the message is transmitted to several recipients, the originator encrypts the secret key once per recipient, using that recipient's public key. For example, if a message is sent to five recipients, five different encryptions of the secret key would be appended to the message.

10.7.3.2 Public-Key Certificates   Digital passports, or public-key certificates, are defined by a standard called X.509. A certificate is the digital equivalent of an employee badge, passport, or driver's license. The certificate and corresponding private key identify you to someone who needs proof of your identity.

Servers can be configured to grant access only to people with particular certificates; similarly, clients can be configured to trust only servers that present certain certificates.

An X.509 certificate is typically a small file that contains the information shown in Table 10.2.

Table 10.2 X.509 Certificate Contents

Field	Description	Examples
Subject's distinguishing name (DN)	Uniquely identifies the owner of the certificate	C=US, O=Connect, Inc., OU=Technology, CN=Norm Hager
Issuer's distinguishing name (DN)	Uniquely identifies the CA that signed the certificate	C=US, O=VeriSign, CN=VeriSign Class 1 root
Subject's public key	Owner's public key	512-bit RSA key
Issuer's signature	CA digital signature from which the certificate derives its authenticity	RSA encryption with MD5 hash (signature itself is not human readable)
Validity period	Dates between which the certificate is valid	Not before Wed, Nov 9, 2001, 15:54:17. Not after Fri, Dec 31, 2003, 15:54:17
Serial number	Unique number generated by the CA for administrative purposes	02:41:00:00:01

Table 10.3 reviews the challenges of public-key technology and exemplifies how industry-standard protocols such as SSL and S/MIME offer solutions for those challenges.

10.7.4 The ANSI Standard

ANSI X9.17 was developed to address the need of financial institutions to transmit securities and funds securely using an electronic medium.

This approach is based on a hierarchy of keys. At the bottom of the hierarchy are data keys (DKs), which are used to encrypt and decrypt messages. They are given short lifespans—such as one message or one connection. At the top of the hierarchy are key encrypting keys (KKMs). KKMs, which must be distributed manually, are afforded longer lifespans than data keys. Using the

Table 10.3 Public-Key Technology Challenges

Requirements	Public-Key Technology	Example of Use
Authentication of users without user name and password in the clear	Digital certificates (X.509)	SSL handshake includes exchange of client and server certificates and corresponding signatures
Single-user login	Digital certificates (X.509)	Servers configured to demand digital certificates rather than user name/password pairs
Scalability to the Internet	Standards-based encryption and message-digest algorithms (RSA, DES) negotiated using industry-standard protocols (SSL)	SSL works both inside and outside the firewall (unlike most proprietary security systems)
Message privacy (real-time as well as store-and-forward applications)	Public-key encryption and decryption (RSA); often used in conjunction with symmetric-key technology (RC2, RC4, DES) for higher performance	SSL protects the session key used to encrypt and decrypt a data stream with public-key encryption; S/MIME uses a similar technique for encrypting and signing E-mail messages in a store-and-forward paradigm
Message integrity	Message authentication codes calculated using message-digest algorithms (MD5, SHA1)	SSL calculates MACs using a message-digest algorithm and a key negotiated during the SSL handshake
Protection of confidential documents from unauthorized access	Digital certificates (X.509) and signatures	Binds users listed in ACLs to certificates or requires that users present a particular certificate (for example, signed by the Netscape Marketing CA) for access

two-tier model, the KKMs are used to encrypt the data keys. The data keys are then distributed electronically to encrypt and decrypt messages.

The two-tier model may be enhanced by adding another layer to the hierarchy. In the three-tier model, the KKMs do not encrypt data keys directly, but encrypt other key-encrypting keys (KKs). The KKs, which are exchanged electronically, are used to encrypt the data keys.

To exchange keys, one of the communicating parties creates a special message defined in X9.17, called a Cryptographic Service Message (CSM). CSMs are fixed-formatted messages used to establish new keys or discontinue use of existing keys. The CSM originator includes a MAC with the message (as specified in X9.9, "Message Authentication Standard" [ANS86]) to guarantee its integrity.

X9.17 describes two other environments for key distribution: key distribution centers and key translation centers. The key centers allow centralized management of keys. Rather than two parties sharing a KKM, each party shares a KKM with the center.

The difference between the two centers is that the key distribution center generates keys for its users. If an originator wants to send an encrypted message to a recipient, the originator submits the request to the key distribution center. The center generates and returns two identical keys to the originator. The first key is encrypted using the KKM shared between the center and the originator. The originator decrypts the key and uses it to encrypt the message. The second key is encrypted using the KKM shared between the center and the recipient. The originator transfers this key electronically to the recipient. The recipient decrypts the key and uses it to decrypt the originator's message.

Key translation centers are used when two parties require the key management functions provided by the center, but one or both of the parties want to generate the KKs and DKs. In this scenario, the originator submits a key and the recipient name to the center. The center encrypts the key using the KKM shared between the center and the recipient and returns the encrypted key to the originator. The originator transfers the key electronically to the recipient.

The advantages of the key centers are flexibility and efficiency. Users only need to exchange and store one KKM (with the center), rather than one KKM per communications partner. The center administers the distribution of KKMs for all its users. Cost is a disadvantage of the key centers but communications partners can reduce cost by exchanging a KK with the aid of a key center and then distributing DKs using a point-to-point approach.

10.8 INTERNET FIREWALLS

An Internet firewall is a device that sits between your internal network and the outside Internet. Its purpose is to limit access into and out of your network based on your organization's access policy. A firewall can be anything from a set of filtering rules set up on the router between you and the Internet to an elaborate application gateway consisting of one or more specially configured computers that control access. Firewalls permit desired services on the outside, such as Internet E-Mail, to pass.

In addition, most firewalls now allow access to the World Wide Web from inside the protected networks. The idea is to allow some services to pass but deny others.

10.9 CONCLUSIONS

Most operating systems have little or no security enabled when initially installed. In order to provide system security, a system administrator must not only be knowledgeable of the different ways to protect a system, but it is also imperative that the administrator implement the computer security plan in a thorough and consistent manner.

10.9.1 Networked/Distributed Systems

Networked systems are much more vulnerable to break-ins because of their accessibility over the network and the use of inherently insecure network protocols. In addition, if one system on a network is broken into, then other systems on the network may be compromised.

Many network protocols are subject to abuse. Each system using common network access procedures must protect against the threats associated with each service used. For example, each system running the UNIX r commands must take precautions to prevent the threats associated with the trusted hosts facility from being exploited. Individual systems must be responsibly administered so that all systems cooperate to achieve a secure network.

Secure gateways provide network security by blocking certain protocols and services from entering or exiting subnets. Secure firewalls have many advantages because security can be concentrated on a firewall. The firewall can be used to filter often-exploited common network access protocols from entering a subnet while permitting those protocols to be used on the inside subnet without fear of exploitation from outside systems.

Robust authentication mechanisms improve the authentication process beyond conventional authentication mechanisms such as passwords.

Local area networking has become a widely used means for organizations to share distributed computing resources. Internet sites often use the TCP/IP protocol suite and UNIX for local area networking purposes, because they offer methods for centralizing the management of users and resources. This aids greatly in reducing the amount of work and overhead involved in managing user accounts and making distributed resources available to users.

It can also be practical to use the same protocols and services for wide area networking as well as for local area networking.

But two factors now make using TCP/IP for local area networking an increasingly risky business: A number of the TCP/IP services are inherently flawed and vulnerable to exploitation, and the tremendous growth of the Internet has greatly increased the likelihood of such exploitation. Crackers often roam the Internet searching for unprotected sites; misconfigured systems as well as the use of insecure protocols make the cracker's job much easier. Two of the TCP/IP services most often used in local area networking, Network Information Services (NIS) and Network File System (NFS), are easily exploited; crackers can use weaknesses in NIS and NFS to read and write files, learn user information, capture passwords, and gain privileged access.

Kerberos and Secure RPC are effective means for reducing the risks and vulnerabilities of local area TCP/IP networks; however, they require modified network daemon programs on all participating hosts. For many sites, the most practical method for securing access to systems and use of inherently vulnerable services is to use a secure gateway, or firewall system.

Public-key technology is also gaining broad market acceptance as the primary means of safeguarding electronic transactions. Public-key technology figures prominently in a large collection of protocols and payment technologies, including Secure Electronic Transactions (SET), the credit card transaction protocol; Electronic Data Interchange (EDI) applications; electronic cash; and micropayment technology.

Building on public-key technology is much more than an investment in a particular protocol or a single vendor's product. It is an investment in a general-purpose technology that is rapidly becoming a foundation for the many applications of secure communications over the Internet.

Distributed Object Technologies

11.1 INTRODUCTION

Distributed computing environments are those which allow for diverse, geographically separate or remote systems to interact and work cooperatively on the same tasks and to interconnect remote sites, facilities, or people.

Distributed computing environments and technologies enable one of the critical challenges of a ubiquitous information infrastructure to be realized: The integration of a diverse set of applications. For example, it enables distributed manufacturing by allowing the interaction of process controllers with remote design databases and engineering design tools and it allows remote experimentation and visualization for educational applications. In this section, we will examine the object-oriented paradigms that enable distribution of function and promote multiprocessing.

11.2 OBJECT TECHNOLOGIES

An object is a programming abstraction that encapsulates logically related data and behavior in a single group. A customer object contains all the data related to a particular object and all the behaviors (called *methods*) for manipulating that data. Before objects, data and behavior were all mixed together. One routine might manipulate billing and customer data while another manipulated customer and order data. This inconsistency made it difficult for programmers to track down bugs in existing systems, especially if they had to be modified.

With object technology, all objects with common behaviors are lumped together in one compartment. This makes things orderly, and it is easy to see exactly what is going on. The container or object's methods protect its data. The methods encapsulate the data, which means they are only accessible by an object's own methods.

For example, if an invoice object needs to know a customer's discount, it does not interrogate the customer object's discount variable. Instead, it calls the customer object's discount method. This has far-reaching implications. When creating the invoice object, the programmer does not need to know anything about the customer object's discount method. Therefore, implementations can be done by different programmers at different stages or even at different locations. In addition, any changes in the discount method are independent of the invoice object.

Understanding how a method can have more than one implementation brings us to the *classes* of objects. Since there are many different aspects of a customer, and a number of methods can be employed to express various functions, the customer object probably is an entire class of objects. Once we group objects into classes, we can group classes into subclasses.

Suppose we have three types of buyers who purchase goods from a company. One is at an enterprise level, one is of medium size, and the third is a small operator. We could assign each buyer into a subclass by itself. In this way, we could apply different discount percentages for each subclass. From the invoice's class perspective, it does not matter how the discounts are computed. We have isolated the public interfaces of the object from their private (subclass) implementations. On the other hand, other classes can use the buyer class's interfaces without knowing its implementation. This allows reuse of objects from application to application, thus reducing code dependencies. Some of the other benefits of object programming are:

☞ Objects lower development time and maintenance costs.

☞ Distributed objects enable flexible and robust application architectures, especially during application execution. These are accomplished without any changes to the fundamental nature of objects. When an invoice object needs service from a buyer object, it calls one of the buyer object's methods by sending it a message. The message contains the identity of the particular object, the method desired, and any parameters for the method.

11.2.1 What Makes an Object Distributed?

To call objects "distributed," we must put some distance between them. The concept of sending a message to an object's interface becomes real. The term *distributed objects* covers a lot of ground. Let me illustrate this concept in two examples:

☞ Assume we have a customer database with information on the customer's financial status as well as product choices. Two different people in the same organization may need to access different data from the same database. They can use two different applications, one to process all the bug reports the customer has logged and the other accounts receivable.

☞ In another scenario, three different departments need to find out the status of the bugs reported by a customer. Sales, core development, and customer support can employ the same application to access the same data but receive a different report format.

11.2.2 Distributed Objects over the Web

The Internet and the Web open up a whole new set of challenges with regard to distributed objects. We are not talking only about distributing enterprise objects around a network; we may want to make them available to our partners and suppliers to enable closer cooperation. We also may make these directly available to our customers to reduce customer service costs. A Web-based HelpDesk is an example in which customers can directly log their complaints/bugs in the supplier database and get status via the Web instantly.

11.2.2.1 Standards   Some products and standards—such as UNIX, the Microsoft Windows family (Windows 3.1, NT, 95, and 98), TCP/IP, DCE, NFS, and CORBA—usually are included because of their importance. For this section, I will concentrate on object technologies that address the distributed nature of computing.

The problem of high-level application interworking and construction is well recognized in the software industry. Enabling diverse applications that are written in many different languages, run on multiple operating systems, and use a variety of networking protocols is a challenging problem. Its solution lies in the marriage of distributed technology to object orientation.

Distribution technology offers the basic infrastructure to abstract the communication layers, while object orientation provides the necessary framework for encapsulation and reuse needed, which is to facilitate application integration. There have been numerous initiatives in this area. While they originate from different perspectives with differing design centers, all offer similar facilities.

Recognizing the urgent need for a standard in high-level application interworking, including across multiple platforms and network architectures, the software industry formed a consensus via the Object Management Group (OMG) and, in particular, the Common Object Request Broker Architecture (CORBA) specification.

11.2.3 A Bit of CORBA

CORBA was designed to provide the specification for an object-oriented "universal middleware" that would allow programmers—without knowledge of how or where the object was implemented—to write objects that could interact with other objects. OMG accomplished this by specifying two primary tools for the architect and programmer: The interface definition language (IDL) and the object request broker (ORB).

CORBA represents the confluence of distributed processing and object orientation. It is the world's first multivendor, industry-supported distributed object standard. CORBA provides a standard method to distribute remote objects across multiple platforms and operating systems in a way that is seamless and transparent to the user. The architecture itself is isolated from the actual transport protocols (e.g., TCP, IPX, SNA) needed to support it, thereby allowing an open-ended standard.

To be sure, there are other ways to distribute services, including Sockets, RPCs, DCE, and reams of *middleware-oriented methods* (MOMs). These tools get the job done with differing levels of complexity and success. Nearly all have been wrapped into object-oriented class libraries, as well. However, none of them was specifically designed to provide the seamless integration of distributed objects in a client/server environment; that is, there is no intrinsic concept of object-passing (by value) or remote inheritance. CORBA dissolves those barriers by allowing distributed objects to behave in precisely the same way as local objects.

The specification is composed of two chief parts: an IDL and language mappings between IDL and implementation languages (e.g., C++, C, Ada95, Java, and Smalltalk). The language mappings relate both to how an object invokes an IDL-defined (CORBA) object and to how an object user should implement an IDL-defined (CORBA) object in a given implementation language.

IDL really is just an object structure that gives developers an API to access the object services while the objects are up and running. IDL lets you build applications and understand the types of objects with which you can communicate when an ORB-based application is up and running.

The IDL serves somewhat the same purpose for objects as English does for our conversing programmers: It provides a common language. However, using the OMG IDL is only part of the battle in getting objects to communicate. The other part involves using a piece of software to arbitrate or broker the requests from the objects.

IDL is used to define interfaces to objects. Remote objects view a CORBA object purely in terms of this interface. IDL provides encapsulation of an object's implementation behind a formal IDL interface that is independent of implementation language, implementation algorithm, location, machine architecture, operating system, network technology, and even ORB architecture. This separation of interface and implementation allows CORBA to be viewed as a *software bus* and is one of its most powerful aspects.

An ORB is a piece of infrastructural technology that aids in the development of CORBA objects and arranges for objects to access each other at runtime as defined by the CORBA specification. The software that brokers request from objects is called an object request broker. If you add a "C" at the start, representing "Common," and an "A" at the end, representing "Architecture," the resulting acronym is CORBA. CORBA, then, is an architecture (or specification) that defines the least common denominator to which all ORBs must adhere in order to be compliant.

The Dynamic Invocation Interface (DII) allows an invocation to be constructed manually, without static (compile time) knowledge of the object being invoked. In return for explicitly building messages and argument lists at runtime, the dynamic API allows decisions to be made much later than the static approach. This is attractive for applications in which insufficient information about remote objects is available at compile time. Such applications include browsers and resource managers.

DII also gives dynamic construction of object invocations. You do not have to call a routine to invoke an operation inside a particular object. The client can set up the objects and operations, including any parameters. With DII, you can make decisions while the objects are running. IDL requires you to set things up beforehand.

The Static Invocation Interface (SII) allows an invoking object to access a remote object using syntax that is natural to the implementation language. The disadvantage of the DII approach is that the API is more complex to use than the SII approach. The ORB development environment ensures that this works.

11.2.4 Database Perspectives

From the database programmer's perspective, the most interesting part of CORBA is found in the Object Transaction Service (OTS), a subspecification of CORBA that defines how atomic transactions can be distributed over multiple objects and multiple ORBs. If you are migrating from a transaction-oriented world, in which the ACID (atomicity, consistency, isolation, and durability) principle governs how your systems handle client interactions with databases, you accept no compromises in your object-oriented systems. Let's look at how OTS brings CORBA benefits to the database world.

The CORBA OTS was designed to interact simultaneously with both ORB-based and traditional TP monitor-based transaction services. This means a client can initiate a recoverable transaction composed of a mix of resources managed by an object as well as resources managed by a TP monitor. The OTS offers the capability of supporting recoverable nested transactions and, in a heterogeneous environment, fully supports ACID and two-phase commit protocols.

Part of the secret behind effective transaction processing lies in good control over concurrency; that is, the locks the transaction places upon the resources during the commit phases of the transaction. CORBA partners OTS with products written to another CORBA specification called the Concurrency Control Service (CCS) to provide these services. The locks available run the gamut from the usual read and write to intention read and intention write. The latter two locks queue reading and writing, respectively, behind currently held locks. In addition, an upgrade lock gives programmers a tool to help prevent deadlocks. These locks can be specified as transactional or nontransactional.

As with traditional, nonobject, transaction processing environments, work in the OTS is divided between clients and servers. Clients issue requests for transaction services, which are filled by transaction servers. A wrinkle added by the object environment is in the recoverable server, which groups all transaction objects for a particular transaction request.

The OTS consists of four important interfaces: Current, Coordinator, Resource, and SubtransactionAwareSource. The *Current* interface lets the programmer establish a context for a transaction. As objects are created and destroyed during the course of the transaction's life, this context is attached to each object and permits the ORB to pass requests from client services to servers controlling resources. When a response from a server object is received at the ORB, the ORB maintains the context of the request and is able to return the desired data to the originating client.

The *Resource* provides an interface to objects implementing the two-phase commit protocol. Multiple resource objects can participate in a transaction but, as with all two-phase commit implementations, each participating resource votes on whether it can fulfill the request submitted to it. If any one resource votes no, the transaction is rolled back or suspended, depending on how the client message was coded. If the vote from a resource object is ambiguous, you can write code to send a forget message to the Current interface, which causes the transaction to drop the resource sending the ambiguous message but allows the rest of the transaction to continue. To increase efficiency in environments in which there is only one resource, OTS current interface provides the option of using the commit_one_phase message, which bypasses the unnecessary overhead of the two-phase commit protocol.

The *Coordinator* interface enables the programmer to invoke services within the CORBA OTS itself. These messages are used primarily by servers to create subtransactions and to coordinate recovery efforts should the current transaction require termination. With the range of messages available in the Coordinator interface, the server-side programmer using the OTS services of the ORB in use has a wide range of granularity available to permit interaction at whatever level of specificity is required. Inter-ORB communication via TCP/IP takes on the greatest significance in the most heterogeneous environment of all.

11.2.5 An ORB

The concept of an ORB grew out of the early days of object-oriented development. As developers learned to leverage objects within applications, they looked to mix and match objects with other applications as well. Because objects are tool-dependent—such as C++, Smalltalk, and PowerBuilder—they do not work and play well with others. Developers needed a binary object standard that would let them mix and match language-independent objects.

ORBs are based on the concept of using standard objects that communicate with other standard objects through a well-defined interface. Like C++ or Smalltalk objects, ORBs invoke each other's methods as well as send and receive data. Because ORBs typically run on any number of platforms, developers can create distributed heterogeneous applications. ORBs are naturally distributed, and they communicate within the same server or with many servers over a network (distributed ORBs or distributed objects).

In their spare time, ORBs pass requests from clients to object implementations on which they are invoked. The client makes the request using the ORB core through the IDL stub or through the DII. The stub provides the mapping between the language of choice (such as C++, Java, or Smalltalk). The ORB has to support the mapping. The ORB core can then transfer the request to the object implementation that receives the message through an up-call using an IDL skeleton or dynamic skeleton.

11.2.5.1 Anatomy of an ORB   The CORBA ORB provides four main components:

- ☞ The orb
- ☞ Object services
- ☞ Common facilities
- ☞ Application objects

ORBs can communicate with other local or remote objects using a well-defined common interface and line protocol. ORBs make requests to other ORBs (using the same standards, such as DCOM and CORBA) and process responses. The power of ORBs is that all of these communications and method invocations take place away from the eye of the user. The applications are built on top of the ORBs, and the ORBs carry on business in the background automatically. This ensures portability and interoperability, either locally or across a network. The CORBA specification simply defines how these ORBs work together.

Object services are groups of services that use an object interface to communicate from one service to the next. Object services provide base services such as security, transaction management, and data exchange. Using this base set of services, developers can build other services on top of them. Object services are mandated by CORBA.

Common facilities are collections of services as well, but they relate more to a client than a server. You can see what common facilities do by looking at component document facilities such as OpenDoc. Common facilities are optional CORBA services.

Application objects support the application directly. These objects are defined by the developer, and they are the portions of CORBA that actually solve the business problem at hand. These are the facilities that are built using the IDL. The IDL assures that they can communicate with other CORBA-compliant ORBs.

11.2.5.2 ORB in Action   Several implementations offer OTS services for their object request broker products. It is possible, incidentally, to use DCE in a CORBA environment, thanks to the Internet Inter-ORB Protocol, because the CORBA specification provides for a General Inter-Orb Protocol (GIOP). The mappings of the GIOP messages to specific transports such as DCE are provided for with mappings such as CIOP to other transports. CIOP stands for the DCE Common Inter-Orb Protocol and describes how the ORBs can take advantage of the fault-tolerant features DCE provides. The essential feature of all other mappings (such as CIOP) is that they use TCP as the bus over which the DCE transport information is overlaid.

VisiBroker for C++ is a complete CORBA ORB implementation that supports IIOP. Because CORBA provides a bus for inter-ORB communication via TCP/IP, VisiBroker can communicate with the VisiBroker for Java ORB. VisiBroker for Java is written entirely in Java and is designed for building, managing, and deploying distributed Java applications.

The CORBA IIOP enables users to break beyond the single-vendor ORB barriers imposed by earlier versions of CORBA. With that software bus and the growing implementation of OTS—particularly its near-seamless integration with X/Open-compliant transaction monitors—the future looks bright for system architects seeking true object-oriented heterogeneous solutions to implementing transaction processing in heterogeneous environments.

11.2.6 IIOP

The CORBA 2.0 specification, published in 1995, introduced important extensions to the features outlined above. A standardized C++ mapping was introduced, protecting developers' programming investment, improving code portability, and further easing software maintenance. The Dynamic Skeleton Interface (DSI) provided a server-side equivalent to the DII that assisted developers in building gateways between CORBA and non-CORBA systems. In addition, the CORBA 2.0 IIOP provides a standardized transport protocol for all CORBA-compliant ORBs.

IIOP is the open Internet protocol for communication between objects and applications. Based on the (CORBA) specification, IIOP not only allows ORBs to interoperate but also enables users to build and distribute multivendor applications across intranets and the Internet. IIOP has become a standard protocol for object-linking across the network and has been adopted by many implementers to allow their browsers to access objects across the Internet or intranet.

11.2.7 CORBA Services

In addition to the standard C++ mapping and IIOP, CORBA includes many services. These include a naming service, event service OTS, initialization service, life cycle service, and persistence. CORBA is suitable for two distinct but related activities:

1. *Writing a distributed system using conventional programming languages,* such as C++, Smalltalk, Ada95, and Java. The requirements here are that the objects of the system can communicate with each other easily, that is with high transparency. By transparency I mean that objects can communicate without considering difficult issues like network protocols, byte streams, network addresses, data representation conversions, and object persistence and replication.

2. *Application integration,* for both new and existing applications, across heterogeneous hardware and software platforms. Applications can provide a number of IDL interfaces and make these available to the overall system. This allows new applications to be written by combining the facilities of existing applications. Since the components of the system are objects whose internals are hidden from their clients, these objects can interface with legacy systems. This support for legacy systems is crucial for some applications.

11.3 CORBA INTEGRATION

CORBA and Common Object Model (COM), from Microsoft, are the two leading technologies for enabling application integration. Although both are object-oriented, they have different origins. COM begins on the desktop, framing application integration in terms of the document and other graphical components. CORBA began at the network, viewing application integration as a messaging layer that successfully routes messages among application components across a network.

Windows-based distributed applications can be written in conventional programming languages, such as C++ or Visual Basic, using the CORBA programming paradigm. COM-based programming systems, such as Visual Basic, can transparently access and distribute CORBA services. CORBA programs running on any machine can transparently access COM objects on Windows. Windows provides four distinct use models for seamless integration of COM and CORBA: COM client/COM server, CORBA client/COM server, client and server in COM, and client and server in CORBA.

11.3.1 COM Client/CORBA Server

Orbix for Windows allows developers to pass Server IDL through the OLE Wizard. The Wizard generates code for either standard COM servers or COM custom controls (ActiveX Controls). These servers can then represent remote CORBA objects on the desktop, and client/server connections are made using standard COM calls. The default Orbix locator transparently manages the locating of remote CORBA objects, leaving the user to concentrate on developing functionality, not network programming.

11.3.2 CORBA Client/COM Server

Orbix for Windows includes a tool that generates IDL from the type information of a COM server. This IDL can be passed through the Orbix Wizard to create an ActiveX Control, which in turn can expose whichever CORBA interface is desired. This ActiveX Control can be placed within the COM server, and the EXE can be registered with Orbix as an active Orbix server. Alternatively, the ActiveX Control can be placed in a proxy application, in order to connect with servers that are not your own.

11.3.3 Client and Server in COM

Users can either write IDL interfaces or generate them (as detailed above) from an existing COM server. This IDL can be used to generate an ActiveX Control with a set of CORBA interfaces. The Orbix Wizard can generate a set of server stubs in various languages, such as Visual Basic and C++.

The server is then implemented by filling in the blanks in the generated stubs, adding additional server functionality. The client is implemented as though it were talking to a local COM server.

11.3.4 Client and Server in CORBA

The user also can choose to implement the distributed system solely using CORBA and C++. Object interfaces are written in IDL, which then generates stub code on the client side and skeleton code on the server side. The server side objects are then implemented as outlined above. On the client side, the stub code marshals the invocation to communicate with the server-based objects.

11.4 CORBA AND THE INTERNET MERGE

Once the Internet and CORBA have been merged by making intelligent objects in the dispersed Internet into a superposition of Java and CORBA using Externalization II, the distribution services of both infrastructures must be rationalized. In CORBA's architecture, the notion of *services* is quite formalized. Each service has standardized IDL interfaces.

In contrast, the Internet services tend to have the ad hoc feel of the Internet itself. For example, there is no official naming service, per se, but DNS has undoubtedly taken on that role for locating host machines, and URL addressing has become the de facto standard for referencing by name individual atomic resources. A similar situation exists for security and other services. Still other facilities, such as concurrency and transactions, have no standards at all in the Internet community. The mechanisms either simply do not exist or are handled in a completely proprietary manner by every resource implementer.

For those cases in which the Internet already has de facto standards for services (e.g., for naming and possibly for security), the CORBA services must adjust themselves to accommodate the larger body of Internet facilities. Of course, the Internet services do not typically have programmatic APIs at all, let alone canonical object IDL interfaces. These IDL services may have to change to support other ways of doing things. For example, the CORBA naming service is intended to be flexible and allow the insertion of foreign name spaces (such as DNS or X.500) into its naming hierarchies.

Also, for those cases in which the Internet has no comparable services today, the sudden arrival of the CORBA services for things like licensing and transactions is certain to be welcomed and to make the whole Internet a much more powerful infrastructure. It is not just the Internet but the superposition of the Internet, Java, CORBA, OpenDoc, and much more. Of course, to the layman, it will probably always be known as the Internet.

11.4.1 Object-Oriented Web Servers

The best object-oriented (OO) Web servers are those whose design and implementation are completely object-oriented, not merely object-based API. There has been a rapid evolution of Web server technology since its relatively recent birth. Web servers started as simple HTML document servers, then were augmented with the Common Gateway Interface (CGI) for invoking scripts and other processes on the server. CGI scripts (mostly written in Perl) combined with HTML input forms create the basis for useful data access utilities and dynamic HTML documents. Developers have been creative in applying the limited CGI interface for connecting to a wide variety of back-end systems.

Through these extensions, the Web server has evolved into a middle layer within an n-tier client/server architecture, connecting Web clients to other database and legacy servers. However, the essential characteristic of a Web server is not its support of CGI extensions, or even that it is capable of delivering static HTML and multimedia files. A Web server is recognized by a client simply because it supports the Hypertext Transport Protocol (HTTP).

Most Web server requests are received as GET or POST commands, and the results are delivered as a data stream with additional MIME-type header information. Because HTTP rides on top of TCP/IP (the language of the Internet), it is easy to add HTTP support as a front-end to almost any network system. For example, embedded systems for real-time manufacturing control were already converting to TCP/IP network communication, and now are adding very lightweight HTTP servers to these embedded systems that allow any Web browser to query their status.

An object-oriented Web server can be created either by adding HTTP protocol support to an existing server platform or by developing an extensible Web server using OO technologies. The best OO Web servers are those with designs and implementation that are completely object-oriented, not merely an object-based API. You can see benefits from two perspectives: Extensible Web server architectures and distributed model-view-controller designs.

11.4.2 Extensible Web Servers

Most client/server systems are designed with a two-tier architecture, a fat client connected to a database server. Even Java-based systems do not deviate from this approach, they simply use Java Database Connectivity (JDBC) in a large client applet to connect to a database. In these systems, the Web server has the trivial role of delivering the applet to the client browser. Object-oriented Web servers are able to take a more active role in a middle tier of the architecture.

OO Web servers often are described as *extensible*, meaning they either expose class interfaces to be implemented or provide superclasses for inheritance, or both. Application-specific subclasses are loaded into the server process and become an integral part of its functionality. There is growing support for a standard *servlet* API so that new subclasses can be written to run on many different servers.

The servlet object is primarily responsible for communicating with the client. For HTTP protocol, this communication consists of retrieving parameters from the GET and POST request, and prepending appropriate headers onto the response. The actual work done by the servlet is performed by other objects instantiated by the servlet object. These other objects might be responsible for database or legacy system connectivity, or they might be skeletons for CORBA-based objects that are implemented on yet another server.

Other previously written, domain-specific classes can be integrated, thus extending the Web server with application logic, business rules, or other middle-tier functionality.

11.4.2.1 Distributed Model-View-Controller Model-view-controller (MVC) designs were popularized by Smalltalk, but have wide applicability in other systems. MVC actually consists of two design patterns: Observer and strategy. The view is an observer of the model, and the controller implements a strategy for handling the view's events. The benefit is realized when an application is split into these logical components, and when different implementations of the components can be interchanged. For example, a model can have several views, and the view/model combination can have several strategies for handling events and coordinating their communication.

With distributed MVC, the view and model run on the client and server, respectively. The controller manages their interaction. Consider a few variations on this pattern. First, for a basic HTML interface, the MVC fulfills the role of a controller handling the HTTP messages from the view in a Web browser client. In this case, the servlet also implements an adapter pattern, acting as an intermediary between the view and the model. The servlet uses data from the client request to invoke methods in the model, then provides HTML translation of the results back to the client view. The model can be an arbitrarily complex object system that is instantiated directly by the servlet, or accessible via a secondary connection such as CORBA's IIOP.

A second scenario would use a Java applet for the view running on the client; but, unlike most applets, this one uses the HTTP POST command to communicate to the servlet running in a Web server. Similar to the first case, the servlet (controller) passes the request along to the model. However, now the servlet can send either formatted HTML or a raw data stream back to the applet, and the applet and servlet could negotiate which return format to use. Compared with the first case, the view is completely new and the model requires no change whatsoever. If HTML is returned to the applet (perhaps to be redirected by the applet to another frame in the browser), then the controller is identical to the first case. An equivalent POST command can be sent either by an HTML form or by an applet, so an equivalent controller can be used.

A third scenario also uses an applet and servlet to fill the roles of view and controller. But in this case, the applet opens a socket connection with the servlet and carries out its communication via a proprietary protocol on this dedicated channel. The model is the same as in the first two cases, but now both view and controller must change to support their new communication design. The view and controller classes probably should subclass general implementations so that the behavior that is common across all three scenarios can be inherited from one code base.

Additional scenarios should be developed that make greater use of distributed objects. For example, the servlet controller might be primarily responsible for returning remote object references to the view, allowing the view to directly execute methods on the remote objects in the model. There is widespread interest in using the IIOP as a replacement for CGI.

11.5 REEVALUATING DISTRIBUTED OBJECTS

Slowly but surely, distributed objects are making their way into the world of client/server. In the '90s, what was supposed to be a revolution turned out to be an evolution of specifications and trial balloons. Today, however, we could be on the verge of moving mainstream client/server development into the world of distributed objects, and the Web could be the way to get there.

Other issues that could move developers toward distributed objects include Microsoft's Distributed Component Object Model (DCOM) and its ActiveX (formally OCX) component incarnation. With Windows NT 5.0 already DCOM-ready and Windows 98 heading there quickly, developers may find that their ORB infrastructure is part of the operating system. Existing OLE-enabled tools are ready to take advantage of the Microsoft give-away ORB.

Components are part of the game, as well. OpenDoc is a component of IBM's Distributed System Object Model (DSOM), which adheres to CORBA.

There are tough decisions in your future, so let's start from the beginning by looking at the concept behind distributed objects, as well as the standards that now compete for the hearts and minds of developers and tool implementers. We will also examine components and their links to distributed object standards, and then how distributed objects are changing the Web.

11.5.1 CORBA

Different object models arise from different requirements. OLE/COM provides interfaces for popular desktop suites and applications. Smalltalk provides an object-oriented application environment. C++ provides a means for object-oriented systems, infrastructures, and component-building. Important standards like CORBA IDL provide a language-neutral and location-neutral messaging interface for component integration. ORB provides the communications backbone with which these different object models can coexist within one enterprise system. Some of the communication models employed in the enterprise model are:

1. *A message bus for CORBA-component objects and servers.* Components can be individual large-grained objects, collaborating groups of objects, or existing nonobject-oriented monolithic applications wrapped with CORBA interfaces. Also called *business objects* and *frameworks*, these building blocks employ object-oriented mechanisms such as inheritance and polymorphism to provide higher-level applications logic.

2. *Fabricating the CORBA components out of smaller, individual objects that cooperate to form components.* These individual objects may perform business rules and support logic such as GUIs. Since they form the plumbing for components, they frequently have more stringent performance characteristics, such as asynchronous messages and event handlers. They frequently are written in an object-oriented language like C++ or Smalltalk.

3. *Assembling and coordinating (scripting) the CORBA components into desktop-centric applications.* This involves connecting OLE/COM/DCOM components and enterprise component (CORBA) objects. Scripting tools at this layer also would make use of tools such as Visual Basic to allow nonprogrammers and power users to build the final stages of the user applications.

The CORBA IDL specification is not an implementation model but, rather, an interface and services model. It is language-neutral and leaves maximum flexibility for underlying implementation details. In fact, recent attempts by some ORB implementers to build enterprises using CORBA IDL as the low-level implementation model have resulted in performance and integration issues that have forced the customers to provide expensive, proprietary extensions to the CORBA-based ORB. This problem could be avoided by using CORBA IDL for distributed component interfaces rather than for individual C++/Smalltalk distributed objects.

11.5.1.1 Component Integration A component of CORBA is intended to behave like an object or object server to a client application, even though it may not actually be written in an object-oriented language like C++. This component *encapsulation* of an application is done by representing it with IDL and hiding the actual details of the application, and its location, from the client. In particular, the CORBA object model provides a strong separation of *interface* from *implementation*. CORBA is oriented to the component subsystem, or server, level rather than the individual object level.

The CORBA IDL is not pure OO technology. While IDL does support interface inheritance, it is more a tool for encapsulating things to make them look like objects to a client. Bindings to convert IDL to languages like C++, Smalltalk, C, COBOL, and ADA allow organizations to describe application objects and services with a well-known IDL interface and provide this interface specification enterprisewide to software developers using many different implementation languages.

The CORBA IDL component is intended to serve as an *interface specification* or *contract* between departments, corporations, larger applications, or entities in a system so that they can provide adequate performance with a synchronous or deferred synchronous (also called *polling*) architecture. In other words, IDL provides a standard client/server interface. A client program requests a server for information, waits until the information is obtained, and continues on to the next activity.

11.5.1.2 Environment Independence

CORBA is not only language-neutral (it is intended to support C++, C, etc.), it also is fairly object-model-neutral. Even though it is an ORB model, it is flexible enough to allow nonobject-oriented modules and applications to fit into the ORB mechanism. Nonobject-oriented pieces can exchange data with one another and with object subsystems as well. Given that not all the components in an enterprise may be object-oriented, CORBA IDL must provide descriptive features that are not tied to any language or object model.

The purpose of the ORB is actually narrow in terms of enterprise application functionality: To provide an interface to remote object components and a *router* between local and remote objects and components. CORBA does not go beyond this base ORB functionality for a reason: There may be many special-purpose ORBs for a variety of application needs, ranging from lightweight embedded requirements to full-service corporate infrastructures. This least common denominator does have a cost, however, in that it cannot directly exploit the features of native object-oriented languages that can enhance functionality or performance.

For example, IDL interfaces currently do not provide for the transmission of full objects between components: There are no C++ like pointers, no event callbacks for asynchronous behavior, no broadcasting/multicasting of objects to multiple receivers, and so on, because these are features that are not common to all languages that need access to the ORB. But they are needed, and so have to be provided at some level in order to build a working system. Discussing the low-level enablers and services of distributed object systems leads naturally to the following discussion of the strengths of a more generic object model for full enterprise-capable applications.

11.5.1.3 Asynchronous Message-Based Communications

The design features for object systems are well-understood: *inheritance, encapsulation,* and *polymorphism*. These object characteristics provide the central design benefit of objects—namely, *reusability*. One factor in reusability is a communications model using a message-based architecture. Messaging is a lightweight communications paradigm, a *send and continue until notified* approach that allows for an object to be available for further requests and activities instead of being tied up while waiting for a server to return a result. With asynchronous messaging, the client can simply be notified when the results are ready instead of waiting, or repeatedly polling, for data. The benefits of asynchronous messaging are evident in a large network with many objects, since the overhead from the synchronous blocking, and for client-side polling, can be quite high.

11.5.1.4 Event-Driven Response and Manageability

Other characteristics of fully distributed object systems (which must be implemented in the server side of the ORB) centered on object-level deployment and management features. In a multiplatform networked environment, systems must transparently migrate and transport objects around the network so that client-level services can be provided independent of location. Also, migration permits services to be load-balanced or failed-over to another system, transparently to the client.

Another feature is event-driven response capabilities: Manageable object systems are able to respond to *events*, which are messages coming from outside the system or control loop. These events can range from networks going down to inventory objects suddenly running low. The system must be able to respond to events like this, asynchronously and in a controlled manner.

The difference in communications requirements between component level and individual object level is this: The latter require lightweight interobject communications that allow objects to *send and continue*—to send the message and then continue on with other activities until they are notified that the request is ready. Events and messages are part and parcel of object systems, especially of distributed object systems with all the complexities of network behavior. Object systems are fundamentally different from synchronous call and wait client/server programs in this regard, and the application of RPC-style call-and-wait communications can bog down a system with numerous objects.

11.5.2 Merging Object Models

The key to building standards-compliant distributed object systems is to use the features of the different object models where they are most appropriate, based on business requirements. Specifically, the enterprise object-oriented application should be driven by lower-level object models for the implementation details, with CORBA IDL used for interface specifications between components. There is at times a language mismatch between the CORBA and OO-language models, given that CORBA is intended for integration with existing client/server and legacy applications while native approaches (like Smalltalk/C++) are intended for low-level modeling of application support and system support objects. Both models are important, and both must be managed and merged for enterprise object systems.

11.5.3 Implementing Message-Based Architectures

One example of this is the need for a low-level interobject communications approach that works well inside components as well as between them. The misapplication of component-level IDL communications models to individual object-level communications leads to several kinds of performance and maintainability issues.

11.5.3.1 Clientside Threads   The individual object relies heavily on IDL's synchronous approach. With synchronous method invocation as the only calling style, client code needs to propagate threads (threads attempt to build asynchronous behavior on top of synchronous calls) to other intermediate software packages. The client must maintain and manage these threads in addition to its own applications.

Threads are powerful enablers for concurrency on the server side, where they provide transparent scalability to many clients. But they should not be the primary means of concurrency for the client side, where they increase the coding burden and make integration more difficult with add-on packages.

11.5.3.2 Interobject Network Coupling   The object messaging/event paradigm is somewhat compromised by the component synchronous/deferred synchronous approach, if it is used for too many low-level objects. When a client object connects to another object, which in turn connects to another object, a *stacking effect* results, in which the intermediate object is blocked and unavailable to other potential clients. This stacking increases behavioral coupling between objects and reduces availability (reusability) to other potential clients. This can be avoided by allowing heavily used intermediate objects to send messages on and then continue with their own control loops in order to service other object requests.

Other ORB implementers have tried to get around these problems with low-level, interobject synchronous communications, but the work-arounds are not optimal for a variety of reasons, including:

☞ One strategy is to simulate asynchronous callbacks with IDL oneway function calls to set up a double oneway connection between the client object and the server object, each managing the connection to the other. Unfortunately, this means that the server is no longer independent of the client and has to be aware of client-side behavior, especially if it has to manage connections to more than one client, which is generally the case.

A better solution would be to allow the client to set up a callback so that it is notified when the server data is ready, since the client and server are decoupled time-wise and more independent of each other. This approach often is needed for numerous objects and is an example of asynchronous method invocation.

☞ Another strategy is the DII *deferred synchronous* method invocation style, which is useful for component clients to poll for data from a server, if they know the waiting period is going to be too long for a synchronous wait. The utility of a polling approach that works for a few large processes is dependent on how many clients are doing it over the network.

The disadvantage of polling is twofold. It may clog the network if done too much and it still requires the client to go back and check for data, thus wasting time managing the information transaction instead of saving its CPU cycles for more useful work. The Extended C++'s asynchronous callbacks permit the client to be notified, and hence interrupted, only when its data is ready. This is effective for large numbers of distributed objects in large networks.

☞ Another approach being used to deal with synchronous calls over a network involves the use of *smart proxies*. This is a caching scheme to duplicate the remote object server into local memory. Essentially, this tactic replicates the data from the remote object into a local object, transparently to the client, to provide better performance. Communication does not actually have to go over the network itself. Of course, an additional copy of each remote server must be placed into local memory, and additional connections exist between server and smart proxy as well as between client and server/proxy. This creates additional overhead.

Interestingly enough, distributed object class extensions make it easier to build these smart proxies, but smart proxies are unnecessary with asynchronous messaging anyway. After all, the whole point of distributed objects is to be able to communicate with remote objects effectively.

11.5.4 Event Management

CORBA standards developers clearly recognize the need for component objects to have an event management interface and so have defined the CORBA services events interface. This provides standard IDL-based APIs for access to send and receive application events by client objects. Event management at the object level has some gaps in the CORBA model and so must be filled in at the implementation layer. While CORBA services standards do exist for the event interface, they are more oriented toward application events. System-related events such as network outages are more implementation-dependent.

11.5.4.1 Transporting and Migration of Objects
Since the CORBA IDL model has to be OO-language independent, any object movement over the wire needs to convert objects to *flat* records or opaque byte streams, and back to objects again at the receiving end. This feature must be used with care in CORBA, since there could be performance hits: One in that this conversion must be done, and another in that now two sets of objects need to be maintained in order to be shipped over the network. A better solution to this conversion process is to provide different access levels in one unified mechanism, so that CORBA and the native object interface could map to a single object transportation engine without a performance penalty.

11.6 WHAT DO DISTRIBUTED OBJECTS DO?

The real benefit of distributed objects is their ability to take a divide and con-
quer approach to client/server development, which enables applications to
provide scalability through distribution.

Suppose a bank application needs to include a loan-processing system,
an investment system, and a system to support new accounts. Rather than
create stand-alone applications to solve each problem, using any number of
client/server development tools, you can take an open ORB approach.

Leveraging ORBs, you can create each application by building it as an
ORB. Creating the loan processing system as an ORB is simply a matter of
defining the application logic inside the ORB using the IDL in the case of
CORBA, or the object definition language (ODL) in the case of COM. You can
even connect the ORB to a database server if you need to. Once created, the
ORB can run anywhere on the network and is accessible by any application
interface that is ORB-aware (for instance, IBM's VisualAge or even Power-
soft's PowerBuilder). The power of such an architecture is this: Because the
ORB is accessible by any application running on the network, the logic is centrally located. Developers can change the ORB at any time for any reason,
automatically changing the functionality of the applications that use it. ORBs
are tool-independent as well, and all sorts of applications can access the services of the banking ORBs. This allows users to reuse the ORBs' application
services throughout the application.

Because the ORBs run remotely, the client does not get burdened with
the application processing (as is the case with traditional two-tier fat client
client/server development). ORBs become an application service layer comparable to TP monitors. Moreover, because the ORBs are portable, you can move
them from platform to platform without worrying about interoperability.

Another issue to consider is the availability of application components
that comply to the ORB architecture. There are two flavors of application components: The CORBA-based OpenDoc, from a consortium of implementers
including Apple and IBM, and the Web-enabled ActiveX, from Microsoft.
OpenDoc was supposed to be the de facto component standard. It is basically a
component-enabled version of IBM's SOM. OpenDoc lets developers plug components into applications or documents as needed, mixing and matching components for whatever reason. It supports multiplatforms as well and is still a
factor on non-Windows workstations, as part of the MacOS and OS/2.

ActiveX is COM's answer to components and to Java. ActiveX is really
just a warmed-over version of OCX, revamped for use inside Web browsers
such as Microsoft's Internet Explorer. You can also find ActiveX components in
ActiveX documents, running on ActiveX-enabled servers such as Microsoft's
Internet Information Server. ActiveX components also can encapsulate Java
applets.

Client/server developers embed ActiveX components inside ActiveX-
enabled client/server development tools such as Visual Basic, PowerBuilder,

and Delphi. The power of ActiveX is not in its architecture and its links to COM but, rather, in the wide array of tools that support it. For example, you can create ActiveX components with any number of tools for any number of applications. Tool support is the key to the acceptance of any standard.

IIOP allows ORBs that reside on a client running inside a browser to communicate with any other CORBA-compliant object running on an intranet or the Internet. ORB implementers such as Visigenic are creating CORBA-compliant ORBs specifically for the Web.

11.6.1 Assessing CORBA

It is hard to argue with the idea of defining vendor-neutral standards for distributed objects. Open standards in networking have made today's connected world possible, with the global Internet providing the most visible example. Without standards, the best we can hope for is a diverse set of single-vendor islands.

But in their hearts, most vendors hate standards. Given a choice, any vendor would prefer to have its own proprietary technology become dominant.

The reality, however, is that each vendor's CORBA-based product is quite different from the others. While some products can interoperate for straightforward requests via CORBA's IIOP, implementers commonly add extra features that rely on their own proprietary protocols. Furthermore, the application programming interfaces seen by developers vary significantly. That is why there is today no serious third-party market in CORBA-based applications.

Many organizations have used successfully CORBA-based products to integrate diverse systems. The technology's great strength is that the successful CORBA-based products—such as Iona's Orbix and BEA's ObjectBroker—all run on a wide range of operating systems. If the goal is to connect a diverse set of multiprocessors together using distributed objects, CORBA-based products are an excellent solution.

Since different products have different programming APIs, different security schemes (when they have security at all), different administrative interfaces, and other variations, sticking with a single vendor's product can make your life much easier. And since a large percentage of the leading CORBA-based products run on most popular operating systems, there typically is no need to use more than one.

11.6.2 Assessing COM/DCOM

Unlike the diversity that exists in the CORBA world, there is only one implementation of COM and DCOM. This homogeneity, together with the tremendous popularity of Windows and Windows NT, has led to an enormous third-party application market. Furthermore, COM is installed today on literally hundreds of millions of machines, and it is a standard part of the operating system. In some areas, in fact, DCOM is clearly ahead: Every copy of DCOM includes solid security services, for example, while most CORBA products provide little or nothing in this area.

For the most part, COM and DCOM run only on Windows and Windows NT. But there are good implementations of COM for the Macintosh, UNIX, and MVS.

Given all of this, it should be obvious why CORBA and COM/DCOM are not really competitors. If the problem you are trying to solve requires connecting objects implemented solely on Windows and Windows NT, you should use DCOM. If, on the other hand, you need to communicate between objects written in multiple languages in a diverse environment that includes UNIX and other non-Microsoft systems (and probably Windows/Windows NT, as well), then you must use a CORBA-based product today. The choice is simple, and debates about which is the better technology are entirely beside the point.

11.6.3 Assessing Java and RMI

It is entirely possible to write Java applications that run on a single operating system. Part of this environment is RMI. RMI is significantly easier to use than either CORBA or DCOM, so developers have flocked to it. Because RMI is designed solely for Java, while IIOP is more generic, there are technical issues that make this a less than perfect solution.

Given that Microsoft provides the operating system for the vast majority of desktops in the world today, organizations that use RMI face a bit of a problem. For organizations standardizing on the Microsoft browser, using RMI means installing the necessary library yourself on every client.

RMI is simple and straightforward to use, but it lacks security and other often important services. But if these limitations are acceptable, if you have a way to guarantee the availability of the RMI libraries on both your clients and servers, and, most important, if the objects on both sides are written in Java, RMI is the way to go. Its simplicity and support for multiple platforms make it too attractive to ignore.

11.6.4 Combining Solutions

Implementers have provided bridges between CORBA and COM that allow tools supporting COM (i.e., Visual Basic and virtually all other development tools) to use CORBA. It is even possible to create specialized ActiveX controls, components that encapsulate remote access to various pieces of server functionality. Once this has been done, those components can be easily plugged into any number of desktop applications, providing a straightforward and reusable mechanism for accessing legacy applications.

While CORBA and COM look at objects in much the same way, it is not exactly the same. The mapping between these two object models, then, has a few problems. As is so often the case, basic functions can work quite well, but more advanced uses become problematic. Gateways between similar but different solutions historically have suffered from these kinds of problems, and the COM/CORBA gateway is no exception; transparent interoperability simply is not reachable yet.

COM and CORBA are not the only two object technologies that can be usefully combined. It also is quite useful to combine both COM and CORBA with Java. CORBA's IIOP can be folded into Java's RMI, making it easy to use IIOP beneath today's RMI API. Microsoft's Java virtual machine includes a transparent two-way mapping between Java objects and COM objects.

11.6.5 Issues

The lack of tools to simplify implementation of business object systems on the Internet/intranet currently is a major inhibiting factor for movement to Java-based client/server applications. The lack of a robust, bug-free Java integrated development environment is a second impediment. The third major handicap for building these applications is the lack of a component-based environment required for building business object architectures.

One of the most encouraging developments for building distributed object applications for the Web is the emerging synergy between Java and Microsoft's ActiveX strategy based on OLE/COM. It turns out to be as easy or easier to use Java for creating COM components as it is to use Visual Basic or C++. In fact, Microsoft has enabled every ActiveX component to look like a Java class to a Java application and every Java class to look like an ActiveX component to a Windows application.

Java's support for garbage collection eliminates the need for reference pointer counting, which is very tedious when you are building COM components in C++. It also hides some of the complexity of the COM interfaces. As a result, it is possible to supply seamless integration between ActiveX and Java components. If properly implemented, it is possible to talk to the same component via DCOM or CORBA protocols.

Most CORBA-compliant ORB implementers will allow DCOM clients to access CORBA objects on the network. This is a primitive capability compared to two-way interoperability between DCOM and CORBA.

11.6.6 The Bottom Line

If, back in 1991, the OMG had chosen to define and publish complete standards for distributed objects, the world today might be a very different place. Furthermore, COM and DCOM are given away for free, always a tough price to beat, and they are well integrated with the dominant tools and applications on their target platforms. For shops committed to Windows NT as a server platform for new applications, DCOM is by far the dominant choice for distributed objects.

For shops that continue to build new applications on UNIX servers and want to use distributed object technology, on the other hand, CORBA may be the right choice. There is another use for CORBA, too, one that has been most common so far in providing integration of existing applications on diverse systems: Even organizations that are not building new applications can make use of CORBA-based products to tie together existing applications.

If your organization has jumped on the Java bandwagon in a major way, get used to RMI. Its simplicity has some drawbacks, such as limited support for security, but Java developers are almost sure to like it. Java's promise of being able to run more or less the same code on all kinds of systems is undeniably attractive.

Ultimately, which technology dominates depends on how popular Windows NT becomes as a platform for building new server applications.

11.7 CONCLUSIONS

The question on everyone's mind is: "Are distributed objects ready for client/server?" Although distributed objects provide an advanced architecture for distributed computing, they are not yet ready for mission-critical applications. For example, most commercial ORBs are slow and inefficient, meaning you can't pump the number of transactions through them that you need for high-end applications. But there are only a few recovery mechanisms built into the ORBs. Most of today's ORBs do not perform garbage-collection functions, load-balancing, or concurrency control, nor do they scale well.

In addition, ORBs remain largely tied to synchronous communications middleware. Missing is support for message-oriented middleware that can operate asynchronously. What is more, the server code is not as portable as it should be. These issues are true for both DCOM- and CORBA-based ORBs.

The new generation of distributed objects is supposed to fix all of these problems. However, products that use them are slow to appear. The best hope for distributed objects is the Web. Hype is driving legions of people to the Web, and users are demanding new, more advanced means by which to deploy applications.

11.7.1 Making Sense of Distributed Objects

Given the popularity of both distributed computing and object technology, it is not surprising that distributed objects are hot. But understanding this technology can be challenging, since it requires a grasp of both networking and objects.

But with a little care, sorting through both the technologies and the competing claims of their proponents is not so hard. And the payoff is worth it: In spite of the hype, distributed objects really do matter.

Allowing objects on different systems to work together requires addressing some fundamental questions. Both CORBA and COM/DCOM provide a language-independent object model, a protocol for communication between objects on different systems, standard interfaces for accessing useful services, and more.

Java also provides most of these things, with the notable exception that there is nothing at all language-independent. Since all three technologies provide solutions to the same set of problems, they seem to be competitors. When you get right down to it, however, it usually is fairly obvious which one you need to solve a particular problem.

11.7.2 Distributed Objects on the World Wide Web

Several important paradigms for distributed computing have been introduced in recent years. This trend began in the last decade with initiatives like OSF DCE and transactional systems, but recently much of the focus has been on applying object-oriented technology to distributed systems. This powerful combination allows network services to be offered in the controlled manner that only object technology, with its principles of data encapsulation and well-defined interfaces, can provide. Bringing together distributed computing with objects has led to a vision of componentized software. Software systems dynamically can be constructed from prefabricated components for network installation.

The explosive number of distributed computing technologies introduced in the last few years has resulted in some powerful models of how an intelligent networked world may operate. Microsoft OLE, the OMG CORBA specification, and Sun's Java specification are all important participants in this brave new world. The primary contentions are that the integration of Java and the WWW to CORBA must happen at the higher semantic levels of the compound document frameworks as well as at the relatively low level of the ORBs, and that the value of Java is for access-by-value objects whereas CORBA offers access-by-reference objects in their superposition.

Ultimately, the WWW and the world of distributed components are merging, and the best capabilities of both domains can be used to enhance each other in the superposition of the two.

Implementations

Technologies Affecting the Future of Computing

12.1 INTRODUCTION

The World Wide Web merges the techniques of networked information and hypertext to make an easy but powerful global information system.

The Web makes any information accessible over the network as part of a seamless hypertext information space. The Web originally was developed to allow information sharing within internationally dispersed teams and the dissemination of information by support groups. It has spread to every facet of life and attracted much interest in user support, resource discovery, and collaborative work areas. It is currently the most advanced information system deployed on the Internet and embraces within its data model most information in previous networked information systems.

In fact, the Web is an architecture that will embrace any future advances in technology, including new networks, protocols, object types, and data formats. Clients and servers for many platforms exist and are under continual development.

The Web consists of documents and links. Indexes are special documents that can be searched. The result of such a search is another (virtual) document containing links to the documents found. A simple protocol (HTTP) is used to allow a browser program to request a keyword search by a remote information server.

The Web contains documents in many formats. Those documents in hypertext (real or virtual) contain links to other documents or to places within documents. All documents—whether real, virtual, or indexes—look similar to the reader and are contained within the same addressing scheme.

To follow a link, a reader clicks with a mouse (or types in a number). To search an index, a reader gives keywords (or other search criteria). These are the only operations necessary to access the entire world of data.

Web browsers can access many existing data systems via existing protocols (FTP) or HTTP and a gateway. In this way, the critical mass of data is quickly exceeded and the increasing use of the system by readers and information suppliers encourages each.

Providing information is as simple as running the Web server and pointing it at an existing directory structure. The server automatically generates a hypertext view of your files to guide the user around.

You can write SGML hypertext files to give an even friendlier view. Also, any file available by anonymous FTP, or any Internet newsgroup, can be immediately linked into the Web. The small start-up effort is designed to allow small contributions. At the other end of the scale, large information providers may provide an HTTP server with full text or keyword indexing. This allows access to a large existing database without changing the way that database is managed. Such gateways have been made into Oracle and Digital's VMS/Help systems.

The Web model gets around the frustrating incompatibilities of data format between suppliers and reader by allowing negotiation of format between a smart browser and a smart server. This provides a basis for extension into multimedia, and allows those who share application standards to make full use of them across the Web.

I will not describe the many exciting possibilities opened up by the Web, such as efficient document caching, the reduction of redundant out-of-date copies, and the use of knowledge daemons. Interested readers will find more information in the online project documentation, including some background on hypertext and several technical notes.

In this chapter, I cover a number of technologies that have become prevalent due to the popularity of the Web. These technologies also are helping to define the new paradigms of network computing.

12.2 INTRANETS

An intranet is any internal network that supports Internet applications. A user on the company's network uses a browser to "surf" the intranet in much the same way one uses a browser to surf the World Wide Web. However, the information that the user sees is internal company information, which is secured from the outside (Internet) by a firewall or other security system.

You can think of an intranet as a scaled-down version of the Internet whose boundaries go no further than your company's walls. You can do anything on this intranet that you can do on the Internet, with the added advantage that no unauthorized snooper from outside your company has access to your information. Of course, you may want to allow access from your intranet to the Internet and vice versa, so that E-mail and other information can be exchanged. In this case, your intranet will have a "gatekeeper," called a *firewall*, sitting between the two nets. This firewall is configured to determine what information can come in and what information can go out.

One of the greatest advantages of an intranet is that it is a kind of mini-World Wide Web. This allows you to use the same software (i.e., Web servers and Web browsers) to browse your intranet and company information and the World Wide Web. This boils down to big cost savings on software development and purchases.

12.2.1 Intranet Design Services

An intranet can be as simple or as complicated as you want to make it. We can design an intranet with content ranging from bare bones information and no employee interaction to one in which each department has its own section and lots of employee interaction. It is all up to you. If it can be done on the World Wide Web, it can be done for you internally. Sites can include several things:

☞ Colored or textured backgrounds, lines, and bullets

☞ Logos

☞ Pictures, images, and animations

☞ Links to pages on the intranet and outside

12.2.2 Intranet Hardware/Software

An intranet can work on any internal network (LAN or WAN). Your network must have TCP/IP connectivity in order to install the Web browsers and servers needed for an intranet. The hardware components involved in setting up an intranet are:

☞ one or more computers that are servers,

☞ a computer sitting on each employee's desktop (i.e., work stations), and

☞ network hubs and cabling to connect all the computers.

If your company already has a computer network setup, you will already have this hardware. The software components include:

☞ A network operating system on the server (Novell or Windows NT)

☞ A network operating system on the work stations (Windows 95 or Windows NT)

☞ TCP/IP network software running on the servers and work stations

☞ A Web server running on one or more of the servers

☞ A Web browser (Netscape or Internet Explorer) installed on all work stations

The intranet seems set for a period of massive growth over the next five years, because it delivers simply and cheaply many of the functions that previous system architectures have failed to provide. Intranets allow the creation of corporate information networks that are easy to use, seamless, and global in coverage.

Intranets are easier to manage and offer a simple, universal, cross-platform client, using smaller applications. They can be installed by piggybacking on existing and more expensive client/server systems, and the client software is either cheap or free. Intranets also cut the cost of software installation, maintenance, and training. And they are ideal for use by new-style virtual organizations or companies with mobile workforces. However, as the applications become more complicated and move beyond information publishing, their cost will increase.

Most intranets today are dedicated to publishing information—such as corporate telephone directories, company procedures, and news items—but this picture is changing rapidly. This means that browsers will offer basic groupware functions, while the separate groupware products will be increasingly confined to high-end applications that augment the functions of the embedded groupware.

The third wave will come with Web-enabled business applications, although much of the complexity that intranets were claimed to avoid will come back when organizations integrate Web technology with business applications.

The fourth wave will be the integration of workflow, or formal collaboration, into intranets. However, today's leading workflow packages may not scale well enough to be used on an intranet.

12.2.3 How to Implement an Intranet

Below are some steps for implementing an intranet:

1. Intranets typically are piggybacked on another IS investment.
2. Start with information publishing applications. Follow with Web-enabled collaboration and transaction-oriented applications.
3. Establish the infrastructure, content, the development environment, and what the intranet will contain. This will avoid trouble later.
4. Roll out your first applications quickly as intranets do not require a 12-month requirements analysis to start.
5. Do not get hung up on the technology evaluation if you want to do Web-based publishing. The available products all offer virtually the same information publishing capabilities and can be swapped out quickly, provided you avoid proprietary features.
6. Most intranet benefits are not directly measured in financial terms, so keep an eye on anecdotal benefits to help justify your intranet.
7. Some users are skeptical about intranets. Implementers have noted that paying attention to user resistance and cultural issues is a key element of ensuring user acceptance. When asked what they could have done better in implementing intranets, organizations said they should have invested more in user education about what intranets were and what they could do.
8. IS drives intranet implementations, but user ownership of the content makes them work.
9. Implementers are keeping an eye on Java and ActiveX, but are currently using CGI and other standard Web technologies.
10. Intranets do not reduce management burden.

New Internet tools are accelerating the growth of corporate networks based on the World Wide Web, allowing companies to develop their own private "intranets" for enterprise applications and communications, both inside and outside the corporate firewall.

New products from Oracle, IBM, Netscape, Microsoft, and others are spurring the rapid evolution of the Web from a venue for posting home page information to a serious network for deploying enterprise applications. The wave of the future in Web sites may be home pages such as those of Federal Express and United Parcel Service, which give customers access to corporate databases to track packages online.

Because of the Internet's universal TCP/IP and HTML standards, using the Web as an applications platform solves one headache for large distributed applications: namely, interoperability. Intranets are becoming a major tool for enterprises.

Security concerns are a key motivation for the creation of an intranet. Simply put, the Internet is not very secure and probably will not be for some time. A security infrastructure is slowly being deployed; however, vendors and users alike are not used to authentication, single-use passwords, and encryption as a normal part of doing business on the Internet. Security concerns aside, intranets are effective and relatively simple mechanisms to improve communications within an enterprise. Some examples of intranets in use are:

☞ The Web sites have an extensive set of "company profiles" and demos that highlight intranets in Action.

☞ At kiosks at Compaq Computer Corp., employees can check on benefits, savings, and 401(k) plans.

☞ FedEx, learning from its highly successful public Web site (which is estimated to save the company $2 million a year), has 60 intranets created by and for employees. The company is equipping all 30,000 office employees with Web browsers to provide access to news sites.

☞ DreamWorks SKG (the new Spielberg, Katzenberg, and Geffen studio) has Netscape browsers on all desktops so production managers and artists can check on the daily status of projects and coordinate scenes.

☞ Silicon Graphics, with an intranet called Silicon Junction, allows employees to access more than two dozen corporate databases.

☞ Ford Motor Company's intranet links design centers in Asia, Europe, and the U.S. This allowed engineers to collaborate on the design of the 1996 Taurus.

☞ Eli Lilly, Genentech, McDonnell Douglas, Mobil, and National Semiconductor all use intranets.

The explosion of intranets will cause a corresponding explosion for Web server software. Many companies already have the infrastructure necessary for intranets. A LAN, a Web server with browsers for the desktop, and a firewall to keep people out are the core elements of an intranet. The Web, which has already provided a unifying view of the Internet, can provide the same service to an enterprise.

Most organizations have jumbled collections of information technologies serving different functions. Payroll, accounting, engineering, purchasing, employee benefits, travel expenses, and so on often function on separate *islands of automation*. The Web presents a unique opportunity to unify these systems into an apparently single system. Unification of these systems is not simple, but a path now exists, an architecture of sorts, which can give users better, more timely access to companywide data, improving communications along the way.

12.3 JAVA RMI

Java RMI is a mechanism that allows one to invoke a method on an object that exists in another address space. The other address space could be on the same machine or on a different one. The RMI mechanism is basically an object-oriented RPC mechanism. CORBA is another object-oriented RPC mechanism. CORBA differs from Java RMI in a number of ways:

☞ CORBA is a language-independent standard.

☞ CORBA includes many other mechanisms in its standard (such as a standard for TP monitors) that are not part of Java RMI.

☞ There is no notion of an object request broker in Java RMI.

There are three processes that participate in supporting remote method invocation:

1. The client is the process that is invoking a method on a remote object.
2. The server is the process that owns the remote object. The remote object is an ordinary object in the address space of the server process.
3. The object registry is a name server that relates objects with names. Objects are registered with the object registry. Once an object has been registered, one can use the object registry to obtain access to a remote object using the name of the object.

Two kinds of classes can be used in Java RMI. *Remote class* is one whose instances can be used remotely. An object of such a class can be referenced in two different ways:

☞ Within the address space where the object was constructed, the object is an ordinary object that can be used like any other object.

☞ Within other address spaces, the object can be referenced using an object handle. While there are limitations on how one can use an object handle compared to an object, for the most part one can use them in the same way as an ordinary object.

For simplicity, an instance of a remote class will be called a *remote object*.

Serializable class is one whose instances can be copied from one address space to another. An instance of a serializable class will be called a *serializable object*. In other words, a serializable object is one that can be marshaled. (Note that has no connection to the concept of serializability in database management systems.)

If a serializable object is passed as a parameter (or return value) of a remote method invocation, then the value of the object will be copied from one address space to the other. By contrast, if a remote object is passed as a parameter (or return value), then the object handle will be copied from one address space to the other.

Serializable objects are something like the concrete objects of C++, but only with respect to remote method invocations. With respect to ordinary method invocations, serializable objects are ordinary objects, not concrete objects. This is confusing, and so in Java one must carefully distinguish remote method invocations from ordinary method invocations. However, one might naturally wonder what would happen if a class was both remote and serializable.

12.3.1 Serializable Classes

Let's consider how to design remote and serializable classes. The easier of the two is a serializable class. A class is serializable if it implements the java.io.serializable interface. Subclasses of a serializable class also are serializable. Many of the standard classes are serializable, so a subclass of one of these is also automatically serializable. Normally, any data within a serializable class should also be serializable. Although there are ways to include non-serializable objects within a serializable object, it is awkward to do so. See the documentation of java.io.serializable for more information about this.

Using a serializable object in a remote method invocation is a straightforward process. One simply passes the object using a parameter as the return value. The type of the parameter or return value is the Serializable class. Note that both the client and server programs must have access to the definition of any serializable class being used. The only serializable class that will be used in this example is the string class.

12.3.2 Remote Classes and Interfaces

Next let's consider how to define a remote class. This is more difficult than defining a serializable class. A remote class has two parts: The interface and the class itself. The remote interface must have the following properties:

☞ The interface must be public.

☞ The interface must extend the interface java.rmi.Remote.

☞ Every method in the interface must declare that it throws java.rmi. Other exceptions also may be thrown.

The remote class itself has the following properties:

1. It must implement a remote interface.

2. It should extend the java.rmi.server and RemoteObject class. Objects of such a class exist in the address space of the server and can be invoked remotely. While there are other ways to define a remote class, this is the simplest way to ensure that objects of a class can be used as remote objects. See the documentation of the java.rmi.server package for more information.

3. It can have methods that are not in its remote interface. These can only be invoked locally.

Unlike in a serializable class, it is not necessary for both the client and the server to have access to the definition of the remote class. The server requires the definition of both the remote class and the remote interface, but the client uses only the remote interface. Roughly speaking, the remote interface represents the type of an object handle, while the remote class represents the type of an object. If a remote object is being used remotely, its type must be declared to be the type of the remote interface, not the type of the remote class.

All of the remote interfaces and classes should be compiled using javac. Once this has been completed, the stubs and skeletons for the remote interfaces should be compiled using the rmic stub compiler. The only problem one could encounter with this command is that rmic might not be able to find the files Hello.java and HelloInterface.java, even though they are in the same directory in which rmic is being executed.

Let's examine how to program the client and server. The client itself is simply a Java program. It does not need to be part of a remote or serializable class, although it will use remote and serializable classes.

A remote method invocation can return a remote object as its return value, but one must have a remote object in order to perform a remote method invocation. So, to obtain a remote object one must already have one. Accordingly, there must be a separate mechanism for obtaining the first remote object. The object registry fulfills this requirement. It allows one to obtain a remote object using only the remote object's name. The name of a remote object includes the following information:

1. The Internet name (or address) of the machine that is running the object registry with which the remote object is being registered. If the object registry is running on the same machine as the one that is making the request, then the name of the machine can be omitted.

2. The port to which the object registry is listening. If the object registry is listening to the default port, this does not have to be included in the name.

3. The local name of the remote object within the object registry.

12.3.3 Programming a Server

The server itself is a Java program. It need not be a remote or serializable class, although it will use them. The server does have some responsibilities:

1. It must create and install a security manager. The simplest way to do this is to use the statement System.setSecurityManager (new RMISecurityManager());

2. At least one remote object must be registered with the object registry. The statement for this is Naming.rebind (objectName, object); where object is the remote object being registered and objectName is the string that names the remote object.

Java RMI limits binding and unbinding requests to object registries running on the same machine, so it is never necessary to specify the name of the machine when one is registering an object. The code for the server can be placed in any convenient class.

12.4 JAVA

Java was designed for creating applications that could be run from a Web browser. It was not the first programming language, or the only one, to offer this feature, but it is one of the most popular.

However, Java is not just a platform for creating small Web applications. It is a general-purpose programming language that can, in principle, be used for any application area. In this section, the Web aspects of Java will, for the most part, be ignored. The emphasis is on Java as a general-purpose programming language.

The Java language often is touted as a variation on C++. Although it has a superficial (syntactic) resemblance to C++, it is semantically different. In many ways, Java is much closer to Smalltalk than to C++.

One also sometimes sees claims that Java is a simpler language than C++. It is not clear what this claim is based on. Java has many features that are built in rather than being supplied by optional class libraries.

These features include a built-in class library, threads, synchronization, security, garbage collection, and reflection. This makes the language much more complicated, as well as a large number of new classes in its development kit. At the same time, Java omits many features of C++, such as overloaded operators, conversions, concrete data types, constants, pointer arithmetic, and templates.

This simplifies the language, but the simplification has a price. Omitting some features of C++ (such as pointer arithmetic) may be an advantage because so many subtle bugs in C and C++ result from the misuse of such features. However, the lack of other features—such as constants, overloaded operators, concrete data types, and templates—means that many important program designs are not expressible in Java.

In any case, since the number of features built into Java compared to C++ is about the same as the number of features Java does not have compared to C++, there is no compelling evidence that Java is either significantly less complicated or significantly more complicated than C++. This was true of the previous version of Java, but there is no question that Java is significantly more complicated than C++.

One important property of Java is that all functions and variables are within some class. There are no "global" variables or functions, as in C. In particular, the main function of any Java program must be a method of some class.

Another property is that functions are always declared and defined at the same time. There is no notion of a "header" file in which classes are declared separately from the file where the class members are defined.

The main function of a Java program has just one parameter: of type String[]. Although arrays in Java are syntactically similar to arrays in other languages, they differ greatly semantically. The array notion in C or C++ is a low-level allocation mechanism that is not well suited to high-level use.

For example, a variable of type int[] in C or C++ is not an object but a constant pointer to the first object in an array of integers. By contrast, the array notion in Java is a high-level notion. A variable of type int[] is a pointer to an object that contains both the length of the array and the actual array of integers. For example, the length of the argv array is written *argv.length*. Once allocated, the length of a Java array cannot be changed.

Standard I/O in Java is handled by the system class. For example, System.out is a static variable that points to the standard output file. It is roughly the same as stdout in C or cout in C++. System.out.println is a method that prints its parameter (usually a string) on the standard output file, followed by a newline character. If this final newline is not desired, one can use the System.out.print method instead.

12.4.1 Control Structures, Expressions, and Pointers

The syntax of control structures (such as *for* and *if*), assignment statements, simple variable declarations, and comments is almost the same in Java as in C or C++. Although commandLine is a pointer to a string object, you do not have to specify that with an asterisk, as in C or C++. Some have claimed that Java does not have pointers. In fact, the opposite is true. Except for variables of the primitive type, every Java variable is a pointer. Because of this limitation, Java has no special notation for declaring a pointer, nor is there any notation for computing an address or dereferencing a pointer.

Interestingly, this is one of the rare examples in which Java and C++ are similar semantically while differing syntactically, rather than the other way around. There are eight primitive types in Java:

1. *Boolean*: Similar to the C++ bool type, but cannot be converted to int. An integer or pointer cannot be used in a boolean context (such as an *if* condition) the way it can in C or C++.

2. *Char*: Similar to the C char type, but uses 16 bits.

3. *Byte*: An 8-bit signed integer.

4. *Short*: A 16-bit signed integer.

5. *Int*: A 32-bit signed integer.

6. *Long*: A 64-bit signed integer.

7. *Float*: A 32-bit floating point number.

8. *Double*: A 64-bit floating point number.

As in most object-oriented programming languages, objects are instances of classes. Each class has a name and members. Each class is also a member of a package of classes. Members can either be data members or function members. Members also can be either static or nonstatic. Data members are called *fields*. If a field is nonstatic, it can have a different value in each object. A static field has just one value, no matter how many instances there are in the class. Function members define the behavior of a class. They are called *methods* in Java.

Each file can define any number of classes, but exactly one must be public. None of the others is visible outside the file. Classes are grouped into packages, a notion that is important for access control (to be discussed later). If no package specification is given, the classes in the file belong to the default package. The name of the file must be the same as the name of the public class together with the .java file extension.

A method having the same name as the class is a constructor for instances of the class. There is no concept of a destructor, as in C++. However, one can define a method called *finalize*, which is guaranteed to be called when the object is deallocated, so it is roughly equivalent to a destructor. This is discussed in more detail in the next section.

All pointer variables are initialized to null unless explicitly initialized to some other value. Variables of the primitive types are initialized to a default value depending on the type, unless initialized to some other value.

Java does not support the C++ notion of a reference type that is used mainly for passing parameters by reference. In particular, Java does not support passing parameters by reference. This makes it awkward to return more than one value from a method. One can achieve the same effect by defining a class so that an instance of the class will contain the desired return values.

One can then define the return type of the method to be this class. There are other techniques you can use to compensate for this limitation of Java, but they are all awkward. The best way to deal with this is to design the program so that it does not need such return values in the first place. Because of this, Java programs tend to be designed differently from programs in other object-oriented programming languages.

There are many other examples of this phenomenon. Despite the superficial similarity between Java and C++, one cannot *port* code from one to the other very easily. It usually is necessary to redesign the entire program structure.

12.4.2 Garbage Collection

New objects are created by the new operator in Java in almost the same way as in C++. This allocates space for the object and also calls a constructor. However, there is no delete operator in Java, and one cannot define a destructor for a class. The Java system automatically deallocates objects when no references to them remain. This is done by a process within the Java run-time system called the *garbage collector*. When an object is deallocated, the finalize method is called. This is roughly analogous to a destructor. However, there is no way to predict when the garbage collector will deallocate an object or, indeed, whether it will do it at all for any particular object.

Garbage collectors are useful for preventing certain errors that can occur when objects are not carefully allocated and deallocated. You can add a garbage collector to any object-oriented programming language, and there are many available for C++. Java and Smalltalk differ from C++ in having a built-in garbage collector.

Many claim that garbage collectors eliminate the problems of dangling references and memory leaks that occur in some programs. A dangling reference is a pointer to an object that has been deallocated. A memory leak is an object that can no longer be referenced but has not been deallocated. Both of these are serious problems. A dangling reference can cause the program to behave unpredictably or even to terminate abnormally. If it involves a large number of objects, a memory leak can cause the program to run slowly and possibly terminate if it can no longer allocate space for new objects because so much space has become unusable.

Unfortunately, it is a myth that a garbage collector will solve either of these problems. Sloppy design and programming can result in situations that are semantically equivalent to a dangling reference or a memory leak, even if you are using a garbage collector. I have seen both of these problems in large Java programs. Indeed, it may be that these problems are more likely to occur in a Java program precisely because one does not think they can, so one does not make any effort to design the program carefully to prevent them. The moral is that good design is necessary, no matter what tools you are using.

12.4.3 Access Control

An important feature of any object-oriented language is *data hiding*. One can restrict access to a member of a class to a specified scope. Access control makes it much easier to determine all of the places where a field or method can be used. This, in turn, makes it much easier to verify that the field or method will be used and modified correctly, according to its specifications.

Java differs from C++ in having a much more complicated and awkward access control mechanism. Java has five kinds of access control specifications compared to the three kinds in C++. Despite this added complexity, it often is not possible to restrict the scope of a variable or method as precisely as you can in C++. In large Java projects, users often allow variables to be visible in a much larger scope than they would like simply because they cannot specify otherwise using Java's access control mechanism. After attempting to use Java's convoluted access control mechanism, many people soon long for the elegant simplicity of C++.

12.5 OLE

Graphical user interfaces popularized the *clipboard* metaphor—with *copy, cut,* and *paste* operations—that greatly simplified the creation of a *compound document* that included text, graphics, and other types of content. Prior to this invention, you had to print the text and graphics separately, then cut and paste them together with scissors and glue.

Although the clipboard works well for the initial creation of a compound document, changing the text might require repositioning the graphics. And editing the graphics requires many difficult manual steps to get the data back into the original format, if that is possible at all. Microsoft created a complex dynamic data exchange (DDE) protocol to simplify these steps.

Out of the DDE protocol grew OLE, which was made available to all developers as a standard. The acronym stands for *object linking and embedding*. OLE greatly enhanced the creation and management of compound documents. All the complexity of editing content was reduced to a double-click of the mouse. The object data was automatically brought back into the original editor.

Small elements of software can be *plugged in* to an application, thereby extending its functionality without requiring changes. In the compound document paradigm, the document editor is a generic *container* that can hold any kind of content object. You can insert charts, sound, video, pictures, and many other components into the container without having to update it.

OLE has been promoted as many things, from Visual Editing and OLE Automation to OLE Controls and Network OLE. OLE might be best understood as a growth curve. In other words, it can be described as an extensible systems object technology whose architecture accommodates new and existing designs. New components, developed by anyone at any time, can be added into the running system, thereby immediately extending the services offered to applications, even if those applications are already running.

A newly installed operating system offers a basic set of services that developers employ in the creation of applications. COM and OLE make it possible for anyone to extend the system with new services without requiring a change to the operating system.

12.5.1 Component Object Model

Component Object Model (COM) is an architecture and a supporting infrastructure for building, using, and evolving component software. This infrastructure contains the standard APIs supported by the *COM Library*, the standard suites of interfaces, and the network protocols used in support of distributed computing.

COM and OLE introduce a programming model based on reusable designs, as well as an implementation that provides fundamental services to make both design and code reuse possible.

12.5.2 Object Concepts in COM/OLE

If you take a language-based *object* and wrap it in COM/OLE interfaces, it is still an *object* when seen from a COM/OLE client. The client sees an entity that is encapsulated. That entity also supports polymorphism and reuse. These are the fundamental concepts behind the *objects* in *object-oriented programming*, and COM supports all three, as described below.

12.5.2.1 Encapsulation All implementation details in OLE are hidden behind the interface structures, exactly as they are in C++ and other languages. The client sees only interfaces and knows nothing about object internals. In fact, COM enforces a stricter encapsulation than many languages because COM interfaces cannot expose public data members—all data access must happen through function calls. Certainly language extensions for compilers can let you express public members in source code; but on the binary level, all data is exchanged through function calls, which is widely recognized as the proper way to do encapsulation.

12.5.2.2 Polymorphism Polymorphism in OLE happens on three different levels:

1. Two interfaces that derive from the same base interface are polymorphic in that base interface, just as they would be in C++. This occurs because both interfaces have vtable entries that look exactly like those of the base interface. The primary reason for this is that all interfaces are derived from IUnknown and thus look exactly alike in the first three entries of the *vtable*. When you program COM and OLE in C++, you actually use C++ inheritance to express this polymorphic relationship. When programming in C, the interface structures are defined as explicit structures of function pointers where polymorphic interface structures share the same set of initial entries in the structure.

2. The object classes (and instances) that support the same interface are polymorphic in that interface. That is, if I have two object classes that both support an interface like IDropTarget, the same client code that manipulates the IDropTarget of one object class can be used to manipulate the IDropTarget implemented in another class. Such client code exists in the OLE system-level drag-and-drop service, which uses this interface to communicate with any potential recipient of a drop operation.

3. The object classes that support the same set of multiple interfaces are polymorphic across the entire set. Many service categories expect this. The OLE specification for embeddable compound document objects, for example, says that such objects always support the IOleObject, IViewObject2, IDataObject, and IPersistStorage interfaces, as well as a few others. A client written to this specification can host any embeddable object regardless of the type of content: chart, video clip, sound bite, table, graphic, text, or something else. All OLE controls also are polymorphic in this manner, supporting a wide range of capabilities behind the same set of polymorphic interfaces.

12.5.2.3 Reuse   Inheritance is not a fundamental OOP concept. Inheritance is how you express polymorphism in a programming language and achieve code reuse between classes. Inheritance is a means to polymorphism and reuse—it is not an end in itself. Many defend inheritance as a core part of OOP, but it is nothing of the sort. Polymorphism and reuse are the things you are really after. We have already seen how COM supports polymorphism. It supports reuse of one component by another through two mechanisms:

1. The first, containment, simply means that one object class uses another class internally for its own implementation. That is, when the *outer* object is instantiated, it internally instantiates an object of the reused *inner* class, just as any other client would do. This is a straightforward client-object relationship, in which the inner object does not know that its services are being used in the implementation of another class—it just sees some client calling its functions.

2. The second mechanism is aggregation, a more rarely used technique through which the outer object takes interface pointers from the inner object and exposes those pointers through its own QueryInterface. This saves the outer object from having any of its own code support an interface and is a convenient way to make certain kinds of containment more efficient. This does require some extra coding in the inner object to make its IUnknown members behave as the outer object's IUnknown members, but this amounts to only a few lines of code. This mechanism works even when multiple levels of inner objects are in use, where the outer object can easily obtain an interface pointer from another object nested dozens of levels deep.

12.5.3 COM and OLE

We have seen why the designs in COM exist and the problems that COM solves. We have seen how COM and OLE complement OOP languages and frameworks, and how COM supports all the fundamental object concepts. Taken by itself, COM is simple.

However, all the layers of OLE that are built on top of COM are overwhelming. There are many API functions and interface definitions. All of this constitutes nearly a thousand bits of functionality that continue to grow. Thus, trying to understand what everything is about is a daunting effort. All functionality in OLE falls into three categories:

1. API functions and interfaces to expose OLE's built-in services, including a fair number of helper functions and helper objects

2. API functions and interfaces to allow customization of those built-in services

3. API functions and interfaces that support creation of "custom services" according to various specifications

The following sections describe each of these in a little more detail.

12.5.3.1 OLE's Native Services   OLE offers a wide range of native services, including these:

☞ Local/remote transparency (remoting and marshalling)

☞ Drag-and-drop data exchange

☞ Task memory allocation

☞ Clipboard data exchange

☞ Implementation location

☞ Default "handling" for embedded objects

☞ Structured storage (described in detail below)

☞ File, item, composite, pointer, and anti-monikers

☞ The "running object table"

☞ Type library and type creation and management

☞ Type conversion routines

☞ Data caching

☞ Helper and wrapper functions, including support for string and array types

The services of implementation location, marshalling, and remoting are fundamental to the ability of objects and clients to communicate across any distance. These services are a core part of a COM implementation on any given system, and they support higher-level interoperability.

OLE's implementation of standard controls the actual layout of data bits inside the files. The software components themselves, however, see stream objects as contiguous byte arrays once more, so the experience you have working with files translates directly to working with streams. In fact, there is a one-to-one correspondence between typical file-system APIs—such as read, write, and seek—and the member functions of the IStream interface through which one uses a stream object.

12.5.3.2 Custom Services   OLE itself can provide only a limited number of native services: Specifically, those that need to be centralized and standardized. There are three primary (and sometimes complex) type specifications, each of which involves a large number of OLE API functions and interfaces:

- ☞ OLE Documents, for the creation and management of compound documents
- ☞ OLE Controls, for the creation and management of custom controls
- ☞ OLE Automation, for programmability and scripting

In addition to these categories, other industry groups have defined service categories for their particular needs. Some examples include real-time market data, health care, insurance, point-of-sale, and process control. No matter who defines the service, the idea is that many people can implement clients or objects according to the specification, which describes the abstraction that either side (client or object) uses to view the other, so that all clients are polymorphic to the objects and all objects of the category are polymorphic to clients.

What is important here is that COM is an open architecture in which anyone can create and define new service categories. COM and OLE enable decentralized and asynchronous innovation, design, development, and deployment of component software—the absolute essential elements of a successful distributed object system.

12.6 ACTIVEX

Microsoft's response to plug-ins and Java was ActiveX, a slimmed down, networkable version of OLE. OLE lets Windows programs communicate with each other automatically. The numbers in a spreadsheet can update the numbers in a document, which in turn generate a chart in a graphics package. Double-click those spreadsheet numbers in your document, and up pops the spreadsheet, ready for editing.

ActiveX technologies create *active* Web documents. ActiveX controls allow developers to create Web pages with actions, such as games, multimedia, animation, and video. ActiveX technologies form a framework for creating interactive content using software components, scripts, and existing applications. Specifically, ActiveX technologies enable developers to build Web content using ActiveX control (formerly OLE Controls), active scripts, and active documents.

A key benefit of using ActiveX is that it allows you to integrate applications into Web browsers so data managed by those applications becomes accessible as Web pages. ActiveX lets you navigate a corporate intranet to view a department's Web page, examine the department's budget spreadsheet, and query the database for sales data from within the Web browser, without having to convert that content into HTML format.

ActiveX server scripts can be written using a host of popular scripting languages, including Visual Basic Script, PERL, and JavaScript. Together, these ActiveX controls and scripts allow Web developers, using familiar tools, to build smart, interactive server applications with little or no programming knowledge.

ActiveX works in a similar way but across a LAN or the Internet. Theoretically, you could give a real-time presentation over the Net, with your accounting staff in another city plugging in the numbers. ActiveX components let Web masters create Web pages with stock tickers, cascading menus, Access databases, or just about anything a Windows-compliant program can produce.

ActiveX does not run within your browser. It downloads freewheeling little programs that can do all sorts of things. In short, ActiveX gives a remote Web site as much connectivity to your system as you have to it. ActiveX programs are powerful, can run faster than Java and some plug-ins, and do not conflict with each other as much as plug-ins do. However, they take up much more disk space, sometimes install themselves where they shouldn't, and run only on Windows systems.

12.6.1 The Uses of ActiveX

To use ActiveX, you need Explorer. If you go to a Web site and do not have the appropriate control, you can download it on the spot. Installation is a bit more automatic than with a plug-in, but you usually have to exit the Internet and reboot your system to finish the job. Not surprisingly, there are far more plug-ins than ActiveX controls.

ActiveX allows controls to be embedded in Internet/intranet sites and to respond interactively to events. It is optimized for size and speed and adds a number of important innovations for the Internet. There are two ways to get a web-enabled application:

1. Have a server-based engine that runs on the Internet/intranet server itself and typically calls HTML pages as its interface.

2. Use the ActiveX control to get the Web to invoke the application, where the application executes on your local computer and within your browser, but the application is still hosted on the Internet/intranet server.

When you run a typical Web-enabled application from a Web page, it looks to see if you have the latest ActiveX controls and the latest application on your local machine. It then transfers both, one, or nothing, depending on your status and the start execution. This approach is suitable when you need a Windows application to be run by a large number of users on a regular basis.

You must be using a browser that supports ActiveX, such as Internet Explorer for 32-bit Windows. This means your browser must be running under Windows 95, NT, or later. It also invokes downloads. You must balance this download traffic against the constant traffic, reliability, and maintenance of using an HTML interface.

HTML is not a good substitute for an interactive Windows program interface. It is good at presenting information, but not at reacting. Using dynamic HTML or Java scripts is an alternative, but again that requires considerable development effort.

12.6.2 ActiveX Controls

When you visit a Web site, your browser downloads a page from a Web server and copies it to your computer. If the browser detects a reference to an ActiveX control from the Web page, it checks to see if the control is present on your computer. If the control cannot be found on your computer, it downloads from a server. ActiveX controls need to be downloaded only once. The size and complexity of ActiveX controls are reduced to allow fast transfer via a network or Internet connection.

ActiveX controls allow Web page developers to add multimedia and mathematical functions to Web pages published on the Internet. Visual Basic programmers can place programs directly into Web pages. Users can run these custom applications whenever they visit sites that are ActiveX-enabled.

An ActiveX control, like a built-in control, is an object you place on a form to enable or enhance a user's interaction with an application. ActiveX controls have events and can be incorporated into other controls. These controls have an .OCX file name extension.

A key advantage ActiveX controls have over Java applets and Netscape plug-ins is that ActiveX controls can be used in applications written in many programming languages, including all of the Microsoft programming and database languages.

Several ActiveX controls available today have functionality ranging from a timer control (which simply notifies its container at a particular time) to full-featured spreadsheets and word processors.

12.7 DISTRIBUTED COMPONENT OBJECT MODEL PROTOCOL (DCOM)

DCOM is an extension of the COM that supports objects distributed across a network. DCOM was developed by Microsoft. The DCOM protocol is an application-level protocol for object-oriented remote procedure calls and so is also called *Object RPC* or ORPC. The protocol consists of a set of extensions, layered on the DCE RPC. There is a natural tendency in a networked environment to create entirely new application-level protocols as each new or seemingly unique combination of client, user agent, and server requirement arises. DCOM (as shown in Figure 12.1) uses the Network Data Representation (NDR) for arbitrary data types supported by DCE RPC.

DCOM leverages the authentication, authorization, and message integrity capabilities of DCE RPC. An implementation may support any level of DCE RPC security. Any connection or call can be made as secure or as insecure as negotiated by the client and the server.

In fact, the bulk of the effort involved in implementing the DCOM network protocol is implementing the DCE RPC network protocol on which it is built. An actual COM network remote procedure call is, in fact, a true DCE remote procedure call.

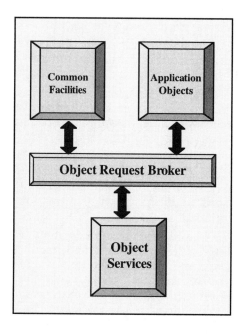

Fig. 12.1 DCOM ORB

12.8 THE ORBIX

An object request broker (ORB) is a piece of infrastructural technology that aids in the development of CORBA objects and arranges for objects to access each other at run-time as defined by the CORBA specification. An ORB mediates between applications, including distributed ones.

IIOP is the open Internet protocol for communication between objects and applications. Based on the (CORBA) specification, IIOP not only allows ORBs to interoperate but also enables users to build and distribute multivendor applications across intranets and the Internet. IIOP is fast becoming a standard protocol for object-linking across the network, and has been adopted by Netscape to allow its browser to access objects across the Internet or intranets.

As IONA has been at the heart of this standardization process, IONA has been able to quickly implement these additions to the CORBA standard, which have been added to Orbix products. All Orbix objects are IIOP-compliant and thus can be accessed by any IIOP-enabled browser, such as Netscape's. IONA's view of CORBA is that it is suitable for two distinct but related activities:

1. Writing a distributed system using conventional programming languages, such as C++, Smalltalk, Ada95, and Java. This is based on the requirements that the objects of the system can communicate with each other easily and with high transparency.

2. Application integration is a strong requirement for both new and existing applications, across heterogeneous hardware and software platforms. Applications can provide a number of IDL interfaces and make these available to the overall system. This allows users to write new applications by combining the facilities of existing applications. Since the components of the system are objects whose internals are hidden from their clients, these objects can interface to legacy systems. This support for legacy systems is crucial for some applications.

Orbix is a mature ORB that implements all of the elements of CORBA, including the stub approach (SII), the Dynamic Invocation Interface (DII), the Implementation Repository (including all of the specified activation modes), the Interface Repository, and the Dynamic Skeleton Interface. It also provides some Orbix-specific enhancements, aimed mainly at allowing application programmers to extend the functionality of the ORB itself, as we will see later. The three main aims of Orbix can be summarized as follows:

1. CORBA and distributed programming in general have been made easy to use by adopting the programming conventions of the chosen language or environment. Hence components of the system can communicate with each other as easily as a program can call one of its own procedures or

functions. This simplifies the construction of new applications and the building of systems from existing applications.

2. Orbix has an open architecture that allows programmers access to a wide variety of hooks. One advantage of this is that Orbix can be integrated with a wide variety of other technologies used to construct real systems.

3. Versions of Orbix run on real-time operating systems. All versions of Orbix benefit because its central core is a straightforward, efficient implementation of CORBA.

12.8.1 Orbix Implementation

Orbix is implemented as a pair of libraries—one for client applications and one for servers—and the orbixd activation daemon. orbixd need only be present at nodes running CORBA servers, and it is responsible for (re)launching server processes dynamically, as required. Nondistributed client and server applications in the same process address space can be built using the server library alone. In this case, references from one object to another are direct (for example, they are direct pointers in C++, and operation invocations are simple C++ virtual function calls).

Because of its library implementation, the Orbix ORB is conceptually omnipresent. There is no distinct component one can identify and as encapsulating the entire ORB. There is no central component through which all object requests must pass. Instead, object requests are passed directly from the client code to the invoked object implementation.

The role of orbixd is to connect clients and servers for the first time. orbixd uses a simple database—the Implementation Repository—to obtain activation information for its servers. For each server the information includes the appropriate CORBA activation mode, the name of the associated executable image, and any command-line parameters. An important component of Orbix is its compiler technology, which translates CORBA IDL into programming language code (for example, C++) that performs remote calls. The generated code is sufficiently sophisticated so that programmers are not burdened with extra programming steps.

Orbix is available on a large number of operating systems, including many versions of UNIX, Windows for Workgroups 3.11, Windows 95, Windows NT, OS/2, VMS, MVS, and Macintosh. The UNIX support includes Solaris, HP/UX, AIX, IRIX, OSF/1, SunOS, Solaris x86, UnixWare, SCO, Sinix, and Ultrix. Both client and server sides are supported on all platforms (including Windows), and full interoperability is provided between all of these.

12.8.1.1 The Messaging Engine This component is responsible for providing request delivery over a variety of underlying transport layers. The engine is split in two halves. A set of generic features—such as request/reply correlation, message caching, message heap management, and threading policies—is implemented in the engine itself. The engine also has an API that allows a variety of different transport mechanisms to be bolted in. This API consists of two major abstractions (expressed as abstract C++ classes in the Orbix source base):

1. This component provides the basic abstraction of a connection between the client and server. Thus, multiple conversations between a pair of objects can be multiplexed over a single channel. In principle, several different channel categories can exist in the same Orbix application: For example, ISIS channels, with MQSeries channels, with regular Orbix TCP/IP channels. In practice, the degree to which this is possible is constrained by the event model adopted by the underlying transports.

2. This component abstracts the notion of the communication protocol used over one or more channels. The Orbix Messaging Engine assumes that every concrete protocol has a notion of request, reply, and exceptional reply. Specific concrete protocols also may have a notion of, for example, connection establishment, graceful connection termination, and priority traffic. However, such refinements are not assumed at the level of protocol.

There are currently two concrete implementations of this protocol:

☞ The OrbixProtocol class, for the proprietary IONA protocol, as used in Orbix before the OMG standardized on a common wire protocol

☞ The IIOP class, which implements the OMG IIOP protocol

12.8.1.2 The Runtime Engine   The runtime implements the CORBA client APIs (e.g., the DII) and server. It also implements the functionality required by the messaging stub code produced by the IDL compiler from IDL source descriptions.

The fundamental classes in the runtime are the request and object classes. The interfaces to both classes are available to Orbix application programmers via the CORBA module. Programmers who choose to use the CORBA static invocation interface need not be particularly aware of these two classes, since the generated stub code largely insulates programmers.

The request class implements the request interface defined in the CORBA specification. It is a part of the DII, and in Orbix is also used by generated stub code. Orbix extends the DII as specified by CORBA, with a stream-based interface. When presented with arguments to an invocation, the request class internally checks whether these are being delivered as part of the DII or from the statically generated stubs. DII arguments are passed into a named-value list (NVList) and their marshaling deferred until Request::invoke is called. Static arguments are marshaled directly.

The object class implements the object interface defined in the CORBA specification. In effect, an instance of the object class has the fundamental information necessary to communicate with a remote object. For each IDL interface compiled with the IDL compiler, there is a corresponding generated (e.g., C++) class: We sometimes call this an IDL class. The object class is the ultimate base class of all IDL classes.

In addition to these two fundamental classes, class TypeCode and any implement their corresponding CORBA specifications. Although *any* and *TypeCode* receive only short descriptions in the CORBA specifications, their implementation is complex and comprises a major part of the runtime source code. A value of *any* is fundamentally mapped—in C or C++—to avoid an "$*$", that is essentially any value whatsoever, including arbitrarily complex structured data. In order to identify the specific kind of value an *any* actually has at runtime, each *any* value also is tagged with type information. The type information in turn is interpreted by TypeCode (and can be generated from the IDL compiler). Marshaling an *any* value can involve deep recursion, based on runtime interpretation of the type code tag.

Apart from these four classes and others that implement interfaces laid down in the CORBA specifications, the runtime includes classes specific to the Orbix implementation. During execution, the runtime builds a *proxy* or *surrogate* for each remote object used by the local process. Each such proxy is an instance of an IDL class. If the IDL class is unavailable to the local process (because the IDL interface was unknown at the time the local process was built) and so there is no IDL stub code available, then the proxy is instead made an instance of class object.

The runtime maintains a table of all proxies and of all implementations of IDL interfaces (these, for example, occur in servers), which in the Orbix source code is called the Object Table (OT). There is one such table per process context (e.g., per UNIX process).

12.8.1.3 Smart Proxies   The default action of the generated stubs of each IDL class is to marshal the request and forward it to the remote object. These stubs are the methods of the proxy objects: Recall that each proxy is an instance of an IDL class.

Using inheritance, the generated stub code can be overridden in a new derived class. Furthermore, the original (generated) code that implements the remote operations is available by calling up the inheritance hierarchy. Orbix also provides a mechanism such that when a new proxy must be constructed for a particular IDL interface at runtime, the proxy can instead be made from a specified derived class of the corresponding IDL class.

In fact, there can be several alternative derived classes for each specified IDL class. When any particular new proxy must be constructed, these classes can collaborate to agree which is responsible for this particular construction, based on the identity of the specific remote object for which the proxy is about to be built.

Smart proxy support for a particular IDL interface typically is provided by a server programmer who wishes to control the behavior of her server, which is presented to its clients in their process contexts. Smart proxy support is typically transparent to an Orbix client programmer.

The most common use for smart proxies is when a server programmer wants to allow her clients to cache state from the server, so as to improve performance and reduce the number of remote calls. It should be noted that while the Orbix client library cannot receive unsolicited incoming requests, it can receive incoming requests, *call-backs*, from a server with which it corresponded earlier. Server call-backs can be used to notify a smart proxy cache of a change of state at its associated server. Smart proxies can have several other uses, for example:

☞ Server rebinding, in which the proxy can be rebound to an alternative remote server when the original server fails

☞ Breakpoints, when debugging and trace code can be executed

☞ Type conversion of IDL types to non-IDL types—for example, converting IDL sequences into conventional linked lists, when migrating legacy applications onto CORBA

12.8.2 Dynamic Invocation Interface (DII)

As we have seen, IDL is used to describe interfaces, and the IDL compiler is used to generate the necessary support to allow clients to invoke remote objects. Specifically, the IDL compiler automatically builds the appropriate code to manage proxies, dispatch incoming requests within a server, and manage the underlying Orbix services.

Using this approach, the IDL interfaces a client program can use are determined when the client program is compiled. Unfortunately, this is too limiting for a small but important subset of applications. These application programs and tools require the use of an indeterminate range of interfaces— interfaces perhaps not conceived of at the time the applications were developed.

Examples include browsers, gateways, management support tools, and distributed debuggers. It certainly is not desirable to limit a browsing tool to a fixed set of predefined interfaces.

Orbix therefore supports a DII that allows an application to issue requests for any interface, even if that interface was unknown at the time the application was compiled. Note that inheritance of interfaces, as supported in IDL, does provide some help in accessing new interfaces. A tool can be written to use a specific IDL interface; but, in fact, that tool can successfully use objects that support any interface derived from that base interface. Sometimes, however, use of inheritance in this way is insufficient: In particular, because the tool would be restricted to using only base interface operations and attributes, and not those added by derived interfaces.

To overcome this general problem, the DII allows invocations to be constructed by specifying, at runtime, the target object reference, the operation/ attribute name, and the parameters to be passed. Such calls are termed *dynamic* because the IDL interfaces used by a program do not have to be statically determined at the time the program is designed and implemented. In contrast, the use of IDL stubs is known as the SII, the Static Invocation Interface.

It is important to note that a server receiving an incoming invocation request does not know or care whether the client that sent the request used the static approach of proxies or the dynamic approach to compose the request.

12.8.3 Dynamic Skeleton Interface

The DII was introduced to allow clients to construct a request by hand and then invoke it. The advantage of the DII is that it allows a client to make an invocation on an object even when the object's IDL interface is unknown at compile time. The DII is a fundamental part of the dynamic CORBA support for clients. Without this support, a client would be able to use an IDL interface only if it was linked with the stub code for that interface.

The Dynamic Skeleton Interface (DSI), on the other hand, is the server-side equivalent of the DII. It allows a server to receive an operation or attribute invocation on any object, even one with an IDL interface unknown at compile time. The server does not need to be linked with the skeleton code for an interface to accept operation invocations on it.

Instead, a server can define a function that will be informed of an incoming operation or attribute invocation: That function can determine the identity of the object being invoked; the name of the operation and the types and values of each argument must be provided by the user. It can then carry out the task requested by the client, and construct and return the result.

Since the introduction of the DSI, the normal way of writing a server—implementing a class that uses the BOAImpl or TIE approach, creating instances of that class, and linking with the skeleton code generated by the IDL compiler—has become known as the Static Skeleton Interface (SSI).

Just as the use of the DII is significantly less common than the use of the SII, the use of the DSI is significantly less common than the use of the SSI.

The client is not aware that the server is, in fact, implemented using the DSI. The client simply makes IDL calls as normal. (Recall from the DII, that a server need not consider whether the client uses the DII or the SII.) To process incoming operation or attribute invocations using the DSI, a server must make a call to the ORB to indicate that it wishes to use the DSI for a specified IDL interface. The same server can use the SSI to handle operation or attribute invocations on other interfaces, but it cannot use the DSI and SSI on the same interface.

12.8.3.1 Filtering Orbix does not directly implement various functions sometimes required in distributed environments. When Orbix is taken out of the box it does not mandate a particular authentication, encryption, auditing, or threads environment. This does not mean Orbix does not support such services. Each of these services can be added by the end user.

One motivation for this is to keep the implementation flexible. It is essential not to insist that every Orbix installation must be configured in the same way. For example, some sites require authentication and some don't. Furthermore, some users may be content to use the Kerberos package as the basis for authentication, while others insist on even stronger requirements.

In a sense, regular Orbix is an ORB and nothing more. It is important to keep its functionality orthogonal and complementary to other software infrastructure packages. This also provides third-party developers with an opportunity to add value-added services to the basic substratum.

Smart proxies allow the behavior of remote representatives of objects to be extended and modified. Conceivably, smart proxies could be used as a way of introducing functionality such as Kerberos into Orbix: A proxy class would have to be provided for every IDL class, and each and every smart proxy class would have to be given such support. Clearly, it would be preferable to have a mechanism independent of all the IDL and proxy classes. Furthermore, proxy classes normally are associated with clients and not with servers: A package such as Kerberos requires support on both sides of a communication channel.

The Orbix runtime allows Orbix programmers to supply filtering code in both clients and servers. Filters are instances of filter classes, which in turn are derived classes of the abstract class Filter provided by Orbix. Filters are formed in a linked list—so an arbitrary number of filters may be installed.

Fundamentally, filters are applied when an operation request or reply is about to be transmitted from a process context, and when such a request or reply is received. The default action (inherited from class Filter) in each case is simply to pass the event on to the next filter in the chain. Having processed an event, a filter can choose to suppress the event from the remaining filters in the chain.

The chief parameter to each filter event is the current request, from which the target object and operation name can be determined. Further parameters can still be marshaled into (or from, as appropriate) the current request by the filter, using the stream-based DII: For example, an authentication token might be marshaled into the request at the time it is about to leave the process context.

Coupling with a threads package is a special case of the filter mechanism. Orbix does not depend on a threads package, because it was envisioned that some applications might not use threading at all. Orbix can be easily combined with a wide variety of threading packages for those who wish to deploy threads in their applications.

In order to integrate Orbix with a given threads package, a ThreadFilter must be written to catch all incoming requests into a process context and dispatch each request on a new thread. The creating thread returns from the filter with the request event apparently suppressed. The new thread continues with the request, applying the remaining filters (if any) in the filter chain, and then calling the target object.

Filtering is a per-process level mechanism and applies (transparently) to all requests and replies leaving and entering a process context. We also have seen how smart proxies can transparently mediate client requests. Orbix provides a second form of filtering that complements smart proxies and operates within servers.

Per-object filtering is a mechanism for providing a filter chain attached to a specific object instance (within a server). The chain can operate independently of other server objects. A per-object filter chain is applied after the per-process filter chain in the case of an incoming request, and before the per-process chain when the reply (if any) to that request is formed.

A further distinction from per-process filtering is that, at the time a per-object filter chain is applied, the actual parameters (if any) to the specific operation have been unmarshaled and are available to the filter code. In effect, then, the filter code is another implementation of the IDL interface associated with the target object: The filter code has methods for each of the IDL operations for the target object. Once again, a filter can choose to suppress the event, so a per-object filter might choose not to pass the request through to its target object and, instead, perhaps generate an exception.

Per-object filtering can have uses similar to those of smart proxies, including assistance in debugging, auditing, and legacy applications. Another use is to transparently propagate a server event across a collection of objects, where such a collection can transparently change. A "move" operation on a graphical object described in IDL could, for example, be notified to a set of attached graphical objects, so that the entire aggregate is moved in unison.

12.8.3.2 Loaders   Orbix does not have any direct support for handling persistent objects—that is, objects whose state can be saved and restored from non-volatile storage. Coupling a persistent store—whether flat-file based, an RDBMS, or an OODBMS—is an important requirement for many applications. The fundamental support for this is the abstract class LoaderClass in the Orbix runtime. Instances of LoaderClass (loaders) are formed in a linked list.

Whenever a new object is built and registered with Orbix, the loaders are notified. A server programmer also can name a new object (using a character string) and this name, if any, is passed to the loaders together with the identity of the object's IDL interface. The name given to the object is called its *marker name*.

The loaders must be coded so that they agree as to which loader is responsible for which object. Typically, there is a single loader, or one loader for a particular set of IDL interfaces. The loader responsible for the new object can adopt the proposed object name (if any) or generate a name for the object. A generated name might be a relational key, for example, which will be used later as a basis for storing the object.

Alternatively, a specific loader can be nominated when an object is registered with Orbix. A class may be written so that all of its constructors ensure that the same loader is used for all of its instances. The loaders are notified when the server process exits, and can choose to carefully store the state of the objects for which they are responsible. A loader also can unilaterally save the state of an object prior to process exit.

When an operation request is received into a server, the loaders are notified if the Orbix runtime cannot locate the target object—that is, if the target is not yet registered in the Object Table (OT). The target object's name also is passed to the loaders, so that the responsible loader can be identified and attempt to restore the object's state from persistent storage. If the target object is successfully retrieved, the OT is updated and the operation request (transparently) resumed—the "object fault" has been successfully handled. If the target object cannot be retrieved or no loader recognizes the object's name, then an exception is returned to the client.

The actual translation of the volatile state of a specific object into and from its persistent state is not handled by Orbix. This is more properly a concern for tools associated with a particular storage manager, rather than the ORB itself. You certainly do not want to constrain the way in which this is done by forcing the use of a specific store.

The default implementation of LoaderClass, the default Loader, names its objects using simple increasing numeric values. It does not attempt to save objects to store, and it ignores object faults.

12.8.4 Naming and the Location Service

In Orbix, an object is named by concatenating the host name of the node at which it was created—along with the name of the server that created it—and the name the object has within that server—its marker name—as previously explained.

The name of a server is, by default, the same name as that of an IDL interface it implements. For example, if we have a server implementation of an interface called *bank*, then the server, by default, will also be called *bank*.

It is common for the same server to implement several IDL interfaces. A bank server also might contain code to implement IDL interfaces for bank account objects, bank statements, the bank manager, and so on. In this case, it is possible to choose the server name by identifying a master interface which abstracts the functionality that the entire server provides and via which all objects managed by the server are obtained. For a banking application, the interface to the bank itself may be such a master interface.

Finally, a server name can be chosen that is independent of any particular IDL interface. For example, we could choose financial Repository as the name of our bank server, even though there is no IDL interface with that name in the application. Server names also can be hierarchically structured, similar to UNIX file names.

The name chosen for a server is significant because it is registered in the Implementation Repository and used by Orbix to identify the executable file that should be used to activate the server. The same executable file can be registered under several server names; that is, different servers can use the same executable image.

When a client program wants to use a particular named service at runtime, it must instruct Orbix to bind the client to a suitable server. One way to do this is for the client to provide Orbix with a character string that represents a full Orbix object reference.

Alternatively, in Orbix, a client can bind to a specific server name at a particular host. The server name must be one of the server names registered in the Implementation Repository at that host—for example, bank or financial Repository as above. The client can go further and attempt to bind to a specific named object at that server, as given by the object's marker name. If the client does not specify a target marker name, then Orbix binds the client to any object within the server which provides an interface compatible with that expected by the server.

The most general form of a client bind is when the client identifies a service, but not a specific host that can provide that service. The service is named by a server name: Zero or more hosts may recognize that server name, based on the information in their respective Implementation Repositories. In this case Orbix must "search" the network, looking for suitable hosts.

Such a search is managed by the location mechanism, implemented in the Orbix runtime by the abstract class locatorClass. This class is called with a service name (as a character string) and is expected to return a list of host names at which the service appears to be present. The locatorClass usually is used transparently to application code.

The default implementation of locatorClass uses a configuration file at each host. This registers knowledge about which hosts, and which groups of hosts, can provide specific services. Each configuration file can contain a pointer to another host to which queries can be forwarded if the information required is not found in the current file. The number of hops used to consult these configuration files is bounded.

The default implementation can, of course, be overruled by providing a derived class of locatorClass and registering an instance of this new locator with Orbix. An alternative implementation, for example, might use a directory service in which the mapping from service names to groups of hosts had been registered.

If the location service identifies several hosts that can provide the target service, Orbix selects any one of these hosts at random. Randomizing the selection helps to spread server loading when multiple clients are using the same service.

12.8.5 Orbix-CORBA Integration

Orbix Desktop for Windows provides the vehicle for our integration of the two systems. Windows-based distributed applications can be written in conventional programming languages, such as C++ or Visual Basic, using the

CORBA programming paradigm. COM-based programming systems, such as Visual Basic, can transparently access and distribute CORBA services. CORBA programs running on any machine can transparently access COM objects on Windows. Orbix Desktop for Windows provides four distinct use models for seamless integration of COM and CORBA.

12.8.5.1 COM Client-CORBA Server

Orbix for Windows allows the developer to pass Server IDL through the Orbix OLE Wizard. The Wizard generates code for either standard COM servers or COM Custom Controls (ActiveX Controls). These servers can then represent remote CORBA objects on the desktop, and client/server connections are made using standard COM calls. The default Orbix locator transparently manages the locating of remote CORBA objects, leaving the user to concentrate on developing functionality, not network programming.

12.8.5.2 CORBA Client-COM Server

Orbix for Windows includes the TLB2IDL tool, which generates IDL from the type information of a COM server. This IDL can then be passed through the Orbix Wizard in order to create an ActiveX Control, which in turn can expose whichever CORBA interface is desired. This ActiveX Control can be placed within the COM server, and the EXE can be registered with Orbix as an active Orbix server. Alternatively, the ActiveX Control can be placed in a proxy application, in order to connect with servers that are not your own.

12.8.5.3 Client and Server in COM

The user can either write IDL interfaces or generate them as detailed above from an existing COM server. This IDL can then be used to generate an ActiveX Control with a set of CORBA interfaces. The Orbix Wizard can generate a set of server stubs in various languages. At present, Visual Basic and C++ are supported.

The server is then implemented by filling in the blanks in the generated stubs, adding additional server functionality. The client is implemented as though it was talking to a local COM server.

12.8.5.4 Client and Server in CORBA

The user also can implement the distributed system solely using CORBA and C++. Object interfaces are written in IDL, which then generates stub code on the client side and skeleton code on the server side. The server side objects are then implemented, as outlined above. On the client side, the stub code marshals the invocation in order to communicate with the server-based objects.

12.9 VISIBROKER

VisiBroker—the CORBA ORB (as shown in Figure 12.2) written in Java—and VisiBroker for C++ provide the means to build and deploy distributed applica-

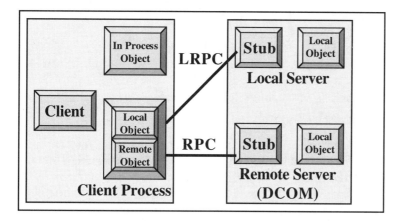

Fig. 12.2 CORBA ORB

tions that are open, flexible, and interoperable across a wide range of platforms.

VisiBroker allows you to take advantage of the opportunities presented by Web-, Internet-, and intranet-based technologies while leveraging the component reuse fostered by object-oriented computing, reducing development cycles and lowering costs. With native support for CORBA's Internet, Inter-ORB truly distributed applications for enterprise computing environments.

12.9.1 Supported Platforms

VisiBroker Integrated Transaction Service (VisiBroker ITS) is the next-generation transaction-management solution for delivering reliable, high-performance distributed object applications. It delivers the features of a traditional TP monitor while meeting the requirements of distributed object applications. VisiBroker ITS simplifies the complexity of distributed transactions by providing an essential set of services—an integrated product set that includes the VisiBroker ORB (naming and event services), which is an implementation of the CORBA Transaction Service (recovery and logging, integration with databases and legacy systems, and administration facilities)—within a single, integrated architecture.

Unlike other implementations, VisiBroker ITS is a fully integrated solution that is CORBA-compliant—a transaction service that is tightly integrated with an underlying object request broker.

12.9.2 VisiBroker Gatekeeper

VisiBroker Gatekeeper allows your enterprise computing environment to extend beyond your corporation's firewall. By transparently providing a proxy mechanism between applets and server objects, VisiBroker Gatekeeper allows applets to escape the limitations of Java sandbox security without compromising functionality such as callbacks.

Support for HTTP tunneling also is built into Gatekeeper, providing even more flexibility to companies concerned with firewall administration and configuration.

12.9.3 VisiBroker Naming Service

VisiBroker Naming Service helps developers cope with the increasing complexity of large-scale distributed computing. Providing a mechanism to associate meaningful names to individual object implementation, VisiBroker Naming Service reduces the complexity of locating and retrieving objects from the thousands of objects available.

An implementation of CORBA Naming Service specification, VisiBroker Naming Service provides a CORBA-compliant solution for heterogeneous interoperability.

12.9.4 VisiBroker Event Service

VisiBroker Event Service, an implementation of the CORBA Event Service specification, extends the capabilities of the VisiBroker ORB to include alternative communication mechanisms needed by event-based tasks. Through support for asynchronous invocations, VisiBroker Event Service allows the decoupling of the traditional clients and servers and transforms applications into information *suppliers* and information *consumers*. This supplier-consumer model reduces server traffic and improves scalability without impacting development efforts. VisiBroker Event Service is a CORBA-compliant, high-performance solution for interoperability within heterogeneous environments.

12.9.5 Visigenic Data Access

The product includes:

☞ VisiChannel for ODBC (Open Database Connectivity), VisiODBC Drivers, and the VisiODBC Software Development

☞ Visigenic distributed object products, including VisiBroker for Java and VisiBroker for C++, both of which are based on CORBA and use IIOP

12.9.6 VisiBroker for C++

VisiBroker for C++ provides a CORBA ORB runtime and supporting development environment for building, deploying, and managing distributed C++ applications that are open, flexible, and interoperable across multiple platforms.

Objects built with VisiBroker for C++ are easily accessed by Web-based applications that communicate using CORBA's IIOP, the emerging standard for communication between and among distributed objects running on the Internet and intranets. VisiBroker provides a native implementation of IIOP, ensuring high-performance, interoperable distributed-object applications for the Internet, intranets, and enterprise computing environments.

12.9.7 VisiBroker for Java

VisiBroker for Java, the first client and server-side CORBA ORB written in Java, provides an ORB runtime and supporting development environment for building, deploying, and managing distributed Java applications that are open, flexible, and interoperable across multiple platforms. Through VisiBroker's implementation of CORBA's IIOP, enterprises can leverage existing corporate applications while developing and deploying new distributed applications.

12.9.8 Leading Java ORB

Unlike other Java ORB implementations, VisiBroker for Java supports both client and server Java applets, providing additional development flexibility. Features like this have made Visigenic the leading supplier of embedded distributed-object technology to the software industry.

12.10 OBJECT-ORIENTED PROGRAMMING WITH SOM

The Object Management Group set its CORBA standards to provide interchangeability of objects. IBM's SOM, Microsoft's COM and DCOM, VisiBroker, Orbix, and others fully conform to these standards. There are two primary ways to provide the services required by computer applications:

☞ The functional or procedural approach to programming provides one or more libraries of functions and procedures with which programmers can operate on device drivers, files, windows, and so on.

☞ The object-oriented approach to programming provides one or more libraries of objects that are computer abstractions of real objects. These objects can interact with each other. For example, the object movie is a software unit that can be played, stopped, and edited. It also can interact with an audio track object to provide synchronized audio and video. The current trend in software engineering is toward object-oriented programming.

The object-oriented approach has several advantages. *Encapsulation*, the key to object-oriented programming, ensures data operations are performed only on appropriate data. Class descriptions can be modified with last-minute design changes without having to recode major sections of the application. Consistent *user interfaces* across many applications are made possible by sharing common objects. *Reusing* the same objects reduces coding time and increases quality.

Hardware engineers do not redesign a circuit board from scratch. They select from a library of prebuilt components with well-defined interfaces and link these together. Object-oriented programming employs lessons learned from the more mature field of hardware engineering.

Object-oriented programming, however, has some disadvantages. Most OOP languages have a tight binding between the object and the programs that use the object. If an object changes, it is often necessary (as in the case of C++) to recompile the application. The binary-level interface to the object is not portable to other language execution environments. Programs written in one language cannot use objects from another language.

12.10.1 Frameworks

In addition to SOM itself (the SOM compiler and the SOM runtime library), the SOMObjects Developer Toolkit provides a set of frameworks (class libraries) that can be used in developing object-oriented programs. These frameworks include DSOM, Interface Repository, Persistence, Replication, Emitter, and Event Management.

12.10.1.1 DSOM Framework
DSOM enables application programs to access SOM objects across address spaces. Application programs can access objects in other processes on the same or different machines. DSOM provides this transparent access to remote objects through its ORB. The location and implementation of the object are hidden from the client—the client accesses the object as if it were local. Currently, DSOM supports the distribution of objects among processes within a workstation (Workstation DSOM) and across a local area network consisting of OS/2 and AIX systems (Workgroup DSOM).

12.10.1.2 Interface Repository Framework
The Interface Repository is a database that holds all the information contained in the IDL description of a class of objects. It consists of the 11 classes defined in the CORBA standard for accessing the Interface Repository. Thus, the Interface Repository framework provides runtime access to all information contained in the IDL description of a class of objects.

12.10.1.3 Persistence Framework
The Persistence framework is a collection of SOM classes that provides methods for saving objects and later restoring them. Since objects can be stored in either a file or a more specialized reposi-

tory, the state of an object can be preserved beyond the termination of the process that creates it. This facility is useful for constructing object-oriented databases, spreadsheets, and other applications that store and later modify data. The Persistence framework includes the following abilities:

☞ Objects can be stored in default formats or in specially designed formats.

☞ Objects can be stored individually or in groups.

☞ Objects of arbitrary complexity can be saved and restored.

12.10.1.4 Replication Framework The Replication framework is a collection of SOM classes that allows a replica or copy of an object to exist in multiple address spaces while maintaining a single-copy image. In other words, an object can be replicated in several different processes while logically it behaves as a single copy. Updates to any copy are propagated immediately to all other copies. The Replication framework handles locking, synchronization, and update propagation, and guarantees consistency among the replicas.

The Replication framework can be exploited only if the applications are structured appropriately. The recommended structure is similar to the Model-View-Controller paradigm used by Smalltalk programmers. The Replication framework proposes a View-Data paradigm. The data object has whatever "state" information the application desires to store in it. The view object has no state, but has methods to show a rendition of the state contained in the data object. In addition, it may have some data that pertain to the image being displayed to the user. For example, in a visual presentation, the colors used for different regions may be in the view object while the content information comes from the data object.

The view and data must have a protocol between them so that when the data object changes, a signal is sent to the view object to note the change and refresh the display. This protocol can be extended to multiple views on the same data object, whereby an update to the data object is automatically seen in all visual presentations. Effectively, the views "observe" the data.

The Replication framework is concerned with data objects only. Application developers must implement the *observation* protocol between the views and the data. The Replication framework requires that data objects be derived from a distinguished framework class SOMRReplicbl.

12.10.1.5 Emitter Framework The Emitter framework is a collection of SOM classes that allows programmers to write their own emitters. Emitter describes a back-end output component of the SOM compiler. Each emitter input has information about an interface, generated by the SOM compiler as it processes an IDL specification and produces output organized in a different format.

SOM provides a set of emitters that generate the binding files for C and C++ programming (header files and implementation templates). For example, an implementor could write an emitter to produce documentation files or binding files for programming languages other than C and C++.

12.10.1.6 Event Management Framework   The Event Management framework is a central facility for registering all events of an application. This registration facilitates grouping various application events and waiting on multiple events in a single-event processing loop. Replication framework and DSOM use this facility to wait on their respective events. Any interactive application that uses DSOM or replicated objects must also use the Event Management framework. These frameworks (class libraries) can provide OO programmers with the following capabilities:

☞ The ability to access objects across address spaces using the DSOM framework

☞ CORBA-compliant runtime access to all information contained in the IDL description of a class of objects using the Interface Repository framework

12.10.2 Implementing SOM Classes

The IDL specification for a class defines only the interface to the instances of the class. The implementation of those objects—the procedures that perform their methods—is defined in an implementation file. To assist users in implementing classes, the SOM compiler produces a template implementation file: A type-correct guide for how the implementation of a class should look. The class implementor then modifies this template to implement the class's methods.

The SOM compiler also can update the implementation file to reflect later changes made to a class's interface definition file (.idl). These incremental updates include adding new stub procedures, adding comments, and changing method prototypes to reflect changes made to the method definitions in the IDL specification. These updates to the implementation file do not disturb existing code in the method procedures.

12.10.3 Invoking Methods on Objects

To invoke a method in C, a client programmer can use the macro <_methodName>. To avoid possible ambiguity, the programmer also can use the long form of this macro. In C, calls to methods defined using IDL require at least two arguments: A pointer to the receiving object and a value of type (Environment*). The Environment data structure specified by CORBA passes environmental information between a caller and a called method.

If the IDL specification of the method includes a context specification, then the method has an additional implicit context parameter. When invoking the method, this argument must follow immediately after the Environment pointer argument. None of the SOM-supplied methods requires context arguments. The Environment and context method parameters are recommended by the CORBA standard.

If the IDL specification of the class that introduces the method includes the callstyle=oidl modifier, the (Environment*) and context arguments should not be supplied when invoking the method. That is, the receiver of the method call is followed immediately by the arguments to the method. Some classes supplied in the SOMObjects Developer Toolkit are defined in this way to ensure compatibility with the previous version of SOM.

If a C expression is used to compute the first argument to a method call, an expression without side effects must be used, because the first argument is evaluated twice by the &ltmethodName> macro expansion. In particular, a somNew method call cannot be used as the first argument to a C method call, because that would create two new class instances rather than one.

12.10.3.1 Obtaining a Procedure Pointer

Method resolution is the process of obtaining a pointer to the procedure that implements a particular method for a particular object at runtime. The method is invoked subsequently by calling that procedure and passing the method's intended receivers—the Environment pointer, the context argument, and the method's other arguments, if any. C and C++ programmers may want to obtain a pointer to a method's procedure for efficient repeated invocations.

Obtaining a pointer to a method's procedure can be done in one of two ways, depending on whether the method is to be resolved using offset resolution or name-lookup resolution. Obtaining a method's procedure pointer via offset resolution is faster, but it requires that the name of the class that introduces the method and the name of the method be known at compile time. It also requires that the method be defined as part of that class's interface in the IDL specification of the class.

Using offset resolution to obtain a pointer to a procedure, the C/C++ usage bindings provide the SOM_Resolve and SOM_ResolveNoCheck macros. The usage bindings themselves use the first of these, SOM_Resolve, for offset-resolution method calls. The difference between the two macros is that the SOM_Resolve macro performs consistency checking on its arguments, whereas the macro SOM_ResolveNoCheck does not. Both macros require the same arguments:

☞ *receiver*: Object to which the method will apply (should be specified as an expression without side effects)

☞ *className*: Name of the class that introduces the method

☞ *methodName*: Name of the desired method

The last two names (className and methodName) must be given as tokens, rather than as strings or expressions.

In addition to methods, SOM objects can have attributes. An attribute, an IDL shorthand for declaring methods, does not necessarily indicate the presence of any particular instance data in an object of that type. Attribute methods are called get and set methods. For example, if a class Hello declares an attribute called msg, then object variables of type Hello will support the methods _get_msg and _set_msg to access or set the value of the msg attribute. Read-only attributes have no set method. The get and set methods are invoked in the same way as other methods.

12.10.3.2 Getting the Class of an Object

To get the class for which an object is an instance, SOM provides a method called somGetClass. The somGetClass method takes an object as its only argument and returns a pointer to the class object of which it is an instance. Getting the class of an object is useful for obtaining information about the object. In some cases, such information cannot be obtained directly from the object, but only from its class.

A class can override the somGetClass method to provide enhanced or alternative semantics for its objects. Because it usually is important to respect the intended semantics of a class of objects, the somGetClass method usually should be used to access the class of an object.

In a few special cases, it is not possible to make a method call on an object to determine its class. For such situations, SOM provides the SOM_GetClass macro. In general, the somGetClass method and the SOM_GetClass macro may have different behaviors. Although this difference may be limited to side effects, it is possible for their results to differ. The macro SOM_GetClass should be used only when absolutely necessary.

12.10.3.3 Creating a Class Object

A class object is created automatically the first time the &ltclassName&gtNew macro is invoked to create an instance of that class. In other situations, it may be necessary to create a class object explicitly.

As seen earlier, it sometimes is necessary to create a class object before creating any instances of the class. For example, creating instances using the &ltclassName&gtRenew macro or the somRenew method requires knowing how large the created instance will be, so that memory can be allocated for it. Obtaining this information requires creating the class object. As another example, a class object must be explicitly created when a program does not use the SOM bindings for a class. Without SOM bindings for a class, its instances must be created using somNew or somRenew. These methods require that the class object be created in advance.

12.10.3.4 Referring to Class Objects

The &ltclassName&gtNewClass procedure initializes the SOM runtime environment, creates the class object (if necessary), creates class objects for the ancestor classes and metaclass of the class (if necessary), and returns a pointer to the newly created class object. After it is created, the class object can be referenced in client code using the macro _&ltclassName&gt.

The procedure takes two arguments: The major and the minor version number of the class. These numbers are checked against the version numbers built into the class library to determine if the class is compatible with the client's expectations. The class is compatible if it has the same major version number and the same or higher minor version number. Major version numbers usually change only when a significant enhancement or incompatible change is made to a class. Minor version numbers change when minor enhancements or fixes are made. Downward compatibility usually is maintained across changes in the minor version number.

The somFindClass or somFindClsInFile methods can be used to create a class object when you are not using the C or C++ language bindings for the class, or when the class name is not known at compile time. Instructions for using these methods can be found in the SOMObjects Developer Toolkit User's Guide.

12.11 CONCLUSIONS

Although CORBA offers many architectural benefits, it is not the only game in town. A few years ago, Microsoft announced its own ORB standard, known as COM. COM is, in every sense, an ORB in that it provides an object standard and a common method of inter-ORB communication using OLE.

As OLE automation became a standard on Windows desktops, client/server tools such as Delphi, Visual Basic, Visual C++, and PowerBuilder began to support COM by giving developers the ability to create OLE automation servers. OLE automation servers come in two flavors:

1. *In-process OLE automation servers* are really just DLLs loaded directly into the memory space of the application to provide all sorts of application functionality. ActiveX controls are examples of in-process OLE automation servers that act like components.

2. *Out-of-process OLE automation servers* are ORBs that function outside the application's memory space. Out-of-process OLE automation servers are .exes, and they run in the multitasking environments of Windows 95 and Windows NT. Out-of-process servers communicate with other OLE-enabled ORBs or applications using an RPC mechanism and the standard OLE interface. Until recently, however, COM could not leverage the power of distributed objects. With the release of Windows NT 4.0, DCOM became a reality for Windows-oriented client/server developers.

12.11.1 DCOM and COM

DCOM lets COM-enabled (OLE-enabled) application-development tools and even office-automation applications access out-of-process OLE automation servers that physically exist on the local machine or on a machine connected by a network. The application simply checks with the Windows NT registry to locate the remote ORB, and then invokes its services. For example, you could create a COM ORB using any number of tools that automatically generate a sales report if a certain method in the ORB is invoked. Other COM-enabled applications existing on the network can access that object by locating and invoking its methods through the DCOM mechanism built into the Windows operating system.

DCOM is different from CORBA because it is built into the infrastructure of the operating system and network, and it is not delivered by an ORB vendor. For existing Windows 95 (where it is soon to be included) and Windows NT shops, this means that it is already there. Although CORBA has yet to attract the mainstream tool market, COM is already a part of most development tools for Windows. However, DCOM is a Windows-only phenomenon, and users who run a hodgepodge of operating systems and processors will not find any value in DCOM.

SOM classes, designed to be language-neutral, can be implemented in one programming language and used by programs written in another language. To achieve language neutrality, the interface for a class of objects must be defined separately from its implementation.

12.11.2 DCOM and DSOM

Both Windows NT and OS/2 Warp have object-orientation facilities built right into the operating system, allowing developers to write distributed applications, portions of which can reside on remote servers anywhere on the network. Microsoft's DCOM and IBM's DSOM basically do the same thing. They allow developers to create objects (packages of data and the operations that can be performed on them) and to have other programs and objects operate on them in a binary-standard manner.

The binary-standard part is significant, in that C++ objects, for instance, exist only for the program in which they were compiled, whereas DCOM and DSOM objects can be written in any language and can communicate with other such objects, no matter what language they were written in—even if they were written by another vendor.

Compound document systems—such as Microsoft's OLE and IBM's implementations of OpenDoc—are built on system object facilities: Specifically DCOM and DSOM.

Both Microsoft and IBM use these object facilities to write large parts of their operating systems. Many of the controls in Windows 95 and Windows NT Explorer are COM objects, and much of the OS/2 Workplace Shell is built on SOM. The advantage of this is that developers can write simple programs to use the same controls that are in the operating system and easily modify their behavior.

12.11.3 Distribution Technologies and the CORBA Standard

The problem of high-level application interworking and construction is well recognized in the software industry. Upon analysis, we see that application integration and distribution are the same thing. Enabling diverse applications—written in many different languages, running on multiple operating systems, and using a variety of networking protocols—is a challenging problem. Its solution lies in the marriage of distribution technology with object orientation.

Distribution technology offers the basic infrastructure to abstract the communication layers, while object orientation provides the framework for encapsulation and reuse needed to facilitate application integration. There have been numerous initiatives in this area. While they originate from different vendors with differing design centers, all offer similar facilities.

Recognizing the urgent requirement for a standard in high-level application interworking (including across multiple platforms and network architectures) the software industry formed a consensus via the OMG and, in particular, the CORBA specification.

CORBA specifies a messaging facility for a distributed object environment: A standard mechanism for objects to access one another's public states and exported functionality.

The specification was composed of two chief parts: An IDL and language mappings between IDL and implementation languages (e.g., C++, C, Ada95, Java, and Smalltalk). The language mappings relate both to how an object invokes an IDL-defined (CORBA) object and to how an object implementor should implement an IDL-defined (CORBA) object in a given implementation language.

IDL is used to define interfaces to objects. Remote objects view a CORBA object purely in terms of this interface. IDL provides encapsulation of an object's implementation behind a formal IDL interface, which is independent of implementation language, implementation algorithm, location, machine architecture, operating system, network technology, and even ORB architecture. This separation of interface and implementation allows CORBA to be viewed as a software bus and is one of the most powerful aspects of CORBA.

The SII allows an invoking object to access a remote object using syntax that is natural to the implementation language. The ORB development environment ensures that this works. Thus, a C++ programmer accesses a remote operation "jump" using the syntax myobject->jump().

The DII allows an invocation to be constructed manually, without static (compile time) knowledge of the object being invoked. In return for explicitly building messages and argument lists at runtime, the dynamic API allows decisions to be made much later than the static approach. This is attractive for certain applications in which insufficient information about remote objects is available at compile time. Such applications include browsers and resource managers. The disadvantage of the DII approach is that the API is more complex to use than the SII approach.

The CORBA specification introduced the important features outlined above, including a standardized C++ mapping, which protected a developer's programming investment, improved code portability, and further eased software maintenance. The DSI provided a server-side equivalent to the DII, which helped developers in building gateways between CORBA and non-CORBA systems. In addition, the CORBA IIOP provides a standardized transport protocol for all CORBA-compliant object request brokers.

Middleware and Distributed Programming

13.1 INTRODUCTION

Distributed computations are concurrent programs in which processes communicate by message passing. Such programs typically execute on network architectures such as groups of workstations or distributed memory parallel machines (i.e., multicomputers such as hypercubes).

Several paradigms are involved. These include networks of filters, clients, and servers; heartbeat, probe/echo, broadcast, and token-passing algorithms; decentralized servers; and bags of tasks. These paradigms are applicable to several practical problems, such as parallel sorting, file servers, computing the topology of a network, distributed termination detection, replicated databases, and parallel adaptive quadrature.

Solutions are derived in a step-wise fashion from a general specification of the problem to a concrete solution. The derivations illustrate techniques for developing distributed algorithms.

Four kinds of processes occur in a distributed program: filters, clients, servers, and peers:

1. A *filter* is a data transformer. It receives streams of data values from its input channels, performs some computations on those values, and sends streams of results to its output channels.

2. A *client* is a triggering process; a server is a reactive process. Clients make requests that trigger reactions from servers.

3. A *server* usually is a nonterminating process that often provides service to more than one client.

4. A *peer* is one of a collection of identical processes that interact to provide a service or compute a result.

In this section, we examine several process interaction patterns that occur in distributed programs. We will also exploit the client/server programming environments using *middleware* processes and programming languages. We will look at the following process-interaction paradigms:

☞ One-way data flow through networks of filters
☞ Requests and replies between clients and servers
☞ Back-and-forth (heartbeat) interactions between neighboring processes
☞ Broadcasts between processes in complete graphs
☞ Coordination between decentralized server processes

13.2 MIDDLEWARE

The need for middleware and its role have been changing as the IT industry has moved through two generations of client/server applications and multiple stages of applications integration. The first phase, called the *rightsizing phase*, was targeted toward limiting the role of mainframes (MVS and VMS) and eventually eliminating them. However, instead of mainframe elimination, rightsizing resulted in the development of additional applications dedicated to one particular department as opposed to an enterprise. An overwhelming majority of these newly developed applications were based on the two-tier client/server model in which a client program accesses a database server.

During the first years of the client/server revolution, many companies realized the limits of a two-tier architecture, including:

☞ Inefficient communication between application tiers

☞ Inability to partition applications logic

☞ Lack of robust security

☞ Lack of scalability

☞ Problems with portability (e.g., stored procedures)

These limitations led to the evolution of three-tier (and beyond) application architectures. Separating the one monolithic application into components that are deployed on three different tiers has a number of significant advantages. The various application components can be located where they are most cost-efficient (e.g., close to the database engine), they can exploit GUI capabilities, and they can be integrated with existing applications or packaged software.

This allows applications to be enterprisewide in scope yet scalable and capable of unifying formerly disparate applications into a single system image for the end user. For example, a bank officer who must view all of a customer's assets, which are spread across separate systems, needs such a single-system image.

The development and deployment of these three-tier distributed applications, combined with an increasing need for applications integration, has caused a wide range of new requirements, including those outlined below:

☞ Application developers need a common and consistent environment that reduces the complexity of developing a distributed application and that allows them to concentrate on solving business problems independent of the operating system, hardware platform, and communication protocol.

☞ Developers need flexible yet robust communication APIs to enable applications to exchange information seamlessly, both synchronously and asynchronously.

☞ Distributed business applications must be secure. Users must be able to rely on the authentication and authorization of clients and application servers, and on the protection and confidentiality of messages that are transmitted across a network.

☞ Corporations that have adopted object-orientation as their strategic direction need a distributed environment that can provide them with a higher level of abstraction than traditional client/server systems.

☞ If possible, applications need to be decoupled—that is, the different components that make up the application should not be strongly dependent on one another. Instead, they should communicate via interfaces; that way, if one application is modified or replaced, the impact on the overall system is significantly reduced.

☞ Organizations should be able to make purchasing decisions based on the functionality of the packaged software rather than on the ability of that software to run in a specific environment.

☞ The life of legacy applications must be extended by integrating them into a client/server context.

☞ Among the foremost requirements is location transparency; that is, an application should not have to spend time searching for the location of another application.

☞ Since organizations have experienced the limitations of first-generation client/server systems, scalability has become another issue that needs to be addressed.

☞ Features such as failover and fault tolerance should be provided by the distributed computing infrastructure, because every component within the distributed environment can fail.

13.2.1 What Is "Middleware"?

Middleware covers such a broad territory of distributed computing that it is almost impossible to frame it in a concrete definition. There are as many definitions as there are opinions about how applications need to be distributed. Some refer to middleware as the glue that holds all components of distributed applications together. Others view it as the component that holds the solution to the scalability maze by creating a layer of distributed infrastructure, on top of which applications are deployed.

Everyone agrees that middleware is an essential component; it fulfills many of the enterprise application requirements we have discussed in previous chapters. These applications typically are part of an environment consisting of heterogeneous operating systems, hardware platforms, communication protocols, databases, and a plethora of development tools. For application developers, dealing with such heterogeneous plumbing quickly becomes a nightmare.

Middleware provides an isolation layer of software, shielding developers from this nightmare by presenting its own enabling layer of APIs. This layer hides the differences inherent in such a heterogeneous environment. In effect, it decouples otherwise coupled applications from dependencies on platform-specific APIs. This leads us to one of the simpler definitions of middleware: Middleware is an enabling layer of software that resides between the business application and the networked layer of heterogeneous platforms and protocols. It de-couples business applications from any dependencies on the plumbing layer, which consists of heterogeneous operating systems, hardware platforms, and communication protocols.

We can classify middleware into five distinct categories:

1. Remote Procedure Calls (RPC)-Based Middleware
2. Message-Oriented Middleware (MOM)
3. Portable Transaction-Processing (TP) Monitors
4. Object Request Brokers (ORBs), including OLE/COM/DCOM
5. Database Middleware

Examples of middleware products available today that have been used for production applications are Information Builders' EDA/SQL, BEA Systems' DECmessageQ, IBM's MQSeries, BEA Systems' Tuxedo and ObjectBroker, IONA Technologies' Orbix, and the various implementations of DCE.

13.2.2 RPC-Based Middleware—DCE

Remote Procedure Calls (RPCs) are one of the more mature mechanisms for building distributed applications. Evolved from UNIX environments, RPCs are widely accepted for building distributed applications. Middleware offerings such as OSF's DCE and Sun's open network computing (ONC) have been built using RPCs. By their nature, RPCs are synchronous and blocking. A client process (or thread) that makes a request to a server is blocked while the server formulates the answer.

RPCs generally enforce a static relationship between different components of distributed applications. For most applications that do not exploit the low-level details of RPCs, this means that once the client has been compiled and linked with the RPC stubs into an executable module, its binding to one particular server procedure is cemented. This is in contrast to the dynamic, environment-dependent server selection that is available with Message-Oriented Middleware and some TP monitors (e.g., load balancing and fail-over) or the object-oriented request-routing supported by Object Request Brokers (e.g., inheritance and polymorphism).

A key component of RPC-based middleware is the Interface Definition Language (IDL). IDL is a high-level universal notational language capable of defining interfaces that represent contracts between client and server applications. While IDL is required from a technical perspective in order to link application components to the distributed infrastructure, it is also useful as a documentation tool for the development process.

Since the RPC technology has been available for several years, most middleware products based on RPC have been consolidated in an open standard middleware offering DCE. DCE is a single-source code offering maintained and owned by the Open Group (formerly OSF); it is available from many major vendors (including Digital, IBM, HP, Hitachi, and Sun).

13.2.2.1 How Do RPCs Work?   In order to connect the client and server components of a distributed application using RPCs, every function that a client application can call must be represented by a *stub* (i.e., a placeholder) for the real function on the server. This stub looks like the remote procedure to the client application and provides location transparency to the client. Using RPCs as the distributed computing model then, it is a relatively straightforward process to build client applications. Clients can call a remote procedure in the same way they would call a local procedure.

Furthermore, the developer does not have to be concerned with synchronization issues between a sequence of requests, because each request is performed by transferring control to the server process. The client process is blocked until the response is returned through the network to the caller (synchronous or blocking communication).

The situation on the server side is similar. Here a stub program calls the procedure on the server in exactly the same way it would be called by the client program if it resided within the client process. However, because the application component on the server is remote to the client, it is not completely transparent to the server developer.

The server must develop a certain amount of *housekeeping* logic in order to make its service available to clients on the network, such as registration with the directory and security services.

Although the stub programs look like the real procedure on the server, they do not contain the business logic. Instead, they contain the logic to accept the parameters for this function call, package them for transport over the network, and perform the reverse operation for the results returned from the server.

13.2.2.2 Interface Definition Language   The translation of the data representation that depends on the hardware and the serialization for the network transport is called *marshaling*. This process requires a complete description of all data involved in a request, including its type, format, and length. This description must be provided by the server application developer in the form of IDL.

IDL is a high-level universal notational language that is capable of defining interfaces that represent contracts between client and server applications. The interfaces are composed of definitions for the function name, parameters that are passed between client and server (either in one or both directions), and possibly a return result.

IDL is programming-language independent, which means that the client does not have to be concerned with the calling conventions of the programming language that has been used to implement the server. As long as a mapping is available between IDL and the programming language of choice, the client can use its native language constructs. Once IDL has been defined, it is used as input to an IDL compiler, which generates the stub routines that must be invoked by the client program and that call the server subprocedure.

While IDL is a key component of RPC-based middleware, it has been rediscovered for object-oriented technologies.

13.2.3 Message-Oriented Middleware

Message-Oriented Middleware (MOM) distributes data and control through the exchange of records known as messages. Messages are strings of bytes that have meaning to the applications that exchange them. Besides application-related data, messages might include control data relevant to the message-queuing system only. This information is used to store, route, deliver, retrieve, and track the payload data. The key feature of the messaging model is that it supports both synchronous and asynchronous communication and lends itself to event-driven rather than procedural processing.

MOM is perhaps the most confusing middleware category today. There is no common source code, as in the case of the DCE from the Open Group. Also, there are no common specifications such as those for CORBA from the Object Management Group.

Further adding to the confusion, there are more than a dozen MOM products spanning a wide range of functionality. Most are driven by the diverse communication models supported by MOM products. As a result, MOM products can be categorized as message passing and message queuing.

RPC-based middleware—such as DCE, MOM, and Database Middleware—offers significant value to a wide variety of applications. However, it does not provide comprehensive support for synchronous transactions that span heterogeneous environments and databases. Many mission-critical applications (e.g., in the financial industry) have an absolute requirement for maintaining the transactional integrity of business functions. These applications can be built using TP monitors.

13.2.3.1 Message Passing
Message passing is a direct, program-to-program communication model by which an application request is sent in the form of a message from one program directly to another. Both programs communicate directly in a connection-oriented way. A logical connection between programs needs to be maintained. This does not make message passing an appropriate model for loosely coupled, time-independent applications.

In message passing the communication mechanism can be either synchronous (i.e., the sender is blocked until the receiver sends a message back, like RPCs) or asynchronous (employing a polling model or callback routines, which make the middleware product suitable for development of event-driven applications). However, a message-passing model is always connection-oriented, meaning that a direct link between two programs must be maintained. Such a direct link generally is supported across the vast majority of communication protocols.

13.2.3.2 Message Queuing
Message queuing is an indirect program-to-program communication model that allows programs to communicate via mes-

sage queues rather than by calling each other directly. Message queuing always implies a connectionless model.

Message queues can be either persistent or nonpersistent. In the latter case, messages are lost in the event of queue manager failure. In the former case, messages are recovered after queue manager restarts. Of course, banking fund transfer applications must choose reliability over performance, and so will select persistent over nonpersistent queues.

Some message-queuing products support triggers, in which an application program is started whenever a request or reply message has arrived on a local queue and the application program is not already active. This feature allows applications to be active only when there is work to be done, which avoids an unnecessary consumption of resources.

Transactional messaging is an advanced feature available with some competitive messaging products. Transactional semantics can be applied to the enqueue/dequeue operations across multiple queues, under the control of a Queue Manager. This allows the split of a synchronous transaction spanning multiple network nodes (and usually updates multiple databases) into a number of smaller transactions. These smaller transactions then can operate asynchronously and are driven by asynchronous messaging. This presents an alternative to using a synchronous transaction with two-phase commit protocol. Database coordination requires a combination of message queuing and a TP monitor or must be handled by the application.

Most message-queuing products support network session concentration. This allows multiple programs to communicate with each other through a lesser number of network connections that are established and maintained between queue managers. This feature can cut both communication costs and network bandwidth requirements.

Overall, message-queuing middleware is an attractive model for the development of enterprise-distributed applications. It presents developers with rich, flexible, yet simple communication models. It lends itself to the development of event-driven applications in which an event (represented by a message) in one application causes some course of action in another. This mirrors complex business processes within an enterprise or across different enterprises.

13.2.4 Distributed Transaction Processing Monitors

For the last twenty years or so TP monitors have been used extensively for mainframe-based, monolithic applications. TP monitors such as IBM's CICS and IMS have been used in many mission-critical applications of major businesses worldwide for ATMs, back office security clearance, and the processing of insurance claims, for example.

Over the last three to five years, most of these TP monitors have become available on additional operating systems such as UNIX and Windows NT. These are in addition to the TP monitors developed from the onset for UNIX platforms. Historically, the purpose of the first TP monitors on UNIX was to reduce the number of connections to the database in client/server environments. Without TP monitors, each client had to be connected to the DBMS, which caused a separate UNIX process to be started. TP monitors act as a database connection concentrator, since the clients are connected to the TP monitor and not to the DBMS directly. This reduces the overhead and increases performance.

A while later this functionality was supported by the RDBMS products themselves, virtually all enterprises today have deployed a vast variety of different DBMSs. A TP monitor is the only solution to guarantee transactional integrity in such an environment. In addition, TP monitors have evolved into more general-purpose middleware capable of supporting large-scale three-tier applications through the extensive suite of middleware services that they offer. Overall, TP monitors represent mature technology and have been providing a unique value proposition.

13.2.4.1 TP Monitors and Middleware Services   Besides providing transactional integrity to distributed applications and resources, TP monitors also include a number of other significant services:

☞ They reduce CPU overhead, response times, and CPU costs for large applications because they can dispatch, schedule, and prioritize multiple application requests concurrently. Furthermore, some support sophisticated features such as load balancing.

☞ TP monitors are designed to support many concurrent users and to handle many database connections. Most have embedded logic to share database connections so that several users can be accommodated without compromising performance.

☞ Many TP monitors support automatic fail-over and possess restart capabilities, thus increasing application up time.

☞ In order to sustain consistent response times, they are capable of starting additional process instances. This is an important feature for any enterprise environment that needs to have ensured scalability.

Given these capabilities, there are two typical scenarios that require the deployment of a TP monitor. These are described below.

13.2.4.2 Distributed Heterogeneous Database Systems   In a distributed environment, updates to multiple resource managers (i.e., databases) must be coordinated across all platforms on which they reside. One way to achieve such coordination is through the use of a two-phase commit protocol. All major relational database management system (RDBMS) vendors have implemented two-phase commit. However, there is one constraint: The transactional semantics (begin transaction, commit transaction, rollback transaction) can only be performed by an RDBMS as long as all databases that participate in the two-phase commit are from the same product.

This does not work if an application attempts to update heterogeneous RDBMSs (e.g., one from Informix Software, Inc., and another from Sybase, Inc.) within one transaction. TP monitors are capable of coordinating and managing transactions across heterogeneous databases since all major TP monitors and RDBMS products are XA-compliant. Adherence to this common protocol allows TP monitors to preserve the integrity of updates across heterogeneous databases.

Furthermore, TP monitors are actively engaged in process management—that is, transactional context is kept across different processes that are part of the same transaction. This way, different processes can update multiple databases with transactional integrity. TP monitors also are capable of coordinating updates to record oriented files and other resource managers, such as queues.

13.2.4.3 Three-Tier TP-Heavy Environments Today's trend to three-tier application architectures opens another domain for the deployment of TP monitors. The business application is usually partitioned into a user interface, an application server, and a database server component. TP monitors can act as the middleware infrastructure that is required to glue these application components together. The three-tier TP-heavy model assumes that the application components perform all operations that require transactional integrity by invoking the specific functions that are provided by a TP monitor, either through a proprietary API or through the mechanisms defined by the X/Open DTP standard. The TP monitor in cooperation with the DBMS engine ensures the ACID properties.

13.2.5 Object Request Brokers

Object-oriented middleware, also referred to as ORBs, fall into two categories:

1. Those products that are conformant to the CORBA standard from the OMG
2. Microsoft's OLE/COM/DCOM technology

13.2.6 Database Middleware

Database middleware is one of the most mature middleware categories. Generally speaking, database middleware provides universal and consistent data access to many data sources used in the modern enterprise IT environment. These might include relational databases, hierarchical databases, object-oriented databases, and even flat files.

The APIs supported by the majority of database middleware products are based either on a de facto standard, Open Database Connectivity (i.e., ODBC) specification, or on a vendor's proprietary API. Regardless, all APIs are SQL-based.

Today, all database middleware products provide similar functionality by providing seamless access to corporate data, regardless of the target data location and data store. Despite such similarities, however, there are substantial architectural differences among different database middleware products. These differences cause performance gaps and variations in functional robustness among different products.

The most common architecture is a three-tier multidatabase gateway, in which the client, the gateway, and the target database(s) are run on different platforms. Using the gateway architecture, each request that is sent to the gateway is parsed, analyzed, optimized, and ultimately translated to the target dialect understood by the target database.

The alternative, less common architecture has no gateways between the data requester (the client) and the data provider (the server). A direct point-to-point connection between the client and the database is established. Generally speaking, point-to-point database middleware can yield better performance than three-tier database gateways.

Database middleware is an attractive solution for multitier decision support applications in which a split-second response time is *not* a requirement and synchronous connection-oriented communication is sufficient. However, database middleware products with built-in efficient optimizers and translators are capable of providing good performance. This is true even when accessing heterogeneous databases.

13.3 PROGRAMMING WITH REMOTE PROCEDURE CALLS

High-level programming through RPCs provides logical client-to-server communication for network application development, without the need to program most of the interface to the underlying network. With RPC, the client makes a remote procedure call that sends requests to the server, which calls a dispatch routine, performs the requested service, and sends back a reply before the call returns to the client.

RPC does not require the caller to know about the underlying network. For example, a program can simply call a C routine that returns the number of users on a remote machine. You can make remote procedure calls from any language and between different processors on the same machine.

13.3.1 The ONC Remote Procedure Call

The remote procedure call model is similar to that of the local model, which works as follows:

1. The caller places arguments to a procedure in a specific location (such as a result register).
2. The caller temporarily transfers control to the procedure.

3. When the caller regains control, it obtains the results of the procedure from the specified location.

4. The caller then continues program execution.

The remote procedure call is similar, in that one thread of control logically winds through two processes, that of the caller and that of the server:

1. The caller process sends a call message to the server process and blocks (that is, waits) for a reply message. The call message contains the parameters of the procedure, and the reply message contains the procedure results.

2. When the caller receives the reply message, it gets the results of the procedure.

3. The caller process then continues executing.

On the server side, a process is dormant, awaiting the arrival of a call message. When one arrives, the server process computes a reply, which it sends back to the requesting client. After this, the server process becomes dormant again. The remote procedure call hides the details of the network transport. However, the RPC protocol does not restrict the concurrency model. For example, RPC calls may be asynchronous, so that the client can do another task while waiting for the reply from the server.

On the other hand, the server could create a task to process a certain type of request automatically, freeing it to service other requests. Although RPC provides a way to avoid programming the underlying network transport, it allows this where necessary.

13.3.2 RPC Procedure Versions

Each RPC procedure is uniquely defined by program and procedure numbers. The program number specifies a group of related remote procedures, each of which has a different procedure number. Each program also has a version number so that, when a minor change is made to a remote service (adding a new procedure, for example), a new program number does not have to be assigned. When you want to call a procedure to find the number of remote users, you must know the appropriate program, version, and procedure numbers to contact the service. This information can be found in several sources.

Typically, a service provides a protocol description so that you can write client applications that call the service. Knowing the program and procedure numbers is useful only if the program is running on a system to which you have access.

13.3.3 Transport Protocol Independence

The RPC protocol is concerned only with the specification and interpretation of messages. It is independent of transport protocols because it needs no information on how a message is passed among processes.

RPC does not implement any sort of reliability. The application itself must be aware of the transport protocol type. With a reliable transport, such as TCP/IP, the application need not do much else. However, an application must use its own retransmission and time-out policy if it is running on top of an unreliable transport, such as UDP/IP.

Because of transport independence, the RPC protocol does not actively interpret anything about remote procedures or their execution. Instead, the application infers required information from the underlying protocol. For example, if RPC is running on top of an unreliable transport and the application retransmits RPC messages after short time-outs, and if the application receives no reply, then it can infer only that a certain procedure was executed zero or more times. If it receives a reply, then the application infers that the procedure was executed at least once.

With a reliable transport, the application can infer from a reply message that the procedure was executed exactly once; but if it receives no reply message, it cannot assume the remote procedure was not executed. Even with a connection-oriented protocol like TCP, an application needs time-outs and reconnection to handle server crashes.

ONC RPC currently is supported on both UDP/IP and TCP/IP transports. The selection of the transport depends on the application requirements. The UDP transport, which is connectionless, is a good choice if the application has the following characteristics:

- ☞ The same procedure can be executed more than once without any side effects. For example, reading a block of data is idempotent; creating a file is not.

- ☞ The size of both the arguments and results is smaller than the UDP packet size of 8K bytes.

- ☞ The server is required to handle as many as several hundred clients. The UDP server can do so because it does not retain any information about the client state. By contrast, the TCP server holds state information for each open client connection, which limits its available resources.

TCP (connection-oriented) is a good transport choice if the application has any of the following characteristics:

- ☞ The application needs a reliable underlying transport.
- ☞ The procedures are nonidempotent.
- ☞ The size of either the arguments or the results exceeds 8K bytes.

13.3.4 External Data Representation

RPC can handle arbitrary data structures, regardless of the byte order or structure layout convention on a machine. It does this by converting them to a network standard called External Data Representation (XDR) before sending

them over the wire. XDR is a machine-independent description and encoding
of data that can communicate between diverse machines, such as a Sun workstation, IBM-PC, or Cray.

Converting from a particular machine representation to XDR format is
called *serializing*, and the reverse process is known as *deserializing*.

13.4 WRITING RPC APPLICATIONS

The RPC (rpcgen) protocol compiler accepts a remote program interface definition written in RPC language, which is similar to C. It then produces C language output consisting of skeleton versions of the client routines, a server
skeleton, XDR filter routines for both parameters and results, a header file
that contains common definitions, and, optionally, dispatch tables that the
server uses to invoke routines that are based on authorization checks.

The client skeleton interface to the RPC library hides the network from
its callers, and the server skeleton hides the network from the server procedures invoked by remote clients. You compile and link output files as usual.
You can write server procedures in any language that has system-calling conventions. To get an executable server program, link the server procedure with
the server skeleton. To create an executable program for a remote program,
write an ordinary main program that makes local procedure calls to the client
skeletons, then link the program.

If necessary, the options enable you to suppress skeleton generation and
specify the transport to be used by the server skeleton. The rpcgen protocol
compiler helps to reduce development time in two ways:

☞ It greatly reduces network interface programming.
☞ It can mix low-level code with high-level code.

For speed-critical applications, you can link customized high-level code with
the rpcgen output. You can use rpcgen output as a starting point, and rewrite
as necessary.

13.4.1 Debugging Applications

It is difficult to debug distributed applications that have separate client and
server processes. To simplify this, you can test the client program and the
server procedure as a single program by linking them with each other rather
than with the client and server skeletons. To do this, you must first remove
calls to client creation RPC library routines (for example, clnt_create).

The procedure calls are executed as ordinary local procedure calls, and
the program can be debugged with a local debugger such as dbx. When the program is working, the client program can be linked to the client skeleton produced by rpcgen and the server procedures can be linked to the server skeleton
produced by rpcgen. There are two kinds of errors possible in an RPC call:

1. *A problem with the remote procedure call mechanism* occurs when a procedure is unavailable, the remote server does not respond, the remote server cannot decode the arguments, and so on. An RPC error occurs if the result is NULL. The reason for the failure can be printed.

2. *A problem with the server itself* occurs if opendir fails; that is why readdir_res is of type union. Handling these types of errors is the responsibility of the programmer.

13.4.2 The C-Preprocessor

The C-preprocessor (cpp) runs on all input files before they are compiled, so all the preprocessor directives are legal within an .x file. The macro identifiers may have been defined, depending on which output file is being generated. Some of these macros are listed below:

Identifier	Usage
RPC_HDR	For header-file output
RPC_XDR	For XDR routine output
RPC_SVC	For server-skeleton output
RPC_CLNT	For client-skeleton output
RPC_TBL	For index-table output

Also, rpcgen does some additional preprocessing of the input file. Any line that begins with a percentage sign (%) passes directly into the output file without any interpretation. Using the percentage sign feature does not guarantee that rpcgen will place the output where you intend it. If you have problems like this, do not use this feature.

13.4.3 rpcgen Programming

The paragraphs below contain additional rpcgen programming information about network types, inetd support, and dispatch tables.

13.4.3.1 Network Types
By default, rpcgen generates server code for both UDP and TCP transports. The -s flag creates a server that responds to requests on the specified transport. The following example creates a UDP server:

```
rpcgen -s udp proto.x
2.5.2 User-Provided Define Statements
```

The rpcgen protocol compiler provides a way to define symbols and assign values to them. These defined symbols are passed on to the C-preprocessor when it is invoked. This facility is useful when invoking debugging code that is enabled only when the DEBUG symbol is defined. For example:

```
rpcgen -DDEBUG proto.x
```

13.4.3.2 inetd Support The rpcgen protocol compiler can create RPC servers that can be invoked by inetd when a request for that service is received.

```
rpcgen -I proto.x
```

In many applications, it is useful for services to wait after responding to a request, on the chance that another will soon follow. However, if there is no call within a certain time (by default, 120 seconds), the server exits and the port monitor continues to monitor requests for its services. You can use the -K option to change the default waiting time. In the following example, the server waits only 20 seconds before exiting:

```
rpcgen -I -K 20 proto.x
```

13.4.3.3 Dispatch Tables Dispatch tables are often useful. For example, the server dispatch routine may need to check authorization and then invoke the service routine, or a client library may need to control all details of storage management and XDR data conversion. The following *rpcgen* command generates RPC dispatch tables for each program defined in the protocol description file, proto.x, and places them in the file proto_tbl.i (the suffix .i indicates index):

```
rpcgen -T proto.x
```

Each entry in the table is a struct rpcgen_table defined in the header file, proto.h, as follows:

```
struct rpcgen_table {
    char *(*proc)();
    xdrproc_t xdr_arg;
    unsigned len_arg;
    xdrproc_t xdr_res;
    unsigned len_res;
};
```

In this proto.h definition, proc is a pointer to the service routine, xdr_arg is a pointer to the input (argument) xdr_routine, len_arg is the length in bytes of the input argument, xdr_res is a pointer to the output (result) xdr_routine, and len_res is the length in bytes of the output result.

The table dirprog_1_table is indexed by procedure number. The variable dirprog_1_nproc contains the number of entries in the table.

13.4.4 Client Programming

The following sections contain client programming information about default time-outs and client authentication.

13.4.4.1 Time-Out Changes RPC sets a default time-out of 25 seconds for RPC calls when clnt_create is used. RPC waits 25 seconds to get the results from the server. If it does not, it usually means one of the following conditions exists:

☞ The server is not running.

☞ The remote machine has crashed.

☞ The network is unreachable.

In such cases, the function returns NULL. Sometimes you may need to change the time-out value to accommodate the application or because the server is too slow or far away. You may change the time-out by using clnt_control.

13.4.4.2 Client Authentication

By default, client creation routines do not handle client authentication. Sometimes, you may want the client to authenticate itself to the server. This is easy to do, as shown in the following coding:

```
CLIENT *cl;

cl = client_create("somehost", SOMEPROG, SOMEVERS, "udp");
if (cl != NULL) {
  /* To set UNIX style authentication */
  cl->cl_auth = authunix_create_default();
}
```

13.4.5 Server Programming

The following sections contain server programming information about system broadcasts and passing data to server procedures.

13.4.5.1 Handling Broadcasts

Sometimes, clients broadcast to determine whether a particular server exists on the network, or to determine all the servers for a particular program and version number. You make these calls with clnt_broadcast (for which there is no rpcgen support). When a procedure is known to be called via broadcast RPC, it is best for the server not to reply unless it can provide useful information to the client. Otherwise, the network can become overloaded with useless replies. To prevent the server from replying, a remote procedure can return NULL as its result; the server code generated by rpcgen can detect this and prevent a reply.

13.4.5.2 Passing Data to Server Procedures

Server procedures often need to know more about an RPC call than just its arguments. For example, getting authentication information is useful to procedures that implement some level of security. This information is supplied to the server procedure as a second argument.

13.4.6 RPC and XDR Languages

RPC language is an extension of the XDR language, through the addition of the program and version types. The XDR language is similar to C. The following sections describe the syntax of the RPC and XDR languages, with examples and descriptions of how the various RPC and XDR type definitions are compiled into C-type definitions in the output header file.

13.4.6.1 Definitions   An RPC language file consists of a series of definitions:

```
definition-list:
definition ";"
definition ";" definition-list
```

RPC recognizes the following definition types:

```
definition:
   program-definition
   declaration-definition
   enum-definition
   typedef-definition
   const-definition
   struct-definition
   union-definition
```

13.4.6.2 Enumerations   XDR enumerations have the same syntax as C enumerations:

```
enum-definition:
   "enum" enum-ident "{"
     enum-value-list
   "}"

enum-value-list:
   enum-value
   enum-value "," enum-value-list

enum-value:
   enum-value-ident
   enum-value-ident "=" value
```

13.4.6.3 Constants   XDR constants are used wherever an integer constant is used (for example, in array size specifications), as shown by the following syntax:

```
const-definition:
   "const" const-ident "=" integer
```

The following XDR example defines a constant DOZEN equal to 12:

```
const DOZEN = 12;
```

The following example shows the corresponding C definition for this:

```
#define DOZEN 12
```

13.4.6.4 Declarations   XDR provides only four kinds of declarations, shown by the following syntax:

```
declaration:
```

```
simple-declaration [1]
fixed-array-declaration [2]
variable-array-declaration [3]
pointer-declaration [4]
```

The syntax for each, followed by examples, is listed below:

Simple declarations
```
simple-declaration:
        type-ident variable-ident
```

For example, colortype color in XDR is the same in C: colortype color.

Fixed-length array declarations
```
fixed-array-declaration:
        type-ident variable-ident "[" value "]"
```

For example, colortype palette[8] in XDR is the same in C: colortype palette[8].

Variable-length array declarations
These have no explicit syntax in C, so XDR creates its own by using angle brackets, as in the following syntax:

```
variable-array-declaration:
    type-ident variable-ident "<" value ">"
    type-ident variable-ident "<" ">"
```

The maximum size is specified between the angle brackets; it may be omitted, indicating that the array can be of any size, shown in the following example:

```
int heights<12>; /* at most 12 items */
int widths<>;    /* any number of items */
```

Variable-length arrays have no explicit syntax in C, so each of their declarations is compiled into a struct. For example, the heights declaration is compiled into the following struct:

```
struct {
    u_int heights_len; /* number of items in array */
    int *heights_val; /* pointer to array */
} heights;
```

Here, the _len component stores the number of items in the array and the _val component stores the pointer to the array. The first part of each of these component names is the same as the name of the declared XDR variable.

Pointer declarations
These are the same in XDR as in C. You cannot send pointers over the network, but you can use XDR pointers to send recursive data types, such as lists and trees. In XDR language, this type is called optional-data, not pointer, as in the following syntax:

optional-data:
   type-ident "*"variable-ident

An example of this (the same in both XDR and C) follows:

listitem *next;

[Return to example]

13.4.6.5 Structures   XDR declares a struct almost exactly like its C counterpart. The XDR syntax is shown below:

struct-definition:
   "struct" struct-ident "{"
     declaration-list
   "}"

declaration-list:
   declaration ";"
   declaration ";" declaration-list

13.4.6.6 Unions   XDR unions are discriminated unions and are different from C unions. They are more analogous to Pascal variant records than to C unions. The syntax is shown here:

union-definition:
   "union" union-ident "switch" ("simple declaration") "{"
     case-list
   "}"

case-list:
   "case" value ":" declaration ";"
   "case" value ":" declaration ";" case-list
   "default" ":" declaration ";"

13.4.6.7 Programs   You declare RPC programs using the following syntax:

program-definition:
   "program" program-ident "{"
     version-list
   "}" "=" value

version-list:
   version ";"
   version ";" version-list

version:
   "version" version-ident "{"
     procedure-list
   "}" "=" value

procedure-list:
   procedure ";"
   procedure ";" procedure-list

procedure:
   type-ident procedure-ident "("type-ident")" "=" value

The list below describes exceptions to the syntax rules described in the previous sections:

1. *Booleans*: C has no built-in Boolean type. However, the RPC library has a Boolean type called bool_t that is either TRUE or FALSE. Items declared as type bool in XDR language are compiled into bool_t in the output header file. For example, bool married is compiled into bool_t married.

2. *Strings*: C has no built-in string type, but instead uses the null-terminated char * convention. In XDR language, you declare strings by using the string keyword, and each string is compiled into a char * in the output header file. The number contained in the angle brackets specifies the maximum number of characters allowed in the strings (excluding the NULL character). For example, string name<32> would be compiled into char *name. You can omit a maximum size to indicate a string of arbitrary length. For example, string longname<> would be compiled into char *longname.

3. *Opaque data*: RPC and XDR use opaque data to describe untyped data, which consists of sequences of arbitrary bytes. You declare opaque data as an array of either fixed or variable length. An opaque declaration of a fixed length array is opaque diskblock[512], whose C counterpart is char diskblock.

13.5 RPC PROGRAMMING INTERFACE

The ONC RPC interface consists of three layers: Highest, middle, and lowest. For ONC RPC programming, only the middle and lowest layers are of interest; the highest layer is transparent to the operating system, machine, and network upon which it is run.

The middle-layer routines are adequate for most applications. This layer is *RPC proper* because you do not need to write additional programming code for network sockets, the operating system, or any other low-level implementation mechanisms. At this level, you simply make remote procedure calls to routines on other machines. For example, you can make simple ONC RPC calls by using the following system routines:

☞ *registerrpc*, which obtains a unique, systemwide procedure-identification number

☞ *callrpc*, which executes a remote procedure call

☞ *svc_run*, which calls a remote procedure in response to an RPC request

The middle layer is not suitable for complex programming tasks because it sacrifices flexibility for simplicity. Although it is adequate for many tasks, the middle layer does not enable the following:

☞ Operating system process control

☞ Time-out specifications

☞ Multiple kinds of call authentication

☞ Choice of transport

☞ Processing flexibility after occurrence of error

The lowest layer is suitable for programming tasks that require greater efficiency or flexibility. The lowest-layer routines include client-creation routines such as these:

☞ *clnt_create*, which creates a client handle

☞ *clnt_call*, which calls the server svcudp_create, a server-creation routine, and svc_register, the server-registration routine

The following sections describe the middle and lowest RPC layers.

13.5.1 Middle Layer of RPC

The middle layer is the simplest RPC program interface. From this layer, you make explicit RPC calls and use the functions callrpc and registerrpc.

☞ *Using callrpc*: The simplest way to make remote procedure calls is through the RPC library routine callrpc. The programming code in the example below, which obtains the number of remote users, shows the use of callrpc.

```
/*
 * Print the number of users on a remote systedm using callrpc
 */

#include <stdio.h>
#include <rpc/rpc.h>
#include <rpcsvc/rusers.h>

main(argc, argv)
    int argc;
    char **argv;

{
    unsigned long nusers;
    int stat;

    if (argc != 2) {
        fprintf(stderr, "usage: nusers hostname\n");
        exit(1);
    }

    if (stat = callrpc(argv[1],
        RUSERSPROG, RUSERSVERS, RUSERSPROC_NUM,
        xdr_void, 0, xdr_u_long, &nusers) != 0) {
            clnt_perrno(stat);
            exit(1);
```

```
    }
    printf("%d users on %s\n", nusers, argv[1]);
    exit(0);
}
```

The callrpc library routine has eight parameters. In the example above, the first parameter, argv[1], is the name of the remote server machine. The next three, RUSERSPROG, RUSERSVERS, and RUSERSPROC_NUM, are the program, version, and procedure numbers that together identify the procedure to be called. The fifth and sixth parameters are an XDR filter (xdr_void) and an argument (0) to be encoded and passed to the remote procedure. You provide an XDR filter procedure to encode or decode machine-dependent data to or from the XDR format.

The final two parameters are an XDR filter, xdr_u_long, for decoding the results returned by the remote procedure, and a pointer, &nusers, to the storage location of the procedure results. Multiple arguments and results are embedded in structures.

If callrpc completes successfully, it returns a zero; otherwise, it returns a nonzero value. The return codes are found in rpc/clnt.h. The callrpc library routine needs the type of the RPC argument, as well as a pointer to the argument itself (and similarly for the result). For RUSERSPROC_NUM, the return value is an unsigned long. This is why callrpc has xdr_u_long as its first return parameter—which means that the result is of type unsigned long—and &nusers as its second return parameter—which is a pointer to the location that stores the long result. RUSERSPROC_NUM takes no argument, so the argument parameter of callrpc is xdr_void. In such cases, the argument must be NULL.

If callrpc gets no answer after trying several times to deliver a message, it returns with an error code. Adjusting the number of retries or using a different protocol requires you to use the lower layer of the RPC library.

The *remote server procedure* corresponding to the callrpc example might look like the one in the example below.

```
unsigned long *
nuser(indata)
    char *indata;
{
    static unsigned long nusers;

    /*
    * Code here to compute the number of users
    * and place result in variable nusers.
    */

    return(&nusers);
}
```

This procedure takes one argument, a pointer to the input of the remote procedure call (ignored in the example), and returns a pointer to the result. In the current version of C, character pointers are the generic pointers, so the input argument and the return value can be cast to char *.

☞ *Using registerrpc*: Normally, a server registers all of the RPC calls it plans to handle, then goes into an infinite loop waiting to service requests. Using rpcgen for this also generates a server dispatch function. You can write a server yourself by using registerrpc.

The example below is a program segment showing how you would use registerrpc in the main body of a server program that registers a single procedure; the remote procedure call passes a single unsigned long.

```
#include <stdio.h>
#include <rpc/rpc.h> /* required */
#include <rpcsvc/rusers.h> /* for prog, vers definitions */

unsigned long *nuser();

main()
{
  registerrpc(RUSERSPROG, RUSERSVERS, RUSERSPROC_NUM,
    nuser, xdr_void, xdr_u_long);
  svc_run(); /* Never returns */
  fprintf(stderr, "Error: svc_run returned!\n");
  exit(1);
}
```

The registerrpc routine registers a procedure as corresponding to a given RPC procedure number. The first three parameters—RUSERPROG, RUSERSVERS, and RUSERSPROC_NUM—are the program, version, and procedure numbers of the remote procedure to be registered; *nuser* is the name of the local procedure that implements the remote procedure; and xdr_void and xdr_u_long are the XDR filters for the remote procedure's arguments and results. (Multiple arguments or multiple results are passed as structures.) The underlying transport mechanism for registerrpc is UDP.

After registering the local procedure, the main procedure of the server program calls svc_run, the remote procedure dispatcher for the RPC library; svc_run calls the remote procedures in response to RPC requests, decodes remote procedure arguments, and encodes results. To do this, it uses the XDR filters specified when the remote procedure was registered with registerrpc.

RPC can handle arbitrary data structures, regardless of machine conventions, for byte order and structure layout, by converting them to a network standard called External Data Representation (XDR) before sending them over the network. The type field parameters of callrpc and registerrpc can be a built-in procedure like xdr_u_long (in the previous example) or one that you supply.

13.5.2 Lowest Layer of RPC

The following capabilities are available only with the lowest layer of RPC:

☞ The ability to use TCP as the underlying transport instead of UDP, which restricts RPC calls to only 8K bytes of data

☞ The ability to allocate and free memory explicitly while serializing or deserializing with XDR routines

☞ The ability to authenticate on either the client or server side, through credential verification

13.5.3 Raw RPC

Raw RPC refers to the use of pseudo-RPC interface routines that do not use any real transport at all. These routines—clntraw_create and svcraw_create—help in debugging and testing the noncommunications-oriented aspects of an application before running it over a real network.

13.5.4 Miscellaneous RPC Features

The following sections describe other useful features for RPC programming.

13.5.4.1 Authentication of RPC Calls
In the examples presented previously, the caller never identified itself to the server, nor did the server require such identification. Every RPC call is authenticated by the RPC package on the server; similarly, the RPC client package generates and sends authentication parameters. Just as different transports (TCP/IP or UDP/IP) can be used when creating RPC clients and servers, different forms of authentication can be associated with RPC clients.

13.5.4.2 Authentication Through the Operating System
RPC calls can be authenticated on the client and server side through the operating system.

☞ *The Client Side*: Assume that a caller creates the following new RPC client handle:

```
clnt = clntudp_create(address, prognum, versnum, wait, sockp)
```

The transport for this client handle defaults to the following associate authentication handle:

```
clnt->cl_auth = authnone_create();
```

The RPC client can choose to use authentication that is native to the operating system by setting clnt->cl_auth after creating the RPC client handle:

```
clnt->cl_auth = authunix_create_default();
```

This causes each RPC call associated with clnt to carry the following authentication credentials structure:

```
/*
* credentials native to the operating system
*/

struct authunix_parms {
    u_long aup_time;        /* credentials creation time */
    char *aup_machname;     /* host name where client is */
    int aup_uid;            /* client's UNIX effective uid */
    int aup_gid;            /* client's current group id */
    u_int aup_len;          /* element length of aup_gids */
    int *aup_gids;          /* array of groups user is in */
};
```

In this example, the fields are set by authunix_create_default by invoking the appropriate system calls. Because the RPC user created this new style of authentication, the user is responsible for destroying it (to save memory) with the following:

```
auth_destroy(clnt->cl_auth);
```

☞ *The Server Side*: It is difficult for service implementers to handle authentication because the RPC package passes the service dispatch routine request that has an arbitrary authentication style associated with it. Consider the fields of a request handle passed to a service dispatch routine:

```
/*
* An RPC Service request
*/

struct svc_req {
    u_long rq_prog;                 /* service program number */
    u_long rq_vers;                 /* service protocol vers num */
    u_long rq_proc;                 /* desired procedure number */
    struct opaque_auth rq_cred;     /* raw credentials from wire */
    caddr_t rq_clntcred;            /* credentials (read only) */
};
```

The rq_cred is mostly opaque, except for one field: The style of authentication credentials:

```
/*
* Authentication info. Mostly opaque to the programmer.
*/

struct opaque_auth {
    enum_t  oa_flavor;      /* style of credentials */
    caddr_t oa_base;        /* address of more auth stuff */
    u_int   oa_length;      /* not to exceed MAX_AUTH_BYTES */
};
```

The RPC guarantees the following to the service dispatch routine:

☞ The rq_cred field of the request is well-formed; that is, the service implementer can use the rq_cred.oa_flavor field of the request to determine the authentication style used by the caller. The service implementer also can inspect other fields of rq_cred if the style is not supported by the RPC package.

☞ The rq_clntcred field of the request is either NULL or points to a well-formed structure that corresponds to a supported style of authentication credentials.

☞ The rq_clntcred field also could be cast to a pointer to an authunix_parms structure. If rq_clntcred is NULL, the service implementer can inspect the other (opaque) fields of rq_cred to determine whether the service knows about a new type of authentication unknown to the RPC package.

It is not customary to check the authentication parameters associated with NULLPROC (procedure number zero). Also, if the authentication parameter type is not suitable for your service, you should have your program call *svcerr_weakauth*. RPC deals only with authentication, not with the access control of an individual service. The services themselves must implement their own access control policies and reflect these policies as return statuses in their protocols.

13.6 DISTRIBUTED COMPUTING ENVIRONMENT

The Distributed Computing Environment (DCE) from the Open Group consists of multiple components (as shown in Figure 13.1) that have been integrated to work closely together. They are the RPC, the Cell and Global Directory Services (CDS and GDS), the Security Service, DCE Threads, Distributed Time Service (DTS), and Distributed File Service (DFS). The threads,

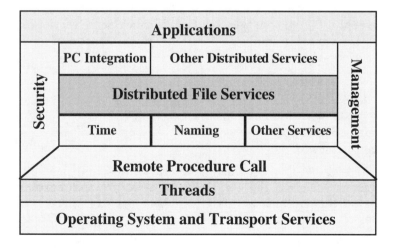

Fig. 13.1 The DCE Architecture

RPC, CDS, security, and DTS components are commonly referred to as the *secure core* and are the required components of any DCE installation.

DCE is called *middleware* or *enabling technology*. It is not intended to exist alone; instead it should be integrated or bundled into a vendor's operating system. DCE's security and distributed file system, for example, can completely replace their current, nonnetwork analogs.

DCE RPC has a number of advantages over ONC RPC. DCE is more secure than ONC RPC and has better security. DCE RPC takes care of many of the minute details, such as locating a server if a server exists on more than one system in the network. It also takes care of retransmissions when using UDP. ONC RPC, on the other hand, requires you get more involved in the network details of your code.

ONC RPC is simpler and has less overhead. DCE RPC's API is more complex, but you gain added flexibility with it. The complexity translates into a steeper learning curve. Distributed applications today are using DCE RPC over ONC RPC.

13.6.1 Overview

Computer users require a communications environment that allows information to flow from wherever it is stored to wherever it is needed, without exposing the network's complexity to the end user, system administrator, or application developer. The architecture of the Open Group's DCE masks the physical complexity of the networked environment and provides a layer of logical simplicity. The offering is composed of a set of services that can be used, separately or in combination, to form a distributed computing environment. The services are organized into two categories.

1. *Fundamental Distributed Services* provide tools for software developers to create the end-user services needed for distributed computing. The Fundamental Distributed Services form the base set of services and tools developers can use to build distributed environments and applications for end users. They include:

   ✗ Remote Procedure Call
   ✗ Directory Service
   ✗ Time Service
   ✗ Security Service
   ✗ Threads Service

2. *Data-Sharing Services* provide end users with capabilities built on the Fundamental Distributed Services. These require no programming on the part of the end user and facilitate better use of information. They include:

   ✗ Distributed File System
   ✗ Diskless Support

13.6.2 DCE RPC

The DCE RPC capability is based on a simple premise: Make individual procedures in an application run on a computer somewhere else in the network. In this way, it distributes application execution. DCE RPC extends the local procedure call model by supporting direct calls to procedures on remote systems, enabling programmers to develop distributed applications as easily as traditional, single-system programs. RPC presentation services mask the differences between data representations on different machines, allowing programs to work across heterogeneous systems.

DCE RPC provides programmers with the powerful tools necessary to build client/server applications. It includes two major components:

☞ A remote procedure call facility developed specifically to provide simplicity, performance, portability, and network independence.

☞ A compiler that converts high-level interface descriptions of the remote procedures into portable, C-language source code. The resulting remote procedure calls behave in the same way as local procedure calls.

13.6.2.1 Features and Benefits

☞ Integration with Threads Service allows clients to interact with multiple servers to handle multiple clients simultaneously.

☞ Directory Service independence allows clients to identify and locate servers by name. RPC applications integrated with the Directory Service are insulated from the details of the service, thus allowing them to take advantage of future enhancements.

☞ RPC features an easy-to-understand interface definition language that allows programmers to specify the operations exported by a server to clients.

☞ Network and protocol independence provides the same behavior for applications regardless of the transport service used; applications need not be rewritten for different transport services. Both connectionless and connection-oriented transports are supported.

☞ Secure RPC provides secure communications between a client and a server, allowing developers to build secure distributed applications. The DCE RPC is fully integrated with the DCE Security Service to guarantee authenticity, integrity, and privacy of communications.

☞ RPC supports large data-processing applications by permitting unlimited argument size, efficiently handling bulk data.

☞ RPC supports data types from multibyte character sets—such as those used by Japanese, Arabic, and Chinese languages—in a manner consistent with ISO standards.

13.6.3 Distributed Directory Service

OSF's Distributed Directory Service provides a single naming model throughout the distributed environment. This model allows users to identify by named resources such as servers, files, disks, or print queues, and to gain access to them without knowing where they are located in a network. As a result, users can continue referring to a resource by one name even when a characteristic of the resource, such as its network address, changes.

13.6.3.1 Features and Benefits   The OSF Directory Service provides a number of features and benefits important in a distributed, networked environment, including:

- ☞ OSF's Directory Service is implemented on top of the OSF RPC, which operates transparently over a wide range of transports. This allows the Directory Service to work in LAN as well as WAN environments.
- ☞ OSF's Directory Service seamlessly integrates the X.500 global naming system with a fast, replicated local naming system.
- ☞ Programmers can move transparently from environments supporting full ISO functionality to those supporting only the local naming service component. The system allows the transparent integration of other services, such as distributed file services, into the Directory Service.
- ☞ The global portion of the Directory Service offers full X.500 functionality through the X/Open Directory Service API and through a standard management interface.
- ☞ The Directory Service allows users or administrators to create multiple copies of critical data, assuring availability across communication and hardware failures. It also provides a sophisticated update mechanism that ensures consistency.
- ☞ Scalability of OSF's Directory Service can accommodate large networks as easily as small ones. The ability to add servers, directories, and directory levels makes painless growth possible.
- ☞ Changes to names or their attributes are automatically propagated to all replicas. In addition, the Directory Service allows names to be replicated near the people who use them, providing better performance.
- ☞ The Directory Service caches the results of lookups, greatly increasing the efficiency and speed of subsequent lookups of the same name.
- ☞ The Directory Service is integrated with the Security Service, which provides secure communications. Sophisticated access control provides protection for entries.

13.6.4 Time Service

Many applications need a single time reference to schedule activities and to determine event sequencing and duration. Different components of a distributed application may obtain the time from clocks on different computers. A distributed time service regulates the system clocks in a computer network so that they closely match one another, providing accurate time for distributed applications.

The DCE Distributed Time Service is a software-based service that synchronizes each computer to a widely recognized time standard. This provides precise, fault-tolerant clock synchronization for systems in both local area and wide area networks. The DCE Time Service software is integrated with the RPC, Directory, and Security services.

To support distributed sites using the Network Time Protocol (NTP), the DCE Time Service also permits the use of time values from outside sources.

13.6.5 Threads Service

The OSF Threads Service provides portable facilities that support concurrent programming, allowing an application to perform many actions simultaneously. While one thread executes a remote procedure call, another can process user input. The Threads Service includes operations to create and control multiple threads of execution in a single process and to synchronize access to global data within an application.

Because a server process using threads can handle many clients at the same time, the Threads Service is ideally suited to dealing with multiple clients in client/server-based applications. The Threads Service is used by a number of DCE components, including Remote Procedure Call; Security, Directory, and Time services; and the Distributed File System.

13.6.6 Security Service

In most conventional time-sharing systems, the operating system authenticates the identity of users and authorizes their access to resources. In a distributed computing environment, however, where activities span multiple hosts with multiple operating systems, authentication and authorization require an independent security service that can be trusted by many hosts.

OSF's Distributed Computing Environment provides such a service. The DCE Security Service is integrated within the fundamental distributed service and data-sharing components. It provides the network with three conventional services: Authentication, authorization, and user account management. These facilities are made available through a secure means of communication that ensures both integrity and privacy.

In order to use authentication and authorization services effectively, users must be able to protect the integrity of communications. OSF's RPC supports secure communications in the distributed environment by detecting message corruption.

OSF's Distributed Security Service incorporates an authentication service based on the Kerberos system from MIT's Project Athena. Kerberos is a trusted service that validates the identity of a user or service, preventing fraudulent requests.

After users are authenticated, they must receive authorization to use resources, such as files. The authorization facility gives applications the tools they need to determine whether a user should have access to resources. It also provides a simple and consistent way to manage access control information. OSF's authorization tools are integrated with the Authentication Service.

13.6.7 Data-Sharing Services

Data-Sharing Services in the OSF DCE are built on the Fundamental Distributed Services. Once integrated with the operating system, they provide end users and developers with key functionality without the need for additional programming.

13.6.7.1 Distributed File System   OSF's key information-sharing component is the DFS. By joining the file systems of individual workstations and providing a consistent interface, the Distributed File System makes global file access as easy as local access.

The OSF DFS uses the client/server model common to other distributed file systems. It is easy to use, provides good performance, and is simple to manage and administer. The file system gives users a uniform name space, file location transparency, and high availability. It performs well across long distances and with large numbers of users.

Reliability is enhanced with a log-based physical file system that allows quick recovery after server failures. Files and directories are replicated invisibly on multiple machines, providing reliable file access and availability even when servers fail. Security is provided through the use of a secure RPC service and Access Control Lists (ACLs).

13.6.7.2 Features and Benefits   The OSF DFS solves the problem of accessing remote files in a convenient, timely fashion, regardless of installation size, geographic location, or hardware types. The Distributed File System appears to the user as a local file system, providing access to files from anywhere in the network for any user, with the same file name used by all. Additionally, the Distributed File System provides these features:

☞ It interoperates with the Network File System (NFS) from Sun Microsystems. The DFS can communicate with and provide file services to clients of other file services.

☞ Copies of currently used files are cached on a user's workstation, providing access without having to go across the network and retrieve them from a file server. This leads to improved performance, reduced network load, better server load balance, and lower communication costs.

☞ The DFS supports both small, local groups of users and groups of thousands across wide-area networks without loss of performance.

☞ It is built on OSF's secure RPC. Users can fine-tune access to their own files and directories through access control lists (ACLs), which allow access to groups and individual users.

13.7 RPC AND MESSAGING-BASED MIDDLEWARE

In this section I compare two middleware categories—RPC-based middleware and Message-Oriented Middleware—on the basis of their underlying communication mechanisms. I refer to them as *RPC* and *Messaging*.

RPCs extend the traditional program call model to a distributed environment. Developers do not have to learn any middleware API. This makes RPCs easy to understand and use. However, the simplicity of the RPC programming model requires developers to use an additional tool: The IDL compiler. Messaging products, on the other hand, require developers to learn new communication APIs; they also must be aware that two (or more) application components are communicating with each other.

RPCs are suited for applications that implement a request/reply model and a sharing of control. Messaging is a better choice for business applications that require more event-driven applications and that are also required to support more complex communication flows between components of the same application, or even between different applications.

One benefit of RPCs is that they provide for automatic conversion of data-type formats. This means that programmers always deal with data in the format of their local operating environments. With messaging, the developer must be concerned with the translation of application data from one format to another. Translations from ASCII to EBCDIC or the conversion between platform-specific number representations must be developed and tested by the programmer if the application is deployed across heterogeneous CPU architectures.

Depending on the type of application, the fact that RPCs usually are synchronous—that is, the client program is blocked until the server returns control—could be a limitation. Messaging supports synchronous (via message passing) as well as asynchronous (via message queuing) communication models. This makes it suitable for event-driven applications.

These applications are better positioned to reflect the dynamic nature of the business, which usually consists of a sequence of business events that must be supported by the application architecture. In addition, this allows for time independence, which is achieved by support for asynchronous communication. For this reason, messaging is an ideal middleware for applications running across intermittent or occasionally connected networks, where network availability and the availability of all application components are not warranted.

In terms of underlying network infrastructure, RPCs are not as flexible. They usually require TCP/IP or UDP/IP as the underlying transport layer, and the physical network protocols need to match between client and server, whereas most messaging products support a number of additional communication protocols. Some messaging products even support a feature called *context bridge*, in which a request from a client to a server can hop through heterogeneous communication protocols.

MOM-based applications are not portable and cannot interoperate across different MOM products. By contrast, DCE from the Open Group is a mature standard for RPCs in which business applications can be deployed using DCE from different vendors.

13.7.1 Messaging and Distributed Objects

As discussed earlier, MOM is a stable and mature technology. It has been used in a large number of mission-critical applications at many customer sites. Most MOM products support scalability requirements, asynchronous transactions, events, and different qualities of service, including guaranteed message delivery. Most also provide excellent platform coverage and offer consistent APIs and functionality across all supported platforms. This feature alone is of particular importance for organizations that require the same API and functionality across all platforms to be used in their enterprise, including the mainframes.

Message-Oriented Middleware provides a rather low level of abstraction to the developer. Many organizations look for object-oriented middleware as part of their overall strategic direction toward development and deployment of object-oriented applications. In fact, some large organizations that have already deployed MOM are looking into distributed objects as the next frontier.

Many companies see these technologies as complimentary rather than competing. As a result, we see a trend to integrate "best of breed" MOM and object-oriented middleware products. This allows an organization to build an application architecture that closely follows its business model using object technologies, without compromising the quality of service of the underlying distributed infrastructure.

It has been proven that MOM is suitable for a wide range of applications that require a different usage model. This is a direct result of its support for diverse communication models, such as synchronous, asynchronous, and publish & subscribe. Contrast this to object-oriented middleware (such as CORBA-compliant products and DCOM), which do not have the same track record for supporting production applications.

Object-oriented (OO) middleware provides an excellent framework for developers. Using either CORBA or OLE/COM, developers have a higher level of abstraction, which does not require them to write any communication code as they may have to using other middleware such as MOM or TP monitors. All the necessary communication code, including the marshaling of application data, is generated from the IDL compiler.

All this, combined with the fact that some OO middleware provides a good integration with Web as well as Java bindings, makes OO middleware an attractive choice for companies committed to the development of multitier object-oriented applications.

At least for now, most ORB products are restricted to the synchronous communication paradigm, which can be used for only a limited domain of applications. The CORBA specification includes only one-way communication and the synchronous request/reply model.

MOM products do not support any formal standards when it comes to interoperability among different MOM products or consistency of the APIs. This means that applications written for one MOM product are not portable to a product from another vendor. In contrast, CORBA's IDL assures reasonable portability of application code across products (unless product-specific IDL extensions are used) and an interoperability standard in the form of the Internet Inter-ORB Protocol (IIOP).

In summary, objects and messaging are two of the fastest growing categories of middleware. Messaging is useful when there is an immediate need to integrate applications on a wide range of operating systems (including legacy applications); when performance and scalability requirements are high; when the same API is required everywhere, including in legacy platforms; and when existing people skills in nonobject-oriented technologies should be leveraged.

Object-oriented middleware is useful for applications in which immediate scalability requirements are somewhat limited. These applications should be part of a long-term strategy toward object orientation, in which an enterprise is committed to exploitation of such benefits as code reuse and assembly of applications from components.

13.7.2 Transaction Processing Monitors and Messaging

We can compare TP monitors and message-queuing systems based on the fundamental differences between synchronous and asynchronous transaction processing. From the onset, TP monitors were designed to support distributed synchronous transactions. While all TP monitors have queuing options built in, they fall short of the full message-queuing capabilities offered by real message-queuing products. As a result, message-queuing products offer more choices for building the kind of application architecture needed by many businesses.

TP monitors support the coordination of distributed transactions through two-phase commit capabilities. Message-queuing products, on the other hand, eliminate the need for two-phase commit by dividing one synchronous transaction that updates multiple databases in different locations into a number of smaller-grained, asynchronous transactions. These smaller transactions communicate via the message-queuing mechanism. This avoids performance problems and the requirement for all participating application components and systems (as well as the network) to be up and running at the same time.

Businesses should consider message queuing when there is no clear-cut requirement for the transactional integrity that only a TP monitor can provide, and when they face the daunting tasks of integrating applications across an enterprise or even across different enterprises. Application integration using asynchronous message queuing is much more practical and efficient than developing synchronous transactions that span applications and enterprises.

TP monitors support a number of important middleware services and can be considered a mature and comprehensive solution. Some of the services unique to TP monitors are load balancing, process management, automatic fail-over, and restart capabilities. However, this comprehensiveness comes at a price.

First, TP monitors are complex. They require a substantial investment in planning and development. Thus, they can be overkill for some types of applications. Second, with the exception of CICS, no TP monitor provides the same platform coverage as message-queuing products. Most support the major UNIX platforms and NT, but do not provide native support for legacy operating systems such as MVS.

Message-queuing products support fewer services. Services such as load balancing and fail-over can be developed, but they are not supported out of the box. Without a TP monitor, the transactional capabilities of message-queuing products are limited to the queues they manage.

In a three-tier *TP-Lite* model, the presentation and application logic are spread over two tiers and the database resides on a third (these tiers can be physical or logical). Only the DBMS is responsible for ensuring the ACID properties (atomicity, consistency, isolation, and durability). No provision is made for synchronous transactional integrity among the various application components. This scenario is suited for MOM products (or DCE and ORBs). They provide all the necessary functionality for developing distributed applications, whereas TP monitors may be overkill, since they introduce unnecessary complexity.

In contrast, *TP-Heavy* model application components perform all operations that require transactional integrity by invoking the specific functions provided by the TP monitor. This guarantees end-to-end protection of all application components that participate in a transaction, including the possibility of transferring control to another process within the boundaries of one transaction. This is ensured by the TP monitor, which also coordinates all data updates with the (potentially heterogeneous) DBMS products involved in the transaction.

13.7.3 Three-Tier Client/Server Applications

The IT industry has witnessed a change in client/server application architectures from two-tier to three-tier systems. The development tools that were chosen dominated two-tier architectures. Tools such as PowerBuilder, Visual Basic, and Delphi dictated middleware functionality. In fact, there was no explicit middleware layer, since all aspects of client/server communication were hidden by the data-access APIs.

Two-tier solutions were (and still are) acceptable for many departmental applications used as decision support systems. For such applications, introducing an independent middleware layer would be overkill, since the benefits of the technology would not be exploited.

The movement toward three-tier infrastructures that can support enterprise-class business applications has changed the rules of the game. Everyone agrees that middleware is an essential component for any scalable enterprise application in which strengths of different operating systems can be fully exploited.

Deployment of a client both on an NT workstation application and a database on an NT server is just one example of the unprecedented flexibility provided by the three-tier approach.

13.7.4 Data-Oriented Legacy Integration

One alternative is to use database middleware products to provide PC-based client applications with access to information stored in legacy like IMS or VSAM. In most cases, this solution is appropriate for decision support systems, since updates to the data sources are still under exclusive control of legacy applications. This approach requires the least effort, since none of the legacy applications has to be changed. However, this approach often is not feasible, since the legacy data is stored in a format that is useless without the application that was designed with these data structures in mind.

Furthermore, this approach ignores all the business rules that have been encoded in the legacy application that normally guards data and that is usually spread across different databases. Ultimately, this is what many organizations want to exploit: Information that is already encapsulated in business rules. These comprehensive business functions can then be used in new projects that are based on client/server application development tools or accessed through the Internet or PC productivity tools.

13.7.5 Application-Oriented Legacy Integration

Another alternative is to use application middleware such as DCE, TP monitors, MOM, or ORBs. This approach requires a greater implementation effort than the data-access approach, but its share among integration solutions is rising substantially.

DCE is a mature technology that can be used to integrate with legacy applications. It provides the same functionality (APIs and services) across all supported operating systems, including MVS. (In fact, it is actually bundled with the new versions of OpenVMS and MVS.) However, the general drawbacks of DCE—such as synchronous, connection-oriented communication, complexity, and low-level APIs—do not make it the best choice for integrating with legacy applications.

There are a few scenarios in which a TP monitor can be used to integrate legacy systems with an open system environment. Except for CICS—which offers the same API and functionality across a multitude of operating systems, including mainframes—other TP monitors require a substantial programming effort for integration with existing mainframe applications.

Products such as Tuxedo, Encina, and Top End have not offered APIs or functionality on the mainframe. Integration between applications developed using these products and existing CICS and IMS applications requires custom programming.

The best choices for integrating legacy applications with open systems are Message-Oriented Middleware and Object-Request Brokers. The key factor in choosing MOM is the variety of communication mechanisms it supports. This provides corporate developers with enough options to work around any restrictions a legacy environment might throw in their way. The process of making a legacy application available to other systems in a distributed environment usually consists of two steps:

☞ One layer of software must be developed to represent specific functions that the application provides to the network, based on the API of the selected MOM product. This layer is responsible for converting data types and parameter lists between the format the legacy application was designed for and the standard format that an organization has agreed upon. In addition, any flow-control logic (i.e., dissecting one request from a client into a sequence of calls to the application) should be implemented here.

☞ Another layer translates client requests into the particular interaction format the legacy application understands. This is the more difficult piece, since the legacy applications were not originally developed with their interface exposed to the external world, and there is no general solution to this problem. Corporate developers will have to use whatever method seems most feasible, such as rewriting parts of the application or simulating terminal I/O via a screen-scraper product.

Another challenge lies in the options (and constraints) in activation of mainframe transactions. By supporting features such as triggering, which allows existing CICS or IMS transactions to be started upon arrival of a message on a specified queue, MOM enables legacy applications to become part of an event-driven application architecture.

Object-oriented middleware (in the form of CORBA and OLE/COM) holds great potential for integration with legacy systems as well. It allows wrapped legacy applications to be reused as an integral part of a component-based architecture. Not only can the legacy application be embraced by a middleware infrastructure and be made available for all other systems on the network, but all the power of object-oriented middleware can be immediately applied to these components. For example, concepts such as inheritance or aggregation can be used, and any repository that is available for the particular object model can manage the components.

Integrating legacy systems with open systems can become part of an approach that starts with an analysis of the business model. Using object-oriented analysis and design tools, a logical and physical model of the application system can be derived. This specification then can be filled in with code that must be developed from scratch and with encapsulated functionality of legacy systems. What is important is that the interfaces to application components are maintained at a higher level of abstraction, and the reuse or extensions to these interfaces can be managed more efficiently.

The drawback of an OO middleware-based solution is that, for the most part (there are some exceptions), ORBs are not available on the mainframe, whereas customers want the same programming model across all platforms. However, by using ORBs everywhere but on the mainframe and using MOM to communicate with the mainframe, a good integration strategy can be achieved. This, combined with a wrapping technique, in which existing applications can be presented as large-grain objects, provides an elegant way of integrating ORB-based applications with CICS and IMS transactions.

By doing this, an organization can combine the strength of MOM with the high level of abstraction that OO middleware provides. This requires careful planning of where (i.e., on which tier or on what system) the different middleware components should be used and of how the APIs these systems provide can be reconciled.

13.8 ENTERPRISE MIDDLEWARE AND THE WEB

Enterprise middleware provides a reliable infrastructure for business-critical applications, accessing transactions and data located anywhere, anytime. However, the unprecedented popularity of the Internet and World Wide Web and its widespread availability and platform insensitivity have led some people to proclaim the Internet as *the platform* of choice.

13.8.1 The Evolution of the World Wide Web

The technologies used to provide access to corporate information services via the Web have developed over time. Initially, static Web pages were used to deliver information from central page stores to Web browsers through the HTTP protocol. This approach is similar to a giant distributed file server system. During the second phase, Web pages could be created dynamically; this allowed for a certain degree of interactivity with the user. The primary mechanism used to support this style of Web middleware was still HTTP, with an extension to the Web server called CGI (Common Gateway Interface), which facilitates connections to databases and server applications.

Then a new portable programming language called Java was introduced. Java can be used to develop small, platform-independent application components. These so-called *applets* can be downloaded from a Web server to a client resident Web browser on demand, and at the same time remain transparent to the end user. Instead of being restricted to passively reading the information conveyed through a static Web page, or to the limited interactive capabilities available with CGI, Java applets have the same power as any conventional desktop application.

13.8.2 The Role of Middleware

Today, the result of this development is that none of the approaches described is sufficient to support business applications that implement electronic commerce over the Web while preserving important characteristics such as scalability and transactional integrity. This has led to an integration of Web technologies and middleware.

Web-based application architectures can be differentiated by the degree of middleware deployment. Overall, middleware can be placed either on the client (and server) or on the Web server only. The different degrees of middleware deployment are defined as follows:

1. *Middleware is placed on the client*: This solution represents a combination of Web protocol (HTTP) and any one of the five categories of middleware. The Web mechanism is used to locate and download a client application component from a server to the user's desktop. It most likely comprises a Java applet (or application) or an ActiveX component.

   Further communication between this client application and a backend service can be conducted using a middleware product that fits the requirements of the business system. This might consist of a direct database access (e.g., via Java's JDBC interface) or any other type of middleware. In fact, the browser-based client could be part of an architecture consisting of any number of tiers. This scenario is used mostly in intranet environments, since it requires that the configuration of the client and server resident parts of the middleware be coordinated.

2. *Middleware is placed on the Web server*: This solution uses the Web protocol (HTTP) between the client (Web browser) and the Web server. This means that the presentation to the end user is prepared on the Web server and the Internet is merely a delivery vehicle.

   It requires that all relevant information be available on the Web server for the construction of a page. Therefore, any of the categories of middleware are deployed on the Web server in order to facilitate access to corporate databases, Data Warehouse systems, or application servers.

The most compelling reasons to use middleware on the server, and not on the client, are the significant reductions in software distribution problems, maintenance effort, and cost. This architecture also is suited for any kind of Internet-based application; that is, it is not restricted to the intranet.

13.8.3 Windows NT

One of the goals of Windows NT's designers was to tightly integrate network protocols and services with the base operating system. Portability to a variety of processors (including RISC and Alpha chips) and scalability, which is made possible through symmetric multiprocessing, make Windows NT Server a desirable superserver platform for developing scalable network-server applications and services.

Packaged with Windows NT and Windows NT Server are several built-in networking protocols and APIs. Windows NT protocols include IPX/SPX, TCP/IP, and NetBEUI. Windows NT Server includes these three protocols as well as AppleTalk. Supported networking APIs include NetBIOS, DCE RPC, and Windows Sockets (Win-Sock).

Another design goal for Windows NT networking was to provide an architecture on which interfaces and protocols can be strategically layered and extended.

Currently, a client/server application can choose to talk directly to Win-Sock or to DCE RPC. Remote OLE is built on top of DCE RPC, using such DCE elements as Network Data Representation (NDR) for data marshaling, authenticated packets, and encrypted sessions.

13.9 FUTURE TRENDS AND DIRECTIONS

One major question is: Can middleware services be delivered as part of an operating system? While companies like Microsoft are trying to push the envelope, by bundling a wealth of functionality into Windows NT operating systems, a majority of software and hardware vendors would confess that middleware covers too broad a ground in terms of functionality to be bundled with operating systems.

Middleware is not just a glue that holds together different components of multitier applications. It creates a level playing field by supporting the same APIs, services, and functionality across heterogeneous operating systems. As long as there are enterprises facing the daunting task of integrating their applications across heterogeneous operating systems, middleware will continue to stand as an essential component that facilitates such integration.

Furthermore, important services provided by middleware products will continue to become more sophisticated and widespread among different products. Services such as synchronous and asynchronous communication with support for different quality of service, naming, security, load balancing, automatic fail-over, events, and others are very important. They are rapidly becoming part of the middleware domain. With at least some of these services already in place, middleware is viewed as a fuel engine that facilitates applications' scalability and integration.

13.10 CONCLUSIONS

The RPC mechanism allows the application programmer transparent use of a server to provide some activity on behalf of the application. This can be effectively used to interact with a computational or database server and has been used on some systems to provide access to operating system services. The latter use is found predominantly in microkernel-based systems rather than in the traditional monolithic kernels found in most UNIX systems; it is especially useful in distributed operating systems.

Remote procedure calls are expressed as ordinary procedure or function calls within the code that uses them. These calls do not require a special compiler for the program source code. The advantages of this include transparency: The RPC layer can be replaced with direct function calls if they become available and the distributed nature of the processing is not needed. Another major advantage (indeed, the driving advantage for the development of RPC) is the familiarity of the interface: Most programmers are accustomed to some form of procedure call. This allows ready adaptation of the RPC mechanism into existing systems, with full understanding of applications being delayed.

The actual calls generated by the compiler are no different than any other calls you define directly in your program. The real differences start once the procedure call is made.

Remote procedure calls are just a way of hiding an underlying message-passing protocol. (What form of interprocess communication is not?) It provides a convenient way of allowing a high-level interpretation of system functionality to be used in programming at the application level, while abstracting the low-level communication mechanisms.

The best-advertised use of RPC mechanisms is to allow an application to make a simple function call to a defined interface. The RPC mechanisms provide a stub that translates any arguments to a flattened form, which may be transmitted over a network to another system, where the arguments are unpacked by another stub in the server process and passed to the actual function or procedure being called. The return value of the procedure is passed back to the caller in a similar manner. While all this overhead has been incurred, the caller has been blocked; it does not resume until the return has been received. One such application of RPC is the Network File System, implemented with Sun's ONC/RPC protocol.

13.10.1 The Process

Each call to an RPC function calls a stub function, which does not actually implement the desired computation but packs its arguments into a flattened (or marshaled) representation. This flattened form is then packed across a network to an RPC server, where the arguments are unpacked and passed to the implementation of the function required. This incurs a moderate amount of overhead but allows a much more flexible environment. The marshaling of the arguments can impose the most significant limits on the passing of complex data structures, since many semantics and multiple-reference structures can be lost in automated translation.

It is important to note that the stubs used at the client and server processes are generated automatically; the programmer need not define flattening and restructuring mechanisms for each function in the interface. This typically requires a large support library as part of the RPC system, but it supports transparency and generality over the network.

The automatic generation of stubs for both the client and server sides of the system is supported by an interface definition language (IDL). This language is used to define the parameter and return types, allowing the stubs it generates to marshal the parameters as efficiently as possible. The advantage of using this intermediate language to define the interface is that it assures the marshaling and demarshaling of the parameters and return value match on each end of the RPC connection, ensuring appropriate interpretation of the data and the ability to define the entire interface in one place.

This class of languages is designed for the cross-platform specification of function call interfaces, much as header files are written to define the interface to a module of C or C++ source code. An interface defined in this way describes the data types used by a set of function, the parameter types and sequence, and the return types.

13.10.2 Future Directions

Interesting work has been done to optimize performance through manipulation of the protocol stack to limit the overhead associated with transferring large data structures.

Systems have been developed to take advantage of the use of automated tools to create these interface definitions to incorporate a distributed object management system into an RPC-based application. This is done with the Object Management Group's CORBA.

Another use of RPC is the provision of operating system services in separate *domains*, where each domain represents a distinct address space. This can be used to provide interfaces to such services as file systems, print spoolers, and even the network layer itself. In this application, in which the client and server reside on the same hardware, significant performance savings can be achieved by avoiding network overhead.

OSF's Distributed Computing Environment is the first of its kind—a fully integrated distributed environment incorporating leading technology from the worldwide industry. OSF's open process provided the means for the computer industry to address and solve its number one problem: Interoperability in heterogeneous, networked environments.

The OSF DCE is a complete set of integrated enabling system services. It provides operating system and network independence, enabling users to obtain the maximum value from their installed systems and networks, while providing an innovative architecture designed to permit the inclusion of new technologies. Each component is a mature, proven technology. Taken as an integrated whole, OSF's DCE forms a comprehensive software platform on which distributed applications can be easily built, executed, and maintained.

As we have seen from the code examples, both ONC and DCE use similar structures in client and server. DCE client stubs look like local procedures, because they can have arbitrary parameter lists. In ONC we would have to write wrappers on client and server side to get the same effect. Apart from that, both RPC protocols need initializations in the client and the inclusion of header files. To hide the actual protocol from the application, it is a good idea to write wrappers anyway.

ONC has no special capabilities that make it hard to port a program designed for ONC to another RPC technology. This is not true for DCE. Any application that makes use of pipes, and especially multithreading on client side, is fairly locked to DCE.

13.10.3 Middleware: The Market Differentiator

Just a few years ago middleware was in its infancy. It provided features such as uniform access to heterogeneous databases and single APIs for program-to-program communication. In that role, middleware facilitated the development of distributed applications independent of communication protocols and databases. Today, we take such features for granted.

Many organizations have recognized that, in order to build a distributed infrastructure that can be used by enterprise-class business applications, they need to select products that offer a wide range of essential middleware services. These services must be consistent across many operating platforms. Support for such services is what differentiates middleware products from one another. Examples include security services provided by DCE; asynchronous, connectionless communication available with DECmessageQ and MQSeries; Encina's support for load balancing; security offered by BEA Systems' ObjectBroker; and the integration with OLE/COM.

It is important to understand that while these middleware services are essential for building large-scale distributed applications, there is no single middleware product that provides them all. However, vendors that offer a multitude of middleware products are in a good position to offer customers a rounded solution. This is especially true when the middleware products foster an opportunity for integration, which has the potential to result in a best-of-breed solution.

In contrast, the process transfer approach implies a direct or indirect communication between two application programs. Both sides exchange messages (either directly or through message queues) based on an application protocol (or "contract") they have agreed upon in advance. The middleware technologies that fall into this category are RPC-based (i.e., DCE), Message-Oriented Middleware, TP monitors, and Object-Request Brokers (including CORBA's ORBs and Microsoft's DCOM).

The data-passing approach makes sense for tactical decision support applications that need to retrieve data from multiple heterogeneous RDBMs. Database middleware products should be optimized to make response time feasible even for decision support systems. Vendors that offer optimization at least when accessing a few supported databases are better positioned than those providing the least common denominator in an attempt to support all possible data sources without any optimization.

The process transfer approach should be used for three-tier and beyond applications in which performance, scalability, and flexible communication models are primary objectives. It should be noted that some middleware products using this approach are designed to provide high-performance communication between application components.

With the data-passing approach, client application issues an SQL request to a database gateway. The gateway can be supplied either by a database vendor or by a middleware vendor and allows access to a variety of heterogeneous databases.

In general, database middleware provides a single, SQL-oriented API (either proprietary in regard to a particular RDBMS or ODBC-compliant, or both) that is capable of accessing heterogeneous databases and files across many different platforms. However, this flexibility comes at a price, as it requires the presence of a translation layer. This layer is responsible for translating the API requests to the native dialect of the target database system. For the most part, the data-passing approach implies a synchronous, connection-oriented communication mechanism. There are a number of scenarios in which this approach should be considered:

☞ *When developing simple, two-tier applications.* In this case there is not any need for middleware. The development tools usually provide ODBC drivers, which form an embedded type of middleware.

☞ *For multitier decision support systems when many applications need to access data from a variety of sources concurrently.* For example, a sales forecasting application needs to consolidate information about a number of geographic regions. The data is collected by the front-end analysis component of this application that resides on distributed systems that house different RDBMSs.

☞ *To avoid changing existing applications.* In some cases, new applications can be developed by accessing existing data sources directly and bypassing the existing application processing that manipulates the data. Even though this approach is limited, it has the advantage of requiring no changes to existing application processing.

As mentioned above, the process-transfer approach implies a direct or indirect communication between two application programs, and it is supported by RPC-based middleware, Message-Oriented Middleware, TP monitors, and ORBs. At least some of these categories offer a variety of communication paradigms, ranging from synchronous, connection-oriented communication to asynchronous (connectionless), message-oriented communication, and publish & subscribe.

The rich set of communication features between application components makes the process-transfer approach much more flexible than the data-passing approach. It can be used to reduce the network bandwidth requirements (which is one prerequisite for scalability), because it is not necessary to transfer large amounts of raw data from a database directly to the client, which would then manipulate the data until (in most cases) a much smaller set of data was derived. The business logic that manages this reduction of data can then be located close to the database. This results in a much smaller amount of data to be transferred over the network to the client.

Some middleware services based on the process-transfer approach support events, which makes them well-suited to model real-business processes more closely. Most of these products have sophisticated communication subsystems built in, thus resulting in subsecond response time.

The combination of the Web and middleware allows an organization to exploit the best of both worlds. The Web paradigm is ideally suited for the distribution and presentation of information, and it provides a uniform way of navigation for the end user. Middleware, on the other hand, provides a flexible way to create this information from corporate data sources and to integrate the Web into the context of mission-critical, transaction-oriented applications.

Managing Distributed Implementations

Managing a Distributed Environment

14.1 INTRODUCTION

Successful operation of distributed systems requires an end-to-end perspective. Since client/server applications are end-to-end entities, it is not enough to manage only the clients, networks, or servers individually. All must be managed in the context of a single, larger system.

In the world of multiprotocols, multiservers, multivendors, and multiplatforms, each platform may have its own management scheme. Technology is progressing at a rapid rate in all of these areas. For example, Novell Servers and applications typically are managed with different tools than Windows NT or UNIX systems. Yet all might exist simultaneously and need management within your own enterprise.

Client/server technology basically seeks to separate the three major components on any monolithic application and redistribute their resources to either the client or the server. These three components are the presentation or user interface, the business process logic, and the data-storage manipulation functions. The glue that holds these components together is the *middleware*. Managing middleware implementation remains one of the great challenges for system integrators deploying a robust and high-performance client/server application.

In the Ethernet era, operating systems were clearly segregated along client/server lines. Client operating systems managed the desktop, and server operating systems managed shared resources. But the intergalactic era requires new hybrid operating systems that do both jobs well. The operating system must provide robust 32-bit preemptive multitasking that protects applications from one another. Clients and servers alike need threads to react quickly to events originating on the desktop and in the global network.

Clients sport an object-oriented user interface (OOUI), which is a place for integrating multiple things that run concurrently. *Things* are on-screen objects that resemble their real-world counterparts. Users interact with things directly, and things exchange information by means of drag-and-drop and live links.

Technologies such as OpenDoc and OLE further the OOUI paradigm, enabling users to assemble, link, script, store, and transport places and the things they contain.

The client also must run the thousands of existing desktop applications, including DOS, Windows, OS/2, and Macintosh programs, as well as the thousands of device drivers users have acquired. It is a daunting task, but that is what it takes to be an integrating client platform in this era.

Of course, developers cannot afford to ship a system administrator with every $99 operating system, so they need a push-button CD-ROM installation, with dynamic discovery and configuration of resources. To achieve shrink-wrapped client/server plug and play, operating systems will bundle the required middleware, including protocol stacks, NOSes, resource binderies, and security features. Some may even have production-strength databases, TP monitors, workflow engines, and ORBs.

To be effective as a server, an operating system must be upwardly manageable. Minimally, it should be able to exploit shared-memory symmetric multiprocessing (SMP) hardware. However, ubiquitous WAN communication also creates the need for massively parallel, *shared-nothing* clustered servers that can service hundreds of thousands of clients and manage tons of data, including video on demand, document databases, high-volume transaction processing, and information warehouses.

In remote data management, the entire application resides on the client, and the data management is located on a remote server/host. Remote data management is relatively easy to program for, because there is just one application program. The client communicates with the server using SQL, the server then responds with data that satisfy the query. RDBMS products that offer remote data management provide a layer of software on the client to handle the communication with the DBMS server. This style represents a more traditional LAN database server or file server approach.

Workstations support the presentation and function logic and interface with the data server through the data manipulation language. Distributed data management is an extension of remote data management and uses the distributed facilities of the DBMS to access distributed data in a manner transparent to users. This is most relevant for architectures with data spread across several servers and when access to a DBMS on another server is required.

14.2 END-TO-END MANAGEMENT

End-to-end management is a cornerstone for successful enterprise management: You must be able to monitor and control every component that is used to deliver functionality to the end user. This means that everything from the server (or mainframe) to the desktop must be managed. End-to-end management is absolutely essential for an organization to measure and manage the quality of service that is being delivered to end users.

Today there are several failure points in establishing end-to-end management. First, most organizations do not monitor or manage all of the components used to deliver the service. Instead, they manage the elements that are easiest to manage. For example, a router that is delivered with an SNMP agent installed probably will be monitored. It is easy to add this piece of equipment to the list of devices managed by an existing network management system (e.g., OpenView or SunNet Manager). Yet, few organizations actively manage the most failure-prone class of components: Application software. In fact, they do not require application software to be instrumented for management. The sparse instrumentation that does exist usually provides little more than error messages written to a log or system console.

The messages themselves tend to be cryptic and are inconsistent between applications. It is imperative that MIS managers demand that applications being delivered are manageable. Otherwise, the MIS organization is doomed to failure.

Today's MIS organizations seem reluctant to even exercise the management capabilities they have. Many make decisions on how to manage networks and systems based on intuition, folk tales, and, in some cases, ignorance. As a result, they create the false impression that they are adequately managing their environments, when they are not.

Consider the use of the Simple Network Management Protocol (SNMP) to manage devices. There is a widely held belief that management traffic across a network can consume vast amounts of bandwidth and jeopardize the network's performance. Because of that belief, many organizations distribute the network management function. Others implement various schemes to limit management traffic; some actually configure their routers to give management traffic a lower priority than the production traffic riding on the network. Others severely limit the frequency with which they permit devices to be polled. No matter what strategy is applied, the result is the same: Managers can be blind to problems that can occur.

In general, management traffic normally utilizes only a minute percentage of the network capacity—hardly a significant impact. If a network is so busy that the consumption of such a small percentage is significant, then the network capacity is inadequate for its task.

Certainly, one can conceive of hypothetical situations in which unusual conditions could cause management traffic to increase significantly for brief periods. For example, a company has a high-speed, international data network; however, there is one low-speed link in the topology, and all management traffic travels across that link. Certainly, in this situation, management traffic can have an adverse impact. However, this is not a normal situation. It is not a problem of network management traffic; it is a problem of network engineering (i.e., inadequate capacity).

Excluding the problems of the special situations and network managers misusing management tools, management traffic typically does not negatively impact a network. Configuring routers to give lower priority to management packets is simply wrong. If you are going to assign different priorities to different types of traffic, management traffic should be given priority above other traffic. Before you disagree, consider this question: If there is a problem in the network, which packet would you prefer to have delivered—one containing a command that will fix the problem, or a routine transaction by an end user?

In a normal, well-managed network, management traffic represents little more than background noise. Network and systems managers must stop letting fear and superstition blind them to problems and rob them of information they need to plan and measure the quality of service being delivered.

There is one more area that must be examined in regard to end-to-end management. It is a rare organization that can actually define what constitutes *quality* in the service it provides to its end users. Even fewer are actually capturing the data required by the definition and reporting it to their clients. After all, MIS organizations exist to deliver high-quality service.

14.3 DISTRIBUTED SYSTEMS MANAGEMENT: GUIDELINES

In its infancy (five or six years ago), client/server showed great promise for cutting costs, allowing faster deployment of new applications, and increasing efficient application processing. Since then, client/server technology has endured prolonged growing pains only to yield disappointing results. It has not emerged as a cheaper solution and has brought forth a systems-management nightmare that tests even the best of IT organizations.

Despite its shortcomings to this point, client/server still offers many potential benefits in the areas of improved productivity, flexibility, and availability. If the chaos of the distributed environment can be harnessed, the technology can lead the way to faster, more powerful, more efficient application processing. Ultimately, the right combination of frameworks and supporting distributed systems management tools determines the difference between victory and defeat with distributed systems.

In addition to increased complexity, distributed system management (DSM) carries a price tag considerably higher than the numbers tallied in the days when a monolithic mainframe environment was the norm. But, most—indeed, the vast majority—of the client/server budget is going for systems management.

14.3.1 Availability

Another attractive payoff comes from the potential of increased—or reclaimed—*availability*. And while the extra availability that DSM tools can squeeze out of distributed systems may not seem substantial when taken in isolation, the incremental growth can actually translate to staggering amounts in corporate revenue. Additionally, significant technology changes occur with regularity within 24-month cycles and should be considered when making DSM investments.

14.3.2 Universality

By providing the middleware to tie together the pieces of distributed applications, frameworks provide helpful capabilities for client/server systems. Yet, while useful, frameworks cannot provide and should not be approached as a complete solution.

Since no framework vendor is adequately accommodating the reality of customer environments, the future scenario is likely to include the use of multiple network and systems management frameworks. Because frameworks do not in themselves constitute a definitive solution, the tools should be the guiding factor in selecting systems management solutions. The right framework is the one that has the tools you need to do the job at hand. It is a particular systems management application that sits right on top of the framework that should govern your choice of products.

14.3.3 Automation

Given the now-standard coexistence of SNMP-based technology and legacy environments using intelligent agents, it is important to have all enterprise elements tied to a central point of command and control, either directly to an enterprise focal point, to an integrated network, or to a systems management platform. In conjunction with this is the need to complement traditional reactive systems management with proactive applications management and monitoring—that is, where the system itself is matching conditions to a prescribed ideal and automatically making adjustments toward achieving the desired state.

An integrated automation engine, then, is a strategic consideration in selecting the most useful systems management tools. Today's most progressive tools can perform advanced correlation and chronic event handling—looking at the defined correct state, constantly assessing current system symptoms, and automatically initiating actions based on machine-speed analysis.

In the distributed systems realm, advanced automation is pivotal to proactive end-to-end availability management of distributed applications. Automation also allows an organization to reduce its dependence on people in certain areas. The operational benefits are immense.

14.3.4 MIS Control

According to research findings, it is the central corporate MIS organization that controls matters related to distributed systems deployment and management. While business units and individual departments may fill the role of *influencer*, it is a central MIS group that makes tactical choices and strategic decisions related to DSM issues and the development and deployment of distributed applications.

14.3.5 Tool Selection

The five criteria considered necessary in choosing tools, in order of importance, are these: Interoperability, scalability, vendor support, ability to support all enterprise elements, and vendor stability.

The significance of product interoperability is underscored by the growth of partnerships between vendors whose solutions serve to extend or complement one another. These vendor alliances are a telling indicator of the degree of interoperability users can expect between the partners' solutions—which is especially important in the DSM arena, where customers look to multiple vendors for a complete solution. Along with extra reassurance that partnered solutions will snap together more easily comes the benefit of better implementation and support for interoperable products.

Customers gain the biggest advantage from systems management vendors who have designed their products to be as open as possible, without boundaries to the type of technology that can be reached.

14.3.6 Scalability

With the growing size and scope of service provided in large distributed environments today, the mainframe-like approach of centralizing all aspects of systems management—applications, knowledge, and GUI—to a single location is obsolete.

DSM products that work this way put their users at unnecessary risk and impose undesirable barriers, since centralizing all analysis and decision making to a single point overloads the network with unwanted messages and polling traffic. In the event of a major malfunction, customers using such products may actually lose the systems management console itself, as it is buried under the weight of a message storm its design cannot handle.

In order to avoid this exposure and achieve a high degree of scalability, the system must use distributed intelligence so that problems are detected, analyzed, and corrected at the local level whenever possible. Only with this distributed approach, geared toward early problem detection and swift automated resolution, can a product deliver the high degree of scalability required by large IT organizations.

14.3.7 The Bottom Line

Although there is no single path to successful distributed systems management, a well-researched and carefully thought out plan can help you avoid the pitfalls and steer toward a winning solution. No single vendor can supply a total DSM antidote. In the pursuit of a workable, effective multivendor management infrastructure, interoperability, scalability, and reach into the enterprise are extremely important. Ensuring that all systems management solutions work together protects your investment in legacy applications and paves the way for the deployment of up-and-coming distribution technologies.

End-to-end availability management for mission-critical applications stands as the vanguard of the IT mission, ready to lead the charge to increased productivity that is substantiated in the bottom line.

14.4 MANAGING DISTRIBUTED SYSTEMS

Network switches are used to increase performance on an organization's network by segmenting large networks into many smaller, less congested LANs while providing necessary interconnectivity between them. Switches increase network performance by providing each port with dedicated bandwidth, without requiring users to change any existing equipment, such as Network Interface Cards (NICs), hubs, wiring, or any routers or bridges currently in place. Switches also can support numerous transmissions simultaneously.

A multilayer switch combines the ease of bridging use within a workgroup with the stability and security of routing among different workgroups. It is capable of providing simultaneous wire speed routing at layer 3, wire speed switching at layer 2, and multiple interfaces at layer 1. Not only is the multilayer switch able to switch at layers 1 through 3, but the latest routing switches are capable of forwarding rates in the range of 35+ million packets per second.

14.4.1 Layers Are Subsystems

Layers are basically subsystems in a network; while distinct from one another, they also are dependent upon one another. The layer architecture of the contemporary network is based on the Open Systems Interconnect (OSI) reference model developed by the International Standards Organization (ISO). These layers are listed below:

1. *Layer 1—Interface.* This layer is responsible for device connectivity.
2. *Layer 2—Switching.* This layer allows end station addressing and attachment.
3. *Layer 3—Routing.* This layer routes data from one node to another, providing logical partitioning of subnetworks, scalability, security, and quality of service.
4. *Layer 4—Transport.* This layer is used for end-to-end integrity of data transmission. Information is broken into sequences of packages and issues such as flow control, retransmission, and reassembly are managed.
5. *Layer 5—Application.* This layer is used for program-to-program communication, providing access either to the end user or to some type of information repository such as a database or data warehouse.

Layer 2 switches are functionally equivalent to bridges. Layer 2 devices improve performance by allowing parallel transfers of packets between pairs of ports. They are able to deliver low latency and fast throughput, but they do have some negative aspects.

A large, flat network is subject to broadcast storms, planning tree loops, and address limitations, which resulted in the placement of routers into bridged networks. The amount of performance improvement attained from a layer 2 switch depends on the pattern of traffic flow, which makes the switch port selection to which a device is attached very important. A major drawback with layer 2 switches is that they have the scalability problems found in bridges, making them truly effective only with smaller topologies.

Bridges and layer 2 switches increase bandwidth with Ethernet by tracking which devices are located on each Ethernet segment and forwarding packets that have to cross the bridge for delivery. Although this functions well for station-addressed packets, for others the bridge has to propagate broadcast packets to all segments, as it has no prior knowledge of where a broadcast packet should be delivered. This results in a broadcast storm in larger topologies, a condition in which the broadcast traffic overwhelms the network.

To overcome this, the layer 3 multiprotocol router is used for LAN segmentation. As a router typically does not propagate broadcast packets, broadcast storms are eliminated, but this becomes difficult to administer. Layer 3 switches integrate routing technology with switching to produce high routing rates in the million-of-packets-per-second range. Vendors have invented a variety of terms to refer to layer 3 switches, such as assisted routing, zero hop routing, IP switching, tag switching, Fast IP, and multiprotocol over ATM (MPOA) routing. But there are basically two types of layer 3 switches.

The packet-by-packet layer 3 switches examine every packet, similar to a router, and forward them to their destinations. They have throughputs of over one-million-packets-per-second. Cut-through layer 3 switches use a short-cut method of packet processing. The cut-through layer 3 switch investigates the first packet or series of packets to determine the destination, then establishes a connection. The flow is then switched to layer 2, allowing for low delay and high throughputs inherent in layer 2 switching.

Layer 3 switches often are implemented to forward information based on the Internet protocol specification, which is the communications protocol governing transmission of data over the Internet. These are capable of routing data packets about ten times faster than traditional routers.

Most networks need to incorporate switching for a variety of reasons, such as subnetwork interconnection, Internet and WAN access, management of alternative paths for load balancing or fault tolerance, and protocol translation between Ethernet and token ring.

Incorporating multilayer switching can be cost-effective, but selecting the right products for the various areas of the network can be difficult. The functional sophistication of network equipment, along with performance and reliability requirements, typically increases with a move from the desktop to the backbone or to central resource sites such as a server farm or data center.

Before deciding on a switching technology, network managers should deploy base-lining and monitoring tools that can be used to discover the amount and destination of traffic and how the volume and patterns are evolving. Next, they should discuss with prospective vendors how a switching product will meet the growing needs of their specific environments. Switching can be carried out at the workgroup, departmental, and backbone levels:

1. At the *workgroup level*, users typically are connected to a shared-media LAN congested with traffic between the desktop and the server or between the server and the backbone. These shared-media hubs can be replaced with a switch that expands the bandwidth of the LAN while segmenting peer-to-peer traffic from client/server traffic. For workgroups, switches are the best price/performance solution. With increasing demand, available bandwidth can be increased by dedicating switch ports for individual workstation nodes.

2. At the *departmental level*, switches can segment the LAN, improve access to the server, and interconnect shared and switched media workgroups. Bottlenecks can be relieved in a cost-effective manner by installing a switch where the high-speed port is connected to the backbone. Many organizations are producing procurements for either routers or switches and not taking advantage of combining the two. Multilayer switching in networks allows an increase in the amount of bandwidth available to LAN users in a cost-effective manner, and preserves the investment in the existing LAN infrastructure.

3. Servers that are on shared 10M bps segments can be moved to switched or dedicated 10M bps segments, and then to switched 100M bps as access demands require. Multilayer switching also can be used for needs beyond the limitations of layer 2. For networks to deliver the performance today's users require, the many components must work together to deliver seamless connectivity between all of the users and the computing systems throughout the enterprise. Flexibility to grow, power to support applications, and seamless connectivity are what users expect in the products they select to build LANs and enterprise networks.

14.4.2 Multilayer Switch Examples

Although each vendor defines a multilayer switch differently, typically it means moving routing into Application-Specific Integrated Circuits (ASICs).

☞ *3-Com*: 3-Com's Corebuilder 3500 is a chassis-based switch that supports Ethernet, ATM, and FDDI and has strong management software (Transcend Enterprise Manager) and an embedded Web server. It does not provide support for Gigabit Ethernet and port density.

☞ *Bay Networks*: The Accelar 1100 is a combination chassis switch and a stackable switch. The Accelar can be configured for VLAN operation with IP routing either through the command-line interpreter or through a Web browser interface or a GUI-based program that can support simultaneous configuration of multiple switches.

☞ *Cabletron Systems*: The SmartSwitch Product Family includes the SmartSwitch 9000 for the data center, the SmartSwitch 6000 for the wiring closet, and the SmartSwitch 2000 for the workgroup. A common architecture used throughout the product line provides consistency in the SmartSwitch Family. The SmartSwitch Family provides redundant, load-sharing power supplies, supports high port densities and frame- or cell-based technologies, and has broadcast control, auto-negotiation, full duplex, and standards-based VLAN capabilities.

☞ *Cisco Systems*: NetFlow LAN switching is included in Cisco's Catalyst Family 5000 series of LAN switches. The Catalyst route switch module (RSM) provides multiprotocol routing and network services, and the Net-Flow Feature Card (a modular feature-card upgrade for the Catalyst 5000 Supervisor) provides hardware-based layer 3 switching. Cisco was the last of the big four networking vendors to market a gigabit layer 3 routing switch.

14.4.3 Managing Distributed Applications

The pain here revolves around the hassles and headaches inherent in designing, deploying, and managing truly distributed applications. The headaches are compounded by the organizational realities of decentralized, autonomous, fast-moving, close-to-the-market business units.

It is hard enough to design, deploy, and maintain a single mission-critical application distributed across a large geographically dispersed organization, such as an airline reservations system or a point-of-sale application. But a headache reaches migraine proportions when you add business-unit-specific applications that are developed, deployed, and managed locally.

Personal computers and client/server development tools now make it possible to design and deploy opportunistic applications rapidly. We seize the day and create new products and services to bring us closer to our customers, including portfolio management applications, online ordering and fulfillment, sales automation, and configuration.

Finally, add in the chaos factor that results from end users procuring software and loading it onto their own machines, departments adding or moving servers, and users hopping from one IP address to another.

Given the virtual unmanageability of today's distributed systems, it is no wonder that the idea of centralized Web servers dishing out information and applets to users equipped with thin clients and browsers begins to sound appealing. There clearly is a rapid upswing in Web-based applications, particularly for delivering applications and information to external customers.

However, the client/server and distributed applications that are running today's businesses and letting us get to the market faster and deliver better service to customers are not going to disappear. Instead, we can foresee a hybrid environment of client/server applications, Web-accessible applications, and downloaded applets and objects installing themselves on our desktops, laptops, and PDAs. This distributed environment is going to become more complex and harder to manage, not easier. So there really is only one solution.

It is time to take seriously the challenge of designing a robust, distributed systems, network, and applications management infrastructure for distributed applications. Even if today's tools and environments are deficient, we need to make the commitment, design the architecture, hire and train the people, and build a manageable distributed systems infrastructure. If we do not, the costs and the headaches may put us all out of business.

14.4.4 Managing Distributed Objects

Distributed systems often must function in the presence of limited or varying network heterogeneity. Connectivity may change dynamically and arbitrary delays occur. In such environments, client applications running on remote machines may not receive information in a timely manner. This is a particular issue when client actions or decisions must be made within a given time frame or information value decreases over time, dropping to zero when critical milestones have passed. A number of basic replication questions must be addressed, including these:

☞ Should you replicate automatically, or on the basis of explicit requests?
☞ How do you determine the boundaries of the set to be replicated?
☞ How do you manage internal component references (links)?
☞ How much information should you replicate, and what are the costs relative to the expected benefit?

In addition, many replicas are likely to be long-lived, existing for an extended period. During this period, updates to replicated objects must be accommodated and reconciled, which introduces additional issues.

Because of the bandwidth and processing limitations, propagation of all updates to all replicas may not be necessary or appropriate. This decision—which I call *information logistics*—may be made on the basis of the value of the information to the receiving application and the availability and cost of communications.

For example, in some circumstances remote systems may be able to model (i.e., simulate) the changes expected to a given object. In such cases, only unexpected changes need be transmitted. In other cases, the client application may specify that it requires only snapshot consistency, so that no further updates would be sent. Obviously, the expected cost of update propagation must be considered as part of the original decision to replicate objects.

Conflicting updates may occur to multiple replicas, and these must be resolved on consistently. A single object may be designated *master*, with the right to mediate conflicts. Alternatively, decisions may be made on a more local basis. Each approach has advantages and disadvantages.

This approach is best suited to applications in which the rate of updates is low relative to the rates of information requests; decisions or actions must be made on the client side in a timely manner; and client applications can accept near-current information.

Two initial implementations of this technology have been developed, including a WWW server that caches remote Web pages and notifies local clients of updates. These focus on applications that perform situation assessment and world modeling.

14.4.5 Managing Distributed Information

When a user updates a document, collaborators see the change in seconds. When the user adds a document to a folder, other users can see and access the new document instantly. This capability is achieved through replication mechanisms hidden from users.

When an object is routed, it is copied and replicated to the locations included in the routing. Shared objects are stored in a database at each site. Within a local database, objects are routed by reference, making for fast communication, removing redundancy in information, and avoiding the problem of out-of-date or out-of-sync copies.

Such operations include destroy, update, read, and so forth. When a user performs an operation on an object, the originating database is contacted to make sure the object is not being modified by another user. Typically, more than one user will open an object on the desktop while another is updating it. Viewing an object does not prevent other users from reading it, since read operations do not change the content of an object. However, multiple users updating an object simultaneously can cause an unpredictable result (i.e., race condition). Thus, a mechanism is required to ensure that each update operation is predictable.

14.5 MANAGING COMPLEXITY

Today's enterprises rely on the transient interaction of thousands of disparate and independent devices, systems, and applications to successfully achieve their business goals. Success requires the collaboration of multiple systems and network elements. The challenges frustrating effective management of distributed systems and networks have become depressingly well-known, including these:

☞ *Complexity*: Distributed systems have many more moving parts than their mainframe counterparts, with correspondingly more that can go wrong. The hardware and software implemented in an independent and piecemeal fashion to solve individual departmental problems further complicates the picture.

☞ *Lack of an end-to-end view of IT services*: Use of IT resources represents a key corporate competitive advantage. However, with distributed applications and transactions spread across systems and networks, it is difficult to track and link to business impact even simple performance metrics such as response time.

☞ *Lack of proactive rather than reactive management tools*: Systems have not been instrumented for self-management; instead, polling and event agents report problems as they occur, providing proactive management only after extensive customization.

Network and systems management tools have focused on the functioning of individual managed elements or on groups of similar devices. These provide little help to managers who require a broader vision of the business and its supporting services.

14.5.1 Corporate Standardization

Single vendor support benefits are tempered by technology lock-in and slow feature enhancement. Corporate standardization of hardware and software represents one response to the complexity inherent in the move to distributed client/server computing. On the plus side, fewer types of systems and network devices reduce support costs. With fewer vendors, it is easier to identify who to call in times of trouble. Also, fewer experts are needed, directly affecting the IT bottom line. This supports the increasing corporate interest in NT as a combined NOS and application server—no more variant OSes that can interoperate.

This approach has several problems. First and foremost is vendor and technology lock-in. The elimination of competition among hardware and software suppliers invariably leads to slowdown in delivery of new functionality as vendors secure in their position become slow to innovate to meet new needs of the client base and slow to integrate enhanced functionality offered through custom consulting services. While very large clients may have some influence on product functionality, vendors tend to be more interested in dealing with broad-based market issues. Thus, vendor professional services provide only custom solutions for individual client problems.

This inflexibility can be costly, particularly in terms of lost opportunities to capitalize on the rapid pace of computing innovation and change. Therefore, we must take precautions before mandating blanket standardization; specialized, nonstandard systems will always have desirable features that will provide business benefits.

14.5.2 Integrated Solutions

IT or off-the-shelf integration solutions require significant commitment and resource allocation.

The lack of a global view of IT resources drives integration demand. Distributed systems require products that collect and process data for multiple systems in a variety of ways to meet specific administrator needs. Different applications provide functions required by different managers. The resulting duplication of function, data collection, and storage creates many problems, including resource waste, database inconsistency, and costly retraining in multiple applications.

The root issue is determining where responsibility for integration implementation and maintenance lies—with IT or with the vendors. Either choice involves significant commitment and resource allocation.

IT integration of best-of-breed products generally provides the most feature-rich solutions with the best fit for an organization's requirements. The downside lies in the amount of internal resources required to design, implement, and maintain the framework as products change over time. IT resources that should be focusing on maximizing a company's competitive advantage are instead sharpening generic operational and development skills.

Many vendor-provided solutions exist, including management platforms, suites, manager-of-managers, data format transformers, and analyzers. To date, these yield mixed results partly because vendor integration has been spotty, partly because of a mismatch between problem definition and targeted solution, and partly because smaller vendors cannot afford the resources to tightly integrate their products into all major platforms. All too frequently, IT must again spend time learning and customizing solutions to their environment.

14.5.3 Distributed Intelligence

In most cases the capability for distributed intelligence is available, but the solution depends heavily on user-defined scripts and rules.

Proactive management reduces emergencies, freeing time to concentrate on designing and implementing strategic business solutions.

Increasing environmental complexity makes out-of-service time more critical, creating pressures to reduce the level of effort required to resolve problems. The result is an increasing demand for systems smart enough to recognize and correct problems before they cause a service interruption.

A self-monitoring system that diagnoses and corrects itself without administrator intervention represents the ultimate goal. Such a solution would reduce the burden on the administrators and management system, as well as enhancing scalability to handle a larger, more complex environment. While today's solutions provide for proactive management capabilities, most leave the implementation of tests and correlation rules to the administrator. All too often, this task is put off by overburdened managers.

14.5.4 Web-Based Management

The interest in Web-based management has been driven by the lackluster performance of current integrated solutions and the explosion of the Internet as a viable information-delivery service.

Web technologies can retrieve, process, and deliver data to universal consoles. With the Internet, the network itself becomes the management platform.

Java-based applets provide the distributed intelligence for proactive management. The browser console can accept and present data from diverse sources, providing the integration point. Complexity is reduced because Java can run on virtually any platform, effectively slicing development time and cost.

With all of these benefits comes one unfortunate problem: Nobody to date has truly implemented, much less tested, this solution for robustness.

14.5.5 The Trends

These trends represent a significant move toward more disciplined management approaches to the currently chaotic distributed environment. Although problems continue and will continue to exist, systems and network management solution providers have begun responding.

Some examples include Hewlett-Packard's enhanced customized consulting services capability; Tivoli's aggressive and innovative efforts to build consensus on standards for the distributed management infrastructure; Amdahl's integrated third-party products; Computer Associates, Inc., and BULL, with powerful, modular tool-kit management platforms.

There is no simple formula for making the ultimate solution provider, as enterprises attempt to select the correct management tool. Success requires a clearly specified scope and more detail in the problem definition. Finding the right solution requires analyzing a vendor's architectural strengths and solution focus, rather than simply comparing feature-functions and vendor stability. Only by doing your homework can you successfully capitalize on these trends and in-house strengths.

14.6 THE NEW AGE NOS

NOSes have always been in the business of hiding the location of resources from applications. But in the client/server era, they must create the illusion of a single system image across, potentially, millions of hybrid client/server machines. Here are some of the elements of that illusion:

1. *Location transparency*: Users, services, and resources join and leave the network constantly, but they are never tied to fixed locations. In this continual flux, the NOS global directory brings people, programs, and things into conjunction to perform work. The global directory is a distributed, replicated object database. Distribution allows autonomous administrative domains to exist. Replication enhances availability and performance. Object-orientation enables the directory to grow organically, like the real-world structures it represents.

2. *Name space transparency*: Everything on the global network must appear to belong to the same namespace. Names must resolve uniquely within a given context or naming authority, but the NOS can grow a tree of federated namespaces, each with autonomous naming authority. Namespaces are like the telephone system's area codes.

3. *Administrative transparency*: The NOS must appear to integrate with the local operating system's management services and provide replication transparency. If a naming directory is shadowed on many machines, for example, it is up to the NOS to synchronize updates. The NOS also must shield users from network failures, transparently handle retries and session reconnects, and synchronize clocks on geographically dispersed machines.

4. *Secured-access transparency*: Users must be able to access any server resource from anywhere—including hotel rooms, offices, homes, and cellular phones—using a single log-on. Security is built on mutual distrust: Clients must prove to servers that they are who they claim to be, and vice versa, by appealing to a trusted third party. MIT's Kerberos, the DCE security system, works this way. After authentication, the server applications use ACLs to regulate clients' access to functions and data.

5. *Communications transparency*: Modern NOSes are learning to hide the complexities of multiple protocols and dissimilar data representations behind a set of abstractions for interprocess communication. All offer peer-to-peer conversational interfaces, and most provide some form of RPC that makes a server appear to be one function call away. Another model—message-queuing or MOM (message-oriented middleware)—is helpful when clients and servers can tolerate communications delay. Current NOSes generally do not come with MOM, but it is available as an add-on.

The Ethernet-era NOSes—including NetWare, LAN Server, LAN Manager, and Windows NT Server—were built for LANs with small numbers of servers. It would be pointless to deploy them in intergalactic environments. However, a new generation of NOSes is on the horizon, and these systems are increasingly suitable for intergalactic environments.

14.6.1 Client/Server Applications

More and more people are talking about a planetary electronic mall, with virtual boutiques, department stores, bookstores, brokerage services, banks, travel agencies, and more. Like Club Med, this mall would issue its own electronic currency to facilitate round-the-clock shopping and business-to-business transactions. Electronic agents would roam the network, looking for bargains and negotiating with other agents. Billions of transactions and oceans of multimedia data would flow through the network every day.

Clearly, we are not talking about today's Internet, where users surf hypertext webs of HTML-tagged information. The volume and complexity of transactions, and the richness of the data on which they operate, will create the need for new enabling technologies, including these:

☞ *Rich transaction processing*: Users will need nested transactions that can span servers, transactions that execute over long periods of time as they travel from server to server, queued transactions for secure business-to-business dealings, and *sagas* that can chain together many pieces of work and selectively undo some of the effects of a transaction. Most nodes on the network should be able to participate in a secured transaction. Superserver nodes will handle the massive transaction loads.

☞ *Roaming agents*: Consumers will have personal agents looking after their interests. Businesses will deploy agents to sell their wares on the network. Sniffer agents will look for trends and gather statistics. Agent technologies include cross-platform scripting engines, work-flow engines, and an infrastructure that lets agents live on any machine on the network.

☞ *Rich data management*: From anywhere on the network, people will create, store, view, and edit compound documents with multimedia content. Most nodes will offer compound document technology (e.g., OLE or Open-Doc) for local document management.

Superservers will provide repositories for storing and distributing massive numbers of documents. Of course, we cannot forget structured data (e.g., SQL databases) either.

What technology base will be used to create these intergalactic client/server applications? The three competing paradigms are SQL databases, TP monitors, and distributed objects. Each can create complete client/server applications, each provides tools to do that (some more than others), and each introduces its favorite form of middleware.

14.6.1.1 SQL Databases SQL database servers dominate the client/server landscape today. SQL began as a declarative language for manipulating data using 10 simple commands. But as SQL applications moved to more demanding client/server environments, it became clear that simply managing data was not enough. There was a need to manage the functions that manipulated the data. Stored procedures, sometimes called *TP lite*, met that need.

A stored procedure is a named collection of SQL statements and procedural logic that is compiled, verified, and stored in a server database. Virtually all SQL vendors support stored procedures along with other SQL extensions (e.g., triggers and rules). The extensions are used to enforce data integrity, perform system maintenance, and implement the server side of an application's logic. No two vendor implementations are alike. Note that stored procedures offer minimal transaction support.

Because SQL standards seem to lag behind vendor implementations by at least five years, almost everything that is interesting in client/server database technology is nonstandard. This includes database administration, data replication, stored procedures, user-defined data types, client APIs, and the formats and protocols on the network. Thus, the best you can do in a heterogeneous database environment is to create a loose federation of databases whose least common denominator typically is dynamic SQL.

SQL does offer three advantages: It is easy to create client/server applications in single-vendor/single-server environments; a wealth of GUI tools makes SQL applications easy to build; and SQL is familiar to millions of programmers and users.

14.6.1.2 TP Monitors
You cannot create mission-critical applications without managing the programs (or processes) that operate on data. That is why, in the mainframe world, a TP monitor comes with every mission-critical database. TP monitors manage processes and orchestrate programs by breaking complex applications into pieces of code called *transactions*. The modern client/server incarnations of TP monitors have not dominated the Ethernet era, but they will be major players in the intergalactic era. It is not farfetched to assume that every machine on the network will have a TP monitor to represent it in global transactions.

Transactions are more than just business events. They have become an applications design philosophy that guarantees robustness in distributed systems. Under the control of a TP monitor, a transaction can be managed from its point of origin—typically, on a client—across one or more servers and back to the originating client. When a transaction ends, all parties involved agree that it either succeeded or failed.

The transaction is the contract that binds the client to one or more servers. It is the fundamental unit of recovery, consistency, and concurrency in a client/server system. Of course, all participating programs must adhere to the transactional discipline; otherwise, a single faulty program can corrupt an entire system. In an ideal world, all client/server programs would be written as transactions.

Transaction models define when a transaction starts, when it ends, and what the appropriate units of recovery will be in case of failure. The flat-transaction model is the workhorse of the current generation of TP monitors (and other transactional systems). In a flat transaction, all work done within a transaction's boundaries occurs at the same level. The transaction starts with a begin_transaction and ends with either a commit_transaction or an abort_transaction. It is all or nothing—there is no way to commit or abort parts of a flat transaction. However, newer transaction models offer finer control of a transaction's threads and can more closely mirror their real-world counterparts.

Most alternatives to the flat transaction extend the flow of control beyond the simple unit of work, either by chaining units of work in linear sequences of minitransactions or by using nested subtransactions. A subtransaction's effects become permanent after it issues a local commit and all its ancestors commit. If a parent transaction aborts, all descendant transactions abort, whether they issue local commits or not. The beauty of this is that subtransactions can run on different nodes.

TP monitors were invented to run applications that serve thousands of clients. By interjecting themselves between clients and servers, TP monitors can manage transactions, route them across systems, load-balance their execution, and restart them after failures. A TP monitor can manage transactional resources on a single server or across multiple servers, and it can cooperate with other TP monitors in federated arrangements. TP monitors also perform a great funneling act that helps the operating system and server resource managers deal with large numbers of clients.

X/Open and the OMG have created complementary standards that define how TP monitors interact with applications, resource managers, and other TP monitors in both procedural and distributed-object environments. You will find some good tools on the market to help you create TP-monitor applications.

TP monitors probably are overkill in single-server, single-vendor departmental applications. That is one reason they have been slow to take off. Moreover, vendors have not yet come to grips with the realities of the shrink-wrapped software market, and they have not been able to explain the advantages of TP monitors. The intergalactic era will make those advantages increasingly self-evident.

14.6.1.3 Distributed Objects

Distributed-object technology promises the most flexible client/server systems, because it encapsulates data and business logic in objects that can roam anywhere on networks, run on different platforms, talk to legacy applications by way of object wrappers, and manage themselves and the resources they control.

When it comes to standards, distributed-object technology is ahead of other client/server approaches. Since 1989, a consortium of object vendors—called the OMG—has been busily specifying the architecture for an open software bus on which object components written by different vendors can interoperate across networks and systems.

The secret to the OMG's success is that it defined how to specify an interface between a component and the object bus—using working technologies as a model—but it did not prescribe how to implement those specifications. Specifications are written in IDL, independent of any programming language. Components specify in IDL the types of services they provide, including the methods they export and their parameters, attributes, error handlers, and inheritance relationships with other components.

IDL becomes the contract that binds clients to server components. The beauty of IDL is that it can be used easily to encapsulate existing applications. You do not have to rewrite your entire inventory of applications to take advantage of distributed-object technology.

The object bus provides an ORB that lets clients invoke methods on remote objects either statically or dynamically. If a component interface is already defined, you can bind your program to an IDL-generated stub to call its methods. Otherwise, you can discover how the interface works at run time by consulting an OMG-specified interface repository.

In addition to defining the object bus, the OMG has specified an extensive set of ORB-related services for creating and deleting objects, accessing them by name, storing them, externalizing their states, and defining complex relationships among them. The OMG also defined a comprehensive set of services for transactional objects. Users are able to create an ordinary object and make it transactional, lockable, and persistent by having it inherit the appropriate services using simple IDL entries.

The OMG created important alliances to make sure its standards are universally accepted. The CORBA-defined persistence service is closely aligned with the new Object Database Management Group (ODMG) specifications for object databases. The object-transaction services can interoperate with X/Open-defined procedural transactions. The OMG also is working with X/Open to help define ORB-based system management interfaces, including security.

It looks as if the object community is on its way to building an object infrastructure that can meet the demands of the intergalactic client/server era. Distributed objects with the proper component packaging and infrastructure may be the ultimate building blocks for creating client/server solutions, including suites of cooperating business objects.

In all honesty, however, the current generation of CORBA-compliant ORBs is not ready for intergalactic prime time. CORBA and the new object services—including transactions, loc king, life cycle, naming, and persistence—must be implemented in commercial ORBs before the technology can take off. The good news is that in this case, unlike in the SQL world, the standards lead rather than lag behind the commercial offerings.

Once distributed-object technology takes off, it will subsume all other forms of client/server computing, including TP monitors, SQL databases, and groupware. Distributed objects can do it all and do it better. Objects can help us break large, monolithic applications into more manageable components that coexist on the intergalactic bus. They are our only hope for managing the millions of software entities that will live on intergalactic networks.

The Ethernet era of client/server saw a file-centered applications wave followed by a database-centered wave. TP monitors and groupware generated minor ripples. Distributed objects are the next big wave.

14.7 MANAGING DECENTRALIZED STORAGE

Storage management can mean anything from backing up data and monitoring the health and performance of disk drives to using new distributed file systems. A better definition looks past the means to the ends of storage management, which is to provide users with optimal system performance and minimum downtime while protecting electronic assets.

As an organization makes data available, it also must aggressively protect it. Implementing rigorous media monitoring, backup, and file-grooming procedures, for instance, may seem like a burden to users, but it is the only way to ensure that the right data will be there when they need it. In fact, as organizations shift from hosts to distributed models—or as their LANs evolve upward to assume more enterprising functions—they are demanding storage management tools as robust and sophisticated as those created for mainframes.

The move to distributed computing thus is being matched by a shift toward centralized storage management. The notion of distributed computing is a distinct issue from distributed storage. Even in the most distributed environments, you are trying to put your data in a centralized place.

Of course, the meaning of centralized can vary: Hard drives and other devices may be physically dispersed in a distributed environment, because storage management is implemented largely at a logical level. Whether data is consolidated on a single giant server or scattered across an array of smaller systems, centralization gives network managers a unified view of storage resources and lets them assert control over otherwise haphazard processes such as drive-performance monitoring and backup.

Asset protection is one of the factors driving storage management into LANs. Sometimes data on the desktop is as valuable—and as strategic—as the data in the server or the mainframe.

Fortunately, implementing storage management need not become another tug-of-war between MIS departments and freewheeling users. If properly executed, storage management not only is transparent to users but ultimately helps them retrieve data more easily, spares them the burden of looking after their own disks and data, and boosts system performance. Unfortunately, many of the storage management products available today for LANs address only part of the problem, and most do not work together in a unified framework.

14.7.1 Hierarchical Storage Management

Assuming you already have adequate security, reliability, and physical management, the key challenge in storage management is to make the best use of your available media with the minimum need for human intervention. This is the area in which Hierarchical Storage Management (HSM) resides.

Some people see HSM as an extension of backup and archiving, but its technology is much closer to that of a cache. As in a cache, the point of HSM is to keep the most current, the most frequently accessed, and the most urgent data as close as possible to the place it is being used, while intelligently discarding that which is no longer needed. The limited space in the cache is at a premium, and not everything needs to be there.

The algorithm that drives backup is based on whether a given file has already been archived and whether it has changed since the last archive. Backups do not delete the source files after copying them to the secondary media. And backup software, which operates in a batch mode, is optimized for backup speed so that the process takes the least possible time and interferes as little as possible with normal system operations. Restores can be done at a more leisurely pace because they are assumed to be infrequent.

HSM is nearly the opposite. Migrating files, which involves making a copy and deleting the original, takes place in continuous sweeps, as thresholds are crossed or trigger events occur (i.e., files pass the one-year mark), and can thus proceed during idle processor cycles with no particular urgency. But demigration must be instantaneous. If you need a file that is no longer online, the load operation should take only marginally longer than it would if the file was on disk.

The algorithms used in HSM to choose which files to migrate weigh several factors. The primary criterion usually is disk capacity: The administrator sets high and low thresholds, or watermarks, and the HSM engine keeps disk capacity between these levels. When the high threshold is crossed, the engine typically looks for the oldest eligible files to move. But to minimize the potential need for demigration, sophisticated algorithms will choose one large but younger file over several small but older ones.

When a file is migrated off the primary storage medium, HSM systems often leave behind a placeholder (or token) that consists of a pointer to the file's new location or an index entry in a server database that tracks the actual location of the file. The latter approach is safer, especially if the database is redundant. Unless the HSM is tightly integrated with the underlying operating system, it is difficult for it to trap disk calls and redirect them to a separate file manager.

The trickiest problem in HSM arises when the user requests a file that needs to be demigrated, but it is too large to fit onto the hard drive. Premigrating means the files are left on the drive and also copied to the next level down; so if you need the space the files occupy right away, you can delete the files from the hard drive and restore them later.

Similarly, some HSM systems fail to quickly remigrate a file that has been demigrated because they see it as having been recently accessed, which fools the algorithm into thinking the file is current. Avail's software solves this by treating remigrated files as if they were premigrated, which means they go back to a lower level in the hierarchy as soon as the next sweep occurs.

HSM is one of the hottest topics in storage management today because it solves several problems at once. Migrating old or infrequently used files onto inexpensive media such as removable optical disks or tape not only frees space on the primary device for more current or important files but also reduces the average cost of storage. HSM is not a substitute for backup; rather, it is complementary.

HSM also increases aggregate network performance by optimizing access time for the data you are most likely to need. With HSM, the focus of network drives becomes speed, not storage. Your concern becomes performance, not capacity. In a complex HSM pyramid, you might have ultrafast cached hard drives that are layered above 10-GB single-spindle Seagate drives, which are layered on top of an optical jukebox for near-line storage, which is layered above a tape library.

HSM comes from the mainframe world, where it was used to minimize storage costs that were 10 times what they are in distributed networks. In fact, the relatively low cost of storage in distributed systems has made implementing HSM less urgent and so has held back its market penetration.

Indeed, the low cost of distributed storage has encouraged users to buy more drives rather than use existing drives more efficiently, and this has ultimately led them to seek HSM for a different reason: As an easy way to implement disk space management.

The basic requirement for an HSM is that it supports a hierarchy of storage devices, ranging from the fastest and most expensive hard drives to low cost-per-megabyte tape autoloaders. Several analysts consider solutions that support only a fixed number of levels to be inadequate.

Using an algorithm that takes into consideration disk capacity thresholds, file aging, and sometimes file type (i.e., you can set the rules so that certain types of files, such as executables or DLLs, are never migrated), a rules engine does the following:

☞ It watches the drives to make sure they stay within their thresholds.

☞ It moves files from one medium to another as necessary.

☞ It tracks file locations in a database. When you try to load a file, the engine intercepts the request and looks it up in the database. If the file needs to be remigrated from tape or an optical drive, it is copied back to the hard disk.

A function that is intimately related to file access might seem like an obvious candidate for inclusion in the operating system, and, in fact, both Novell and Microsoft are moving to support HSM. However, as with other third-party functions that get added to the operating system, their support will consist of a simple out-of-the-box implementation coupled with an API that allows richer external products to plug in.

14.7.2 Unified View

One problem faced by network administrators is the proliferation of network management consoles on their desktops. Eliminating multiple displays requires integrating management applications into a common framework. Because of the widespread adoption of Simple Network Management Protocol (SNMP), most internetworking devices such as hubs and routers can report their status to and be managed from a single console. But storage management systems have remained largely isolated.

14.7.3 Future Files

If storage management in distributed environments raises problems and requires solutions that did not exist in centralized systems, it is only the tip of the iceberg. Just around the corner are fundamental changes in the conception of file systems and documents that may require a rethinking of storage management altogether.

The technological shifts underlying this trend are the emergence of *locationless* network services and the rise of objects and object file systems. In today's computing model, a file stands on its own and resides in a specific place. Advanced operating systems like Windows NT support rich data typing, yet files still are backed up and migrated using conventional attributes such as date/time stamp or archive bit. Obviously, backup and HSM for compound documents will have to respect links, grouping related files together.

Whether you use a GUI or some other scheme for finding and manipulating files—and whether you back up via disk mirroring, RAID, optical jukeboxes, or tape libraries—the ultimate goal of storage management is to ensure that data are there when you need it.

By implementing sophisticated backup, HSM, physical resource management, and access control, you are actually making data more available. And implementing centralized storage management does not contradict a movement toward distributed computing. Virtually, the data is distributed to clients; physically, it is grouped at servers; logically, it is centralized. The network makes these distinctions invisible to the user.

14.8 MANAGING CHANGE

Why focus on software distribution management in something as complex as the modern networking environment? It is because of that very complexity, and because of the evolutionary changes in networking and the scarcity of enterprise resources that require such a selection of priorities.

The first wave of personal computers sidestepped MIS bureaucracies to capture desktops across the enterprise and spawn easily configurable networks. The result was a LAN explosion for local file and print sharing—mostly unsupervised and unmanaged by MIS departments.

Clearly, individual productivity benefits dramatically from the powerful and highly personalized PC. All too often, however, the individual gains contribute little to group results because of the increased isolation of the individual and the reinforcement of islands of automation across the enterprise.

Today's desktop environment approaches chaos, with its escalating demands on management time and expertise. Local experts and ad hoc systems managers have difficulty responding to rising job loads with their often shrinking staffs. Centralized IT groups try to pick up the slack, but similar pressures frustrate their efforts. Scarce resources must be focused on solving problems important and large enough to yield significant benefits. Automated software distribution management fits that profile. Unfortunately, most observers look at software distribution as a stand-alone solution and completely miss the larger issue involved in managing ongoing changes in software configurations across the enterprise.

A comprehensive solution includes automated tools to track platform configurations, build required software packages, and schedule changes, as well as to combine workflow management and organizational modeling. The solution infrastructure encompasses all tools that enable, implement, and manage the enterprise software change processes. These basic premises include:

☞ Software change management represents a significant business problem today.

☞ Change management and desktop infrastructure link intimately.

☞ Existing products provide a good starting point.

Product architecture exerts the greatest long-term effect on a product's scalability and flexibility. Solutions must adapt to the inherent dynamism of commercial desktop and corporate networked environments.

The emerging area of *process and organizational modeling* provides the ability to systematically represent organizational hierarchies and access control. Process modeling allows managers to document the workflow of administrators involved in the software change management process. Organizational modeling allows managers to represent the enterprise as dynamic, logical groups (e.g., accounting, sales, and engineering) to simplify software policy making.

Configuration management covers the ability to record platform inventories and develop software profiles as well as record and test scheduled activity. It enables the end user to control the implementation of change.

Change management is concerned with scheduling software distribution and installation and with distribution policy management. It also involves modeling how configuration changes affect the desktop so that problems can be determined before the distribution is scheduled.

Distribution describes features that automate distribution tasks, reduce transmission costs, and determine the ability to handle different types of software packages and installation situations.

Administration evaluates the tools needed to create an effective management environment. These include remote management, secured administrative access, and error handling capabilities.

14.9 CONCLUSIONS

Managing distributed computing is becoming more complex than ever. A multitude of computing types is available on the Internet and through mobile computing, and there are applications that must work between different enterprises. All of these now compete against typical client/server environments.

Enterprises are evolving toward the *computing-defined* organization, in which technology allows entire new classes of business activity to emerge. Because of the great dependence on technology, once an enterprise becomes computing-defined, it cannot go back and operate in any other way.

As this occurs, MIS organizations have to redefine their essential purpose to the enterprise. Successful MIS managers will lead the transition to a business-centric set of competencies, including project leadership, change management, and solutions integration.

Large enterprises face some of the most profound changes in software since the introduction of online processing 25 years ago. The different types of computing now available—on the Internet and through mobile computing, as well as applications that must work between different enterprises—will compete against typical client/server environments and combine to make managing IT resources and MIS organizations more complex than ever before.

The management of widely distributed databases is becoming a difficult problem. Database systems span large geographical areas, yet must be kept current. Models of database management are being developed to assist in this problem.

The use of a data warehouse in an organization's private intranet or throughout the Internet is becoming important in the future. When it comes to managing distributed systems, a growing number of network managers are opting to steer clear of highly touted SNMP-based platforms such as Hewlett-Packard's OpenView or Sun Microsystems' SunNet Manager, preferring to use lesser-known products or devising customized solutions instead.

A look at a cross-section of network managers reveals that the tremendous variation inherent in network environments has engendered an equivalent diversity in management mechanics. Not only do differences in budgets, staff resources, personal skills, and attitudes dictate the way network management is performed, but these differences also manifest themselves in individualized tool kits, staff structures, and overall network philosophy.

The trend toward distributed processing has significantly increased the awareness of data as a key corporate resource and underscored the importance of data management. In spite of this, there is a lack of empirical investigation of issues related to data resource management in distributed processing environments.

These trends represent a significant move to introduce more disciplined management approaches to the currently chaotic distributed environment. Although problems continue and will continue to exist, systems and network management solution providers have begun responding.

Summary and Conclusions

15.1 INTRODUCTION

Companies today face an increasing need to be competitive in their product offerings to take advantage of shifting market conditions and new business opportunities. This competition takes place in the context of market globalization and a significantly reduced time frame for making decisions and implementing new business strategies. This has affected the role of information technology and its relationship to lines of business. Increasingly, as information becomes a strategic weapon in corporate competition, it is no longer simply accepted that centrally planned IT infrastructures and applications determine the way a company conducts business.

Requirements have changed throughout the '90s, as business moved from downsizing to bringing the whole enterprise back together. The information that was spread throughout various business applications in different departments now must be made available to workers in a transparent and seamless fashion. Stovepipe systems need to be integrated, and islands of automation must become part of an enterprisewide flow of business logic, in which a business event in one line is propagated to another line.

Although the first wave of client/server applications has been successful by most accounts, these applications did not often face the challenge of scalability. As companies attempt to grow these applications from departmental usage to enterprise usage, the challenges of scalability are just around the corner.

Many experts agree that middleware is the answer to both problems companies face today: Applications integration and scalability. For this reason, middleware has moved to center stage in most new IT initiatives.

Originally, middleware evolved around the database access model. This model usually is characterized by two-tier applications, in which a "fat" client application retrieved and updated information that was maintained by a relational DBMS. Early solutions were proprietary in nature. Then the SQL standard emerged and provided a common language for data access (obstructed by the proprietary vendor extensions). Finally ODBC set a de facto standard that enables most users to speak to databases in the same language. Such support for heterogeneous environments is crucial today, as most organizations now use, on average, five different types of database systems. However, even for applications focused on data access rather than on process distribution, support for standard ODBC is not enough, since access to data must be efficient and optimized.

While the data access model is a valid approach for some distributed two-tier applications, limitations have become apparent, particularly in large enterprises. Organizations that have a strong need for scalability have begun building applications following a new model—that of distributed application components, mostly in the form of a three-tier architecture. This architecture extends the two-tier model by adding a tier between the client and the server. This tier is called an *application server.*

In a three-tier model the client tier becomes thinner. It focuses on providing an easy-to-use graphical user interface, while some of the business logic moves from the client tier to the application server. At the same time, business logic that used to be buried in proprietary database extensions (i.e., stored procedures) has moved to the application server as well. In general, this model provides more choices in how business rules of distributed application can be partitioned across the different tiers. This, in turn, enables better exploitation of resources and supplies an infrastructure that meets scalability requirements.

As the move to the three-tier model continues, middleware is evolving to support this new model as well. Early middleware products capable of supporting the three-tier model did not provide much more than a higher-level abstraction of communication protocols. Using this approach, the application developer could use a higher-level API instead of a low-level API such as TCP/IP Sockets, SNA LU6.2, or DECnet. Such APIs masked the substantial differences between native APIs provided by communication protocols. Today, however, this functionality cannot be considered sufficient for the development of robust, scalable production applications that are enterprise-wide in scope. As a result, a competitive middleware offering must provide an extensive suite of services, such as naming, security, and reliable and flexible communication. These are essential in any serious effort to design, develop, and deploy complex mission-critical applications.

Parallel to the evolution of vendor technology, standards have been emerging. DCE from the Open Group was the first available. It provides not just a common set of APIs and a consistent programming model (i.e., Remote Procedure Calls) across multiple operating platforms, but also a comprehensive set of distributed computing services. Nonetheless, many user companies have realized they need a higher level of abstraction. Along with the move toward object-oriented programming languages and tools came the requirement for a middleware infrastructure that could support distributed objects and a new paradigm for application development: the assembly of applications from small building blocks, known as components.

CORBA from the OMG recently became available in products from a variety of vendors. Although this can be considered an open standard in the classical sense, Microsoft has countered this model with OLE/DCOM. This has established a de facto standard, supported by a large number of ISVs and user companies. While it creates another option, it also puts an additional burden on technology planners who must learn the pros and cons of these technologies and make strategic decisions for their organizations.

When an organization decides to build distributed applications, it must also decide what should be done with existing applications (in-house developed or purchased). These applications represent a major investment and, for the most part, cannot be abandoned. Many enterprises are looking for solutions that enable the integration of these legacy environments with the new breed of distributed applications, as well as integration between existing applications caused either by mergers and acquisitions or by a company's desire to move into a new and uncharted business activity.

Distributed multiprocessing is progressing from a simple client/server computing model to far more scalable, robust, and manageable architectures. The promise of these new distributed computing paradigms can be fully realized only when enterprises can clearly understand and successfully manage the technology benefits and drawbacks.

15.2 TRADITIONAL CLIENT/SERVER APPROACHES

As depicted in Figures 15.1 to 15.3, traditional client/server computing uses the processing power of both desktop and server machines. The client/server architectures evolved from a simple terminal-oriented application at the mainframe being accessed via a so-called *dumb terminal* (IBM 3270s), as shown in Figure 15.1.

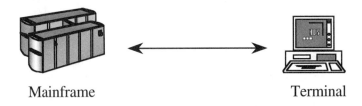

Mainframe   Terminal

Fig. 15.1 Traditional Terminal-Oriented Client/Server

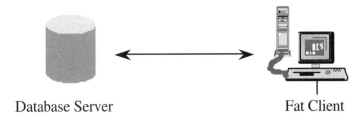

Database Server   Fat Client

Fig. 15.2 Traditional Two-Tier Client/Server

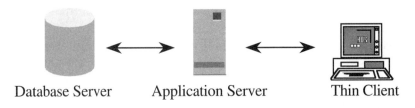

Database Server   Application Server   Thin Client

Fig. 15.3 Thin Client Architecture

The traditional client/server received a real boost when the IBM PC became popular. This gave birth to a two-tier client/server, as shown in Figure 15.2. It places the application on the client, which communicates with the server over a network.

15.2.1 Problems

While this two-tier client/server approach works well for smaller applications, significant performance and maintenance issues prevent it from scaling well to large or enterprise applications.

Such performance problems usually are termed *fat client syndrome*, since the application is resident on the client. Because all processing takes place on the client, large quantities of unnecessary data is sent over the network, which places an enormous burden on it.

For example, a financial application that analyzes a historical record of commodity prices to make sell/buy recommendations may need to pass thousands of bytes of data over the network at a time. In addition, data errors over the network could cause delays in final application executions. On the other hand, it is much more efficient if all the computational numerical analysis is performed on the server where the data resides, saving the network bandwidth and preserving the integrity of the data. Of course, only the final results are passed to the client over the network.

This approach also has significant maintenance problems, because the client application is monolithic and the client software must be redeployed at each desktop, every time a change is made. Redeployment is particularly troublesome. Every time a business rule changes, the organization must redeploy an application to many clients in the enterprise. This negates any flexibility that client/server architecture has over the mainframe type of setup.

15.2.2 Thin Client Architecture

With the proliferation of the Internet, *thin client* architecture was developed in the client/server space (Figure 15.3). This attempts to address the redeployment problem by separating the client presentation service (graphics user interface) from the rest of the application. This is not a traditional client GUI but rather an HTML page that is downloaded to the client on demand or via the "push" mechanism.

Because this GUI resides on the server and is downloaded each time it is required, it may be updated at will, thereby lowering maintenance and network costs and enhancing flexibility.

Unfortunately, such an approach does not address the monolithic nature of the client application. Therefore, it usually is classed as a natural descendent of the traditional client/server architecture. It does not even begin to address the distributed environments of multiprocessing computing.

15.2.3 n-Tier Architectures

To address the problems discussed previously, a new generation of client/server technology has emerged. This technology supports an n-tier (≥ 3-tier) model of application development as shown in Figure 15.4. In this approach, the application is partitioned into three or more tiers: The client, business objects, and the server.

The client is primarily responsible for interaction with the user and other pertinent tasks, while the server plays the traditional role. The nth-tier (business objects) reflects core business tasks such as statistical analysis, inventory control, conversion middleware, and order processing, which may be shared among enterprisewide applications. There are several key benefits of this middle tier of shared business objects.

15.2.3.1 Improved Performance   Processing can take place where it is most efficient. Separately shared business objects can run on various machines, including the machines on which the DBMS is located. In addition, multiple instances of the same application/business object can be used via load balancing to further improve performance. The multiprocessor systems can take additional advantages of the business objects located in their vicinity, without having to depend on network delays.

15.2.3.2 Improved Reliability and Fault Tolerance   Business objects may be made redundant. If one should fail, another can take its place.

15.2.3.3 Simplified Maintenance   Business rules do not have to reside on the client. They can reside in a shared object on a centralized server, where they

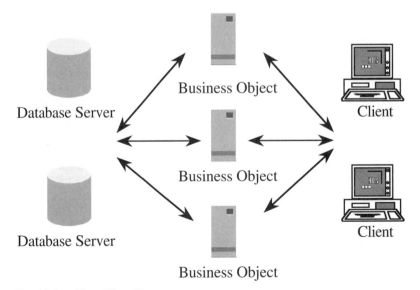

Fig. 15.4 n-Tier Client/Server

can be better managed on an enterprise basis. With increased modularity, changes to individual business objects can be made without affecting other business objects.

15.2.3.4 Reduced Development   Multiple applications can reuse the same business objects.

15.3 ENTERPRISE DISTRIBUTED INFRASTRUCTURES

The business benefits of an n-tier client/server architecture are compelling. The enterprise reality is far more complex than most n-tier implementations exhibit. In fact, such an approach can deploy multiple servers, multiple databases, and multiple processors. However, two problems must be addressed: Synchronization and resource sharing.

With respect to distributed computing, the typical enterprise has a combination of most, if not all, of the architectures described above. It usually has some mainframe-critical applications it has no intention of replacing. These might include financial applications such as accounts receivable and accounts payable. Such enterprises also have a mix of fat client and thin client applications with Internet access.

All these applications may be interconnected and need to share the data. As shown in Figure 15.5, a Web-based application (thin client) provides presentation services to external customers that may be accessing applications residing on the mainframe. Another system (n-tier setup) is accessing a number of other objects as well as the mainframe. It is also accessible via the thin

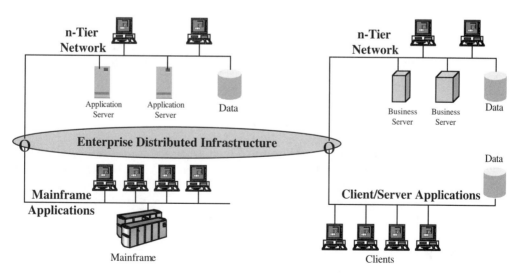

Fig. 15.5 Enterprise Distributed Infrastructure

client. In addition, all of these applications and their related data resources are being accessed for application management purposes, as well as for corporate summarizations at the end of the day.

15.4 TYPES OF INFRASTRUCTURES

A large number of infrastructures are deployed in the industry. Four of these—transaction processing, messaging, application management, and object RPC—are most common.

15.4.1 Transaction Processing

TP monitors and systems are designed to coordinate transactions across many processes. In addition, transaction-processing monitors provide load balancing, activation, and thread pooling.

15.4.2 Messaging

Messaging is widely used in mission-critical applications. It offers offline processing, guaranteed delivery, and improved overall performance through asynchronous processing.

15.4.3 Application Management

Using their own protocols, such tools monitor applications for remote systems. However, in order to save life-cycle costs, applications must also rely on the same protocols in addition to their native protocols.

15.4.4 Object RPC

DCOM and CORBA are the major object RPCs implemented extensively in n-tiered applications. However, unbundled RPCs are cumbersome in developing and debugging n-tier applications.

15.5 INFRASTRUCTURE CONNECTIVITY

Each of the applications, whether mission-critical or generic, is built on a different software infrastructure. Therefore, connectivity requires a special-purpose custom coding, involving impedance matching of particular distributed infrastructures. In any enterprise, the distributed computing connectivity falls into two major groups: Bundled and unbundled.

15.5.1 Bundled

This includes any application or tool that comes with its own infrastructure: For example, applications from SAP and most 4GL tools from Forte and Power-

Soft. The primary advantage of such tools is that they are seamlessly integrated with the application, resulting in reduced development overhead. However, such tools often are proprietary and rarely follow industry standards, such as CORBA. Thus they create problems for interoperability, migration, or best-of-breed enhancements.

15.5.2 Unbundled

This includes a standalone infrastructure such as IBM's MQSeries Messaging. The distributed infrastructures for unbundled groups fall into the following categories:

☞ Messaging systems, such as IBM's MQSeries and DEC's MessageQ

☞ Transactional systems, such as BEA's Tuxedo and Microsoft's Transaction Server

☞ Object RPC systems, such as Microsoft's DCOM and CORBA object-request brokers

☞ Systems and application management protocols, such as CMIP, SNMP, OpenView, and Tivoli's TME framework

Each of the these categories provides special-purpose capabilities. As a result, making a connection across applications that use heterogeneous infrastructures becomes challenging. However, the distinctions among categories are blurring as technologies and implementations merge. Still, the categories remain relevant because a particular category may offer more advantages in one implementation than another. Therefore, it may be some time before the complete benefits of connecting architectures are realized.

15.6 EVOLUTIONARY TRENDS

Two major trends are influencing the evolution of distributed multiprocessing: Enterprise-distributed multiprocessing and the development of business-to-business distributed computing applications in which connectivity is provided by the Internet.

15.6.1 Enterprise-Distributed Architecture

There are two fundamental reasons for creating enterprise-distributed architecture. One is to reduce the integration costs by replacing the plethora of special-purpose hard-coded integrations with a more general-purpose architecture. The second is to reduce management costs by unifying the disparate and disconnected infrastructures under a single, manageable distributed computing architecture.

As shown in Figure 15.6, each of the diverse distributed computing systems is tied to a backbone. This backbone is robust and scalable to integrate the enterprise.

15.6.2 Business-to-Business Applications

Enterprises have seen the benefits of providing services such as customer support, order fulfillment, and catalog access/search via the Internet. Such business-to-business connectivity is provided by electronic commerce applications and is advancing by leaps and bounds.

Vertical integration is only one of the opportunities made possible over the Internet. Horizontal integration also is beginning to pick up momentum.

15.7 CONCLUSIONS

In this book I have described distributed multiprocessing and its problems. The primary problems in the design of a distributed operating system that must be addressed are listed below:

Network latency: The advantages of the resources gained through collaboration are offset by the increase in communication times between machines.

Coherency: The workstations must conspire together to produce the illusion of a single virtual memory. The choice of coherency mechanism may have an impact on the amount of network traffic generated.

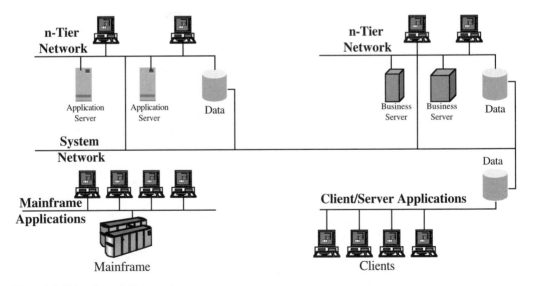

Fig. 15.6 Distributed Enterprise

Heterogeneity: The collaborating machines probably will not all be code- or data-compatible. The translation of data and the use of "fat8" binaries can address this problem, but every effort must be made to avoid their costly use at runtime.

Fault tolerance: Distributing a process and its memory over a number of machines increases its vulnerability to host and network failures.

One of the early promises of client/server distributed processing was to reduce IT expenditures. In many cases, this has not been fulfilled. The cost of owning a large number of PCs running distributed applications over a network has turned out to be much higher than expected, in particular when hidden costs like internal professional services are accounted for. This is compounded by the fact that these new business systems have empowered users to be more productive, which means they consume more resources. At the same time, the mainframe has not been unplugged; it still runs major mission-critical applications that must be maintained. It also carries an additional burden of increased networking with intelligent clients.

Originally, the move to client/server was driven largely by a rightsizing strategy. At the same time, corporate hierarchies have been flattened and individual departments or lines of business have been empowered to make their own decisions about information technology. This has led to solutions that fit the narrow focus of individual departments. They form islands of applications and technologies that cannot provide a single system image to end users who need information that spans departments. It also makes necessary manual steps in order to conduct a business workflow across different lines of business. Because of the lack of integration, these islands of automation cannot support the flow of information and control.

Finally, increased global competition, mergers and acquisitions, and the need to react quickly to emerging market opportunities have contributed to the drastic reduction of acceptable application development cycles. What used to be developed in 18 months must now be done in 3 to 6 months. This need to support a faster time to market means that, for many new business systems, one cannot afford to build from scratch. This leads to questions like, which pieces of a legacy system can be salvaged? And how can they be converted into reusable building blocks? Not only can this compress development time, it also can increase the return on investment, since legacy applications already have been paid for.

Distributed multiprocessing and the Internet are at the core of future innovations. The potential benefits this marriage offers are enormous. However, the costs involved in integrating and managing the complex, heterogeneous distributed computing infrastructures will continue to climb for the foreseeable future.

GLOSSARY

Access Control List (ACL). List that grants the user access to an object and defines its capabilities (i.e., what the user can do to the object). An access control list specifies the privilege attribute(s) needed to access the object and the permissions that can be granted, with respect to the protected object, to principals possessing such privilege attribute(s).

ACM. Association for Computing Machinery.

Ad Hoc Query. Request or query about which the system has no prior knowledge or built-in functions for servicing. Ad hoc queries are distinguished from standard reports, where specific information is sought in a certain format about specific subjects on a regular basis.

Ad Hoc Query Tool. An end-user tool that accepts an Englishlike or point-and-click request for data and constructs an ad hoc query to retrieve the desired result.

Adapter. A board installed in a computer system to provide network communication capabilities to and from that computer system. Also called a Network Interface Card (NIC).

Adobe Acrobat. Cross-platform software that allows you to view and print formatted documents accessed from the Web or a file server.

AFS. Andrew File System (protocols).

AFTP. Anonymous File Transfer Protocol.

Agent. An entity that performs operations on behalf of other objects, systems, and agents.

Aggregation. In the broad sense, used to mean aggregating data horizontally, vertically, and chronologically.

AIX. Advanced Interactive Executive [IBM].

Alerts. A notification from an event that has exceeded a predefined threshold.

Alternate Routing. A mechanism that supports the use of a new path after a failed attempt to set up a connection along a previously selected path.

American Standard Code for Information Interchange (ASCII). The code that most computers use to represent displayable characters. An ASCII file is a straightforward text file without special control characters.

ANSI. American National Standards Institute.

APPC. Advanced Program-to-Program Communications [IBM].

APPI. Advanced Peer-to-Peer Internetworking.

Applet. A small application program written in Java and commonly distributed in an attachment in a Web document to be executed by a Java-enabled web browser.

Application. A program or a set of programs that provide functionality to the end user.

Application Layer. Layer 7 of the OSI Reference Model; implemented by various network applications including file transfer, electronic mail, and terminal emulation.

Application Objects. Applications and their components that are managed within an object-oriented system. Example operations on such objects are "Open," "Install," "Move," "Re-move," and "remove."

Application Programming Interface (API). A set of callable routines that a programmer uses to interact with an application.

Application-Level Firewall. A firewall system in which service is provided by processes that maintain complete TCP connection state and sequencing. Application-level firewalls often readdress traffic so that outgoing traffic appears to have originated from the firewall rather than the internal host.

APPN. Advanced Peer-to-Peer Networking [IBM].

Architecture. A definition and preliminary design that describes the components of a solution and their interactions. An architecture is the blueprint by which implementers construct a solution which meets the users' needs.

ARPANET. Advanced Research Projects Agency Network.

ASCII. American Standard Code for Information Interchange.

ASCII File. Document containing only unformatted standard text characters without any graphics or special coding.

ASIC. Application-Specific Integrated Circuit.

Assignment. Copying the values of one object into another object. The details of such an assignment vary according to the implementation language used.

Associations. A statistical measure that shows the degree to which two variables are related.

ASYNC. Asynchronous.

Asynchronous. Referring to two or more signals that, though they have the same nominal rates, actually operate at different rates.

Asynchronous Message Communication. Provides the capability for objects to send messages, even without the existence of the receiving object at the instant the message is sent. The receiving object can retrieve messages at its convenience. There is no blocking or synchronization required between objects. Asynchronous message communication is a foundation for constructing concurrent computing environments.

Asynchronous Operation. An operation that does not cause the process or thread requesting the operation to be blocked from further use of the CPU. This implies that the process and the operation are running concurrently.

Asynchronous Protocol. A type of transmission in which information is sent at any speed and at random with no routing information.

Asynchronous Request. A request in which the client object does not pause or wait for delivery of the request to the recipient, nor does it wait for the results.

Asynchronous Transfer Mode (ATM). (1) The CCITT standard for cell relay wherein information for multiple types of services (voice, video, data) is conveyed in small, fixed-size cells. ATM is a connection-oriented technology used in both LAN and WAN environments. (2) A fast-packet switching technology allowing free allocation of capacity to each channel. The SONET synchronous payload envelope is a variation of ATM. (3) An international ISDN high-speed, high-volume, packet-switching transmission protocol standard. ATM currently accommodates transmission speeds from 64 Kbps to 622 Mbps.

Atomic Data. Data elements that represent the lowest level of detail. For example, in a daily sales report, the individual items sold are atomic data, while rollups such as invoice and summary totals from invoices are aggregate data.

Attribute. An identifiable association between an object and a value. An attribute A is made visible to clients as a pair of operations—get_A and set_A. Read-only attributes only generate a get operation. A characteristic or property of an object. Usually implemented as a simple data member or as an association with another object or group of objects.

Authentication. The process of assuring that data has come from its claimed source or of corroborating the claimed identity of a communicating party.

Authentication Protocol. A formal procedure for verifying a principal's network identity; Kerberos is an instance of a shared-secret authentication protocol.

Authentication Token. A portable device used for authenticating a user. Operates by challenge/response, time-based code sequences, or other techniques. This may include paper-based lists of one-time passwords.

Authorization. The process of determining what types of activities are permitted. Usually, authorization is in the context of authentication—once authenticated, a user may be authorized different types of access or activity.

Authorization Rules. Criteria used to determine whether an individual group or application may access reference data or a process.

Availability. A measure of the percentage of time that a computer system is capable of supporting a user request. A system may be considered unavailable as a result of events such as system failures or unplanned application outages.

Bandwidth. (1) Measure of the information capacity of a transmission channel. (2) The difference between the highest and lowest frequencies of a band that can be passed by a transmission medium without undue distortion, such as the AM band, 535 to 1705 kilohertz. (3) Information-carrying capacity of a communication channel. *Analog bandwidth* is the range of signal frequencies that can be transmitted by a communication channel or network. (4) A term used to indicate the amount of transmission or processing capacity possessed by a system or a specific location in a system (usually a network system).

Baud. Rate at which data is transmitted over a modem connection. *See* bps.

Bidirectional Extracts. The ability to extract, cleanse, and transfer data in two directions among different types of databases, including hierarchical, networked, and relational databases.

Bin. Common UNIX term for a directory where executable programs are stored in binary form.

Binary. Number system based on two components, usually the digits 0 and 1. The method most computers use to handle data.

Binding. The selection of the method to perform a requested service and of the data to be accessed by that method.

BIOS. Basic Input/Output System.

Bit. Binary digit, either 0 or 1.

Bit-Mapped Indexes. Indexing techniques that use binary encoding to represent data. Originally used only for low-cardinality data, recent advances, such as Sybase IQ, have allowed this technique to be used for high-cardinality data as well.

Bps. "Bits per second"—the rate at which data is transmitted between two computers or between one computer and a peripheral.

Bridge/Router. A device that can provide the functions of a bridge and router or both concurrently. Bridge/router can route one or more protocols, such as TCP/IP and/or XNS, and bridge all other traffic.

Browser. Application that provides a graphical interface for exploring the Web; or the client machine that requests WWW information from a Web server.

Bulk Data Transfer. A software-based mechanism designed to move large data files. It supports compression, blocking, and buffering to optimize transfer times.

Business Architecture. One of the four layers of an IT architecture—information, business, applications, and technology. Describes and defines the business processes used within an organization.

Business Data. Information about people, places, things, business rules, and events. Used to operate a business. It is not metadata. (Metadata defines and describes business data.)

Business Rules. The statements and stipulations that a corporation has set as "standard" in order to run the enterprise more consistently and smoothly.

Byte. The most common unit of computer storage.

Cache. A high-speed dynamic memory used as a buffer between the CPU and physical disk storage to mitigate or eliminate potential speed differences between access times to physical disks and faster system memory. In storage arrays, cache implementation is usually nonvolatile to ensure data integrity.

Caching. The technique of copying data from a server machine (its central storage place) to a client machine's local disk or memory; users then access the copy locally. Caching reduces network load because the data does not have to be fetched across the network more than once (unless the central copy changes).

Capacity Planning. The process of considering the effects of a warehouse on other system resources such as response time, DASD requirements, etc.

Cardinality. The number of data occurrences allowed on either side of a data relation. In the common data architecture, cardinality is documented with data integrity, not with the data structure.

Catalog. A component of a data dictionary that contains a directory of its DBMS objects as well as attributes of each object.

CDR. Common Data Representation.

Cell. The basic unit of operation in the DCE. A cell is a group of users, systems, and resources that are typically centered around a common purpose and that share common DCE services.

Cell Directory Service (CDS). A distributed, replicated naming service.

Central Warehouse. A database created from operational extracts that adheres to a single, consistent, enterprise data model to ensure consistency of decision-support data across the corporation. A style of computing where all the information systems are located and managed from a single physical location.

CGI (Common Gateway Interface). Standard method for providing a gateway between browsers and programs (usually written in Perl or C) running on a Web server.

CIOP. Common Inter-ORB Protocol.

Class. In object programming, a type or group of objects, all having the same properties, operations, or behavior. Types classify objects according to a common interface; classes classify objects according to a common implementation.

Class Attribute. A characteristic or property that is the same for all instances of a class. This information is usually stored in the class type definition.

Class Hierarchy. Embodies the inheritance relationships between classes.

Class Inheritance. The construction of a class by incremental modification of other classes.

Class Member. A method or an attribute of a class.

Class Method. A class method defines the behavior of the class. Such a method performs tasks that cannot or should not be done at the instance level, such as providing access to class attributes or tracking class usage metrics.

Class Object. An object that serves as a class. A class object serves as a factory.

Classification. The process of dividing a data set into mutually exclusive groups such that the members of each group are as "close" as possible to one another and different groups are as "far" as possible from one another, where distance is measured with respect to specific variable(s) you are trying to predict. For example, a typical classification problem is to divide a database of customers into groups that are as homogeneous as possible with respect to a creditworthiness variable with values "Good" and "Bad."

Client. An object that requests a service from a server object in a client/server relationship. The code or process that invokes an operation on an object.

Client/Server. A distributed technology approach where the processing is divided by function. The server performs shared functions—managing communications, providing database services, etc. The client performs individual user functions—providing customized interfaces, performing screen-to-screen navigation, offering help functions, etc.

Client/Server Processing. A form of cooperative processing in which the end-user interaction is through a programmable workstation that must execute some part of the application logic over and above display formatting and terminal emulation.

Collaboration. Two or more objects participating in a client/server relationship in order to provide a service.

Collection. A set of data that resulted from a DBMS query.

COM. Microsoft's Common Object Model.

Common Object Request Broker Architecture (CORBA, CORBA 2). A specification for objects to locate and activate one another through an object request broker. CORBA 2 extends the specification to facilitate object request brokers from different vendors to interoperate.

Component. A conceptual notion. A component is an object that is considered to be part of some containing object. Classes, systems, or subsystems can be designed as reusable pieces. These pieces can then be assembled to create various new applications.

Composition. The creation of an object that is an aggregation of one or more objects.

Conceptual Schema. A schema that represents a common structure of data that is the common denominator between the internal schema and external schema.

Configuration. Settings that control program or system behavior. Usually, a system must be configured before it is used and often may be reconfigured between uses.

Connectivity. The ability of a device to connect to another. This includes the physical issues associated with the busses, connector topologies, and other components as well as the support of the protocols required to pass data successfully over the physical connection.

Consistent Data Quality. The state of a data resource in which the quality of existing data is thoroughly understood and the desired quality of the data resource is known. It is a state where disparate data quality is known, and the existing data quality is being adjusted to the level desired to meet the current and future business information demand.

Constraint. A relational or behavioral restriction or limit. Usually regarded as a property that must always hold true.

CORBA. Common Object Request Broker Architecture.

Coupling. A dependency between two or more classes, usually resulting from collaboration between the classes to provide a service. Loose coupling is based on generic behavior and allows many different classes to be coupled in the same way. Tight coupling is based on more specific implementation details of the participating classes and is not as flexible.

CPU (Central Processing Unit). The "brain" of a computer, where most data is processed.

Data. Items representing facts, text, graphics, bit-mapped images, sound, or analog or digital live-video segments. Data is the raw material of a system supplied by data producers and is used by information consumers to create information.

Data Access. Equipment and/or software applications that permit connection and attachment to data stores. Commonly means access to relational databases.

Data Access Tool. An end-user-oriented tool that allows users to build SQL queries by pointing and clicking on a list of tables and fields in the data warehouse.

Data Accuracy. The component of data integrity that deals with how well data stored in the data resource represents the real world. It includes a definition of the current data accuracy and the adjustment in data accuracy to meet the business needs.

Data Aggregation. A type of data derivation where a data value is derived from the aggregation of two or more contributing data characteristics in different data occurrences within the same data subject.

Data Architecture. (1) The science and method of designing and constructing an integrated data resource that is business-driven, based on real-world objects and events as perceived by the organization, and implemented in appropriate operating environments. The overall structure of a data resource that provides a consistent foundation across organizational boundaries to provide easily identifiable, readily available, high-quality data to support the business information demand. (2) The component of the data resource framework that contains all activities, and the products of those activities, related to the identification, naming, definition, structuring, quality, and documentation of the data resource for an organization.

Data Attribute. Represents a data characteristic variation that is used in a logical data model.

Data Capture. The collection of information, usually at the time a transaction occurs, in a form that can be used by a computer system (for example, the recording of a withdrawal from an automated cash machine). The term also applies to saving on a storage medium (a disk) a record of the interchanges between the user and a remote information utility.

Data Cardinality. A property of data elements that indicates the number of allowable entries in that element. For example, a data element such as "gender" only allows two entries—"male" or "female." Data elements that have few allowable entries are said to possess "low cardinality." Those, such as "age" or "income," for which many allowable entries are possible, are said to have "high cardinality."

Data Characteristic. An individual characteristic that describes a data subject. It is developed, directly through measurement or indirectly through derivation, from a feature of an object or event. Each data subject is described by a set of data characteristics.

Data Cleansing. The process of manipulating the data extracted from operational systems so as to make it usable by the data warehouse. When loading data from existing operational systems, it is likely that few if any of the operational systems will have data to present in a format compatible with the data model developed for the warehouse. For example, a product number may be held as a numeric field in one system while a second system appends an alpha suffix to the number for reporting purposes.

Data Cluster. A temporary group of data subjects for a specific purpose. It can be any useful combination of data subjects for any specific purpose that cannot be met by any of the other categorical levels.

Data Collection. The process of acquiring source documents or data; also, the grouping of data elements into a coherent whole through classifying, sorting, ordering, and other organizational techniques.

Data Compression. Mathematical techniques used to reduce the amount of storage required for certain data.

Data Concurrency. The situation in which the replicated data values are synchronized with the corresponding data values at the official data source. When the data values at the official data source are updated, the replicated data values must also be updated so they are consistent with the official data source.

Data Consistency. The result of using a repository to capture and manage data as it changes so that decision-support systems can be continually updated.

Data Conversion. The process of changing data from one physical environment to another. This process makes any changes necessary to move data from one electronic medium or database product to another.

Data Delivery. The electronic movement of data stored in remote locations to a user's desktop.

Data Denormalization. The process of developing internal schema from conceptual schema.

Data Dictionary. A database about data and database structures. A catalog of all data elements, containing their names, structures, and information about their usage. A central location for metadata. Normally, data dictionaries are designed to store a limited set of available metadata, concentrating on the information relating to the data elements, databases, files, and programs of implemented systems.

Data Distribution. The placement and maintenance of replicated data at one or more data sites on a mainframe computer or across a telecommunications network. The part of developing and maintaining an integrated data resource that ensures data is properly managed when distributed across many different data sites. Data distribution is one type of data deployment, which is the transfer of data to data sites.

Data Element. The most elementary unit of data that can be identified or described in a dictionary or repository and that cannot be subdivided.

Data Encryption. Encoding of file contents so that they are unreadable or difficult to read without the original encoder key.

Data Encryption Standard (DES). A popular encryption scheme.

Data File. A representation of a data entity from the logical data model that is implemented with a physical data model. It is a physical file of data that exists in a database management system, as a computer file outside a database management system, or as a manual file outside a computer that represents a data entity.

Data Fragmentation. A nonorderly process of placing data at various data sites. It is not done within the common data architecture, is not well-managed or documented, and results in unknown, undocumented, redundant data.

Data Generalization. The process of creating successive layers of summary data in an evaluational database. It is a process of zooming out to get a broader view of a problem, trend, or situation. It is also known as rolling up data.

Data Integrity. The formal definition of comprehensive rules and the consistent application of those rules to assure high-integrity data. It consists of techniques to determine how well data is maintained in the data resource and to ensure that the data resource contains data that has high integrity. Data integrity includes techniques for data-value integrity, data-structure integrity, data-retention integrity, and data-derivation integrity.

Data Key. A set of one or more data characteristics that have a special meaning and use in addition to describing a feature or trait of a data subject. Data keys are important for uniquely identifying data occurrences in each data subject and for navigating through the data resource.

Data Layer. A separate and distinct set of related spatial data that is stored and maintained in a spatial database. It represents a particular theme or topic of interest in the real world and is equivalent to a data subject.

Data Management. Controlling, protecting, and facilitating access to data in order to provide information consumers with timely access to the data they need. The functions provided by a database management system.

Data Mapping. The process of assigning a source data element to a target data element.

Data Mining. (1) The process of utilizing the results of data exploration to adjust or enhance business strategies. It builds on the patterns, trends, and exceptions found through data exploration to support the business. Also known as data harvesting. (2) A technique using software tools geared for users who typically do not know exactly what they are searching for, but are looking for patterns or trends. Data mining is the process of sifting through large amounts of data to produce data content relationships. Also known as data surfing.

Data Model. A logical map that represents the inherent properties of the data, independent of software, hardware, or machine performance considerations. The model shows data elements grouped into records and the association those records share.

Data Normalization. A process to develop a conceptual schema from external schema.

Data Optimization. A process that prepares the logical schema from the data view schema.

Data Partitioning. (1) The formal process of determining which data subjects, data occurrence groups, and data characteristics are needed at each data site. It is an orderly process for allocating data to data sites that is done within the same common data architecture. (2) The process of logically and/or physically partitioning data into segments that are more easily maintained or accessed. Current RDBMS systems provide this kind of distribution functionality. Partitioning of data aids in performance and utility processing.

Data Quality. Indicates how well data in the data resource meets the business information demand. Data quality includes data integrity, data accuracy, and data completeness.

Data Refining. A process that refines disparate data within a common context to remove data variability and redundancy, and develop an integrated data resource. Disparate data is the raw material and an integrated data resource is the final product.

Data Refreshing. The process of updating active data replicates based on a regular, known schedule. The frequency and timing of data refreshing must be established to match business.

Data Replication. (1) A formal process of creating exact copies of a set of data from the data site containing the official data source and placing this data at other data sites. (2) The process of copying a portion of a database from one environment to another and keeping the subsequent copies of the data in sync with the original source. Changes made to the original source are propagated to the copies of the data in other environments.

Data Repository. A logical (and sometimes physical) partitioning of data where databases applying to specific applications or sets of applications reside. For example, several databases (revenues and expenses) that support financial applications (A/R, A/P) could reside in a single financial data repository.

Data Resource. A component of information-technology infrastructure that represents all the data available to an organization, whether automated or nonautomated.

Data Sharing. The process of understanding the content and meaning of data, identifying and selecting the appropriate data to meet business needs, and sharing that data.

Data Source. A site where data is stored and from which it can be obtained. Any source of data from a specific organization, such as a database or data file. A data source may include nonautomated data, but it does not include unpublished documents containing data.

Data Store. A place where data is stored; data at rest. A generic term that includes databases and flat files.

Data Structure. A representation of the arrangement, relationship, and contents of data subjects, data entities, and data files in the common data architecture. It includes all logical and physical data within the common data architecture.

Data Summarization. The process of summarizing primitive evaluational data or derived evaluational data to create more generalized derived evaluational data.

Data Synchronization. The process of identifying active data replicates and ensuring that data concurrency is maintained. Also known as data-version synchronization or data-version concurrency because all replicated data values are consistent with the same version as the official data.

Data Terminal Equipment (DTE). The part of a data station that serves as a data source or destination or both. DTE provides for the data communications control function according to protocol and includes computers, protocol translators, and multiplexers.

Data Transfer. The process of moving data from one environment to another. An environment may be an application system or operating environment.

Data Transformation. The formal process of altering data in the data resource. It includes transforming disparate data to an integrated data resource, transforming data within the integrated data resource, transforming disparate data, and transforming operational, historical, and evaluational data within a common data architecture.

Data Translation. The process of converting data from one form to another when moving between different DBMSs.

Data Type. The form of a data value, including dates and numbers and string, floating-point, packed, and double-precision.

Data Value. The individual facts and figures contained in data characteristics and their variations, data attributes, and data items.

Data Visualization. The process of creating and presenting a chart from a set of data based on a set of attributes. It required recognizing patterns, trends, and relationships in historical data and providing visual information based on them.

Data Warehouse. (1) A subject-oriented, integrated, time-variant, nonvolatile collection of data in support of management's decision-making process. A repository of consistent historical data that can be easily accessed and manipulated for decision support. (2) An implementation of an informational database used to store sharable data sourced from an operational database-of-record. It is typically a subject database that allows users to tap into a company's vast store of operational data to track and respond to business trends and facilitate forecasting and planning efforts.

Database. A collection of logically related data.

Database Administrator (DBA). The individual or group of individuals responsible for a database. Typically, the DBA is responsible for determining the information content of the database, determining the internal storage structure and access strategy for the database, defining data security and integrity checks, and monitoring database performance and responding to changing requirements.

Database Management System (DBMS). A layer of software between the physical database and the user. The DBMS manages all requests for database action (for example, queries or updates) from the user. Thus, the user is spared the necessity of tracking the physical details of file locations and formats, indexing schemes, and so on. In addition, a DBMS permits centralized control of security and data integrity functions.

Database Schema. The logical and physical definition of a database structure.

DB2. Database 2 from IBM.

DCE. OSF's Distributed Computing Environment. It includes data communications equipment, distributed computing environment (OSF), or distributed computing equipment.

DCF. Data Communication Facility.

Decentralized Database. A centralized database that has been partitioned according to a business- or end-user-defined subject area. Typically, ownership is also moved to the owners of the subject area.

Decision-Support Systems (DSS). Software that supports exception reporting, stop light reporting, standard repository, data analysis, and rule-based analysis. A database created for end-user ad hoc query processing.

Denormalized Data Store. A data store that does not comply to one or more of several normal forms. *See* normalization.

Derived Data. Data that is the result of a computational step applied to reference or event data. Derived data is the result either of relating two or more elements of a single transaction (such as an aggregation) or of relating one or more elements of a transaction to an external algorithm or rule.

Design. A process that uses the products of analysis to produce a specification for implementing a system.

Dial Up. A type of communication that is established by a switched-circuit connection using the telephone network.

DII. CORBA Dynamic Invocation Interface.

DIR. Dynamic Implementation Routine.

Disparate Data. Data items that are essentially unalike, or are distinctly different in kind, quality, or character. They are unequal and cannot be readily integrated to meet the business information demand adequately. Heterogeneous data.

Disparate Databases. Databases or database management systems that are not electronically or operationally compatible. Disparate databases are known as heterogeneous databases.

Disparate Operational Data. The current-value operational data that supports daily business transactions. It is the disparate data, including both tabular and nontabular data, that most organizations use to support their daily business operations.

Distributed Database Management System. A software product that manages and maintains the distributed database and makes it transparent to clients. Data flows freely over any network or combination of networks using one or more network protocols.

Distributed Database System. (1) A combination of distributed databases and distributed database management systems. Any database management system can interact with any other database management system across multiple system configurations to provide data to clients. (2) Systems in which the database storage is dispersed across multiple machines and physical locations.

Distributed File Service (DFS). A file service that joins the local file systems of several file servers, making the file systems equally available to all DFS client machines.

Distributed Object Computing (DOC). A computing paradigm that distributes cooperating objects across a heterogeneous network and allows the objects to interoperate as a unified whole.

Distributed Processing. Spreads the work of program execution and data retrieval over multiple machines. It is the opposite of having one huge computer that serves all users simultaneously.

Distributed Time Service (DTS). Synchronizes the clocks in networked systems and is responsible for propagating a consistent notion of time throughout a cell.

DME. Distributed Management Environment.

DNS (Domain Name Server). Server that matches IP addresses with their associated machine names.

Domain. A formal boundary defining a particular subject or area of interest.

Domain Naming Service (DNS). A distributed directory service used on the Internet. Along with GDS, it provides a global name space that connects local DCE cells into one worldwide hierarchy.

DOS (Disk Operating System). Command-line operating environment used on some PCs (for example, Microsoft's MS-DOS or IBM's PC-DOS).

Download. To transmit a file from a remote computer to a local one.

Drill Down. A method of exploring detailed data that was used in creating a summary level of data. Drill-down levels depend on the granularity of the data in the data warehouse.

DSOM. Distributed System Object Model.

Dynamic Invocation. Constructing and issuing a request whose signature is not known until runtime.

Dynamic Link Library (DLL). A dynamically loaded runtime library.

Dynamic Object-Based Application. The end-user functionality provided by one or more programs consisting of interoperating objects.

Dynamic Password Authentication Servers. Products consisting of server software that generates constantly changing passwords and two-factor software- or hardware-based passwords.

Dynamic Queries. Dynamically constructed SQL that is usually constructed by desktop-resident query tools. Queries that are not preprocessed and are prepared and executed at runtime.

Dynamic Routing. Routing that adjusts automatically to changes in network topology or traffic.

EBCDIC. Extended Binary Coded Decimal Interchange Code [IBM].

EIS. Executive Information System.

Embedding. Creating an object out of a nonobject entity by wrapping it in an appropriate shell.

Encapsulation. The technique used to hide the implementation details of an object. The services provided by an object are defined and accessible as stated in the object contract. (Often used interchangeably with information hiding.)

Encryption. Applying a specific algorithm to data to alter the data's appearance and prevent other devices from reading the information. Decryption applies the algorithm in reverse to restore the data to its original form.

Enterprise. A complete business consisting of functions, divisions, or other components used to accomplish specific objectives and defined goals.

Enterprise Data Model. A blueprint for all of the data used by all departments in the enterprise. Resolves all of the potential inconsistencies and parochial interpretations of the data and presents a consistent and commonly understood and accepted view and definition of the enterprise data.

Enterprise System Connection Architecture (ESCON). An IBM mainframe channel architecture commonly used to attach storage devices.

ESIOP. Environment-Specific Inter-ORB Protocol.

Ethernet. (1) A baseband LAN specification invented by Xerox Corporation and developed jointly by Xerox, Intel, and Digital Equipment Corporation. Uses CSMA/CD to run over coaxial cable. (2) A common method of networking computers in a LAN. Ethernet will handle about 10 megabits per second and can be used with almost any kind of computer.

Event. (1) A happening in the real world. (2) A significant change in the environment or the state of an object that is of interest to another object or system.

Exchange Format. Form of a description used to import and export objects.

Executive Information Systems (EIS). Tools programmed to provide canned reports or briefing books to top-level executives. They offer strong reporting and drill-down capabilities and allow ad hoc querying against a multidimensional database. Most offer analytical applications along functional lines such as sales or financial analysis.

Export. To transmit the description of an object to an external entity.

Extranet. An instantiation of an Internet in which an organization allows its external partners to participate in the internal data warehouse.

Fault Tolerance. The characteristic of a system that allows it to handle the loss of a particular component without interrupting normal operations.

File Server. Computer used to store files and share them with other computers on a network.

File Sharing. Use of file servers to exchange files between networked computers.

File Transfer Protocol (FTP). (1) An IP application protocol for transferring files between network nodes. (2) An Internet protocol that allows a user on one host to transfer files to and from another host over a network.

Firewall. (1) Isolation of LAN segments from each other to protect data resources and help manage traffic. (2) Hardware or software that restricts traffic to a private network from an unsecured network.

Fractional T-1. A WAN communications service that provides the user with a portion of a T-1 circuit that has been divided into 24 separate 64-Kbps channels. Fractional E-1 is the European version.

Fragmentation. The process in which a packet is broken into smaller pieces, fragments, to fit the requirements of a physical network through which the packet must pass.

Frame Relay. High-performance interface for packet-switching networks. Considered more efficient than X.25, which it is expected to replace. Frame-relay technology can handle "bursty" communications that have rapidly changing bandwidth requirements.

Framework. A set of collaborating abstract and concrete classes that may be used as a template to solve a specific domain problem.

Fraud Detection. The use of technologies such as data mining to look through large amounts of data and discern patterns that may indicate fraudulent use of a company's product. For example, credit card companies review transaction data to see if a customer's usage profile has suddenly changed.

Frequently Asked Questions (FAQ). Usually appears in the form of a "read-me" file in a variety of Internet formats. New users are expected to read the FAQ before participating in newsgroups, bulletin boards, video conferences, and so on.

FTP (File Transfer Protocol). The most common protocol for transferring files between machines on the Internet; FTP supports the transfer of both binary and ASCII files.

Functional Interface. Interface that defines the operations invoked by users of an object service. The service consumer, the user of the service, is the audience. The interface presents the functionality (the useful operations) of the service.

Garbage Collection. The recovery of memory occupied by unreferenced objects, usually implemented by the language or environment.

Gateway. A software product that allows SQL-based applications to access relational and nonrelational data sources. Connection between a local system of networked computers and a remote machine or network.

Gigabyte (GB). Approximately one billion bytes, or 1,000 megabytes. Also referred to as a "Gbyte."

GIOP. General Inter-ORB Protocol.

Global Directory Service (GDS). A distributed, replicated directory service based on the CCITT X.500/ISO 9594 international standard. Along with DNS, it provides a global name space that connects local DCE cells into one worldwide hierarchy.

Global Name. A name that is universally meaningful and usable from anywhere in the DCE naming environment. The prefix /... indicates that a name is global.

Graphical User Interface (GUI). Any interface that communicates with the user, primarily through graphical icons.

Handle. A value that identifies an object.

Hash. Data allocated in an algorithmically randomized fashion in an attempt to evenly distribute data and smooth access patterns.

Heuristic. A rule of thumb or guideline used in situations where no hard and fast rules apply. An empirical rule, or educated guess, based upon past experience.

HTML (HyperText Markup Language). Command formatting language for WWW documents.

HTTP (HyperText Transfer Protocol). Set of rules allowing access to and interaction with hypertext documents. The protocol most commonly used in the World Wide Web to transfer information from web servers to web browsers. The protocol that negotiates document delivery to a web browser from a web server.

Hypertext. A way to link related information; clicking on the text allows movement between linked documents. The World Wide Web uses this format.

ICMP. Internet Control Message Protocol.

IDL (Implementation Definition Language). CORBA Interface Definition Language. A notation for describing implementations. The implementation definition language is currently beyond the scope of the ORB standard. It may contain vendor-specific and adapter-specific notations.

IEEE. Institute of Electrical and Electronics Engineers.

IIOP. Internet Inter-ORB Protocol.

Implementation. A definition that provides the information needed to create an object and allow the object to participate in providing an appropriate set of services. An implementation typically includes a description of the data structure used to represent the core state associated with an object, as well as definitions of the methods that access that data structure. Typically, it also includes information about the intended interface of the object.

Implementation Inheritance. The construction of an implementation by incremental modification of other implementations. The ORB does not provide implementation inheritance. Implementation inheritance may be provided by higher-level tools.

Implementation Object. An object that serves as an implementation definition. Implementation objects reside in an implementation repository.

Import. Creating an object based on a description of the object transmitted from an external entity.

IMS. Information Management System.

Information. (1) A collection of data that is relevant to one or more recipients. It must be meaningful and useful to the recipient at a specific time for a specific purpose. Data in context that has meaning, relevance, and purpose. (2) Data that has been processed in such a way that it can increase the knowledge of the person who receives it. Information is the output, or "finished goods," of information systems. Information is also what individuals start with before it is fed into a data capture transaction processing system.

Information Systems. A component of information technology infrastructure that represents the implementation of business activities, using the data resource, and residing on the platform resource.

Information Technology. Constantly evolving body of knowledge pertaining to networking, computing, and communication resources.

Inheritance. The construction of a definition by incremental modification of other definitions. *See also* Implementation Inheritance.

Initialization. Setting the initial attribute values of a new object.

Input/Output (I/O). Transmittal of information between a computer processor and its peripherals, such as terminals and storage devices.

Instance. An object created by instantiating a class. An object is an instance of a class.

Instantiation. Object creation.

Integrated Digital Network (IDN). The integration of transmission and switching functions using digital technology in a circuit-switched telecommunications network.

Integrated Services Digital Network (ISDN). (1) The recommendation published by CCITT for private or public digital telephone networks in which binary data, such as graphics, digitized voice, and data transmission, pass over the same digital network that carries most telephone transmissions today. (2) An overall application of the technology to provide for both newer digital and more traditional telephone services in an integrated network, incorporating the new network and interfacing standards that are being adopted worldwide. (3) Method for carrying many different services over the same digital transmission and switching facilities. (4) A digital telephone system made up of two 64-Kbps "B" channels for data and one "D" channel for message trafficking.

Integration. Used here in the broad sense to mean the transformation of disparate data into an integrated data resource.

Intelligent Agent. A software routine that waits in the background and performs an action when a specified event occurs. For example, agents could transmit a summary file on the first day of the month or monitor incoming data and alert the user when certain transactions have arrived.

Intelligent Caching. Prefetching and storing disk-resident data in memory based on algorithms that identify access patterns, rather than on simple frequency of access.

Interface. A description of a set of possible uses of an object. Specifically, an interface describes a set of potential requests in which an object can meaningfully participate.

Interface Definition Language (IDL). When used in conjunction with an ORB, IDL statements that describe the properties and operations of an object. A high-level declarative language that provides the syntax for interface definitions.

Interface Inheritance. The construction of an interface by incremental modification of other interfaces. The IDL provides interface inheritance.

Interior Gateway Routing Protocol (IGRP). Learns best routes through LAN Internet (TCP/IP).

International Organization for Standardization (ISO). Best known for the seven-layer OSI Reference Model.

Internet. A collection of networks interconnected by a set of routers that allow them to function as a single large virtual network. Global network supporting E-mail and many different information systems.

Internet Access. The method by which users connect to the Internet. Also called an IP address. It is a 32-bit address assigned to hosts using TCP/IP. The address is written as four octets separated with periods (dotted decimal format) that are made up of a network section, an optional subnet section, and a host section.

Internet Protocol (IP). A Layer 3 (network layer) routing protocol that contains addressing information and control information that allows packets to be routed.

Internet Service Provider (ISP). (1) Any of a number of companies that sell Internet access to individuals or organizations at speeds ranging from 300 bps to OC-3. (2) A business that enables individuals and companies to connect to the Internet by providing the interface to the Internet backbone.

Internetwork. A collection of networks interconnected by routers that function (generally) as a single network. Sometimes called *an* Internet, which is not to be confused with *the* Internet.

Internetworking. General term used to refer to the industry that has grown around the problem of connecting networks together. The term can refer to products, procedures, and technologies.

Interoperability. The ability of two or more ORBs to cooperate to deliver requests to the proper object. Interoperating ORBs appear to a client to be a single ORB.

Intranet. A private network that uses Internet software and standards.

IOP. Inter-ORB Protocol.

IP. Internet Protocol. A family of network protocols defined by the U.S. Department of Defense.

IP Address (Internet Protocol Address). Unique four-number code that identifies a specific computer ("node") on the Internet to the rest of the computers on the network.

IP Spoofing. An attack whereby a system illicitly attempts to impersonate another system by using its IP network address.

IPX. Novell's Internet Packet Exchange.

IR. CORBA Interface Repository.

ISDN (Integrated Services Digital Network). Expensive high-speed dedicated system of telephone lines for remote-access communication.

ISO/OSI. International Organization for Standardization/Open Systems Interconnection (model).

ISP (Internet Service Provider). Organization that provides Internet access (E-mail, World Wide Web, etc.) to its customers.

Java Database Connectivity (JDBC). A standard implemented by Sun Microsystems that allows developers to write applications in the Java language, without having to use environment-specific code.

Joins. An operation performed on tables of data in a relational DBMS in which the data from two tables are combined in a larger, more detailed joined table.

Kerberos. The authentication protocol implemented in DCE. Kerberos was developed at MIT. In classical mythology, Kerberos was the three-headed dog that guarded the gates of the underworld.

Key. A value used to encrypt and decrypt data.

Key Access. Extension available on the Applications volume of ACS Room Service that you must install in order to run a KeyServed application on your Macintosh.

Kilobyte (KB). 1,024 bytes (often approximated as 1,000 bytes).

Legacy Data. Another term for disparate data because they support legacy systems.

Legacy System. A previously existing system or application.

Link. Relation between two objects (a concept).

Load Balancing. Distributing system load evenly across server machines by placing identical copies of frequently accessed information among available server machines.

Local Area Network (LAN). (1) A set of computers sharing a network that does not include bridges or Wide Area Network links. (2) A network covering a relatively small geographic area (usually not larger than a floor or small building). Compared to WANs, LANs are usually characterized by relatively high data rates.

Location Independence. The ability of a file to change location without the affecting the pathname.

Location Transparency. The pathname does not indicate the location of the object.

Mach. Machine in the ACS Server Cluster used for computational research and programming.

Manageability. The collective processes of storage configuration, optimization, and administration, including backup and recovery and business continuance.

Managed Object. Clients of system management services, including the installation and activation service and the operational control service (dynamic behavior). These clients may be application objects, common facilities objects, or other object services. The term is used for compatibility with system management standards (the X/Open GDMO specification and ISO/IEC 10164 System Management Function, Parts 1–4).

Mapping. A rule or process, the OO equivalent of a mathematical function. Given an object of one set, a mapping applies its associative rules to return another set of objects. Member function. *See* method.

Massively Parallel Processing (MPP). The "shared nothing" approach of parallel computing. A technology that tightly couples many processors, each with its own copy of the operating system and memory. Coupling the processors and coordinating their activity allows the processors to work in parallel on complex problems that would otherwise take too long on a single processor. MPP is a competing technology to Symmetric Multiprocessing (SMP), in which multiple processors share a single copy of the operating system and also share memory and peripherals.

Megabyte (MB). Approximately 1,000 kilobytes, or a million bytes.

Message. The mechanism by which objects communicate. A message is sent by a client object to request the service provided by the server object.

Metadata. (1) Traditionally, metadata was data about the data. In the common data architecture, metadata is all data describing the foredata, including metapredata and the metaparadata. It comes after or behind and supports the foredata. Examples of metadata include data element descriptions, data type descriptions, attribute/property descriptions, range/domain descriptions, and process/method descriptions. The repository environment encompasses all corporate metadata resources—database catalogs, data dictionaries, and navigation services. Metadata includes the name, length, valid values, and description of a data element. Metadata is stored in a data dictionary and repository. It insulates the data warehouse from changes in the schema of operational systems.

Metaobject. An object that represents a type, operation, class, method, or object model entity that describes objects.

Metatype. A type whose instances are also types.

Method. Code that can be executed to perform a requested service. Methods associated with an object are structured into one or more programs.

Methodology. A system of principles, practices, and procedures applied to a specific branch of knowledge.

MIB. Management Information Base.

Middleware. A communications layer that allows applications to interact across hardware and network environments.

MIME. Multipurpose Internet Mail Extension.

MIPS (millions of instructions per second). Measure of logical and integer-type operations, MIPS is used for interactive processes. MIPS is mistakenly considered a relative measure of computing capability among models and vendors. It is a meaningful measure only among versions of the same processors configured with identical peripherals and software.

MIS. Management Information System or Multimedia Information Sources.

Modem. A device that modulates and demodulates signals transmitted over communication facilities. Peripheral that allows connection to a network over phone lines. Short for "modulator-demodulator."

MPP. Massively Parallel Processing.

MTS. Message Transfer Service/System or Multichannel Television Sound.

Multidimensional Analysis. Informational analysis of data that takes into account many different relationships, each of which represents a dimension.

Multidimensional Database. (1) A database constructed with multiple dimensions prefilled in hyperdimensional "cubes" of data rather than the traditional two-dimensional tables of relational databases. (2) A database concept designed for decision-support systems in which related data is stored in multidimensional "hypercubes." This data organization allows for sophisticated and complex queries and in certain cases can provide superior performance over traditional relational structures.

Multidimensional Database Management System (MDBS and MDBMS). A powerful database that lets users analyze large amounts of data. An MDBS captures and presents data as arrays that can be arranged in multiple dimensions.

Multiple Inheritance. The construction of a definition by incremental modification of more than one other definition.

Multithreading. A program execution environment that takes instruction from multiple independent execution threads.

Multiway Joins. A join operation that involves more than two tables.

Netscape. Program with graphical interface used to browse the World Wide Web.

Network. Computers that share data with one another. A collection of computers and other devices that are able to communicate with each other.

Network Computing Architecture (NCA). An architecture for distributing software applications across heterogeneous collections of networks, computers, and programming environments. NCA specifies the DCE Remote Procedure Call architecture.

Network Connection. Usually refers to a direct connection to a network's backbone rather than simply a modem accessing a single machine. Often allows a faster and more versatile form of communication.

Network Data Representation (NDR). The transfer syntax defined by the Network Computing Architecture.

Network Driver. Low-level software that permits higher-level applications (such as Netscape) to communicate with network hardware.

Network File System (NFS). A protocol for remote file access developed by Sun Microsystems, Inc.

Network Information System (NIS). A protocol for remote distribution of common configuration files developed by Sun Microsystems, Inc.

Network Layer. Layer between the computer's hardware and the network applications that manages the accurate transmission of data.

Network Protocol. A communications protocol from the network layer of the OSI network architecture, such as the Internet Protocol.

Neural Networks. Nonlinear predictive models that learn through training and resemble biological neural networks in structure.

NIC. Network Information Center [Internet] or Network Interface Card.

Normalization. The process of removing all model structures that provide multiple ways to know the same fact; a method of controlling and eliminating redundancy in data storage.

Object. A data structure that implements some feature and has an associated set of operations. In terms of an object-oriented system, an object is an entity that combines descriptions of data and behavior. An object is an instance of a class.

Object Adapter. The ORB component that provides object reference, activation, and state-related services to an object implementation. Different adapters may be provided for different implementations.

Object Component. (1) A group of collaborating objects. (2) A discrete repackaged application that provides a large-grained piece of business application functionality.

Object Creation. An event that causes an object to exist distinct from any other object.

Object Database Management System (ODBMS). A system that provides for long-term, reliable storage, retrieval, and management of objects.

Object Implementation. The code executed for an object or a component in Extended C++. Uses C++ idioms and mechanisms to build a distributed version of C++ that works like the regular nondistributed C++ language.

Object Interface. A description of a set of possible uses of an object. Specifically, an interface describes a set of potential requests in which an object can meaningfully participate as a parameter. It is the union of the object's type interfaces.

Object Library/Repository. A central repository established expressly to support the identification and reuse of software components, especially classes and other software components.

Object Management Group. A nonprofit group, consisting of users, vendors, and university researchers, dedicated to promoting object-oriented technology and the standardization of that technology.

Object Name. A value that identifies an object.

Object Reference. A value that precisely identifies an object. Object references are never reused to identify another object.

Object Request Broker (ORB). Provides the means by which objects make and receive requests and responses. The middleware of distributed object computing that provides a means for objects to locate and activate other objects on a network, regardless of the processor or programming language used to develop and implement those objects.

Object Services. The basic functions provided for object life-cycle management and storage. Includes creation, deletion, activation, deactivation, identification, and location.

Object System. A system used to model/simulate attributes, behavior, and communication of objects.

Object Type. A type the extension of which is a set of objects (literally, a set of values that identify objects). In other words, an object type is satisfied only by (values that identify) objects. *See also* interface type.

Object UUID. The universal unique identifier for a particular RPC object. A server specifies a distinct object UUID for each of its RPC objects; to access a particular object RPC object, a client uses the object UUID to find the server that offers the object. *See also* object, universal unique identifier.

Object-Based. A characteristic of a programming language or tool that supports the object concept of encapsulation but not inheritance or polymorphism.

Object-Oriented. Any language, tool, or method that focuses on modeling, real-world systems using the three pillars of objects: Encapsulation, inheritance, and polymorphism.

Object-Oriented Analysis. The process of specifying what a system does by identifying domain objects and defining the behavior and relationships of those objects.

Object-Oriented Design. The process of developing an implementation specification that incorporates the use of classes and objects. It encourages modeling the real-world environment in terms of its entities and their interactions.

ODBC (Open Database Connectivity). A standard for database access developed by Microsoft with OMG.

ODP. Open Distributed Processing.

OIDL. Object Interface Definition Language.

OLAP. On-Line Analytical Processing (software).

OLE. Microsoft's Object Linking and Embedding mechanism.

OLTP. On-Line Transaction Processing.

OM. Object Manager.

ONC. Open Network Computing [Sun].

Online Analytical Processing (OLAP). Processing that supports the analysis of business trends and projections. It is a counterpart to Online Transaction Processing. Allows users to derive information from data warehouse systems by providing tools for querying and analyzing the information in the warehouse. Allows multidimensional views and analysis of that data for decision-support processes. Also known as decision-support processing.

Online Transaction Processing (OLTP). Processing that supports daily business operations. Also known as operational processing.

OODB. Object-Oriented Database.

OODMS. Object-Oriented Database Management System.

OOL. Object-Oriented Language.

OOPL. Object-Oriented Programming Language.

OOPS. Object-Oriented Programming and Systems.

Open Connectivity Architecture. A standard way of connecting applications to enterprise services.

Open Systems Interconnection (OSI). A seven-layer architecture model for communications systems developed by ISO. Used as a reference model for most network architectures.

Operation. A service that can be requested. An operation has an associated signature that can restrict which parameters are possible in a meaningful request.

Operational Data. Data used in the operational processing of business transactions that support day-to-day business operations. It is detailed, largely primitive data. Continually changes as updates are made and reflects the current value of the last transaction.

Operational Database. The database of record, consisting of system-specific reference data and event data belonging to a transaction-update system. It may also contain system control data such as indicators, flags, and counters. The source of data for the data warehouse.

ORB. Object Request Broker.

ORB Core. The ORB component that moves a request from a client to the appropriate adapter for the target object.

OS. Operating System.

OS/2. IBM's Operating System/2.

OSF. Open Software Foundation.

OSI. ISO's Open Systems Interconnection.

OT. Object Technology.

Parallel Processing. A technique of tightly coupling multiple processors and associated software to coordinate the efforts of the multiple processors so that they can act in parallel to solve problems that are too large and/or complex for single processors.

Parallelism. The ability to perform functions in parallel.

Partition. Decomposing a type into its disjoint subtypes, parts, etc.

Password. A group of characters assigned to a user by the system administrator and used for accessing or entry to a system or database. A string presented by a principal to prove its identity. The login facility transforms this string to generate an encryption key that is used by the Authentication Service to authenticate the principal.

Password Authentication Protocol (PAP). A simple password protocol that transmits a user name and password unencrypted across the network.

PCI. Peripheral Component Interconnect/Interface. Allows data transfers at a clock rate of 33 Mhz. PCI puts a complex managing layer between the CPU and peripherals that buffers the signals allowing ten peripherals to maintain high performance.

PCI-Bus. A set of industry standards that defines the mechanical, electrical, and protocols required to interface peripheral controllers to a CPU.

PCMCIA. Personal Computer Memory Card International Association.

PDN. Public Data Network.

Perimeter Firewall. There are two types of perimeter firewalls, static packet filtering and dynamic. Both work at the IP address level, selectively passing or blocking data packets. Static packet filters are less flexible than dynamic firewalls.

Persistent Object. An object that can survive the process or thread that created it. A persistent object exists until it is explicitly deleted.

Physical Data Model. A data model that represents the denormalized physical implementation of data that supports an information system. The logical data model is denormalized to a physical data model according to specific criteria that do not compromise the logical data model but allow the database to operate efficiently in a specific operating environment.

PIN. Personal Identification Number or Process Identification Number.

Pointer. A variable that can hold a memory address of an object.

Polymorphism. The concept that two or more types of objects can respond to the same request in different ways.

Port. The identifier (16-bit unsigned integer) used by Internet transport protocols to distinguish among multiple simultaneous connections to a single destination host.

POSIX. Portable Operating System Interface for UNIX. A set of standards intended to provide portable interfaces to operating systems services.

PPP (Point-to-Point Protocol). A modem connection method that allows computers to run IP and Apple protocol software over phone lines.

Primary Data Source. The first data site where the original data is stored after its origination.

Primary Key. A set of one or more data characteristics whose value uniquely identifies each data occurrence in a data subject. A primary key is also known as a unique identifier.

Principal. An entity that is capable of believing that it can communicate securely with another entity. In DCE, principals are represented as entries in the security database and include users, servers, computers, and cells.

Print Server. Computer that accepts printing jobs from other networked computers and sends them to one or more printers.

Protection. The ability to restrict the clients for which a requested service will be performed.

Protocol. Set of rules governing the transmission and reception of data. (1) A formal description of a set of rules and conventions that govern how devices on a network exchange information. (2) The set of rules governing interactions between two or more parties. These rules consist of syntax (header structure), semantics (actions and reactions that are supposed to occur), and timing (relative ordering and direction of states and events).

Protocol Address. Also called a network address. A network layer address referring to a logical, rather than a physical, network device.

Protocol Stack. Related layers of protocol software that function together to implement a particular communications architecture. Examples include AppleTalk and DECnet.

Proxy. The mechanism whereby one system "fronts for" another system in responding to protocol requests. Proxy systems are used in network management to avoid having to implement full protocol stacks in simple devices, such as modems.

Query. A (usually) complex SELECT statement for decision support. *See* ad hoc query.

Query Tools. Software that allows a user to create and direct specific questions to a database. These tools provide the means for pulling the desired information from a database. They are typically SQL-based tools and allow a user to define data in end-user language.

RACF. Resource Access Control Facility.

RAID. Redundant Arrays of Independent Disks.

RAM (Random-Access Memory). Computer's temporary work space in which all processing is done.

RASAPI. Remote Access Service Application Programming.

RDBMS. Relational Database Management System.

Redundancy. The storage of multiple copies of identical data.

Redundancy Control. Management of a distributed data environment to limit excessive copy, update, and transmission costs associated with multiple copies of the same data. Data replication is a strategy for redundancy control with the intention of improving performance.

Redundant Data. The situation in which the same data characteristic exists at two or more data sites. Redundant data is created, stored, and maintained independently and the existence of the redundancy is often unknown to the organization.

Refresh. Once a data warehouse is implemented, the contents of the warehouse must be periodically updated to reflect changes in the legacy systems from which the data is gathered. These update cycles are known as refreshes.

Relation. An object type that associates two or more object types. A relation is how associations are formed between two or more objects.

Relational Database. A type of database that stores information in tables and conducts searches by using data in specified columns of one table to find additional data in another table. In a relational database, the rows of a table represent records and the columns represent fields. In conducting searches, a relational database matches information from a field in one table with information in a corresponding field of another table to produce a third table that combines requested data from both tables.

Relational Database Management System (RDBMS). A database management system that uses the concept of two-dimensional tables to define relationships among the different elements of the database.

Remote Access. The process of allowing remote workers to access a corporate LAN over analog or digital telephone lines.

Remote Access Server. Access equipment at a central site that connects remote users with corporate LAN resources.

Remote Procedure Call (RPC). A call to a procedure in a different address space. In a traditional procedure call, the calling and the called procedures are in the same address space on one machine. In a remote procedure call, the calling procedure invokes a procedure in a different address space and usually on a different machine.

Replicated Data. Data that is copied from a data source to one or more target environments based on replication rules. Replicated data can consist of full tables or rectangular extracts.

Replication. The process of keeping a copy of data, either through shadowing or caching. Replication is supported by the security, directory, and file services in DCE. Replication can improve availability and load balancing.

Repository. A location, physical or logical, where databases supporting similar classes of applications are stored.

Request. An event consisting of an operation and zero or more actual parameters. A client issues a request to cause a service to be performed. Also associated with a request are the results that can be returned to the client. A message can be used to implement (carry) a request and/or a result.

Requirements. A statement of the capabilities a system is supposed to offer, from a user's point of view. This statement is input into the object-oriented analysis process, where it is transformed into a more precise description.

Response Time. Time it takes for the computer to comply with a user's request.

Reuse. Reuse is the process of locating, understanding, and incorporating existing knowledge, design, and components into a new system. Reuse should occur at all levels of system development: Analysis, design, implementation, testing, documentation, and user training.

ROLAP (Relational OLAP). Performing OLAP functions against a relational DBMS. Many relational products offer star and snowflake schema for accepting OLAP queries in a relational environment.

Role. A sequence of activities performed by an agent.

ROM (Read-Only Memory). Memory chip that permanently stores instructions and data, the contents of which are created at the time of manufacture and cannot be altered.

Route. A path through an internetwork.

Router. (1) An OSI layer 3 device that can decide which of several paths network traffic will follow based on some optimal metric. Also called a gateway (although this definition of gateway is becoming increasingly outdated), routers forward packets from one network to another based on network-layer information. (2) A dedicated computer hardware and/or software package which manages the connection between two or more networks.

Routing. The process of finding a path to the destination host. Routing is very complex in large networks because of the many potential intermediate locations a packet might traverse before reaching its destination host.

Routing Information Protocol (RIP). An IGP supplied with Berkeley UNIX systems. It is the most common IGP in the Internet. RIP uses hop count as a routing metric. The largest allowable hop count for RIP is 16.

Routing Protocol. A protocol that accomplishes routing through the implementation of a specific routing algorithm. Examples of routing protocols include IGRP, RIP, and OSPF.

Routing Table. A table stored in a router or some other internetworking device that keeps track of routes (and, in some cases, metrics associated with those routes) to particular network destinations.

RPC Interface. A logical grouping of operation, data type, and constant declarations that serves as a network contract for calling a set of remote procedures. *See also* interface definition language.

Scalability. (1) The ability to scale to support larger or smaller volumes of data and more or fewer users. The ability to increase or decrease size or capability in cost-effective increments with minimal impact on the unit cost of business and the procurement of additional services. (2) The ability of a system to accommodate increases in demand by upgrading and/or expanding existing components, as opposed to meeting those increased demands by implementing a new system.

Schema. (1) A diagrammatic representation of the structure or framework of something. (2) The logical and physical definition of data elements, physical characteristics, and interrelationships.

Secure HTTP (SHTTP). An extension of HTTP for authentication and data encryption between a web server and a web browser.

Security. Protection against unwanted behavior. The most widely used definition of (computer) security is *security = confidentiality + integrity + availability*.

Security Policy. The set of rules, principles, and practices that determine how security is implemented in an organization. It must maintain the principles of the organization's general security policy.

Segmentation. Techniques for deriving clusters and classes by creating two-way and multiple-way splits from a dataset according to specified variables.

Server. (1) A service that provides standard functions for clients in response to standard messages from clients. A commonly used definition of server also refers to the physical computer from which services are provided. (2) A computer or program that provides a particular operation (a "service") for the benefit of other machines on a network (often "clients"). (3) The party that receives remote procedure calls. A given application can act as both an RPC server and an RPC client.

Server Object. An object providing response to a request for a service. A given object might be a client for some requests and a server for other requests.

Simple Mail Transfer Protocol (SMTP). Protocol governing mail transmissions.

Single Inheritance. The construction of a definition by incremental modification of one definition.

Skeleton. The object-interface-specific ORB component that assists an object adapter in passing requests to particular methods.

SLIP (Serial Line Internet Protocol). A modem connection method that allows computers to run IP (network) software over phone lines.

Small Computer System Interface (SCSI). A standard for connecting peripheral devices to computers. The standard defines a physical connection scheme as well as a set of protocols for controlling the flow of data across the interface.

SNA. IBM's System Network Architecture.

SNMP. Simple Network Management Protocol.

SOM. Start of Message or IBM's System Object Model.

Source Database. An operational production database or a centralized warehouse that feeds into a target database.

SPARC. Scalable Processor Architecture.

Specific Object. An object (relative to a given object service) whose role is to provide a part of the object service whose interface it carries. The concept is that a limited number of implementations (and potentially a limited number of instances) of these objects exist in the system, commonly as servers.

SQL (Structured Query Language). A structured query language for accessing relational, ODBC, DRDA, or nonrelational compliant database systems.

SQL Query Tool. An end-user tool that accepts SQL to be processed against one or more relational databases.

SQL-Compliant. Conforms to ANSI standards for SQL specifications.

SQL/DS. IBM's Structured Query Language/Data System.

SSL. Secure Sockets Layer.

Standard Query. A stored procedure of a recently executed query. Technically, a standard query may be stored on the desktop as "canned" SQL and passed as dynamic SQL to the server database to execute. This is undesirable unless the stored query is going to be seldom executed.

State. Information about the history of previous requests needed to determine the behavior of future requests.

Static Query. A stored, parameterized procedure, optimized for access to a particular data warehouse.

Stovepipe Decision-Support Systems. Independent, departmental data marts incapable of making accurate decisions across the enterprise because they have no way to consistently define data.

Striping. A RAID technique that breaks up blocks of data into parallel "stripes" which are stored on different disks in order to enhance performance.

Stub. A local procedure corresponding to a single operation that invokes that operation when called.

Subnet. Group of computers within a domain sharing specific network functions.

Subnetwork. Collection of OSI end systems and intermediate systems under the control of one administrative domain and using a single network access protocol. For example, private X.25 networks or a series of bridged LANs.

Subtype. A specialized or specific object type.

Summary Data. Data aggregated according to specific criteria. For example, individual daily sales may be aggregated to weekly totals.

Symmetrical Multiprocessing (SMP). The "shared everything" approach of parallel computing.

Synchronous Request. A request in which the client object pauses to wait for completion of the request.

System Object Model/Distributed System Object Model (SOM/DSOM). SOM is a class library, and DSOM is an ORB. Both are provided by IBM.

Systems Architecture. One of the four layers of the information systems architecture. The systems architecture represents the definitions and interrelationships between applications and the product architecture.

T1. (1) Digital transmission facility operating with a nominal bandwidth of 1.544 Mbps. Also known as Digital Signal Level 1 (D1). Composed of 24 DS-0 channels in many cases. The T1 digital transmission system is the primary digital communication system in North America. (2) A high-speed 1.5 Mbps leased line often used by companies for access to the Internet.

Table Partitioning. The process of identifying the tables needed at each data site.

Target Database. The database in which data will be loaded or inserted.

Target Object. An object that receives a request. (Synonymous with server object.)

Targeted Marketing. The business technique for isolating the most likely set of potential customers for a given product and/or product profile.

Telnet. Protocol and program for TCP/IP networks that permits a network connection to a remote machine.

Temporal Data. Any data that represents a point in time or a time interval. It is data with a time component.

Temporal Database. A database that has the capability of storing temporal data and managing data based on those temporal data. It can re-create data values for past or future dates based on the temporal data values. These databases are also known as time-relational databases.

Terabyte. Approximately a thousand gigabytes, or a trillion (1012) bytes.

TFTP. Trivial File Transfer Protocol.

Thread. A single sequential flow of control within a process.

TLI. Transport Layer Interface.

Transaction. The occurrence of two or more related actions that result in a transfer from one party to another or from each party to the other. Transactions include order entry, point-of-sale exchanges, teller machines, etc.

Transaction Data. Data captured during an exchange between two or more systems that accomplish a particular action or result. For example, a point-of-sale terminal will provide data about the latest sale processed.

Transmission Control Protocol/Internet Protocol (TCP/IP). (1) The common name for the suite of protocols developed by the U.S. Department of Defense in the 1970s to support the construction of world-wide internetworks. TCP and IP are the two best-known protocols in the suite. TCP corresponds to layer 4 (the transport layer) of the OSI reference model. It provides reliable transmission of data. IP corresponds to layer 3 (the network layer) of the OSI reference model and provides connectionless datagram service. (2) The collection of transport and application protocols used to communicate on the Internet and other networks. (3) A protocol (set of rules) that provides reliable transmission of packet data over networks.

Transport Independence. The capability, without changing application code, to use any transport protocol that both the client and server systems support, while guaranteeing the same call semantics.

Transport Layer. A network service that provides end-to-end communications between two parties, while hiding the details of the communications network. The TCP and ISO TP4 transport protocols provide full-duplex virtual circuits on which delivery is reliable, error free, sequenced, and duplicate free. UDP provides no guarantees.

Transport Protocol. A communications protocol from the transport layer of the OSI network architecture, such as the transmission control.

UDP. User Datagram Protocol.

UFS. UNIX File System.

UI. UNIX International or User Interface.

Universal Unique Identifier (UUID). An identifier that is immutable and unique across time and space.

UNO. Universal Networked Objects.

Upload. Loading data or modules from client to server.

URL (Uniform Resource Locator). String of characters that identifies a computer resource or object (an image or document, for example) on the World Wide Web, such as http://www.uchicago.edu.

VAX/VMS. DEC's Virtual Address Extension/Virtual Memory System.

VB. Microsoft's Variable Block or Visual Basic.

VBA. Microsoft's Visual Basic for Applications.

Virtual Memory. Technique that simulates more memory than actually exists and allows the computer to run several programs at a time. Virtual memory breaks up a program into segments, called pages. Instead of bringing the entire program into memory, it brings as many pages as it can fit, based on the current mix of programs and leaves the remaining pages on disk. When instructions are called for that are not in memory, the appropriate disk page is called in, overlaying the page in memory.

Virtual Private Network (VPN). A network service offered by public carriers in which the customer is provided a network that in many ways appears as if it is a private network (customer-unique addressing, network management capabilities, dynamic reconfiguration, etc.) but which, in fact, is provided over the carrier's public network facilities.

VRML (Virtual Reality Modeling Language). Code for creating virtual reality programs for the World Wide Web.

WAN. Wide Area Network.

Web. Web, used as a noun, is shorthand for the World Wide Web.

Web Gateway. An interface between some external source of information and a Web server.

Web Page. An HTML document on the Web, usually one of many that together make up a Web page. Any document that can be accessed on the Web. Web pages are linked into the Web via hypertext.

Web Server. Networked computer that contains documents that can be accessed on the Web.

Web Site. Group of related Web pages on a Web server. A Web server can contain a number of Web sites.

Wide Area Network (WAN). A network that includes computers spread across a large geographical distance, usually involving several cities or states.

World Wide Web (WWW). Networked, distributed information system that provides hypertext, sound, images, movies, and other media over the Internet. Also called "the Web."

World Wide Web Servers. Also called http servers for the underlying protocol with which they communicate with Web browsers, the HyperText Transport Protocol.

XA. Extended Architecture or Extended Attribute.

BIBLIOGRAPHY

Adve, S. V., and M. D. Hill. "A Unified Formalization of Four Shared-Memory Models," *IEEE Trans. on Parallel and Distributed Systems* 4(6): 613–24 (June 1993).

Agarwala, A., and C. R. Das. "Experimenting with a Shared Virtual Memory Environment for Hypercubes," *Journal of Parallel and Distributed Computing* 29(2): 228–35 (September 1995).

Agrawal, D. et al. "Mixed Consistency: A Model for Parallel Programming," *Proceedings of the 13th ACM Symposium on Principles of Distributed Computing—PODC '94* (August 1994).

Ahamad, M., P. W. Hutto, and R. John. "Implementing and Programming Casual Distributed Shared Memory," *Proceedings of the 11th International Conference on Distributed Computing Systems—ICDCS-11*: 274–81 (May 1991).

Ahn, J. H., K. W. Lee, and H. J. Kim. "Architectural Issues in Adopting Distributed Shared Memory for Distributed Object Management Systems," *Proceedings of the 5th IEEE CS Workshop on Future Trends of Distributed Computing Systems*: 294–300 (August 1995).

Amaral, P., C. Jacquemot, and R. A. Lea. "Model for Persistent Shared Memory Addressing in Distributed Systems," *Proceedings of the Second International Workshop on Object Orientation in Operating Systems—IWOOOS '92*: 2–12 (September 1992).

Ambegaonkar, Prakash, ed. *Intranet Resource Kit*. New York: Osborne/McGraw Hill, 1997.

Amza, C., A. L. Cox, S. Dwarkadas, P. Keleher, H. Lu, R. Rajamony, W. Yu, and W. Zwaenepoel. "Shared Memory Multiprocessors," *Proceedings of Supercomputing '95* (December 1995).

Ananthanarayanan, R., S. Menon, A. Mohindra, and U. Ramachandran. *Integrating Distributed Shared Memory with Virtual Memory Management*. Technical Report GIT-CC-90/40, College of Computing: Georgia Institute of Technology, 1990.

————. "Experiences in Integrating Distributed Shared Memory with Virtual Memory Management," *ACM Operating Systems Review* 26(3): 4–26 (July 1992).

Ananthaswamy, Anil. *Data Communications Using Object-Oriented Design and C++*. New York: McGraw-Hill, 1995.

Argile, A. D. S. "Distributed Processing in Decision Support Systems." Ph.D. diss., Nottingham Trent University, 1995.

Argile, A. D. S., and A. A. Bargiel. "XDSM—an X11 based Virtual Distributed Shared Memory System," *Proceedings 2nd Int. Conference SMSTP* (1994).

Bal, H. *Programming Distributed Systems*. Englewood Cliffs, NJ: Prentice Hall, 1990.

Banatre, M., A. Gefflaut, P. Joubert, C. Morin, C, and P. A. Lee. "An Architecture for Tolerating Processor Failures in Shared Memory Multiprocessors," *IEEE Transactions on Computers* 45(10): 1101–15 (October 1996).

Banâtre, M. A., and P. Joubert. "Cache management in a tightly coupled fault tolerant multiprocessor," *Proceedings 20th Int. Symposium on Fault-Tolerant Computing*: 89–96 (June 1990).

Banerji, A., D. Kulkarni, J. Tracey, P. Greenawalt, and D. L. Cohn. "High-Performance Distributed Shared Memory Substrate for Workstation Clusters," *Proceedings of the Second IEEE International Symposium on High Performance Distributed Computing—HPDC-2* (1993).

Baratloo, A., P. Dasgupta, and Z. M. Kedem. "CALYPSO: A Novel Software System for Fault-Tolerant Parallel Processing on Distributed Platforms," *Proceedings of the Fourth IEEE International Symposium on High Performance Distributed Computing—HPDC-4*: 122–9 (August 1995).

Barbosa, Valmir. *An Introduction to Distributed Algorithms*. Cambridge, MA: MIT Press, 1996.

Barker, K., R. Peters, and P. Graham. "Distributed Shared Memory for Interoperability of Heterogeneous Information Systems—Position Statement," *OOPSLA Workshop on Interoperable Objects—Experiences and Issues* (October 1995).

Beck, Kent. "Patterns and Software Development," *Dr. Dobb's Journal* 19(2), February 1994.

Beck, Kent, and Ralph Johnson. "Patterns Generate Architectures," *European Conference on Object-Oriented Programming* (1994).

Bell, G. "Scalable, Parallel Computers: Alternatives, Issues, and Challenges," *International Journal of Parallel Programming* 22(1): 3–46 (January 1994).

Ben-Ari, M. *Principles of Concurrent and Distributed Programming*. Englewood Cliffs, NJ: Prentice Hall, 1990.

Bennett, J. K., S. Dwarkadas, J. A. Greenwood, and E. Speight. "E. Willow: A Scalable Shared Memory Multiprocessor," *Proceedings of Supercomputing '92*: 336–45 (November 1992).

Bernard, Ryan. *Corporate Intranet.* New York: John Wiley & Sons, 1996.

Berners-Lee, Tim. "Of Webs and Objects." Object World Keynote Address, Boston, 6 March 1997.

Bhatt, S.N., G. Pucci, A. G. Ranade, and A. L. Rosenberg. "Scattering and Gathering Messages in Networks of Processors," *IEEE Transactions on Computers* 42: 938–49 (1993).

Blount, M. L., and M. Butrico. "DSVM6K: Distributed Shared Virtual Memory on the Risc System/6000," *Proceedings of the 38th IEEE International Computer Conference—COMPCON Spring '93*: 491–500 (February 1993).

Booch, Grady. *Object-Oriented Analysis and Design With Applications.* Redwood City, CA: Benjamin/Cummings, 1994.

———. *Object-Oriented Design with Applications.* Redwood City, CA: Benjamin/Cummings, 1994.

Brown, L., and J. Wu. "Dynamic Snooping in a Fault-Tolerant Distributed Shared Memory," *Proceedings. of the 14th International Conference on Distributed Computing Systems—ICDCS-14*: 218–26 (June 1994).

———, "Snooping Fault-Tolerant Distributed Shared Memories," *Journal of Systems and Software* 29(2): 149–65 (May 1995).

Burett, Marie. *Data Replication.* New York: John Wiley & Sons, 1997.

Chapin, J., M. Rosenblum, S. Devine, T. Lahiri, D. Teodosiu, and A. Gupta. "Hive: Fault Containment for Shared-Memory Multiprocessors," *Proceedings of the 15th ACM Symposium on Operating Systems Principles—SOSP '95*: 12–25 (December 1995).

Chaudhuri, S., S. Kanthadai, and J. Welch. "The Role of Data-Race-Free Programs in Recoverable DSM," *Proceedings. of the 15th Annual ACM Symposium on Principles of Distributed Computing—PODC '96* (May 1996).

Cheng, J., U. Finger, C., and O'Donnell. "A New Hardware Cache Coherence Model," *Proceedings of EUROMICRO '94*: 117–24 (September 1994).

Cheriton, D. R., and H. A. Goosen. "Paradigm: A Highly-Scalable Shared-Memory Multicomputer Architecture," *IEEE Computer* 24(2): 33–46 (February 1991).

Chorafas, Dimitris. *Object Oriented Database.* Upper Saddle River, NJ: Prentice Hall, 1993.

Choy, M., H. V. Leong, and M. H. Wong. "On Distributed Object Checkpointing and Recovery," *Proceedings. of the 14th Annual ACM Symposium on Principles of Distributed Computing—PODC '95*: 64–73 (August 1995).

Coad, Peter. "Object-Oriented Patterns," *Communications of the ACM* 35 (9): 152 (1992).

Colouris, G., J. Dollimore, and T. Kindberg. *Distributed Systems—Concepts and Design*, 233–43. Reading, MA: Addison-Wesley, 1994.

Comer, D., and J. Griffioen. "A New Design for Distributed Systems: The Remote Memory Model," *Proceedings of the Summer 1990 USENIX Conference*: 127–35 (June 1990).

Corner, Douglas E. *Internetworking with TCP/IP*. Vol. 1. Englewood Cliffs, NJ: Prentice Hall, 1991.

Coulouris, G.F., and J. Dollimore, J., *Distributed Systems—Concepts and Design*. Reading, MA: Addison-Wesley, 1988.

Coulouris, George, Jean Dollimore, and Tim Kindberg. *Distributed Systems: Concepts and Designs*. Reading, MA: Addison-Wesley, 1994.

Cox, Brad. *Object-Oriented Programming: An Evolutionary Approach*. Reading, MA: Addison-Wesley, 1986.

Crichlow, Joel M. *An Introduction to Distributed Computing*. Upper Saddle River, NJ: Prentice Hall, 1997.

Crichlow, Joel, *An Introduction to Distributed and Parallel Computing*. Upper Saddle River, NJ: Prentice-Hall Professional Technical Reference, 1996.

Dennett, Daniel. 1995. *Darwin's Dangerous Idea: Evolution and the Meanings of Life*. New York: Simon and Schuster, 1984.

E. Moser, Y. Amir, P. M. Melliar-Smith, and D. A. Agarwal. "Extended virtual synchrony," *Proceedings of the Fourteenth International Conference on Distributed Computing Systems, IEEE*, Poznan, Poland: 56-65 (June 1994).

Fischer, Michael J., Nancy A. Lynch, Michael S. Paterson. "Impossibility of Distributed Consensus with One Faulty Process," *Journal of the ACM* 32(2): 374–82 (April 1985).

Gamma, Erich, Richard Helm, Ralph Johnson, and John Vlissades. *Design Patterns: Elements of Reusable Object-Oriented Software*. Reading, MA: Addison-Wesley, 1994.

Goldstein, Neal, and Jeff Alger. *Developing Object-Oriented Software for the Macintosh*. Reading, MA: Addison-Wesley, 1992.

Goscinsk. A. *Distributed Operating Systems: The Logical Design*. Reading, MA: Addison-Wesley, 1991.

Hart, Johnson M., and Barry Rosenberg. *Client/Server Computing for Technical Professionals: Concepts and Solutions*. Reading, MA: Addison-Wesley, 1995.

Heath, L.S., and A. L. Rosenberg. "Laying Out Graphs Using Queues," *SIAM Journal of Computing* 21: 927–58 (1992).

Heuring, Vincent P., and Harry F. Jordan. *Computer Systems Design and Architecture*. Reading, MA: Addison-Wesley, 1992.

Honeyman, Peter. "Distributed File Systems," 27–44. *Distributed Computing: Implementation and Management Strategies*. Edited by Raman Khanna. Upper Saddle River, NJ: Prentice-Hall Professional, Trade, Reference,1994.

Hutchinson, Norman C., Larry L. Peterson, Mark B. Abbott, and Sean O'Malley. *RPC in the x-Kernel: Evaluating New Design Techniques*. New Castle, UK: International Thomson Computer Press, 1997.

IBM Corporation. *OSF DCE for AIX, OS/2, and DOS Windows Overview, IBM Document Number GG24-4144-00*, 1st ed., 27, New York: IBM Corporation, July 1993.

IBM Corporation. *AIX Versions 3.2 and 4.1 Performance Tuning Guide, IBM Document Number SC23-2365-03,* 4th ed. New York: IBM Corporation, August 1994.

Islam, Nayeem. *Distributed Objects: Methodologies for Customizing Systems Software.* Los Alamitos, CA: IEEE Computer Society Press, 1996.

Jenkins et al. *Client/Server Unleased.* Indianapolis, IN: SAMS, 1996.

Jones, Capers. *Programming Languages Table Monograph,* 8th ed. Boston: Software Productivity Research, 1996.

Kay, Alan. "The Early History of Smalltalk," *History of Programming Languages.* Edited by T. J. Bergin and Richard G. Gibson. New York: ACM Press, 1996.

Khanna, Raman. *Distributed Computing.* Upper Saddle River, NJ: Prentice Hall Professional Technical Reference, 1994.

Larson, James A. *Database Directions.* Upper Saddle River, NJ: Prentice-Hall, 1995.

Larson, James A., and O. R. Beaverton. *Database Directions: From Relational to Distributed, Multimedia and Object-Oriented Database Systems.* Upper Saddle River, NJ: Prentice Hall Professional Technical Reference, 1995.

Larus, J. R., S. Chandra, and D. A. Wood. "CICO: A Practical Shared-Memory Programming Performance Model," *Portability and Performance for Parallel Processors.* Edited by Ferrente and Hey. New York: John Wiley & Sons, Ltd., 1993.

Leighton, F.T., B. M. Maggs, and R. K. Sitaraman. "On the Fault Tolerance of Some Popular Bounded-Degree Networks," *33rd IEEE Symposium on Foundations of Computer Science*: 542–52 (1992).

Lerner, Moisey. "Software Maintenance Crisis Resolution: The New IEEE Standard." *IEEE Software* 11: 65-72 (August 1994).

Levy, Eliezer, and Abraham Silberschatz. "Distributed File Systems: Concepts and Examples," *ACM Computing Surveys* 22(4): 321–74 (1990).

Levy, Steven. *Artificial Life: A Report from the Frontier Where Computers Meet Biology.* New York: Vintage Books, 1993.

Loomis, Mary E. S. *Object Databases: The Essentials.* Reading, MA: Addison-Wesley, 1995.

Maggs, B. M., and R. K. Sitaraman. "Simple Algorithms for Routing on Butterfly Networks with Bounded Queues," *24th ACM Symposium on Theory of Computing,* 150–61 (1992).

Manger, Jason J. *Java Script.* New York: Osborne/McGraw Hill, 1996.

Marc, Rozier, Vadim Abrossimov, François Armand, Ivan Boule, Michel Gien, Marc Guillemont, Frédéric Herrmann, Claude Kaiser, Sylvain Langlois, Pierre Léonard, and Will Neuhauser. "CHORUS distributed operating systems," *Computing Systems Journal* 1(4): 305–70 (December 1988).

Martin, James, and Joe Leben. *Client/Server Databases*. Upper Saddle River, NJ: Prentice Hall, 1995.

META Group, Inc. "Making the Case for Use Case," *Advanced Information Management,* File 324, 13 February 1995.

Minoli, Daniel. *Internet and Intranet*. New York: McGraw Hill, 1997.

Mowbray, T. J., and R. Zahavi. *The Essential CORBA: Systems Integration Using Distributed Objects.* New York: Wiley/OMG, 1995.

Mullender, Sape J., ed. *Distributed Systems.* Reading, MA: Addison-Wesley, 1994.

Mullender, Sape J., ed. *Distributed Systems*, 2d ed. Reading, MA: Addison-Wesley, 1993.

Nelson, Carl. "A Forum for Fitting the Task," *IEEE Computer* 27(3): 104 (March 1994).

Nelson, Ted. *Computer Lib/Dream Machines*. Self-published, 1974. Republished by Microsoft Press (Redmond, WA), 1987.

Nutt, G. *Centralised and Distributed Operating Systems*. Englewood Cliffs, NJ: Prentice Hall, 1992.

Object Magazine. "Executive Brief: Objects important to redesign, O-O 4GLs outracing Smalltalk?" *Object Magazine* 5: 3–10 (June 1995).

Obrenic, B., M. Herbordt, A. L. Rosenberg, C. Weems, F. Annexstein, and M. Baumslag. "Achieving Multigauge Behavior in Bit-Serial SIMD Architectures Via Emulation," *3rd IEEE Symposium on Frontiers of Massively Parallel Computation,* 186–95 (1990).

OpenForum '92 Technical Conference, 323–36, Utrecht, The Netherlands, (November 1992).

Orfalli, Robert, Dan Harkey, and Jeri Edwards. *Essential Client/Server Survival Guide.* New York: John Wiley & Sons, 1994.

———. *The Essential Distributed Objects Survival Guide.* New York: John Wiley & Sons, 1996.

Peterson, Larry L., Norm Hutchinson, Sean O'Malley, and Mark Abbott. "RPC in the x-Kernel: Evaluating new design techniques," *Proceedings of the Twelfth ACM Symposium on Operating Systems Principles.* Litchfield Park, AZ: 91–101 (November 1989).

Pfister, Gregory F. *In Search of Clusters*. Upper Saddle River, NJ: Prentice Hall, 1995.

Raynal, M., and J-M Helary. *Synchronization and Control of Distributed Programs*. New York: John Wiley & Sons, 1990

Reiter, Michael, Kenneth P. Birman, and Li Gong. "Integrating security in a group-oriented distributed system," *Proceedings of the IEEE Symposium on Research in Security and Privacy*: 18–32 (May 1992).

Renaud, Paul E. *Introduction to Client/Server Systems*. New York: John Wiley & Sons, 1996.

van Renesse, Robbert, Hans van Staveren, and Andrew S. Tanenbaum. "The performance of the Amoeba distributed operating system," *Software—Practice and Experience* 19(3): 223–34 (March 1989).

Rosenberg, A. L., V. Scarano, R.K. Sitaraman. "Fine-grain parallel computation on reconfigurable rings of processors," *6th IEEE Symposium on Parallel and Distributed Processing* (1994).

Rosenberry, W., D. Kenney, and G. Fisher. *Understanding DCE*. Sebastopol CA: O'Reilly & Associates, Inc., 1992.

Ryan, Timothy W. *Distributed Object Technology*. Upper Saddle River, NJ: Prentice Hall, 1997.

———. *Hewlett-Packard. Distributed Object Technology: Concepts and Applications*. Upper Saddle River, NJ: Prentice Hall, 1997.

Salemi, Joe. *Client / Server Databases*. Emeryville, CA: Ziff Davis Press, 1995.

Satyanaranan, M., "Distributed File Systems," *Distributed Systems, an Advanced Course*. Edited by S. Mulender, 361–8. New York: ACM Press, 1989.

———. *A Survey of Distributed File Systems, Research Report CMU-CS-89-116*, Pittsburgh: Carnegie-Mellon University Computer Science Department, 1989.

Shah, G. et al. *Architectural Mechanisms for Explicit Communication in Solution*. New York: McGraw Hill, 1995.

Shavit, N., and D. Touitou. "Software Transactional Memory," *Proceedings. of the 14th Annual ACM Symposium on Principles of Distributed Computing—PODC '95* (August 1995).

Shelton, Robert. "The Distributed Enterprise." *The Distributed Computing Monitor* 8(10): 3 (October 1993).

Shirley, J., *Guide to Writing DCE Applications,* 1st ed., 145. Sebastopol, CA: O'Reilly & Associates, Inc., 1963.

Shuey, Richard L., Cavid L. Spooner, and Ophir Frieder. *The Architecture of Distributed Computer Systems: A Data Engineering Perspective on Information Systems*. Reading, MA: Addison-Wesley, 1997.

Siegel, Jon. *CORBA Fundamentals and Programming*. New York: John Wiley & Sons, 1996.

Signore, Robert, John Creamer, and Michael O. Stegman. *The ODBC Solution*. New York: McGraw Hill, 1995.

Singh, Harry. *Interactive Data Warehousing via the Web*. Upper Saddle River, NJ: Prentice Hall Professional Technical Reference, 1998.

———. *Data Warehousing: Concepts, Technologies, Implementations, and Management*. Upper Saddle River, NJ: Prentice Hall Professional Technical Reference, 1997.

———. *Heterogeneous Internetworking: Networking Technically Diverse Operating Systems.* Upper Saddle River, NJ: Prentice Hall Professional Technical Reference, 1996.

———. *UNIX for MVS Programmers.* Upper Saddle River, NJ: Prentice Hall Professional Technical Reference, 1996.

Singhal, Mukesh, and Niranjan G. Shivaratri. *Advanced Concepts in Operating Systems.* New York: McGraw-Hill, 1994.

———. "Communication Primitives," *Advanced Concepts in Operating Systems*, Section 4.7. Piscataway, NJ: IEEE Computer Society Press, 1996.

Sinha, Pradeep K. *Distributed Operating Systems.* Piscataway, NJ: IEEE Computer Society Press, 1997.

Sitaraman, R., and N. Jha. "Optimal Design of Checks for Error Detection and Location in Fault Tolerant Multiprocessor Systems," *IEEE Transactions on Computers* 42 (1993).

Spertus, Mike. "Garbage Collection in C++," *Object Magazine* 5: 6 (February 1996).

Stallings, William. "Operating Systems," *Distributed Process Communication,* Section 9.4, 536–47. New York: Macmillan, 1992.

Sterling, Bruce. "Internet," *The Magazine Of Fantasy And Science Fiction* (February 1993).

Stevens, W. Richard. *TCP/IP Illustrated.* Vol. 1 of *The Protocols.* Reading, MA: Addison-Wesley, 1994.

Stokes, D., "A Comparison of DCE DFS and AFS," */AIXtra* 2(4): 58–66 (October 1992).

Strayer, T., B. J. Dempsey, and A. C. Weaver. *XTP: The Xpress Transfer Protocol.* Reading, MA: Addison-Wesley, 1992.

Stroustrup, Bjarne. *The C++ Programming Language.* 2d ed. Reading, MA: Addison-Wesley, 1991.

Sutherland, Jeff. "Road Kill on the Information Highway: JavaDay," *Homepage Journal.* New York: ACM Press (February 1996).

———. "Smalltalk, C++, and OO COBOL: The Good, the Bad, and the Ugly," *Object Magazine* (1995).

Sutherland, Jeff et al., eds. *Proceedings of the OOPSLA '95 Workshop on Business Object Design and Implementation.* London: Springer-Verlag, 1997.

Sutherland J. V., M. Pope, and K. Rugg. "The Hybrid Object-Relational Architecture (HORA): An Integration of Object-Oriented and Relational Technology," *Proceedings of the 1993 ACM/SIGAPP Symposium on Applied Computing*, Indianapolis, 14–16 February 1993, Edited by E. Deaton et al., 326–33. New York: ACM Press (1993).

Tannenbaum, Andrew S. *Distributed Operating Systems.* Upper Saddle River, NJ: Prentice Hall, 1995.

————. *Modern Operating Systems.* Upper Saddle River, NJ: Prentice Hall, 1992.

————. *Computer Networks.* Upper Saddle River, NJ: Prentice Hall, 1961.

Tay, B. H., and A. L. Ananda. "A Survey of Remote Procedure Calls," *Operating System Review* 24(3): 68–79 (July 1990).

Taylor, David A. *Object-Oriented Information Systems.* New York: John Wiley & Sons, 1992.

————. *Object-Oriented Technology: A Manager's Guide.* Reading, MA: Addison-Wesley, 1996.

Wegner, Peter. "Why Interaction Is More Powerful Than Algorithms," *Communications of the ACM* 40(5): 80–91 (May 1997).

Wiggin, Richard W. *The Internet for Everyone.* New York: McGraw Hill, 1995.

Wong, William. *Plug & Play Programming—An Object-Oriented Construction Kit.* Redwood City, CA: M&T Books, 1993.

Zahn, Lisa. *Network Computing Architecture.* Upper Saddle River, NJ: Prentice Hall, 1990.

Zomaya, Albert, ed. *Parallel and Distributed Computing Handbook.* New York: McGraw Hill, 1996.

O

X

Back   Forward   Reload   Home   Search   Guide   Images   Print   Security   Stop

http://www.phptr.com/

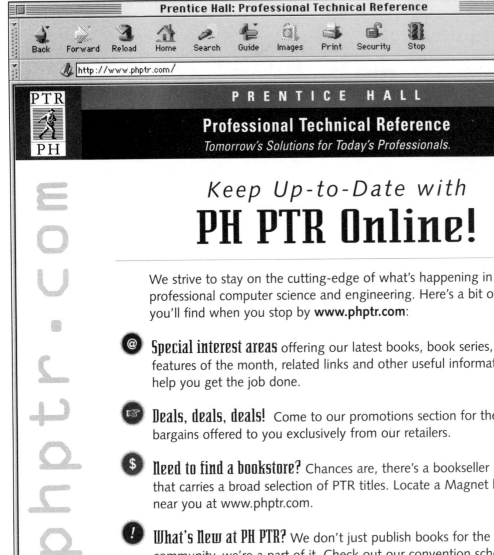

PRENTICE HALL

Professional Technical Reference
Tomorrow's Solutions for Today's Professionals.

Keep Up-to-Date with
PH PTR Online!

We strive to stay on the cutting-edge of what's happening in professional computer science and engineering. Here's a bit of what you'll find when you stop by **www.phptr.com**:

@ Special interest areas offering our latest books, book series, software, features of the month, related links and other useful information to help you get the job done.

☞ Deals, deals, deals! Come to our promotions section for the latest bargains offered to you exclusively from our retailers.

$ Need to find a bookstore? Chances are, there's a bookseller near you that carries a broad selection of PTR titles. Locate a Magnet bookstore near you at www.phptr.com.

! What's New at PH PTR? We don't just publish books for the professional community, we're a part of it. Check out our convention schedule, join an author chat, get the latest reviews and press releases on topics of interest to you.

✉ Subscribe Today! Join PH PTR's monthly email newsletter!

Want to be kept up-to-date on your area of interest? Choose a targeted category on our website, and we'll keep you informed of the latest PH PTR products, author events, reviews and conferences in your interest area.

Visit our mailroom to subscribe today! **http://www.phptr.com/mail_lists**